T0367491

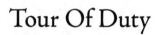

Tour Of Duty

TOUR of DUTY

COMPLEXITY of POLICE WORK

STEVE P. DANKO SR.

TOUR OF DUTY
COMPLEXITY OF POLICE WORK

iUniverse books may be ordered through booksellers or by contacting:

iUniverse
1663 Liberty Drive
Bloomington, IN 47403
www.iuniverse.com
1-800-Authors (1-800-288-4677)

Because of the dynamic nature of the Internet, any web addresses or links contained in this book may have changed since publication and may no longer be valid. The views expressed in this work are solely those of the author and do not necessarily reflect the views of the publisher, and the publisher hereby disclaims any responsibility for them.

Any people depicted in stock imagery provided by Thinkstock are models, and such images are being used for illustrative purposes only. Certain stock imagery © Thinkstock.

ISBN: 978-1-4917-7825-8 (sc)
ISBN: 978-1-4917-7826-5 (e)

Library of Congress Control Number: 2015917712

Print information available on the last page.

iUniverse rev. date: 11/05/2015

Dedication

To my wife and soul mate, her encouragement inspired this book and its writing aided in my recovery from a medical problem. Her steadfast support worked and I am forever in her debt. Her acceptance and loyalty through my long police career was remarkable. Mother of two she managed a successful career of her own while raising two fine sons, she is a friend to all, and a mentor to our now second close knit generation.

Contents

Introduction

————⟫∘∘∘⟪————

My reason for writing this book is to show the general public how exhausting and demanding the job of police officer is, both physically and mentally. To reveal to the citizens how many hats he or she has to wear, how many things they must learn and use to do their job effectively while being alert to the dangers and crime, and keeping themselves and others from physical harm. We pay them such an insignificant amount that after long years of service, they retire hoping their financial situations hold. Most have to go on to additional occupations to supplement their income. Away from their families on shifts, they accidentally neglect their children while their husbands or wives wonder on a daily basis if they will come home from their shift.

During my tour with the Baltimore city police, I witnessed, met and worked with some of the finest to take the oath and wear the uniform. Including plainclothes personnel and detectives, in their relentless efforts to prevent or solve crimes. These are the men and women I attempt to bring to you in the true situations and stories shared in this book, to show them through my experiences, as examples. These situations and cases are just an example of what all police officers face. Think of the hundreds of thousands who serve across this country when you read this. I hope you have a stronger regard for them afterward.

I know it was a blessing to work with and know so many great officers and people I meet while doing this job. Every day they do things like I describe in these pages, including far more dangerous and immensely detailed accomplishments during investigations than you can imagine. These investigations involve deep undercover work and lengthy joint enforcement investigations that result at times in lifesaving actions. They involve drugs and weapons cases, white collar fraud and much more than I can relate in these pages. They do this all the while fearlessly protecting you and yours from crime and its ramifications. Every minute of the day you, the general public, are enabled to go about your business and normal daily activities because of those who stand between good and evil, the law abiding and the lawless.

The stories, cases and situations related in this book are true to the best of my knowledge. Names and locations in some of the events detailed have been changed or deleted to protect the innocent parties involved.

Growing Up in Baltimore

I was born in Baltimore and, except for my first two years, lived at two locations on Linden Avenue, which was just three blocks south of Druid Hill Park. Our rental apartments were located in the Central and Northern districts, in the heart of town, just north of the downtown area and blocks below its large inter-city park area, Druid Hill Park, which housed the Baltimore Zoo. At the time, the area was considered a rather seedy section compared to most. North Avenue divided the two police districts, Northern and Central District.

Over the years, my mother and grandparents rented apartments on both sides of North Avenue. My grandfather Charles R. Franklin died at home of a severe stroke when I was just 10 years of age. He had worked up until that time as a bus repair mechanic at the Baltimore Transit Company at Washington Boulevard and Monroe Street. He made inexpensive repairs to the neighbors' cars on the weekends for extra money. Every Friday he would take me to the local Five and Dime Store and buy me some penny candy and a ten cent toy, usually a model plane. My grandfather was one of few at that time who had won the Dale Carnegie Medal. He had attempted to rescue a swimmer in distress in 1937, not knowing how to swim himself.

After the death of my grandfather, my mother became the sole supporter of the family, working as a telephone exchange operator for the City Of Baltimore at City Hall, until retiring in 1985. She passed two years later. Although some would consider this broken

3

home disruptive to a child's development, I knew that my parents, who were mentors to other relatives and myself, loved me. Like others, I was not disturbed as a result of coming up in what was considered to be a broken home at the time. I never held any malice toward my known father, who died in 1995 without ever having contacted me. He walked away from his family when I was two years old, never to return or be heard from again.

Both my mother and grandmother were caring people, remembered as being thoughtful and so beloved. They never ridiculed the father that had deserted us. If he was mentioned, they only agreed that marriage wasn't meant for him. So often, the one that leaves a relationship is blamed. Perhaps because he wasn't the target of their anger, it made it easier not to dislike him. Some abandoned children grow up with a desire to locate, seek out and meet their long-lost parents; I never remember thinking that way. My thought was that he was the adult, I was his child, and it was his mindset about the matter that would have governed our meeting.

In my neighborhood and in most parts of Baltimore City, overall, we lived a quiet life. It was a different world and a different time. Baltimore was made up of poor ethnic groups that lived in their own cultural sections Polish, Italian, German, Greek, etc. Everyone tended to live together in their own ethnic groups and clans, all based on their languages and cultures. For the most part, blacks and whites lived separately with their own. Although Eutaw Street on the west side, just a block from Linden Avenue, was the end of our neighborhood and the dividing line between the races, we lived peacefully.

Ours was a mixed, blue-collar, multicultural neighborhood, with no particular ethnic group being largest in number. The men supported their families as best they could. They worked five-day long and hard weeks at various occupations, and the majority drank the weekends away as a release from their financial problems and life's responsibilities. While my mother worked her five-day week as a telephone operator at "The Hall," my grandmother ran the household and worked seven days weekly keeping the house and making meals. As loving and caring as my grandfather was, he needed the weekends to cope. It was hard on him knowing that his labors as a mechanic for the Baltimore Transit were just enough to cover the bills.

My first job was delivering newspapers at the age of twelve. I worked hours each weekday and extra time on the weekends to collect payments for the papers. My meager salary was determined by the successful payment collections, since the papers were paid for based on the number dropped from the truck. It was not very provable. Can you imagine how easy it was not to pay a kid and promise next week you would catch up?

I attended Polytechnic (Poly) High School, which was then located on North Avenue at Calvert Street; presently the same building houses the city's Board of Education. At the time of my decision to attend, it was based not on the fact that the school was rated one of the top ten in the country at the time, but because the other guys in my neighborhood were going there. I went to an engineering school with a lot of mathematics, and attended Eastern High almost every summer to make up for those math courses.

Nevertheless, poly was a fabulous high school. My development there was bolstered by the school's policies and emphasis on life skills. We dressed in white dress shirts and ties, always were treated as men, had our own student council which monitored the halls and held hearings for student rule violators, and directed as well as produced a yearly fundraiser, the Poly Follies. Instead of using numbers for the snap count during my football year, we used the school principal's name instead. They not only educated you but they instilled self-reliance and the responsibility of manhood. It felt more like a college than a high school.

My family was poor, like most in the neighborhood, so a lot of my time was spent playing sports in a schoolyard as a means of free recreation. Almost every day we rushed from our respective schools, first by streetcar and later by bus, in order to be at Elementary School #61's yard and be picked for the first team for whatever sport was in season. We played winners up, so you did not want to wait for the first game to end. Get there first for the pick and your team may play all day. Get there late and play one game that day. The game would abruptly end when the ball was lost in a yard where the old man residing there would not return it, or when it made its way down a sewer hole, or out on the street and could not be recovered, or when it was too dark to see. Many times I was held by my ankles; face down in a sewer hole, hoping that a lost ball could be reached to continue play. That schoolyard supported all manner of seasonal sports.

We played football, sometimes tackle, on the macadam and slid around monkey bars that were just out of bounds after a missed diving tackle. We played baseball, occasionally watching balls fly through school windows. The season would start with us playing with new balls we got on a birthday or holiday, and then eventually those baseballs would look like taped hand-me-downs, their original covers torn off or damaged. Basketball, step-ball and fast pitch rounded out our typical sports year in the neighborhood.

Our sporting equipment usually came from Simon Harris, a sports store that sold secondhand or damaged goods. Frequently, we would walk the two miles to Gay and Fallsway streets for baseball gloves, bats and spikes, and to bicker over the sales prices. My first and only bicycle came from the Goodwill. As far as indoor sports, we had a converted church with a basketball floor a third the size of a standard court, located on Bolton Street, which also served as our teen center. My first organized sport was baseball, at the age of thirteen, for a team sponsored solely by one guy in the neighborhood. Our uniforms were 100% wool at the time and were passed on from one age group to the next younger age group and so on. We played in an Optimist League, never in comfortably fitting uniforms, but always warm, to warm actually.

Neighborhoods were tightly knit and outsiders were not warmly welcomed. We frequented the Arundel Ice Cream store located on North Avenue, and were separated by age groups. When the older guys were there, we were not allowed in the booths at the same time. We'd watch films at the two movie houses on each side of North Avenue, the Rialto and the Linden, and on occasion pitched black Juicy Fruits at one another during the movies. At the Rialto, you always sat in the aisle seats to get away from some unwelcome movie-going companions: bugs. Occasionally, you would see roaches crawling on the walls when the lights went down. I guess you could consider that VIP seating.

The lowest price I can remember to attend a movie was eighteen cents; I was in my early teens at the time. I remember seeing Jesse Owens at a promotional movie held at the Linden Theater. Owens was the winner of four gold medals during the 1936 Olympic Games in Hitler's racist Germany. Soda and candy cost five cents at the time. Chocolate sundaes were twenty five cents. Penny candy and nuts were in vending machines. Popcorn cost fifteen to twenty five cents depending on the box size. A dollar bag of ten cent hamburgers from the Little Tavern would last you through the Saturday double feature, which also included two or three cartoons, a weekly serial attraction, and the coming attractions. This constituted five to six hours of entertainment at either of the weekend movie houses.

After serving papers on Sundays, it was a ritual for four friends to meet at the schoolyard and play fast pitch, two against two. We would stop first at a bakery on North Avenue, get gills of milk and donuts, and play a nine-inning game. Strikeouts outs and caught balls were outs everything else was a singles.

Beyond the movie houses and schoolyards, we also had board games to occupy our wandering minds, in particular a baseball game called All Star Baseball. You chose the teams based on player cards for the named big league players at the time. The circular cards were divided into numbers with different sizes based on the individual's professional hitting percentages. The cards were placed on a spinner and spun to determine what number you hit. This game was a ritual played out in the summer on my shaded back porch, while we ate hot cherry pie baked by my grandmother. The fruit in the pie was from several cherry trees just behind the shopping area on Whitelock Street. Naturally, we always said that the nice man that owned the trees willingly gave us the cherries. He probably did, but we never got the chance to ask him. Whenever we thought we had enough cherries "collected" in our paper bags, or maybe when he decided we had enough, he would appear at his back door and chase us almost every time, though never manage to catch us.

It was a simpler time, a quiet neighborhood where everyone knew each other. The kids knew one another and the adults knew the kids.

The neighbors had a right to correct you, with the permission of your parents, if you did wrong. You best never be taken home by the policeman for something you did; the punishment would be far worse than if you were arrested. Everyone's personal life and property was respected. On weekends, we had chores: sweep the gutters and sidewalks in front of your house, wash the marble steps and the inlaid stone vestibule, and cut the grass and clean the backyard. You could sleep away the hot summer nights in your vestibule or on the steps safely. Even if you left your door unlocked, your home was safe. Although 90% of the neighborhood was relatively poor, most were respectable and honest. People frequently feel their lives are similar to most others. Except for those who were in the military or from other ethnic backgrounds, I think my upbringing was similar to most that joined the Police Department.

Often you hear people talk about the good old days and say that they were the best, much better than things today. Of course, over the years you mature and therefore have a different outlook as you age. Events impact your lifestyle and attitude toward certain things and you change over the years with experiences. Your views on life in general, work, politics, religion do change. But if you have no reason to let go of the past, to let go of your youthful memories then don't, they were good, fond, strong, lasting, fine memories to be savored for a lifetime. Friends from that period of my life are still as close to me as they were then. They are fewer as the years pass, but are never forgotten.

My dearest friend passed during the writing of this book, Robert Schaffer. Friends since the age of ten, we met in the 5th, grade. Growing up as brothers, we did everything I have mentioned together. Bob was a rare person, accomplished in business, family and friendships. He was always there for anyone who ever needed him. He was the best man at my wedding; so nervous that he handed the minister his Poly ring when asked for the wedding band. He was my eldest son's godfather and presented him with a basketball at his birth when he first saw him at the hospital. He was of the Jewish faith and he and his children looked forward to spending every Christmas in our home with our family. He was financially independent in his business ventures, but that was a minor accomplishment compared to his grace, kindness and love for others. Needless to say, we had more experiences over the years than can be mentioned. We played Little League baseball and basketball together. He helped me with my paper route, and rode behind me on my runaway bike and ran in front of me when dogs chased us. Our families grew up with each other and I am blessed with knowing him and his loving family.

There are some things you can't explain in life. One is that I was reviewing these exact pages of the book when he passed; that was truly much more than just irony, I feel it was a continuance of our relationship. The other seemingly inexplicable thought is why and how could I have met such a man at such an early stage in my life and be so honored with a lasting friendship of sixty years. Family and friends are all you can hope for in life, and I found a lasting friend who was only ten years old at the time of our first meeting. All the lasting fond memories of our lives made it possible to endure his passing.

At just nineteen years of age, I married my girlfriend of five years, Lorry, which was a nickname for Lorraine. In 1960, getting married young was common. I had found a life mentor and soul mate in Lorry and we remain happily married to this date. We had two sons, the oldest three years senior to his brother. Neither had been born when I joined the police department in 1962. Our marriage would last, even with the shift work and the inherent dangers of the job, over fifty years to date. Yes, we danced at our 50th anniversary, and our mutual lives together continue on. Apparently, she overlooked the many mistakes of my youth, adjusted and continued to forge our family. Like most good women she raised both my sons and I. We had an unspoken routine when I left for work. There was never a cross word between us at that time, nor were family problems discussed. Both of us felt that if I were injured or worse during my shift, we didn't want harsh words between us to be our last.

Like most men, I did not think of the pressures endured by my wife because of the job and raising the children, who came along in 1965 and 1968, raised basically alone due to shift work. They say a man is always proud of his sons; in my case, I am humbled by their never ending love and affection for us. My wife deserves more credit than I could ever express for the men they have become.

When the boys aged, Lorry went to work and became a successful realtor, and later a loan officer. Her earnings offset the consistently low salary of the police department. When I was hired in 1962, I made $4,200 a year. We saved and bought our first home in the city before we considered having children. Education, as far as I was concerned, was quickly secondary to the excitement and experiences learned on the streets. I often teased Lorry that she raised three kids, two sons and a husband. I was child like because I was thrilled by my newfound, exciting occupation. I was once told that to be happy, you had to work at a job that brought you satisfaction. I was one of the lucky ones, I had found it.

Initially, I was talked into the job by Officer Harold Rose, a foot patrolman whose post was where I lived and worked. It made the decision easier knowing that the B.C.P.D. provided shift work that would allow me to attend college and complete a degree. Ironically, later Rose would work side partners (officer on the next foot or car post) in Northern District Car 501 when I was in Central District car 105. Our assignment areas divided at North Avenue, as did the districts. Talk about parallel careers: Officer Rose and I were both in Homicide at the same time, but on different shifts, we never worked a case together. I liked action on the job and at that time would not consider being tied to a desk job.

I had also considered the fire department in as much as it also offered shift work, which allowed time for college courses, but like most people, I had an inherent fear. Mine was and is a fear of heights. I never even considered that would come into play with police work, until responding to nighttime calls that had me clamoring across third-floor rooftops in pitch dark pursuit of burglars, prowlers and peeping toms. I guess it would not have mattered anyway, six of one and a half dozen of the other. With Officer Rose being very persuasive, the die was cast, and I do thank him.

Once on the job, I loved the excitement and thrill of it all. It was why young men volunteered and fought in wars. I was youthful enough to think I was invincible and had no rational thought of ever being injured. It was never a reality to me at that time; like all young headstrong men,

I never considered that possibility. It would always be the other guy that got hurt, hopefully the bad guys if necessary, never one of us, never a police officer. I would not be injured; if harm came to those who joined, it would always befall someone else, and I always thought and prayed they would survive. These thoughts proved to be naive wishes. There were just too many dangerous situations and too many bad people out there, naturally some of us would end up injured or killed.

We had all signed up for hazard pay just like solders in wartime on the front lines, even if we didn't comprehend it at the time. Although I quickly learned the proper protective methods to remain safe, and remembered the defense training I was taught at the academy, along with the arrest procedures. I realized that in any possible situation I could be injured.

Located on the second floor of the old Northern District, on Keswick and 34th streets, the academy offered classes on law, procedure, public relations, uniform attire, marching, driver training, street and monument locations to assist the public, as well as physical training, including self-defense tactics.

After sixteen weeks, our small class of thirty rookies was released for two weeks of traffic control in downtown Baltimore to learn on the job. This job was truly an art form: the art of directing thousands of pounds of vehicles occupied by drivers who were not paying attention while nonchalant pedestrians crossed the street when and were ever the spirit told them. I quickly learned from the first traffic officer I was assigned with how to survive. When I asked, "How do you handle this mess?" He replied, "Kid, whatever you do, don't get hit. Let them that can protect themselves, and don't worry your self about the rest. They seem to get by even without our help." It was not necessarily a direct answer to my question, but as the day wore on, it seemed to work. The drivers managed to drive somewhat alertly and the pedestrians stayed upright, even though neither seemed to pay attention to us.

I recall one afternoon of traffic training in particular that still makes me chuckle. I was in full uniform in late October of 1962 with my traffic-training officer at Light and Lombard streets. At the time, a building on the southwest corner was being demolished to make room for another, with dump trucks filled with debris from the site coming and going on eastbound Lombard Street. It was well into lunchtime and we had worked traffic control since morning rush hour. I turned away from the intersection and heard the tires on one of the trucks squeal as the driver reacted and stopped suddenly. The abrupt stop sent pieces of concrete over the truck cab from the bed, over the windshield, and down the hood and into the street at my feet. Dust and broken pieces of concrete, from baseball size to heavy slabs, fell into the intersection from the overloaded bed of the truck, denting the truck hood as they fell.

I looked up at the light and it was still green. Why had the driver stopped? I walked over to the driver and asked why he had stopped so quickly? He looked disgusted and replied, "You signaled for me to stop." I thought about what he had said for a second and then I realized what had happened. When I turned toward him, I adjusted my hat; he saw my hand go up and thought I was signaling him to stop, which he definitely did. He was the first conscientious driver I had encountered during traffic training. I did help him pick up some of the debris after he parked; after all, it was my fault, at least he thought it was. Of course, we had to clear the roadway. His reaction in stopping the truck and the look he had given me when he told me why he stopped convinced me that my hat adjustment had caused this messy intersection.

Once on the street, I quickly learned that attitude and physical size was most important. Those who looked up at you usually would not try you. I learned to read people by whatever attitude they responded with when they were approached; consider their actions and what led up to their response if possible. If they could be calmed, be considerate of their problems; if they continued to be disrespectful, react so that they would understand you were in charge. If you found the person or persons to be polite and respectful, confront the situation with forethought and consideration, be more respectful than they were. In a situation with a violent individual, adapt to the situation and be as physical as necessary. It did not take long to understand that the strength of character and a willingness to express it physically was the only thing some understood. Force, although infrequently used, was all that some individuals understood.

During my police academy days, I was paired against an ex-military boxer. We got along well personally, but he probably hit me two or three times for every one blow I landed. But I was persistent and hung in with him when we boxed, although each time we fought, I wished and prayed I were better. Our instructor said not to worry about it; I showed enough gumption to survive. Just remember, if it gets bad, hit them with anything. You're issued gear first, that's what it's for. Next, resort to anything you can pick up and use. Once in a while, you find a whole family of police fighters, all with the same disrespectful attitude, who would actually all fight physically against the arrest of one. I had a straightforward opinion that if anyone resisted a legal arrest by a uniformed police officer, they had no respect for the law itself. If they fought a uniformed representative of the law, they would fight anyone. It was not an assault on me or another officer; it was a total disregard for the legal system.

When I was new, each of the bars on my post and the characters that frequented them had an unwritten code, physically try the new postman. Consuming alcohol didn't help this attitude. Or perhaps it was just the desire to act as if they were the toughest person in the neighborhood and needed to uphold their already established reputation. But once you weathered one or two such confrontations, the word on the street was that you were tried and tested, and you were not another victim. Your authority was accepted and street respect given.

Central District

A fter my traffic training, which I never cared for, I reported to my first assignment: the Central District at Fayette and Fallsway streets. The building also housed the Police Department Headquarters, its related offices and the various detective units. At the time, out of thirty class members, I was one of fifteen assigned to the Central District. The antiquated building was dedicated around 1921. It looked and smelled old when we walked in, but we did not particularly notice. We were too excited by our new uniforms and the youthful dream of becoming working policemen.

The Central District itself took up about one-third of the first floor and was located at the south end of the building, overlooking Fayette Street. It consisted of one large open room that served as a roll call room. The desk sergeant's office used for booking arrested subjects was just off this room to the north. There were small offices off the south end for ranking staff officers, followed by larger offices for captains. A double door opened onto the ramp parking lot. An outside garage opened to the west and housed lockers for the radio crews. A small hall from the garage opened to the desk sergeant's booking area and to the cellblock across from his desk area. The cellblock had two entrances on both the south and north. These doors opened into one of the two District Courts, one on the north end of the block-long building and the other located on the southeast corner of the first floor.

The basement area of the District and Headquarters building was literally a gas station and a storage area accessible by ramps leading downward to enter the garage and one ramp leading upward and out. Probably the building for its time and building codes was magnificent, but consider modern architects designing a building and approving codes for a block-long, multi-storied Police Headquarters building being built with open gas pumps and gas storage tanks in the basement. Today's building and safety codes would have labeled the building much too dangerous of a concept to be considered today. What a target.

Serving in the Central was my best opportunity to learn how to work with all types of people. The District encompassed the downtown area as well as economically depressed neighborhoods surrounding downtown businesses. The people you met varied from professionals to laborers, and the housing could be anything from offices and homes of grandeur to slums. I learned from and enjoyed the diversity of it all.

During my Central District assignment, I was readily accepted by my shift lieutenant, despite a dispute with a driving instructor that preceded my time at the District. The instructor was a sergeant in charge of the driving safety program, but I had been informally introduced to the good sergeant, using the term "good" loosely, once before in an academy classroom. The sergeant asked all of the class to put their driver's licenses in front of them on their desk, and then asked those of us who could drive a stick shift to raise our hands. During what I think he considered his class presentation, he walked to one of the seated recruits, casually removed the man's driver's license from his desk and tore it up because the recruit was not paying attention, in his mind. He then announced to those who could only drive automatics rather than stick shift cars that they could not drive and they may as well not report for the driver's test because they could not pass the driving test and could not drive departmental vehicles.

The sergeant was a loudmouth, a heavy-set, boisterous controlling personality who was also an overweight person bursting out of an extremely ill fitting, unkempt uniform. He came across as arrogant, thinking he was always in control. For the first time during training, I had met a man in the same uniform as me who I felt could possibly be the worst representative of the Department possible. Perhaps they had seen fit to hide him away at the driving academy to keep his physical appearance and disagreeable personality from the public. Days later, the rumor went around the academy that this very sergeant had actually been charged at one time with automobile manslaughter. No one knew the circumstances, but he was the highest-ranking officer at the driver's academy.

In those days, you spent a day at the driving school, which was located in Clifton Park, at the completion of your sixteen week training period. You actually took a physical driving test around Lake Clifton at that location, including pursuit driving. At a random point unknown to the driver during the staged pursuit, a .22-caliber blank was fired and you were required to apply the brakes to test your response time.

After my driving test was over, the charming sergeant in his controlling, rough voice informed me I had passed but said there was no need for my license because "rookies would not drive anyway if they had less than five years on the job." Naturally, that comment made no sense to me. He had just said I passed. I asked for my license. A uniformed officer seated next to him to the left of his desk got up and stared me down without a word. I stood up and stared back at him. What he was doing in regards to my upbringing posed a physical threat as far as the way I was brought up. The sergeant realized the situation, asked what I was doing and told me to leave, saying that I would not get my license. I replied by asking, "What is this patrolman standing over me for?"

I was greeted at the Central by Lieutenant Thomas Middleton who, in a tough, raised voice that matched his large physical appearance, yelled at me asking, "Why would the good sergeant want to report the situation to me?" The demanding lieutenant could have been the Commissioner of Police as far as I knew about the rank and his District authority, not having been in the military and not having known the status of a District lieutenant at the time. After hearing my side of the story, he dismissed me from his office saying, "You have just arrived and there's a problem already." When I reached the door, hat in hand, I felt I was going to get fired before hired, what a way to start off. He said, "Wait a minute, I'll send you back and you will get your license. My son was in your class and he thinks you are all right; he might have been correct. If you don't care for the sergeant, he's a goof." Until that minute I had no idea that his son was in my class or that he liked me one way or the other, but the lieutenant definitely disliked the sergeant in charge of the driving school.

Lt. Middleton proved not only a mentor but also a policeman's police. There was an incident in which a local government official's son was arrested and charged with rape. Rather than have the two radio car men that had made the arrest appear in District Court for the court procedure and politically risk their future careers, Lt. Middleton appeared in the District Court and presented the case himself. He retired years after with the same rank of lieutenant, although he deserved and would have achieved a higher rank if he had not stepped up in that situation.

A few months later after my conversation with the lieutenant, I had to take the driving test again and I got my license; although, it was begrudgingly issued by the previously mentioned good sergeant, who frowned at me, handed it to me without a word and dismissed me by pointing to the door. Over my years in the district, I cannot count the ways Lt. Middleton impressed so many of us with his knowledge and dedication to his men and the job. Nothing was said about my first test, and my protest, so I knew Lt. Middleton had spoken to the sergeant probably in no uncertain terms.

I mentioned that Lt. Middleton was a man's man. He told everyone at one time or the other that if we needed help in arresting a resisting subject to call him. And if we had a known bad actor wanted on a warrant, he would always tell the postman he wanted to be there personally when the warrant was served. Once during our roll call he proved his point to all of us.

At the time, we stood for roll call in lines in the largest of rooms at the district. The lieutenant or sergeant reading roll stood at a podium on a one-step platform near the double rear door to the District, which overlooked a ramped parking lot for the radio cars. One of the guys in either Squad seven or eight was called down for talking while Lt. Middleton was reading. A few minutes later, the same rather large man was called down a second time. The third time was a charm. Lt.

Middleton unstrapped his gun belt, flung it on top of the podium, pointed to the man and invited him out on the ramp. Telling the officer if he could not be quite during roll call he he was going to beat him until he could not utter a word. A quick apology followed and silence fell over the entire room.

Now a story about myself, the old adage, "If you can't laugh at yourself you should not laugh at others" I am the one writing this? The Police Department had proved itself to be somewhat like the stories you hear from wartime heroes. With all the horrors of war from the soldiers who had seen active duty, only the funny stories survive to be told over and over by those who witnessed the events. I'm sure it's because they want to forget the ones that could cause them nightmares. And so it was with the Department.

Thankfully, this story had no witnesses. I was still what they called "extra," which meant I had not been assigned a post and worked various posts each time I came in. This particular night I was working the 12 P.M. to 8 A.M. shift and a post down on Lombard Street that incorporated small streets south of Lombard. My first night on the post I was unfamiliar with the area, but like a "good rookie" I was going to "try up" every possible door. "Trying up" was checking every commercial establishment during your tour to make sure it had not been broken into and that the property was securely locked.

Walking the post on foot on Salisbury Lane, I tried the door of what appeared to be an auto repair shop and found it open. Like any new, energetic rookie, I thought I had a burglary and I was about to apprehend my first part one crime, "a felony." It was around two in the morning and the buildings were dark, with only dim street lighting reflecting off the entrance door and window glass. I entered the garage front entrance holding the flashlight away from my body as taught in my left hand and my revolver in my right hand. Once inside it was impossible to see in the darkness. I stumbled on a metal tool that clanged on the concrete floor, leaving me with the thought that if anyone other than myself were in the building, they now knew I was there also and I was about to be hit in the head with another metal tool, this one wielded by the burglar. The first room was clear, but a door on the west side of the area was open and led to another room located behind the building next door.

I entered that room still spotlighting my flashlight and the first thing my light hit was a large opened safe on the west wall. I turned off my light, now thinking in my mind that I had an actual commercial burglary. I stepped into the room and turned the flashlight on again. This time it focused directly on a fully dressed man standing in the far northwest corner. I raised my gun, pointed it at the man and yelled for him not to move. He didn't, nor did he speak. As a matter of fact, he did not even flinch. Seconds later, I realized that my target was bald headed. Not a normal hairstyle at the time. I realized that the figure was not a burglar trying to hide in the corner, but a well-dressed male mannequin. It was dressed in a shirt, pants, sport coat and even wearing shoes. The only thing that prevented shots from being fired after I yelled was that the figure, although fashionably and fully dressed, was bald headed and motionless.

Next, my light hit the large, open safe. Upon examination of the safe, I found it to be open wide, but with dust and cobwebs on the empty shelves and door. The station called in the night reference, and the responding young owner explained away what I thought was my first big case. The door had been accidentally left unlocked. The previous building owner had left the safe about three years ago because of its size and weight. Unlocked and empty, too heavy to be removed, it had never been used by the present business. The mannequin was used to display restored cars. They used it to sit in the cars as if it was the driver. Baldy was part of the display and all was explained away. I tried not to show my disappointment in not having what I thought was a good case. The owner was impressed that I had found the open door; there wasn't a word from my supervisors about me finding the place open.

About every two years, one of the local newspapers would have a field day with anything they considered embarrassing to the department. I could see the headlines now, "Dummy shoots dummy." Needless to say, I was embarrassed. Many people to this day have not been told this story. I have told a few of my close friends, after realizing it was funny.

My first arrest came early in my career while I was still an extra, just a month or so after my assignment to the Central District. I was working the day shift on a downtown post, wandering around on foot within the boundaries of my assigned post. At that time, the heart of our shopping district was Howard Street, which was lined with major department stores that drew daily crowds from both the city and the surrounding counties. Vehicular and foot traffic was heavy everywhere in the downtown area. I was still trying to get used to the unwanted attraction that the uniform caused me, trying to act as casual as possible even though I was a youthful, inexperienced rookie.

I guess now that I think back on it, most who gave me a glance, knew I was a rookie fresh on the street from the academy. A tall youthful, lanky drink of water in a blue uniform, not confident enough to twirl my nightstick in front of the public for fear they would laugh at the mistakes, or end up hitting myself with it. That's all I had to do, hit myself with that stick publicly. I walked for hours, wandering about my post, taking in the sights and sounds of downtown.

That was the only problem with being a loan out, you didn't know anything about the post, the people, the businesses, and even the area was unfamiliar. I watched the traffic as I walked: the pedestrians hurrying to and fro stores and those who worked in the area running from their rushed lunch breaks. I found the call boxes located on my post and made sure that I made prompt calls on my designated time.

Like any rookie, I wondered about what eventful calls or situations could occur in such a busy commercial area that would require police action. And like any one on a new job I wondered if I had the ability to handle whatever developed. As I walked, I thought of a few such situations, but things had been so uneventful up until this time, I was considering my hourly calls as probably the most memorable experience I would take away from this post assignment. Walking down Liberty Street and turning west on Fayette Street, I first noticed a crowd gathering at the curb, attracted by something taking place in the street. I approached to see what the trouble was. As I got closer to the crowd, I heard someone say, "One's a cop." I pushed my way through the group of onlookers and observed a stocky man fighting with a uniformed traffic police officer.

This wasn't a situation where I had to make a decision as to right or wrong; it was right in front of me and obvious. I ran to the officer's assistance and helped him subdue his attacker, who was holding his own as far as the fight was concerned when I reached them. All that happened to me at the time was a glancing blow from the man, which bounced off my right shoulder, when he turned toward me and realized I was coming to join in the fighting. Two against one was no odds for the guy, who gave up when he realized his chances of winning this battle were slim at best. Someone had apparently called the altercation in, as the patrol wagon arrived within minutes, about the same time two radio cars screeched to a halt with their lights on and their sirens wailing. At that time, there was not a cell phone in every pocket, or for that matter that many conveniently placed public phones. Probably someone had called who had seen the fight from one of the buildings overlooking the street.

The wagon pulled up and I followed the traffic officer's lead and helped him pitch the man head first into the back of the wagon, with his hands cuffed behind him. His body made a rather loud thud as it struck the metal wagon floor. As the sound and view of the man hitting the inside of the wagon filtered outside, the downtown crowd who had watched the brief altercation actually cheered. People from all walks of life, young, old, black, white, male and female shoppers, businessmen and women, in short, the citizens of Baltimore applauded.

That's how dramatically times have changed today; you would have fifty people recording every aspect of the arrest on their smart phones, being sure to capture scenes of those reported blows landed by the police on the defenseless suspect. Some that hadn't even seen the situation would be blaming everything on the police, including being responsible for initiating the disturbance. Most of the photos and videos would show the police hitting the man, but for some reason there would be no frames showing the police being struck, or how it began. Needless to say, throwing the guy into the wagon would inspire complaints to Internal Affairs before the wagon could leave the scene.

But not back then there were no complaints, not even from the man himself. It really was a more forthright period; people took responsibility for their actions and accepted the consequences. I gave the officer my name and district and he told me he would write the report; good thing, I was so new I would have to get someone in the District to show me the proper report form.

A month or so later, I was one of the first in my class to be summoned to Criminal Court on a case. Others and my self had testified in District Court for minor arrests that in those days were tried the next morning, but few had been involved in cases that went uptown. District Court had its merits: trials being the next day, the judge usually saw the defendant in the same or near condition he was in at the time of his arrest. Criminal Court had changed over the years since those days in regards to appearance time because of the volume of cases. Today it takes months for a court appearance after one or two granted postponements, sometimes six to eight months after the original arrest.

The man arrested had been charged with assaulting two police officers and resisting arrest. After the traffic officer testified, I was called to the stand to testify to what I had witnessed and what action I had taken as a result. During my testimony, the defense attorney, after establishing my part in the arrest, looked me straight in the eye and asked, "What was my client wearing at the time you two arrested him?" I thought about the question he had asked and stated, "I don't recall exactly the color, he was wearing a suit."

The lawyer, confident that he had found a flaw in my testimony, lashed back, "You mean you arrested this man, and you can't tell us the color of the suit he was dressed in at the time!" I looked him directly in his face this time and replied, "I arrested him for what he was doing, not for what he was wearing at the time he was fighting with a uniformed police officer." A few muffled laughs came from the gallery and the judge leaned forward with a slight smile he could not control. Leaning over the front portion of the bench, the judge whispered to the defense attorney, "Well, you asked and he answered." The attorney thought over my answer for a minute, then stated, "No further questions of this witness." My first criminal trial testimony had concluded, rather favorably I thought. The trial ended and the man was found guilty of all the charges.

I often found myself anxious to return to work on my days off. At the time, we had one day a week off and one optional day a month. I seldom considered taking the optional day. In those days, police walked their post and watched call box lights between their appointed check-in calls. Your call times were predetermined and you were allowed fifteen minutes past the allotted call in time before counted as overdue. The purpose of the call was to assure that you were safe. Items such as cell phones were not even thought of at the time. If the light on the call box came on, it was your responsibility to contact the call box operator by means of a phone inside the call box to see if they wanted you to handle a complaint on your post.

The posts were roughly three to four square blocks. On the 4-to-12 and 12-to-8 shifts, the officers were responsible for finding any commercial break-ins, or burglaries, on their respective posts. Shift sergeants would "tell tale" the commercial properties and schools with either black thread, which would break when walked through, or a piece of paper that would fall from a door when shaken while being checked to see if it was locked. The officers were responsible for finding the break-ins on the evening shifts or held accountable. The district had night references should a property be found damaged or broken into. If Sgt. John Grempler was working, you could bet he checked and marked the properties and definitely expected the rookies to find them. He was a quiet man, one of few words at any given time. As a matter of fact, his quietness along with his sometimes gangly gestures and slow speech made you question his very intelligence.

One night after I had tried up "Antique Row," which was located in the 800 block of Howard Street, an extended block loaded from one end to the other with storefronts. I made my call at Madison and Tyson and headed north on foot on the 800 block of Tyson. Meandering casually south in what we called an alley street because it was so narrow it was just wide enough for one-way traffic was Sgt. Grempler. We met about halfway down the block. Grempler smiled with a greeting and asked if I had tried up the row, meaning Howard Street. I replied I had just finished. He glared at me with a stern look on his face and asked, "Then why are the tell tales still in place?" I told him where about ten of them were wedged between the doorframes and the door, and named the businesses where they were found. He asked, "Why are they still there?" I answered, "If they are on the ground when I go back, someone had tried the doors. If I move them from where you placed them, then you think someone else has tried the door."

He smiled at me and said, "I stop and stand in secluded spots on your post and wait to see how often you get in the area. You're alright, keep up your frequent patrol and don't bother me, it works two ways, I won't bother you." After that statement, he walked away southbound on the street. I continued up Tyson Street, smiled and realized I had been accepted as far as he was concerned. Over my patrol years, I grew to respect this conscientious, quiet man. He taught me many things about the job and how it worked without me realizing his intent.

Over the years, I discovered that I had been completely wrong in judging Sgt. Grempler's intelligence. One instance occurred when Officer Ralph Eicher and I were on the 12-to-8 shift in a radio car and in between calls. Ralph was driving and had been studying for weeks for the pending sergeant's examination. Without a word in regards to what he was doing, he drove us to Madison Street and Martin Luther King Blvd. There, standing at the call box, apparently waiting for us was Sgt. Grempler. He got into the back seat of our radio car and leaned back casually, and as usual silent, while Eicher asked him question after question for at least a half an hour about everything on the pending sergeant's test. Grempler answered every question, elaborated on a few, and added a few questions on his own. This apparently quiet, unassuming man knew the Digest of Laws backward and forward.

In the case of arrest, the subject arrested had to be taken to a call box on foot by the officer and, if combative, handcuffed to a pole or metal step railing. After subduing the arrested suspect the officer would walk to the nearest call box and call in the whereabouts of the person arrested.

Our equipment issued upon graduation from the academy consisted of: one revolver, which was a .38-caliber Colt revolver; an issued nightstick that was so light it blew in the wind; a pair of handcuffs; the uniformed leather gun belt with attachments for the revolvers, holster and cuffs; along with a badge, cap device and uniform.

You quickly learned how difficult it was to replace any torn or worn clothing. The issued nightstick was so light it had to be replaced with solid, heavier wooden sticks. Red wood was my preference. And yes, although not sanctioned by the Department, it was an era in which the police learned how to twirl their sticks. Twirling the nightstick is an art form mainly forgotten in this age, as conventional nightsticks have given way to hard rubber batons. Optional equipment frequently carried included slapjacks and the iron claw. The iron claw was a device shaped like a single handcuff with a ratchet handle. The officer would clamp the open cuff on the suspect's wrist and turn the ratchet handle to tighten the cuff portion to the suspect's wrist.

There was an art to the use of the iron claw. Using one extended finger of the same hand, almost in one motion, you had to open the claw, slap it on the wrist of the suspect and close the cuff-like ratchet before the subject realized it was on his wrist. Only a few carried and used this device effectively. The slapjack was leather with a weighted piece of metal in the head portion and a shaped handles and strap to hold it with, it was a seriously effective weapon if used properly. If anyone took a hard blow from a slapjack and continued to fight, you knew you were in for a battle.

The police department was considered a semi-military organization at the time; set rules were to be followed while in the public eye. Those who smoked were not allowed to smoke in public. If you wanted or had to smoke, you had to sneak into an alley like a child hiding from their parent.

We were to appear in full uniform at all times when dealing with the public. Caps were to be worn at all times, when on foot patrol and when exiting the car. On one occasion, I was driving off duty when I observed a uniformed officer from another district involved in a street altercation with a subject. I pulled my car out of traffic and ran to his aid, not even thinking about my hat on the car seat, just the altercation in front of me. While both of us tried to subdue the man, an unknown police lieutenant walked up to the fight, did not assist, and ordered me to put on my hat. I yelled some profanity at him and he turned and walked away. He was never identified to me, but it was obvious that he was a book man, not a street cop.

Other pieces of issued equipment I almost forgot to mention included a metal whistle and a call-box key. The purpose of the key is obvious. The whistle was in case you were injured on the street. A necessary special tool, as was your nightstick, should you be injured on the night shift and needed help. You would blow the whistle at intervals until you were located, or bang your stick on the pavement until found. Most never considered how alone out there we were.

My mentor, Lt. Middleton, once caught me with a plastic whistle and commented, "Good, get beat up, find yourself hurt and bleeding, unable to walk, needing help, and fall during the fight, breaking that plastic thing, lose your stick in the fight, and get yourself killed because others won't be able to find your bleeding, stupid, dumb ass." His point was well taken, and still remembered. Often, we did not think about it, about who we were and what we did; out in a world by ourselves with to many pitfalls to imagine or consider armed with the tools of the trade that dated back to the turn of the century.

There were only five two-man cars in the district; the closest car would back up an arrest if in service, meaning not on call them selves. There were two wagons, known as "Cruising Patrols," to haul away those who were arrested. They patrolled half the district, each waiting for arrest calls, and ran into each other's territory on calls if the assigned cruiser was out of service. No handheld radios were available for years. The only communication was through the call boxes. Yes, the system was archaic. No instant communication was available and that constantly wasted response time on calls and jeopardized the safety of the officers on the street and the public who were in need. What if an officer were injured and alone? If so, they had up to one hour before there was a thought of locating and rescuing them? What if the injury occurred in the dead of night at an isolated location?

The potential for injury wasn't even the biggest concern. The days the powers to be were removed the foot officers and we were motorized did irreparable harm. Militant groups like the Black Panthers were on the rise, causing civil unrest and more than just the usual disrespect toward police officers, with their hate speeches in the streets. Two Central District officers, Sager and Serikowski, had been shot while seated in their patrol car. The shooter, later identified as a Black Panther, walked up to their car and fired at them point-blank. Officer Sager died of his wounds at the scene. Officer Serikowski survived his wounds after over a year of hospitalization and multiple operations.

The resulting situation, with no police available to the public unless they were called to the respective scenes, made for miscommunication and mistrust between the police and the public. We had lost our street intelligence. Police would respond, take action and leave until the next call. More than once I heard, "You come, lock someone up and then you're gone until the next time." Neither the public nor the police liked the new system. Not a positive or productive situation at all. Gone were the foot patrolmen who knew everyone on their post, who knew who were the lawless and who to talk with to find out information on a wanted criminal. No longer was the beat cop known to the individual, just a man in a uniform, liked and respected in the community, who was concerned with their problems and helped decent people like a friend. Gone were the police like "Hawk," who I'll share some stories about in a few pages.

At the worst time in our history, mobilization caused a situation where the general public thought it was us against them. It's ironic now, in this age of police chief associations around the country talking about bringing back the foot officers. Without the human police element reaching out to the public, we were left with the Black Panthers' propaganda, street drugs and gang control was understood and accepted more than the Department's influence.

I will never forget an incident where a parent commented to his five year old, "See that cop he will hit you with that stick if he ever gets you." I replied that, "Police are the only reasonable people to come to if the child is lost or hurt. Never teach them that police are not their friends. Police are, in truth, the only safe way home." But now we were even strangers to that kid; he would never willingly meet one of us on the beat with time to stop and talk unless his father heeded the advice I had given.

Foot patrol was a work in progress. It was your responsibility to learn the good guys from the bad. Be able to identify them.from the honest daily workers, storeowners and residents on your post from the strangers. Know their hours, their properties, their vehicles and their work habits. Show that honestly you cared and were there to protect them; let the bad know they would go to jail if you caught them. Patrol the streets on the evening shifts long after most have left the area, looking for those willing to commit crime aided by the darkness. Interact with those on your foot post; they were the ones that knew what was happening and who was responsible, and what problems existed, they lived with it. Gain their confidence and listen. Often, information sounded like just conversation because the person relating it to you lived there twenty four hours a day; fearful of retaliation, but still wanted to help. I talked to everyone about whatever they wanted to talk about, usually starting the conversation with "Hello" or "Nice day." If they shunned conversation, it sparked your interest in them.

You learned to distinguish between serious crimes that required arrest and those minor violations that if overlooked would lead to valuable information. Once I stood outside a liquor store at Madison Street and Martin Luther King Blvd., watching a neighborhood resident I knew well work for over ten minutes stealing five cigars. The man was working harder at the theft than if he had been at work. Every time one of the three clerks in the store was busy with customers or not looking in his direction, he would snatch another cigar. He was so preoccupied with what he was doing that he did not notice me leaning against the outside window watching. Finally, he strolled out of the liquor store without an apparent purchase and a smile on his face. Seeing me as soon as he came out, he walked over and started a nervous, but somewhat casual conversation. I interrupted him and advised I had watched him for minutes and asked if he wanted to go to jail for the theft. Of course, I knew his answer before I asked. I sent him back into the store and had him replace the cigars on the promise that if he was caught replacing them, he was going to jail. I waited and watched him; honestly, it took him longer to put them back than it had taken to steal them. But he finally replaced them without being noticed by the store help. When he came out, he thanked me and told me I was all right with him. I told him that was the first and last break he would get from me. From that day on, anything he saw or witnessed in the neighborhood that would interest me, I knew.

One part of the job I was not anxious to do: issue parking tickets around Maryland General Hospital, although you could probably issue a book a day. Parking was limited to those who had business at the hospital and restricted to the public and staff, with parking meters everywhere. Workers, nurses and those visitors of the sick and dying had more far reaching problems and issues during their visits than the time left on their parking meters or the inconvenience of a ticket. I had a new sergeant tell me to give out a book of tickets before I was reassigned to the radio car. That meant twenty five tickets. I had not given out twenty five tickets in the two plus years I was assigned the post, with no intentions of reaching that high number. I always considered parking tickets terrible public relations.

On an unrelated matter, one of the things that benefitted me greatly on foot post was conversations with various tradesmen: bricklayers, carpenters, electricians, concrete finishers, street finishers and road workers, all at various places on my post at different times. Ask anyone how they perform their job and they willingly tell you, its human nature. They take pride in their work; and the thought that someone else appreciated it enough to ask about it usually started the conversation and led to discussing how they performed their various occupations. Living payday to payday at the time, I learned to build my own brick barbeque, in the style at the time and did all the wood and electrical work in my first clubroom and several others as we moved from one house too the next over the years.

While on foot, I caught my first armed hold-up man. There used to be a corner liquor store at Martin Luther King Blvd. and Linden Avenue called Oriole Liquors. One night, my mother and her boyfriend brought me lunch. I was seated in the boyfriend's car having a sub and soda on the parking lot of the State Office Building near the intersection of Eutaw Street and Martin Luther King Blvd. when I observed a man running from Oriole Liquors, west toward Eutaw Street. At first, I thought nothing about his actions, just another petty theft from the owner Irv, probably a neighborhood boy known to him. Seconds later,

Irv came out of the store and watched the man run, shouting something at him and waving his fist in his direction. Just the fact that Irv took the time to come outside making an attempt to see which way the man ran tipped me off. Irv's appearance told me that something was wrong. He was used to the neighborhood thefts and played little to no attention to those who stole off the counters of his business. For Irv, small losses never mattered. He worked the liquor store mainly alone and did not want to confront small petty thefts for fear it would result in an altercation and injury. I excused myself from my company saying I had to go.

I jumped from the car and chased the man down Eutaw Street; he was the closest he would be to me for several blocks until his apprehension. At that point, I was probably a half block from him, but he wasn't looking back in my direction. He had ran to the corner of Eutaw and Martin Luther King Blvd. and turned south on Eutaw. At the intersection of Madison and Eutaw streets, he turned north on Madison Avenue and then west on Orchard Street toward Druid Hill. At that point, I was probably still a quarter of a block from him, but I had still not been seen; he was too busy in what I realized was turning into a frantic escape attempt. Why was he running so far? Why not relax, walk and look like an innocent person out for a walk? I caught up to him on Orchard Street near Druid Hill Avenue, where Cliff's bar was located.

It was a mild night with lots of people on the street, sitting on their steps and in front of Cliff's. I heard someone on the street yell, "Run faster, he's catching you." Most who witnessed the chase saw two men with guns in their hands and realized what was happening, and were running for cover at this point. Whoever had yelled from the crowd alerted the runner and he turned for the first time to see me chasing him. Suddenly he decided to stop running just before he reached Druid Hill Avenue in front of Cliff's Bar. At the time, there was about a car length between us. He turned to face me with a gun in his right hand. That was the first time I actually saw the weapon.

I raised my service revolver and we stood for a split second looking at one another with about twenty feet between us, the length of a parked car. Both of us were in the street at the time. He was at the front of a parked car and I was at the trunk area of the same car when I yelled, "Why did you hold up the store?" But he did not reply. He just stood there pointing his gun at me, holding it waist high. I did everything taught to me in the police academy. I turned to my left to give him a smaller target. I raised my revolver to eye level and cocked it. At that time, I heard shouts from those still on the street and doors slam. I aimed my revolver, single action, steadied my aim and prepared to shoot, thinking at the time I would at least be wounded but not killed.

When I aimed my revolver, the hold-up man lowered his gun to his side. He gave me a look of disappointment and exhaustion at the same time, and surrendered without a word. He dropped his gun hand to his side and I ordered him to drop the gun, which he did. As I walked up to him, I asked, "Why did you hold up the liquor store?" He didn't answer, reached in his pocket and handed me a handful of money. I retrieved the pistol from the ground after having him back up, prone on the hood of a parked car, and threatening to shoot him if he moved. Both out of breath and with him cuffed, I walked him a short distance to a call box just south of Orchard Street on Druid Hill Avenue to call for the wagon.

A man who must have watched us came out of Cliff's Bar, staggered over to us at the call box on Druid Hill Avenue and said, "We are not going to allow you to take him. We are going to take him away from you." I had just finished calling for the cruising patrol and was standing at the call box with my prisoner pushed up against the box with two handguns, my service revolver in my right hand and the holdup man's gun in my left hand. I looked at the bar patron and concerned citizen and said, "Which one of these would you like to get your sorry ass shot with?" He turned and walked away without another word. A foolish man with a drunken thought to become a neighborhood legend had thought it over and decided it wasn't worth it.

Now thinking back on the arrest, I think it represented what we as police were and still are always faced with, one minute, things were fine, no problems, you were in control of whatever the situation; the next, your safety or your life could be in jeopardy. The holdup man had been taught enough in his home life or in the military not to take a life. The street person was cold enough or drunk enough to walk into a dangerous situation and attempt to start trouble. We were always in the position to meet either personality, but we didn't have the advantage of knowing which type or when we would encounter them.

Since I had bailed out of the car from my mother's company without a word and chased the man down the street, I did call her to ensure that her only son was all right. Ironically, within minutes of this arrest, the officer working the top end of the same sector arrested an attempted rape suspect, caught at the home of a potential victim in Bolton Hill. Two officers working in the same small bailiwick, usually quiet posts, in the same area had made two felony arrests within minutes.

Later it was learned that the man that I had arrested was AWOL from the military. He said that he robbed the liquor store because he needed money. His frantic run around the neighborhood made sense after all; he was not familiar with the area. After all that running, he had only gone a little over two blocks from the liquor store. When asked why he hadn't shot at me when arrested, he said, "I was taught never to shoot policemen. If you hurt or killed a cop, other ones would kill you." It was lucky for me he had that old-school upbringing. Thinking back on the possibilities of two armed men shooting at each other with only twenty feet or so between them, well, I was fortunate to say the least, maybe the luckiest ever in my career. If I were destined to be shot on the job, that's when it would have happened.

The runner was tried in our jurisdiction and found guilty of the use of a handgun during the commission of a commercial robbery and the armed robbery itself. Another aspect of the trial that stood out in my mind was when a young state's attorney who handled the case asked if he could have the subject's gun. "Could I get it from evidence control for him?" he inquired; I abruptly refused, quite angered at the time. Irv and I could have been shot with that gun, maybe killed, that youngster of a lawyer was not going to get it.

Usually, during my entire tour with the Department, gun charges were often dropped as part of the pre-trial agreements between the two attorneys and the judge during motions. This practice allowed the most serious charges to stand. You know without it being said that they never give out statistics on how many gun charges are agreed to be dropped. Gun possession during the commission of a crime carried a ten year sentence in itself.

Today, the politicians rant and rave about tighter handgun regulations to prevent armed robberies and shootings. They don't enforce the laws that are already on the books, and they attempt to pass laws yearly to prevent citizens from carrying weapons for their own protection. They harp about gun violence at every opportunity, but never talk about the statistics in "right to carry states," where robberies and burglaries are lower. Stands to reason, would you rob someone or break into their homes if you knew they were armed or had the right to be?

Cliff's Bar

In 1962, Cliff's Bar located at Druid Hill Ave. and Orchard St. was rated one of the top ten most violent bars in the city. One of its victims was a man who was shot because he played the wrong song in the jukebox after the other had given him the nickel to play his requested song. Both were drunk at the time and that did contribute to the misunderstanding, but over a nickel in the jukebox? The victim of the shooting was pronounced dead at the scene. Of course, the thirty some witnesses did not see anything; some said they didn't even hear the shot.

We received more calls for serious assaults there than you can count. Every time you walked in on a call and interviewed customers of the bar present at the time of the arguments that led to shootings and stabbings, they were covered with the blood of either the assailant or the victim and would swear to not having any knowledge of the assault or to not have even witnessed the event.

Initially in the early 1960's, the weapons of choice were razors and knives. Most of the patrons of Cliff's wore their wounds visibly, with scars from these weapons on their faces and arms, even boasting about the fights and proud of their previous battles. Gradually, handguns came on the scene; revolvers primarily back in that period.

My personal thought about the use of handguns was that not only was it more injurious to the victims but it allowed the assailant to stay out of arm's reach, out of range from his victim and their weapons, especially the razors. No longer were they toeing and wrestling over a knife or razors; the use of guns allowed them to inflict more injury and afforded the assailant protection. No longer were they in physical contact with a potential victim or assailant. Personally, I think that it removed up-close contact with a combatant and allowed you to assault him without the threat of personal harm.

Another misnomer that I think society has bought into is the fear of black people in confrontations. People are people, one on one in a physical or forceful situation; both combatants are equally upset and frightened. The majority of assaults and robberies occur with more than one suspect against a single victim. There is support, confidence and physical strength as well as safety in numbers.

On one occasion, I walked into Cliff's shortly after I had been assigned to the post, recalling the warning how bad the bar was and to expect anything, and to exert control over any situation or become the victim. Two drunks were fighting, which was not that uncommon a situation for that bar. I separated them and one failed to calm down. He kept running his mouth at the other and tried several times to get around me to restart the fight. When he did not settle down, I placed him under arrest. I grabbed the back of his belt and started toward the front door of the bar with him in front of me. The bar aisle was only wide enough for one person to walk, with the bar stools on the right side and booths on the left side. We were probably fifteen feet from the door when he planted his feet and announced, "You are not taking me out of here." My first thought was he might be right.

The man was larger than me and actually it surprised me that he had stopped our exit. My nightstick was in my right hand and his belt in my left. I didn't say anything to him. I swung as hard as I could in the confined space we were in, bringing the stick around from behind me and cracking him on his right knee. He buckled under the blow, fell toward the bar where he caught his weight, straightened back up and limped to the entrance with me pushing him forward. Everyone in the bar looked and became silent. The statement he had just made to about twenty people in the bar had been forgotten when he slumped in pain. Their laughs faded and they parted, allowing us a path to the door. I walked him to the call box located on Druid Hill Ave., about a quarter of a block from Cliff's, and placed him in the wagon when it arrived. All this occurred without another word from him or any further resistance, or interference from the bar onlookers for that matter, half of which had witnessed the arrest inside of the bar and spilled out onto the sidewalk in front.

The next day, I walked into the bar just on routine patrol. When the bartender saw me, he shouted, "This man don't take any shit. "When he grabs you, you go." That was my first and last trial at Cliff's. From there on, I was "Mr. Steve" and not to be messed with. The bouncer at the time became a personal friend and provided information on the patrons, out of reach of their hearing. This was a dangerous thing to do; if they knew, he would surely be found seriously injured or dead. But I knew from seeing him in action it would take two or more to get him. He was fearless and ran that bar; I never met anyone who could beat him, if they were foolish enough to try.

Ironically, years later after I was assigned to homicide, I saw him on a call off of Greenmount Avenue, where he was living at the time. Now a gentle elderly man with fading scars from the fights he had handled at the bar, he still projected the image of a man who could handle himself, and well, he could, he put many of Cliff's patrons in the hospital while settling arguments. It was great to see him healthy and doing well. Seeing him brought back a lot of old memories about him, the old post, its people and things that happened there.

One incident in Cliff's and I was accepted. They had decided that as far as the regulars were concerned, I was in charge. If outsiders started anything inside the bar, patrons actually offered their help, or at least stood back. I never had anyone try to hinder me during any arrest or challenge my actions when making an arrest, except with that one armed robbery suspect I arrested outside. That drunk who staggered over to the call box and said they were going to take him away from me wandered away with no support from anyone. I never saw him afterward. He was never in Cliff's when I was working, and the regulars at the bar claimed not to know him.

Another run-in with not one but two hold up men was at a small, family grocery store located on 21st Street between St. Paul and Calvert streets. At the time, Officer Ronnie Lamartina and I were working a marked car, both assigned to car 105. Ron had replaced Officer Douglas Cash, when Cash went to detectives. I was driving at the time the call came over.

We were just blocks from the call when we received report of a robbery in progress. We responded without the emergency lights or siren on, feeling we were close enough to catch the robber in the act. We double parked in the street just below the store entrance so we would not be seen from the store windows and ran to the front of the building. We arrived quickly at the scene. There was no pedestrian traffic on the street and the vehicle traffic was light. As we both ran to the store address, I called to Ron to be careful; our response was quick enough that the suspects could still be there if the hold-up call was legit.

The entrance was to our left and inside of a small vestibule on the first floor. Apparently, the entrance and the first-floor area had been converted from a normal row house into a small neighborhood grocery. We had approached the storefront from the west and had not crossed in front of the store window, which would have exposed us to anyone inside. We paused for a few seconds inside the vestibule, both of us not knowing what to expect; then without a word, we pointed to the doorknob. We looked at each other and motioned with our heads to enter, pointing our weapons at the door. We opened the door and rushed in.

Ron grabbed one of the armed holdup men, who froze when he saw us, and threw him into a vegetable counter facing the front window. He pinned the guy's right hand, which held a 38 revolver, and shoved his own service revolver into the man's chest. His quick physical response startled the suspect and he was easily subdued and disarmed without a shot being fired.

A second man ran around the back of a meat counter and attempted to open the back door to escape. The door was locked with three or four different types of bolts and his attempt at unlocking the door frustrated him to such a degree that he turned toward my pointed gun and surrendered. He was not armed. I had drawn down on him with my revolver, reaching over the meat counter and yelling for him to raise his hands, with which he complied. He saw no other option than to surrender. Ron had already successfully subdued his armed subject and was out of harm's way. Both men were apprehended and cuffed without a shot being fired.

The store itself amounted to one large room, a mom and pop operation, with two suspects, the owners, man and wife, and two policemen we had a full house. After all the excitement, we were practically on top of each other in this small neighborhood store. There were no injuries as a result of the arrest. The owners had only been verbally threatened before our arrival and had not turned over any money. They were so excited about the robbery being halted that I think they thanked us; I'm not sure, they fell back into their native language, jumped about laughing and smiling, patted us on the backs, and I think they cursed the two unsuccessful holdup men, at least their gestures indicated that.

First Assignment & "The Hawk"

My first assignment after months of being an extra was a hospital post. Extra meant that you worked a different post almost every day. It was a method of learning the district and at the same time covering the post for those off duty. The officers at hospitals were responsible for all reports, meaning that anyone who came into the hospital with an injury as a result of a violation of the law had to be interviewed as to the nature of the assault, the cause, the perpetrator if identified to them, a description if not and a written report documenting the incident. Needless to say, I quickly learned a lot about report writing and observed every injury imaginable that could be caused by a multitude of criminal acts and traffic accidents.

My post was the center of three, located at the southern end of the bailiwick. The entire bailiwick constituted of six individual posts, three on the upper north end and three to the south. Usually you worked either two or three of the bottom post, never just a single post, or just yours. The bailiwick was diverse in its area makeup. On the top, or the north post, you ranged from projects on the west to the Maryland Art Institute on the east, with middle to upper-class residents. In the middle and east, you had a very refined, upper-class residential area called Bolton Hill.

The three posts on the bottom, or south end, were as diverse. On the west end, you had Cliff's Bar and black residential row homes. The middle post was comprised of low-income white residents on Eutaw

Street, with Antique Row to the east in the 800 block of Howard Street, as well as white middle-class residential homes and apartments on Park Avenue. Like the entire makeup of the district, the diversity taught you how varied the situations could be that you would be confronted with. The area encompassed all walks of life.

During the day, or 8-to-4 shift, a legend in the police department at the time worked the upper post: Officer Hawkins or, as we knew him, "The Hawk." He was a short, completely gray-headed, jolly man. Probably in his early or mid seventies at the time, he was set in his casual approach to everything and a real member of the community. Hawk knew everyone on the post he worked. He lunched at the homes in Bolton Hill, carried the ladies' groceries for them, and he walked them to and from the grocery stores. He was truly a throwback to when policemen were members of the neighborhood. He was a respected friend, a member of the community and a gentleman to almost all of the residents. Known by most, you could not count the number of questions asked about Hawk if he was missing from the post and you were covering the area. The neighborhood concern for this man was such that you spent hours explaining to residents that he was well and just on leave every time you worked the area.

Because of his age, Hawk worked only the day shift, and when he was tired, he would call in on the call box and announce that he was weary and leaving for the day. On our calls, we would be told if he had left for the day and one of us would pick up his post assignments. Hawk had been on the job forever; no one knew exactly how long, not even the supervisors, nor apparently took the time to find out. They just accepted him as public relations plus to the area he worked. He had been around so long that he dated most of our supervisors. All knew he was senior on the job and up in age because of the stories he told, but it was back in the day when you looked after one another.

Hawk had put in his time, paid his dues and was going to be protected and looked after until he decided to retire another respectful act that has been lost in time. Often he related that he remembered the days he would have to commandeer a car driving down Howard Street, jump on the running board, gun in hand and bounce over the street car tracks, directing the driver to chase a suspect trying to escape by car or on foot down Howard Street dodging the street cars and traffic. Picture this, but of course you have seen this scene over and over in the movies; Hawk actually did this. He was a legend, and now a community "PR Man," a tribute to Bolton Hill and the job. The elderly residents on his post felt they were more than adequately protected from crime by a real gentleman who listened and cared about their daily concerns and just happened to be in a police uniform. In reality, he had reached such an elderly age himself that only his side arm, nightstick and his wealth of street ingenuity could protect him physically from harm during an arrest.

One warm early afternoon, Hawk walked up to me on my post and said, "Boy, come with me, I want to show you something." I didn't question him, but followed as he waved me on. It was the beginning of a summer day and the heat and humidity was already setting in. It was going to be a hot one. Baltimore always had its own race with the weather: Was the heat going to outdo the humidity, or was the humidity going to outpace the temperature?

We walked for almost half a mile, walking off my assigned post and finally, because of his slow and deliberate pace, we reached one of his assigned posts located on Bolton Street. Once in the residential area, he talked about the different residents as we passed each house. He did know everyone, their habits, traits, hours to and from, comings and goings, their cars, their churches, their religions. He was a man who really impressed me with regards to really knowing and taking an interest in those on your post. Any deviation from their daily routine would indicate to Hawk that something was wrong.

As enlightening as the conversation and Hawk himself was, I was young and getting impatient regarding what he wanted to show me; plus, I was off my post, leaving it unattended for longer than I had thought I should. At the same time, it was getting awfully hot. But still we walked on at such a slow pace that I felt we would never get there, wherever we were headed. As we tracked on, still not a hint as to what he wanted to show me. Again, the stories about the neighborhood lunches, walking them to the stores, how nice Mr. or Mrs. so and so was, what a nice car Mr. so and so had. His post and its residents became a steady topic of conversation as we walked on at a snail's pace. He started talking about the special lunches they made for him and how many asked him to stay for dinner when he got off. If for no other reason, Hawk was well worth his weight in public relations, having convinced an affluent neighborhood that they were safe in his aging hands.

At this point, we had walked for about fifteen minutes and after telling him I had to get back to my post, he replied, "Just a little further, boy," still not saying what he wanted me to see. Finally, we turned into an alley, walked south about forty feet and stopped. We were on the west side of Sutton Place, a newly developed high-rise apartment complex with an adjoining swimming pool. Again, conversation about the neighbors continued. A little impatient now, I asked, "Hawk, what do you want to show me?" Hawk looked at me a little disgustedly and said, "You rookies, always in a hurry. We are here." I looked around and seeing nothing out of the ordinary, I asked, "Where?" "Right here," Hawk exclaimed. "On a hot day, if you ever work my post, this is the coolest place in the entire bailiwick; there is always a constant breeze here," he said. I smiled, thanked him for showing me the spot, said my goodbye and walked back to my post. Smiling again as I thought about him telling this story to one of his many friends on his post, I could already hear Hawk sharing his tale: "I'm worried about these new kids; they don't seem to know or appreciate anything."

Another funny incident occurred during my first twelve to eight tour on my assigned post. For any of you that have walked the streets late at night, sounds travel far and wide and you hear the sounds echoing from different directions if you are not used to it. Well, I was walking my post about 3:00 A.M. when I heard a woman's scream. The screaming continued periodically, although I could not locate the direction the screams were coming from. Up and down the streets I walked rapidly, thinking again as once before that I had a big case, a rape in progress, and naturally a part one arrest would follow. After walking at least two blocks, the woman's screams became louder. I was finally getting close and was about to make the arrest, I thought.

I had hurried to the 800 block of Linden Avenue, the hospital was on my right and the rear yards of Eutaw Street tenements were on my left. I first looked toward the various yards on my left, thinking that the victim had been pulled into one of the yards. I realized the screams were coming from my right as I walked. I looked at the open second-floor window and heard an unidentified woman shriek again. She was in the process of giving birth on a hot summer's night.

I learned four things from this experience. One, I was glad that being a man meant that I would never bear a child. Two, it was easier to laugh at yourself when you were alone in the dark. Three, street noise does carry. And four, the hospital's delivery room was located on the second floor of the hospital overlooking the emergency area drive, often with their windows open on a warm summer's night.

While on patrol, I was very fortunate in the southwest district as far as making arrests. At one point, I used to tease that I did better accidentally, not even having to try, in the southwest than I did working in the central district. The first such case came when I was driving to work on the four to twelve shifts, east on Pratt Street. Pratt and Lombard streets are one way, running east-west. Periodically, the city has a habit of changing the east-west one way directions of these streets.

I was driving in uniform at the time and driving with my convertible top down. I observed an elderly white female turn the street corner from Schroeder Street onto Pratt, running east after a young black male teenager who was waving a purse in his right hand as he ran pumping his arms. Well, the situation was pretty self-explanatory. The young male had grabbed the purse from the elderly female, and she was not going to let it go without pursuing the boy. The newspapers later wrote the story that I had jumped from my car seeing the situation and apprehended the youth with the purse after a foot chase. Actually, it was pleasant out that day weather wise and I was enjoying my convertible with its top down on my way into work. Seeing what was going on, as the boy ran up the street on my left, I just sped up and pulled to the curb in front of him. I took out my revolver and yelled for him to stop as he reached my car. He was no more than fifteen feet away from me at the time; he looked in my direction as I yelled to him to put up his hands. He immediately threw up his hands seeing the gun pointed at him, came to an abrupt stop and surrendered.

I was thankful he had surrendered rather than realizing I could not chase him with my car. I stepped from the vehicle and handcuffed him as the irate old lady ran up and actually threw a couple of punches at the youth. He must have stopped out of fear that I would have shot him, but now he was just as bad off. I had to step in between them to stop the feisty old woman from beating him to death. I had a purse-snatcher on one side and one angry lady on the other. She told me she was seventy one years young once she calmed down and realized I had her valuable purse to return. Later I found out why she was so worked up. If this kid got away with her purse, she would have lost the purse and its contents of $10.42 in currency and coins. She had chased the youth some three blocks and wasn't as breathless as she was mad. The 16-year-old youth was charged at the district.

My second arrest in the southwest occurred when Officer Douglas Cash and I were driving off duty to a birthday party on the west side for a friend, a newspaper reporter for The News American, John Jennings. John and I shared the same date of birth. He was one year my senior. Cash, by then, was my side partner in Car 105, having replaced Ralph Eicher upon his promotion. Jennings was a soft-spoken gentleman, almost frail in his appearance, average height and slender build. He had the police beat for The News American newspaper and he loved police officers. He was the type of person that if he arrived on a scene and there was a fight, he would jump right in on the side of the police. He was a fine reporter who wrote well and honestly.

Doug and I often took credit for introducing him to his then girlfriend, Marilyn. They later married and had a wonderful life together. John would later work at a Philadelphia newspaper after The News American went out of business. He would, unfortunately, pass away in his early 60's. Perhaps for a reason, he would not respect or take part in what they consider journalism today. Sorry, I was sidetracked by my affection for the two.

Anyway, we were driving on Pratt Street at the time and stopped for a light when we noticed a male duck out through the lower portion of a broken glass commercial door front and run into the alleyway located next to the store with what appeared to be a television set. He met another man parked in the alley; both were attempting to place the television into a parked car. We caught a glimpse of him running into the alley, noticing that he had run from the front door of S&N Katz, a jewelry store. They were committing a commercial burglary. We jumped from my car and ran over to the front of the store while both of the suspects were busy at their car in the alley. At the time, we hugged the front of the building so they could not observe us from the alley. With our weapons drawn, we turned into the alley and observed one male still working at placing the television set into the backseat of a car facing Pratt Street, with the other man standing next to the vehicle. When we announced for them to halt, the one inside the car backed out with his hands up; the other subject who was standing in the alley ran north, with Doug chasing after him. I grabbed the one at the car and asked if he or his partner had a gun, with a threat that if he lied I would shoot him. He answered quickly, "No, neither one of us has guns. He is not armed with anything, I don't have anything." It was dark and I did not want Doug running into a shooting.

Doug came back with the second guy in tow about ten minutes later. Neither of them looked as if they had been in a battle. Later I found out, that during the chase the second subject had stopped to hide behind a parked car and had been discovered by Doug. We ran the car they were using and found that it was stolen with the assistance of the responding officer. We got the night reference, both youths were taken to the southwest district where they were charged with the burglary and stealing a car. We found out later that one of the youths had helped the burglary detectives by supplying them the name and address of their fence. One of the subjects was tried as an adult and received five years for the burglary and the possession of a stolen vehicle. The other was just sixteen and was given probation after one year in a juvenile facility.

For those local police and those who know Doug personally, I have to stand as a witness with regards to him running down the one suspect. Everyone who knows Doug knows he would lose a foot race with a turtle. He is so deliberate a walker that when you are walking with him, you have to slow your pace. But he did catch the guy, honest. When he took after that kid, it was the fastest I had ever seen him move. Needless to say, we missed the birthday party for John Jennings.

The manager of the burglarized jewelry store cooperated with testimony in both cases. In an unrelated, non-criminal matter, he later explained to my mother how he had met us when she was in an Eastern Avenue S&N Katz store where he had transferred He had recognized the family name while she was buying something.

The Projects

The projects consisted of both two-story brick row housing and high rises. The initial intent, like most good ideas and well-meaning deeds, was to provide housing for low-income residents. Before the social experiment was over, these high rises provided the grounds for countless killings, drug activity, robberies, assaults, and poor living conditions for the honest, frightened inhabitants.

Our bailiwick contained several blocks of low rises on the west end, which were relatively quiet when compared to the high rises and its crime. The biggest problem we had in the area was stolen car recoveries. The cars were always found parked on the side streets in front of the two story projects. Although the subject was never apprehended for these periodic thefts, the thought with so many recovered stolen cars in the same area was that a young resident of the low rises was stealing cars and abandoning them after using them as a joyride home. The recovery point of the stolen vehicles was established, but the individual cars were being stolen from all over the city. Our car thief apparently traveled far and wide around the city and stole cars when the thought and opportunity presented itself. No known car thieves lived in the area and no information on this well-traveled car thief's identity was ever developed.

The only serious call I remember having at the low rises was one up off of McMechen Street on Webb Court one night on the 12-to-8 shift. I was driving Car 105 with a loan-out officer accompanying me at the time Officer Jim Kelly. He was normally a foot officer assigned to the No. 2 bailiwick. He was a tall man, slender build, almost gaunt in appearance. Because of his slender build, and his long narrow face, he had been appropriately nicknamed Abe Lincoln by someone in his squad, and the nickname had stuck. He was tall, slender and gangly and walked slowly because of leg problems, missing work frequently for that reason.

The call came in for a disorderly man at a reported address. We drove to the address and exited the car in front of the three stories, red brick apartment complex. We walked past the chain stretched between short metal posts in front of small grass lawns not quite big enough for a push mower, down the concrete walkway to the metal front door. We announced our arrival by tapping on the door with our nightsticks. A minute later, an elderly woman met us at the front door, saying she was concerned for her son. He was upstairs and without reason had become extremely upset and began speaking unintelligently, running upstairs to the third floor in an excited state. We told her to be calm and that all would be well as we entered, with her following us to the second floor. Upon reaching the second floor, we heard her son ranting and raving senselessly from the third floor. Before we could start up the stairs, the woman asked us to stop. We assumed that the rant was from drinking. There was something else she had to tell us. Her son had just been released from a mental hospital a few weeks ago. He was back working since and had appeared normal until this episode. He had a history of violence and was a physically strong individual, who when in these fits did not know his own strength; apparently, him not taking his medicine caused his relapse. My first thought was for Abe Lincoln, as frail as he was with his leg problems to consider. Would he be hurt if this guy was to fight?

There was a sofa near the front windows of the room and the steps leading to the third floor were on the east wall near the sofa. I told Abe to position himself behind the back corner of the sofa so that it would be between him and the subject should a fight develop. He admitted his legs were weak and that the sofa was a good idea. We stepped toward the stairs with Abe behind me near the sofa as the man's mother said,

"Please be careful and try not to hurt him. He really does not know what he is doing." Before taking the first step upward, and thankful that I did, I looked up and saw the son standing at the top of the stairs. He had a crazed look on his face, and was leaning forward ready to lunge. A large, muscular built man, he appeared to be about two hundred and fifty pounds, short, with a solid frame.

Our eyes met as he threw himself headfirst with a defying scream down the concrete steps, capped with metal stripped edges. He had flung him self at us. We had just enough time to step back and watch the huge man dive headfirst onto the concrete floor at the base of the stairs. At first we thought he had broken his neck or back. He landed headfirst with a heavy thud, the sound of flesh hitting concrete. The man's face was covered with blood, but his slight movements indicated he didn't kill himself; he was semiconscious. Still, I thought it was remarkable that he had not killed him self, he had flung his full weight into a headfirst dive down twelve steps onto a concrete floor.

His irrational act had solved one potential problem: neither one of us had to contend with fighting him in the condition he was in. Abe's fragile legs were safe from harm. Who knows what injuries he might have come away with if we had to fight this madman? Its true people in that state of mind do not realize their own strength and sometimes will fight through their injuries. We cuffed him there on the floor and let him lie until we could get him treated. An ambulance was called while we did our best to keep the mother out of the son's reach as he lay there on the floor. After the ambulance crew was warned of his mental condition, they examined him in place and strapped him down on a stretcher and left for the nearest hospital. His mother thanked us and apologized for her son. As we walked back to the car, Abe said, "Jesus, did you see that? That guy would have killed us if he hadn't almost killed himself. There's no way my legs could have taken a fight with a man that size, and out of his mind, to boot, or handle the impact of his dive at us." Who knows what the results would have been if it had turned into a free-for all with a crazy. I think the incident turned out the best it possibly could have.

For the most part, the people we found were like this lady and her son. Low rises were the homes of hardworking, lower class people facing their own everyday problems. This family lived the best they could and faced what life had given them. This woman's concern for her son was evident. I hoped he would eventually improve and in doing so bring her some peace of mind. The housing overall was modest but well kept and clean, and the people living there were generally respectful when we received calls, and for the most part honest.

The high rises were a different matter. They fell into disrepair, profanity written on the walls everywhere, the smell of urine in the halls, stairwells and elevators, with trash, garbage and even an occasional soiled diaper thrown about anywhere a thoughtless person would disregard it. Drugs were openly sold inside and out, within the shadows of the buildings. Drug dealing became the source of the community's income. Almost any type of crime imaginable flourished.

These high rises were located in the western district, blocks from the central. Our cars frequently backed up assist calls in the areas. Upon arrival, we were faced with urine that was poured down and broken bottles thrown at us from the balconies when we left our units and attempted to enter the buildings. The various glass and debris that was thrown from the upper floors had some degree of accuracy once we were close enough to be targets.

Occasionally we had jumpers, or those thrown off the balconies during a fight. Once in a while an occasional shot would ring out from one of the floors, directed at the uniforms that scurried about under whoever had fired the shot. At night it was impossible to even spot the people responsible or the balconies they were on. Eventually, city planners to some degree abated this problem. In their grand wisdom, they finally fenced in the balconies from top to bottom, side to side. This greatly reduced the problem for responding police, but I often wondered how much it restricted the safety of those who lived there. True, the building, halls and walls were all concrete and cinder block, but closing off the balconies left only the front doors of the apartments as an escape exit in case of an emergency and the narrow steps to and from the interior located at each end of the building as possible fire exits. Elevators were not to be used in the case of fire, and the concrete stairs at each end of block-long buildings would not support the amount of foot traffic should a serious fire break out. The smoke caused by the fire and the limited escape routes could cause mass fatalities.

Crime was rampant around these homes, as I have mentioned. Our drug units picked up children for selling openly on the street. Ten and twelve year olds who could only furnish their handler's street names because that was all they knew. Arrest one of these child street dealers and another would take his place. Using children was another way not to be identified. They only knew the dealer's street names. Drug and robbery shootings were almost daily occurrences, as were the police chases that resulted from these drug activities.

Crime reached such a point that uniformed armed guards were placed inside of the high rises in command booths on the first floors and marked security guards patrolled the grounds in marked cars. These officers were known as Housing Authority Police. Still the crime continued. Like the old saying, "Where there's a will, there's a way." In this case, "Where there is a prime location, there's action." The high rises housed and drew more bad guys than good, and the population of the apartments made the number of addicts plentiful.

One night, two men involved in narcotics sat and waited for the time of a pre-arranged appointment before exiting a cluttered apartment to make the deal. One laughed about the easy money they were making while he inhaled from his rolled marijuana cigarette; the other took what was to be his last drink of Jack Daniel's. They decided it was time for them to leave. They gathered themselves, both placing handguns under their shirts, concealed from view. The men tightened their belts, pulled down their wide-brimmed hats, threw on their colored dress coats, smiled at one another and closed the apartment door behind them. They walked to the elevator talking in a cheerful mood, probably thinking of the waiting deal and the money it would bring. They looked forward to their upcoming meeting with another area drug dealer. Both expressed their feelings that they were about to become bigger than ever in their chosen field as a result of this pending meeting. Things were looking up and they were going to be rich.

The elevator arrived on the upper floor and they got in, with one of them pushing the floor button for the lobby. They were both smiling as the elevator stopped and the door opened, thinking again of how this was the deal of all deals, the one that would make them known. They would be respected on the street after this one. In truth, they would only be talked about until the next neighborhood shooting.

Standing in front of the elevator, drawing their handguns as the double doors of the elevator opened, were two men who started shooting as soon as the elevator doors opened at the lobby and the two passengers could be identified. Neither of the two elevator riders had a chance to reach for their weapons. A hail of bullets fired from outside ripped into both of their bodies. When the sound of gunfire stopped, and as the smoke literally cleared from in front of the elevator, the two fatally wounded men fell to the floor, both either dead or near death. Their lives in the drug world ended; they would be remembered on the street not as they had hoped. Not for being big known street dealers, but just two more wannabes assassinated in the high rise elevator. In the homicide office, their deaths were noted as two more open cases.

The shooters turned, walked by the occupied guard office while they concealed their weapons, and calmly exited the front door. The drug dealers were found to have been shot numerous times, three bullet wounds to the center chest area of one and the other was hit both in the face and chest. A witness near the front entrance at the time, about thirty feet from the elevator where the shooting occurred, gave us the account of the shooting and descriptions of the shooters later in their apartment, not wanting the neighborhood to know they had helped.

There were three armed uniform guards on duty at the time of the crime; all were in the guard station approximately fifteen feet from the elevator at the time of the shooting, two males and a female guard. All stated that they could not identify the assailants, although the two responsible for the crime had walked away within feet of their station. None drew their weapons or made any attempt to stop the shooters. Between the three of them, they did give a suspect description that to some degree matched the one given by the man that had witnessed the shooting from the door. Although they were the legal authority charged with the protection of those living there, with arrest powers if necessary and armed at the time, they refused to take action and later swore through their attorneys that nothing could have been done. Our state's attorney's office denied further action to seek investigative information, as did the city government for fear they would not be able to hire guards if they forced these three to cooperate.

The gunmen were suspected as being in a rival drug gang. They were identified on the street through informants as possibly being responsible but not charged. If indeed they had done the shooting, they later met their respective fates, but not through the courts. One was found shot to death on a quiet city street in the western district weeks after the high rise shooting, possibly a revenge killing for the two neighborhood dealers killed. The other, after his arrest for a robbery, was unwilling to admit to any involvement in the elevator shootings, but went to prison for fifteen years for a store robbery that occurred just before the killings. He died after three years in prison as a result of a stabbing during a fight with another inmate.

The project high rise homes were a fine example of those liberal minded people with power and influence over the majority trying to enhance the lives of those they had decided needed a hand up. Their hope of inexpensive apartments for those who could not afford more did not happen. Instead, it led to overcrowded and poor living conditions, broken schools, crime, drugs, and more often than not countless deaths that destroyed generations of families.

The Famous Ballroom

O ne night on the twelve to eight tour, an "assist an officer" call came over the radio for a situation in progress at the Famous Ballroom, located on the 1700 block of N. Charles Street. The ballroom was right next to the Charles Theatre, which showed artsy movies then and now. Upon our arrival, we were told that during a struggle some unknown male had managed to steal one of the special officer's revolvers from his holster. The other guards had secured the emergency exits and were convinced that the thief was still on the premises. Upset and disorderly, the large crowd there was not quieted by our presence; we seemingly added to the chaotic situation.

Our only solution for recovering the stolen weapon was to search everyone as they came from the second-floor dance area down the steps to the main entrance. The only exit from the second floor was now the wide stairs from the entrance to the second floor located on the north wall. We started allowing people down the stairs in an orderly manner, but naturally those who were anxious or drunk and disorderly had other ideas. Shortly after we started the procedure, people were pushing and shoving through the crowd headed down the stairs. I heard the sound of breaking glass behind me and looked to see Officer George Winn fall to the floor from in front of a broken glass display box on the wall behind him. That was it. That's all it took. We were swept away on a wave of fleeing, drunken, hysterical people running down the steps toward the front doors and the street.

Some ran from the scene and others stayed to do battle with us. Remember there is always safety in numbers. Safety for your assailants in this case; we were outnumbered, ten or maybe fifteen to one. It was so crowded that during the melee we could not make arrests, or for that matter seldom could you tell who was trying to hit you. I broke the first finger of my left hand sometime during that fight, trying to hit a man with a punch that landed to high on his head. With the sound of approaching sirens, the fight was over as quickly as it had started. The crowd had come to one decision in mass; it was more thoughtful to run than to stay for the arrest. The crowd spilled onto the 1700 block of N. Charles Street and ran in all directions.

Naturally under the circumstances, the stolen revolver belonging to the special officer was not recovered in the attempted search of the patrons of the dance nor was it found during a search of the ballroom. That would have been the easiest way to get rid of the weapon. Knowing a search was coming, the answer would be to throw it down or hide it in one of the bathrooms and retrieve it later; that way the original thief would not be caught with the weapon. But whoever took the gun originally, or whoever managed to end up with it, escaped with the revolver still in their possession.

I was treated at Mercy Hospital for the injury and followed up with the Medical Section of the department. I was told at one time I would never use the shattered finger again and possibly would be retired as a result. The Medical Section thought the break was to my right hand first finger, not my left. The thought was that I would be unable to qualify with my revolver because of the injury. The injury healed and I never have had any lasting effects from the finger injury. Even with age, I have not developed arthritis in the hand or finger.

Officer Winn, who was elderly at the time of the ballroom assault, retired as a result of his back injuries incurred when thrown into the advertising display. Needless to say, we never recovered the stolen pistol, and to my knowledge it was not reported as being used in a crime, but the odds were it was.

Central Car 105

ithin two years, I was assigned to a radio car 105 with Ralph Eicher, the senior man. Lt. Middleton no doubt was behind the assignment, but he never mentioned it. Although I had more than the usual loan-out assignments to cars 104 and 105, and wore a car coat on patrol instead of the standard three-quarter heavy coats worn at the time, Middleton said nothing when I was assigned except wishing me well and saying that I deserved it.

In those days, there were only five cars in the district and we responded to all serious calls for service. Ralph was a great teacher, a fair person and an intelligent man. He knew the book, The Digest of Laws, and never in all the years abused his police authority while in patrol and later in Operations. Throughout my career, Ralph was not only a friend but also a mentor. He passed away shortly after his retirement, but his wife and my family exchanged Christmas card greetings until her death in 2010.

At that time, the car men had the option to remain at the scene when responding on serious calls and awaiting the arrival of the detectives, having the postmen (foot officer) stay with the car. I now had the opportunity to be physically on the scene of all types of calls; assaults, robberies, burglaries, homicides, etc. Any part one crime I wanted, adding to my on-the-job education, allowing me to learn about scene processing and the actions of the detectives on serious cases.

When Ralph was promoted to sergeant, Douglas Cash took his

place. Cash was my ex-side partner from the foot patrol days and remains a dear friend and golfing partner to this day. We made a good pair. Our personalities were different enough that one or the other brought sensible solutions to the various problems we encountered on our numerous calls.

Our car worked an area located in the middle center, top part of the district. We had central district cars 104 to the west to Druid Hill Avenue and 103 to the east to Greenmount Avenue. Often in the summers we handled eighteen to twenty four calls a shift. Frequently we worked in the other two car areas most of the shifts, because they were out of service themselves on calls.

Our area was made up of commercial establishments such as restaurants, small businesses, movie houses, a college and a mix of rental properties in the downtown area. The other two car areas were made up of lower income row housing and inexpensive, rough corner bars. We seldom answered calls in our area.

Initially, Baltimore's welfare building was located at Greenmount Avenue and Oliver Street and, although not in our patrol area as previously stated, we frequently handled calls in the area. At the end of each month, the Welfare Department issued checks and it was amazing. Male drivers sat in their expensive cars which bore license plates from Pennsylvania, New Jersey, New York, D.C. and Virginia, waiting for their female passengers who were inside picking up their State of Maryland checks. Men would leave their homes locally on dates of checks or inspections from the Welfare Department, because their women claimed they were not there to provide support to them or the children. We witnessed these abuses in the early 1960's. The abuse of the system was evident from the beginning, but not addressed. The population at the time increased with those coming to Baltimore and other cities just to join the welfare rolls. So also did the crime rate. I'm still bothered by this fact because I know it continues to this day.

Even back then, we arrested subjects for drugs and robberies to find out they also sublimated their activities with welfare money. Don't get me wrong, for those who truly need help, it's a great program. But it is meant to be temporary assistance, not a lifestyle. By the time I retired, we saw second and third generations of welfare recipients. Who knows, except for the grace of God go I and mine, but it was not meant for those who are taking the money because they found an easy paycheck and having children so they can declare additional dependents.

Years do make a difference. My generation came from hardworking, poor people, to proud not to have a job; working at anything to provide for their family, striving to get ahead through hard work and nighttime education. Now we have generations sitting around waiting for the check in the mail, with no self-pride or initiative.

Provident Hospital

———————————◦◦◦◦———————————

Provident Hospital at the time was located in the 1500 block of Division Street and primarily served the black community unless there was a critical victim and they were transported to the nearest hospital. My first experience with the hospital was when I was assigned to the radio car and learned that victims of shootings and stabbings were transported there from the scenes of their assaults in the central district if Maryland General Hospital was overwhelmed with patients at the time.

Mainly because of its location, the hospital serviced those from the western district. Unfortunately, Provident was usually not up to the task with regards to the number of assaults they received, especially on the weekends. They had moved their location several times over the years, attempting to upgrade their building and the patient number they could handle, but remained in an antique building with aged beds and facilities.

The first time I walked into the accident room I could not believe what I saw. I passed through the small, overcrowded courtyard filled with flashing lights from ambulances and police cars and approached the first-floor ward area. There it was: an open ward of beds with white metal headboards, row after row filled with patients with their various ailments and complaints. I heard moans of pain from around the room. While the nursing staff scurried about trying to help those in need. Seeing the sight, my first thought was a scene from a World War I military hospital ward. It reminded you exactly of those scenes, except the doctors and nurses were not covered in their patient's fresh blood.

Ralph advised me that the hospital had a poor reputation with many who had been treated there in the past. He advised that most of the victims with injuries that required hospitalization would much rather be taken to Maryland General Hospital rather than there. This proved to be a tool in solving some of our cases. The victims of assaults, stabbings and shootings would often readily give up the circumstances leading to their injuries and name those responsible for a verbal promise to take them to Maryland General rather than Provident if they told us the truth and identified the suspects responsible for their injuries. Some of those injured would actually plead, and occasionally argue, with us to take them to Maryland General instead. The reputation Provident had at the time helped us solve more than a few cases before a crime report that would contain the information was actually written.

On one occasion, we walked into Provident Hospital's admittance section looking for the victim of an assault case that occurred in the central. While looking for our complainant/victim, I was making small talk with a man who appeared to be in his late 50's. It was summer and he was wearing a T-shirt, shorts and tennis shoes. He was very personable and rather talkative, having greeted me with a hello when I entered and looked at him. While we talked, I noticed that he did not have a number. I'm sure they really were price tags; they had the same shape. At the time, the accident room gave out numbers written on what looked like these sales tags you would see on merchandise in a store with the string attached to indicate what order the patient would be treated in.

As usual, the waiting area was full of people with more complaints than you could count. Probably there were twenty people from infants to aged, colds to wounds. I asked the man, "Where is your tag?" He smiled and turned his right shoulder toward me with his answer. I was looking at a hunting knife buried to the hilt in his right shoulder, and his blood soaked shirt from the knife hilt to his waist. The tag with the number indicating the order in which he was to be treated was tied to the knife handle. I looked at the number inked on the price tag; he was only four away from treatment. He seemingly accepted his plight well, not complaining, but not willing to implicate anyone in his assault.

He stated that he had been stabbed during a bar fight on "The Avenue," aka Pennsylvania Avenue, by a young buck who wanted to be famous, meaning the young guy wanted to be known. He stated, "These young bucks are crazy, they'll kill you for nothing." He was right. All we could do was to wish him well. His assault had not occurred in our district and he had made up his mind how it would be handled. As I walked away from him I thought, you don't only have to worry about the young bucks who want to make a name for them selves; you have to worry about the old bucks that have resolve.

Another story about the hospital comes from a friend of mine, a detective in another unit, who had served in the western district as a patrolman prior to his assignment in Auto Theft. While in the district, he was detailed to guarding a patient at Provident Hospital on the midnight shift. He found himself at the bedside of a seriously injured man who was a victim of a shooting, but also under arrest for shooting the other man he was involved with. Bob Puepke wondered about the details. He found himself in the World War I ward with so much noise from the patients that he knew it would be a long night. He asked for a chair and then had to scout out one for himself.

Seated at the detail's bedside, he realized that this man who was hospitalized with gunshot wounds was no threat. This guy was not going to attempt any type of escape. He was attached to numerous machines, seemed unconscious, and had hardly moved since his arrival. The night wore on and left him wondering why the patient had not been checked for a while by one of the nurses. Concerned, he looked long and hard at the shooting victim and did not recognize any signs of movement or for that matter any signs of respiration. Convinced in his mind that the man was dead, Bob called a nurse. The nurse, who seemed slightly disturbed by Bob's diagnosis, reluctantly checked the patient and announced, "You're right, he's gone."

Running Down a Thief

On one occasion working day work, Ralph Eicher and I received a call for a disorderly man at the grocery store located on Linden Avenue above Dolphin Street; before the location was torn down to redevelop the area. Ironically, the grocery store was one that Hawkins used to walk his Bolton Hill residents to and from. As we pulled up in front of the grocery store, a man in his early 20's ran from the entrance carrying something in his hands. He ran south to Dolphin Street and turned west, still running toward Eutaw Place. I went to the door and was told that he had just struck the cashier and fled with steaks he had grabbed from the checkout counter. The manager stated that the female cashier was not injured.

I immediately ran after the subject. He was a solid block ahead of me when I turned onto Dolphin Street. I was young and fit at the time, and did not give a thought about chasing this guy down. Off I went after him, leaving Ralph with the car and the manager in front of the store. I chased the subject to the rear of Pennsylvania Avenue, crossing Eutaw Place, Madison Street and Druid Hill where he turned south into the rear alley. At this point he had deserted his prized meat in the gutter during the chase and seemed intent on making good his escape, knowing that I was closing from behind.

He had run about a quarter of a mile at that point with me behind him, but steadily gaining. After reaching the corner of the next block, he abruptly hesitated and turned into a corner lot with an eight foot high, solid wooden fence surrounding the backyard. As I turned through the open yard gate into the yard, I saw the subject run up the back wooden steps to the second floor area and enter the open rear doorway. I ran up the steps and stopped on the second floor landing outside of the house. What stopped me was seeing the man crossing the second floor in what looked like a skipping motion.

I looked down at the floor and saw only floor beams, no floor, just bare beams. Apparently, the house was in the process of being renovated but the workers were not there at the time. The suspect was attempting to climb out the frameless front window as I scampered across the beams, with him probably some fifteen feet in front of me. He must have been holding onto a portion of the roof when I reached him, because his legs were the only things I could see and reach from the window he had climbed out. I grabbed his legs and thought about it. Was I going to pull him down and cause him to fall onto the concrete pavement on Pennsylvania Avenue below us? Maybe kill a man who had just pushed a cashier and stolen some meat that he no longer had?

As soon as I let go of his legs, he disappeared. I heard him running toward the back of the house on the roof. I turned and skipped across the beams for the second time, probably some ten feet above the first-floor area. As I did, I heard him drop onto the rear steps, landing with a thud, and saw him standing there briefly. He was running off the bottom step by the time I reached the landing. I was still a good twenty feet from him again, but gaining as I crossed the yard after him. He ran to the back of the yard and attempted to jump up and scale the wooden fence. The solid wood fence made a stressful creaking sound under his weight and fell inward toward the yard and landed on top of him. As the fence fell, I saw my radio car and Ralph standing next to it on the alley side. Ralph stepped over to the man, who was now pinned by the fallen fence that had trapped him, reached down, placed his hand on the man's shoulder and announced, "You are under arrest."

Ralph smiled at me and gave his patented snicker of a laugh. I knew I was in for days of ridicule after this escapade. Exhausted from the chase, I sat on the back steps of the house under renovation to catch my breath and thought about the fact that despite all my efforts to run this guy down, Ralph had merely followed the chase in the radio car and effortlessly made the arrest. Ralph looked away from the arrested man and smiled at me again. Nothing had to be said. The man was still pinned down by the fence. Ralph looked down and told him not to move, as he called for the cruising patrol, grinning at me the whole time. Another lesson learned, but not necessarily heeded: I was quick to react to other situations during my radio car experiences, and maybe a little lucky, since acting before thinking could get you hurt or worse.

Cab Driver Rape

One case has always stuck with me because of the implications of it regarding the life of the accused. It occurred when Officer Eicher was still my partner. One evening on the 4-to-12 shift, we received a call to Preston and Charles streets to meet a woman. We were met by an attractive white woman who was around thirty years old. She explained she was a dancer on "The Block," the Baltimore Street strip club area known the world over because servicemen from all branches frequent it. She stated she had just been raped. The woman was dressed nicely and bore no marks or injuries that were visible on her body, no torn material or disarrayed clothing or hair. Thinking the scene would be in the area, we asked her where the rape had occurred. At the time, many people working on The Block lived on Preston Street, near Charles Street.

She stated that the assault took place somewhere off of Gwynns Falls Parkway, another district away. She had just left her day shift job, hired a cab and the driver took her to his apartment and raped her. Her story instantly caught my interest and I called for the postman to fill in the car for me. She was not telling the truth about what had happened; she had not been raped. She was asked if she was physically forced or if the assault took place after she told the man to stop. She replied that he forced her, although she did not have any signs of injury, by threatening her with a knife. The woman detailed how he had thrown her on the bed and restrained her during the assault. Afterward, he drove her home

65

to an address on Preston Street. Right away the story didn't ring true, but the sex crimes unit had to be notified and the victim checked at the hospital regarding the assault. She provided the cab number and the description of her assailant on the way to the hospital.

Our dispatcher was contacted and the identified numbered cab driver was requested to respond to the district through the cab company dispatch. It took over an hour to contact the driver of the cab who responded when he finally got the request. The complainant was physically examined at the hospital and it revealed she had sexual intercourse, but had no signs of bruising or lacerations caused by forced intercourse. The sex crimes unit had all they needed along with the facts of what would be in the report. I transported the victim to the central district and waited for the arrival of the driver. Not much of this story made sense.

In burst a young black male who must have been told by someone that he was in trouble. Once he was calmed down and told about the rape, he went into telling his side of the story without being asked. He said he had picked the woman up on The Block. After conversation, they went to his apartment. They had consensual sex in his bed and then left. She was all right with the sex, never complained about anything. While they were at his place they both had drinks, and afterward he returned her to her home address. He swore he was innocent and requested a polygraph, calling the woman's story a lie and a false charge. He was definitely frightened and appeared sincere, although scared by the ramifications of such charges.

The overall story was not logical. Why would a man easily identified by the cab company and the cab number as the driver commit such an act? Who would take the victim to his own apartment to assault her and then take her home afterward? It was a ridiculous story, but until clarified it was the only one we had. Believe me, I had already learned stranger reports and situations had proven to be correct.

Having not taken a formal report from the woman, I told her that once the report was taken and written as stated, if we found afterward that what she stated was false, she could be charged with a false report. She had sex admittedly, proven by her hospital examination, but nothing substantiated the rape. No marks or scratches on her body, and strange circumstances. Two glasses reportedly still on the night tables, with both their prints. A suspect identifiable by his cab medallion uses his home address for the assault, decides to commit the act while working, and afterward he drives his victim to her front door.

"Tell me the truth and I'll write it, either you were raped or you were not," I said. The woman lowered her head and admitted it was consensual sex: "He was a good-looking man and I was interested. On the way back to my house, I thought it out and panicked. I realized I was ovulating, if I conceive, my husband would have killed me if I had a black baby."

The rape allegation was false and the cab driver was more than relieved, thanking everyone he came into contact with. Both involved were more than relieved for different reasons: her for telling the truth and not getting charged with a false report, him for not being charged for some crime he had not committed. The sex crimes unit detective had no confidence in her story when interviewing her at the hospital. After hearing the latest version of her story, they readily dropped their involvement.

Yet another memorable call was for an incident at North Avenue and Charles Street. Upon our arrival, a female bystander yelled, "That man has a gun!" With that statement, a man ran north on Charles Street and turned east on North Avenue. I jumped from the car and ran after him. Like I said earlier, I respond before I think. I still had not learned from the runner with the steak and the renovated house. The suspect was young and fast enough at the time that I was 70 to 100 feet behind him during the chase across North Avenue. When he reached Calvert Street, two blocks from where the chase started, he turned south on Calvert. When I reached the intersection and turned south, he had disappeared.

On that corner at the time was an apartment house. I looked up the stairs at the double-door entranceway just in time to see one of the two doors slightly moving before it closed I ran up the steps through the double entrance doors and onto the first-floor landing. The steps leading to the second floor were straight ahead I could hear the sound of someone moving across the second-floor area on the wood floors. I drew my gun and walked up the steps as quietly as I could, watching the second-floor level closely in case the subject decided to jump out into the stair area and fire.

When I reached the second floor area, I noticed a fireproof door opened and partially closed against the wall behind it. The open door revealed a hall leading to the second floor apartments. I pointed my gun at the fire door and ordered that the weapon be dropped. From behind the door came an exhausted sounding voice requesting that I don't shoot, and then the sound of a weapon being dropped to the wood floor. With the wooden floors and the size of the area before the hall leading to the apartments, I thought the noise from the object he had dropped sounded like a 45 or 357 revolver. I ordered him to step out with his hands up and he complied, "Don't shoot, I'm unarmed." I handcuffed the man and looked toward the weapon on the floor. Just behind the door was a foot long iron blade, the hilt of which was about three inches wide, with a point like an arrowhead. The type of knife you would generally find in a commercial kitchen. On our way back onto the street he explained that he was carrying it for protection and that someone must have seen it over on Charles Street.

Ralph had pulled the radio car to the corner having seen me turn from North onto Calvert. He called in for a wagon and waited until the subject was being taken away in the cruising patrol before he turned and yelled at me: "No matter what happens on the street, what you get into, what you see, don't ever leave your partner. You're not safe and you're partner is alone, not safe either. Always know where your partner is and what he is doing. There's always more safety in numbers. If a suspect gets away, he gets away. It's more important not to get hurt. The hell with them, we count, we go home."

This time was not as casual as the man under the backyard fence; this time it was serious, a man with a gun, although it turned out to be a knife that looked like a small sword. It's still better for the good guys when it's our two against their one. There are plenty of other stories about reacting instead of thinking the situations through first, but I did learn from my mistakes. Just because reaction seemed to work for me does not mean it's the best choice.

Cadet Experiences

Department policy was to send Police Academy students out on the weekends to get firsthand training working with experienced officers in the radio cars. If your regular partner were off, then more than likely you would have a trainee for a partner. At the time the department was becoming, in their words, "more community oriented" What we would now call "liberal." The pairing of trainees with their assigned officers made for some good stories. Here are a few that I witnessed.

We received a call for a domestic complaint in car 104's area on Mount Royal Avenue. We heard the argument while knocking on the door of the first-floor apartment. A man opened the door and continued the verbal abuse he previously had directed toward the wife. He used every imaginable curse word, adding "G.D. police" to almost everything spilling out of his mouth and concluding with the question, "What in the hell are you doing here?" Without an answer, I pushed by him and entered the apartment, which he either allowed or was taken off guard when I walked past him.

We entered the apartment and attempted to calm down the male and his female companion. The man was asked several times to stop yelling and using vulgar language. Out came one more "G.D. police" instead. That was enough. We had tried; remember, handle people as they act toward you. I turned to the subject, told him to calm down and that it was for the last time. I told him he had made a big mistake;

69

he let us in. Now his home was mine If he didn't shut up, he would calm down in the lock-up, and he would get there the easy or hard way. Evidently I had gotten through to both; they both calmed down, as often in domestic cases, she helped her man to do so, pleading with us not to arrest him. Afterward we left quietly, not having to arrest either, with the promise if we returned he would leave with us.

Once we were back in the car, the rookie could not wait to speak up. He nervously stated that I had cost him his job; was something wrong with me? We couldn't treat the public that way. We would have an Internal Investigation Division number the next day. I simply told him what worked for me: Learn to treat people the way you find them. Kill them with kindness if they are reasonable and under control with you; threaten them with physical harm and arrest if they are disrespectful to the uniform. Some of these people will hurt you; they will fight at a drop of a hat and use anything they can get their hands on while they do it. They'll use guns and knives, or use anything possible that can be used as a weapon. Use your common sense and evaluate the situations you find yourself in. No two situations are alike. When things happen, you'll be lucky to have someone with you, much less any of the ones that taught you to think the way you do now. That "yes sir" and "no sir" approach they teach you at the academy is sometimes interpreted as a sign of weakness to some of the people out here, not a sign of mutual respect. You're alone out here; learn what works and what approach will keep you safe most of the time.

The rookie leaned back in his seat, thought about what I had said, and replied, "Maybe you are right, but that's not what they teach in the academy." I just smiled back at him, started the car, pulled from the curb and turned to him and said, "You will have to learn on your own, whichever works."

Another incident with a loan-out officer occurred on St. Paul Street on a call to meet an upset landlord. When we got to St. Paul, the woman expressed concern about a retired military man renting a room on the second floor. At the time, the area was clean and well kept by homeowners and renters alike who were middle-class people. She stated she had not seen or heard from her tenant in a day or two and thought he was ill, lying in his room alone. We were told that he seldom had visitors and none for over a month.

The landlord accompanied us to the tenant's room on the second floor. The house appeared to have freshly painted woodwork, good carpet throughout the halls and steps, and a nice looking, subtle, flowered wallpaper pattern covering the walls. When we reached the man's room, the landlord unlocked the door and I told her that we would handle it from there and for her to go downstairs. The odor of a decomposing body could be detected at the door; an odor distinctive, and hard to describe, but one you always remembered after your first time. On some of these calls, the air was so heavy with the stench that your eyes burned.

I turned to the rookie and told him what to expect: the remains of a human that could well be unrecognizable, blackened and decayed to an incredible extent. The weather had been hot and does contribute to decomposition, so we could expect his body to be in any type of condition. I told him if he should become uncomfortable or ill at any point to leave the room. It was a normal response and his first experience with such a sight may be tough to handle. Some people readily accept what they see, others don't. It's in your makeup, or it's not. Whatever we saw in the room was not to be disturbed; I reminded him not to move or touch anything he saw. I told him that from the smell, something or someone was dead in the room, but until we found out how they died, it was still a potential crime scene.

We walked into the room and found the retired military man lying full length, face up in his bed; his legs covered with the bed covers to his knees, clad only in a pair of boxer shorts, and the semi-skeletal remains of his head resting on a pillow. His hands were crossed, lying on what was at one time his upper chest; his chest now caved into what remained of his organs from advanced decomposition. The overall body appeared almost skeletal except for his chest area, which was decayed and liquefied.

The rented room was comprised of an area about fifteen by twelve square feet, and there was no bathroom. A table used for meals sat in one corner and a desk and chair were centered between the windows overlooking St. Paul St. The room was neat and clean, everything had a place and everything was in its place. It reflected that of a military man as far as its neat appearance. There was no apparent disturbance to anything in the room or no indication of foul play anywhere.

The rookie, while I was not looking, picked up a gun holster from beneath the bed and attempted to hand it to me. I asked where he had gotten it and told him to put it back, just as the maggots crawled from the holster and up his right hand and forearm. Seeing the maggots, he dropped the holster and looked ill. He had just contaminated what could be a possible homicide scene, apparently he didn't listen after being told seconds before not to touch anything in the room. Were these guys listening and learning the right things at the academy or not? One thing was sure, this one would think twice before picking up anything at his next crime scene and not doing what the senior officer advised.

It turned out that it was a suicide. According to the autopsy, the victim had shot himself in the head, right to left, with a small caliber .22 automatic. After he had shot himself, his hand dropped to his chest and decomposition caused the gun to fall inside his chest cavity. Decomposition was so advanced that the head wound was not observed at the scene and the weapon was located and recovered during the autopsy from fluids and decomposed matter inside the victim's chest cavity.

My first experience finding a dead body occurred in the summer of 1963, the inaugural year of my assigned foot post on the 800 block of Eutaw Place. I received a call from the call-box operator giving the address of a possible death. I was met by the building owner, who began to explain how he leased single rooms monthly and he was concerned about a tenant. He had not seen the man he leased to in weeks nor had the man paid his rent, even though he usually complied without being asked.

The landlord unlocked the tenant's room after the knock at the door was unanswered. A pungent odor difficult to describe caused by a decaying human hit my nostrils for the first time. I entered the sparsely furnished, unkempt room and found the occupant lying on the floor in the reflected sunlight coming from the room's closed window. There were no signs of a struggle or disturbance in the room. Not having ever experienced this before, I remember thinking the poor man on the floor did not appear to have previously been a human being.

The body was in a rather advanced state of decomposition because of the room temperature, but showed no indications of foul play when examined as best I could. The medical examiner's office was notified and responded to take charge of the remains. When the attendant walked into the room and noticed the smell, he offered me a cigar. Smoking and chewing gum were methods used to compensate for the odor. Later the autopsy revealed no indication of an assault or violent death, and the manner of death was ruled a heart attack.

The worst call I ever had regarding a decomposing body occurred in 1965 just north of Police Headquarters, about a block away on Gay Street. I had just finished roll call on the four to twelve shift once again on a summer's day. Pulling down the district ramp in my marked radio car, I was flagged down by a parking lot attendant on a lot I used if I was reporting late to roll call and had to rush. The man ran over to the car and indicated that there was a bad odor coming from one of the buildings that faced Gay Street and backed up to the west side of the parking lot area. He pointed the building out and walked back to his ticket booth. My regular partner was off at the time and I had a loan-out officer riding with me.

We parked on the lot, called out of service and walked over to what we discovered was a three-story vacant building with boarded doors and windows. It was one of several buildings pending destruction by the city to make way for redevelopment in the block. Walking into an alleyway between two of these buildings we noticed an odor. Something was decomposing, and the odor was coming from within the rear room we were standing outside of. We pried off the boards marked "City of Baltimore Property" and peered into total darkness, the bright sunlight contrasting with the pitch black interior. With the window now open, it was evident we had located whatever had died inside, but we were blinded by the contrasting light.

I stepped carefully into the darkened room through the window's broken frame, leading with my right leg first, feeling for the floor which

I hoped still existed as part of this abandoned property. As I settled down on what felt firm and shifted my weight, I felt myself slowly sink another six or so inches. My eyes adjusted to the different light and I looked down, realizing that I had just stepped into the chest cavity of what remained of a man. The homeless person had entered the property by some other means and had nestled down under the window, because it was his only source of light in the room, and died. The autopsy revealed he died of natural causes. Naturally, I needed new shoes, socks and uniform pants before my tour continued.

During our calls and investigations, we found people and bodies in all various forms of injury and death; that was part of the occupation, both in uniform and in plainclothes. You quickly discovered whether you could adjust to the sights and sounds of the street life are odd in that way some people handle certain situations that others cannot.

Being prepared for all sorts of situations was exactly what happened when a rookie loan-out witnessed me do battle with an irate husband during a domestic call at an apartment on Calvert Street. We walked in and the husband jumped me. It was all I could do to get the better of him. He ended up lying face down on the kitchen floor, cuffed and under arrest. The fight had destroyed most of the room, as well as breaking the table and one of the chairs. The whole time the rookie stood back and watched. Once the husband was subdued and in the wagon on his way to jail, we called in service and continued our patrol.

After our in service call to our dispatcher, I asked the rookie why he had stood back during the fight. He answered by saying he thought I could handle the situation. I asked if he was frightened by the altercation and he responded as if questioning himself that he was not. I looked him in the eye and said, "If you are afraid to fight, find a different type of work. You're surely not fitted for the job; you will get yourself or others hurt or killed." Showing any sign of refusing to fight was an action for dismissal from the department. Failing to assist another officer was unacceptable. It weighed heavy on my mind for several days whether or not to write the rookie up for the incident. Maybe he had answered me honestly; he thought I could handle the situation. Maybe being new he was reluctant to get involved, while in the academy not knowing what ramifications would follow? Maybe some strange instructor at the academy had instructed him not to hurt anyone? If I did write it, he would be fired; if I didn't, he could cause a fellow officer to be injured. A consideration that eased my mind was that altercations were actually few and far between the police and the public. I decided against writing him up, and worried about my decision for a while.

Less than a year later, the same rookie was dead, not because he was reluctant to fight when called upon to do so, but perhaps because he decided to transfer. I found out about his transfer immediately after he had graduated from our academy. He had transferred to one of the county police departments, where he was involved in a fatal departmental accident while responding to an emergency call.

Another loan-out officer from the academy was one I did not want to even remember by name. The guy was so sure of himself, shortly after he got in the car he looked me in the eye and stated, "If we get into a fight with anyone tonight, he could probably take care of it without my help." I could not keep myself quite: "If you think you are the deadliest kid on the block, you will get your ass handed to you more often than you can imagine, and if you happen to challenge the wrong person while you are at it, they'll do more than that. If you beat someone for no reason, or he thinks it, they will come at you with a gun or knife, or two or three friends when he gets the opportunity. Just you making that statement made me think not to rely on you if anything really does happen." He thought over what I had said and apologized. The shift went well and he behaved on every call for service. When you hear such statements, it makes you think, is he trying to reassure himself? Is he really too quick to react to situations, or is he afraid to react? One thing's for sure, that smart-aleck attitude will spark unnecessary conflict and will get someone injured.

Domestic Call

O fficer Eicher and I answered a domestic call one day in car 103's territory because they were out of service when the call came over the radio. It was on Preston Street, just off of Greenmount Avenue. We were ushered in by the husband who, in a routine manner, said we were there for nothing. "Every once in a while, the old girl and I get into it over nothing," he commented. On the other hand, the wife was more than upset. Both were in their mid to late fifties. It took minutes to calm her and, because she occasionally lunged toward her husband while explaining that he was a drunk and useless as far as working, we decided to separate the two of them. Ralph stayed downstairs with the calmer husband while I willingly took the rather robust wife upstairs after advising her it would be best to separate them for a time to allow them both to calm down.

The second floor landing was narrow and the first doorway led to their rather small bedroom. The woman walked gingerly up the steps and into the bedroom, saying separation was a good idea. I followed her and when I entered the room she was standing over by an old dresser, which was scratched and faded with water stains. She apologized to me about us having to come there, as I entered the dingy room that was dimly lit even for the noon hour. I heard nothing from downstairs and had to assume that all was well with Ralph and the husband. The woman leaned back against the dresser and after she apologized again, she started telling me how impossible living with her husband had become. She complained that he was abusive when he drank, he beat her often as a result, and he was often fired from jobs after a few weeks for the same reason: his drinking. He either gets too drunk to work the next day or he is caught drinking on the job. "It's just the same old thing, too much for me to contend with," she said.

All the while, even as I tried to calm her, she was working herself into frenzy. She smiled, reached down on top of the dresser and started past me with a knife in her hand, saying, "Don't worry, officer, I'm going to kill him. I don't want to hurt you, just his sorry ass." The woman outweighed me at the time by I would imagine about one hundred pounds. I stepped in front of her, blocking her path, and she continued to try and get past me, trying to exit through the door. She actually smiled at me and said, "Please, I told you, you won't get hurt. I just decided to cut that bastard and be done with him." At that point, we were wrestling for possession of the knife, which appeared to have been brought up from the kitchen. She never made a move aimed at me or attempted to hit me, so I took her at her word. Because of her size, we landed on the bed still wrestling over the weapon before I got it away from her. She calmed at that point, "You're right, that son of a bitch is not worth me going to jail for, but some day he'll hit me and I'll have to kill him."

Ralph was not aware of what had occurred just some eight feet above him in the upstairs bedroom. Once I told him, we agreed that she should be arrested. If not, a half hour after we left them alone, one would have killed or injured the other. My bet was that the wife would survive; she had shown enough intent and desire to carry out her threats.

This was an example of two very important lessons learned. Never get separated to the point that you do not know what your partner is doing or what situation he is faced with. I know I had a bad habit of doing just that, reacting instead of thinking, and I honestly worked on that and it did get better. Your partner's safety depended on you and vice versa. The second point was always being conscious that the call is a domestic matter. Blood is thicker than water. Both parties arguing with each other at one point may turn and unite in a physical assault against both or one of you. Usually this occurred when there was an arrest and the other realized that their mate was going to jail. We knew an entire adult family that argued with one another until the police arrived and then united against us at some point after our arrival. Police realized that, rationally, with all the passion and sometimes-actual hatred that develops between married couples as well as sometimes between siblings, domestic calls could be explosive and potentially dangerous calls to respond on.

As far as entire families that fought, I was never called to the home of the ones we had identified up near North Avenue. But one of the family members was involved in another one of my calls. I was working foot patrol on the upper portion of our assigned bailiwick when I received a call for a disorderly man at the Mt. Royal Tavern on Mt. Royal Avenue just north of Oliver Street. It was about 10:30 P.M. when I entered the seemingly always busy tavern. The bar was located between two buildings used by the Maryland Art Institute and therefore whenever it was open, college youth were there. There was a crowd of about thirty people in the bar at the time, about a dozen in their thirties; the rest were males and females in their early twenties, the usual crowd. Music was playing and it was a lively group. A small number were in the back shooting pool. I did not have to ask the bartender why he had called.

There was a man staggering in front of the bar and cussing with every other word he uttered. Those standing around him backed away and were trying to avoid him. I glanced at the bartender and nodded as if asking through eye contact if this was the man he called on. The bartender answered silently with a nod of his head as if indicating yes. I walked up to the man who was about my weight but shorter, and as I approached him he turned and said, "Well, look who's here, the G.D. cops. I guess you f------ called them?"

That was enough; he was drunk and combative. When I reached for him, I grabbed him by the belt and turned him toward the door saying, "That is it, you're under arrest." His staggering slowed us slightly as we exited, and I noticed that most of the people in the tavern I glanced at had a look of relief on their faces. We had no trouble walking down the light marble steps that led onto the street from the tavern. Once down the eight or ten steps, I pointed him across the street by pushing him forward. A call box was located directly across the street from the tavern in front of what was then a large Goodyear Tire store. There was no problem walking him to the box, actually not a word. When they are quiet like that, you always wondered what they are thinking, what are they contemplating?

When we reached the call box, I opened it and called for a wagon. Up until that point, the man had remained silent, which both surprised and prepared me. He was certainly vocal when I walked into the tavern and he first saw me. He was thinking about something. He was facing the call box and without trying to turn he asked, "Do you know who I am? I'm one of the Ross's." I had finally met one of the notorious members of the fighting family. Theirs was a family that seemingly called police just to fight with those who answered the call. I pushed him forward, head into the base of the phone inside of the call box and answered, "Yes, I know who you are, and if you as much as flinch I'm going to slam this iron door shut on your head. You don't have half the family to help you now."

He remained quiet and still while I walked him to the wagon. Once the wagon arrived, I advised the wagon crew who he was and to be careful. Like so many, he was willing to fight when the odds were in his favor, when the family outnumbered the police. But with the odds lowered, one on one, he was not nearly as heroic.

Jumpers

I was a rookie working the post that I had been assigned six months earlier. It was a nice summer's day with a mild temperature, one of those afternoons that brought people out on the street to enjoy the weather. Pedestrians were walking about, with some folks seated in the grassy areas of the State Office Building on Preston and Eutaw streets having their lunches.

A glance in the direction of the hourly picnickers brought to mind how often on Fridays at noon I would respond to the office building for a false fire alarm. The alarm would force hundreds of workers from the building onto the surrounding grounds. We were sure that the alarm was being used to allow the building's number writer space to wander among workers and take their bets. But no matter how many times the alarm sounded, we were unable to find our suspected writer. After the people went back inside to their respective jobs, all we had left were the men and fire equipment leaving the scene of another false alarm.

I looked back up the street and noticed that the recall lamp on the call box at Madison Avenue was on. The light was the only way at the time to alert an officer that an area call for service had been received. I walked to the call box, unlocked it and grabbed the phone inside. The call-box operator explained that there had been a call for a jumper a block off of our Park Avenue post in Love Grove Alley and no other officers were available.

As I walked to the area, I thought about it being my first call for a jumper, a person who had decided to leap to their death from a building. What condition would the body of the victim be in? What should I expect to find? As I thought about these and other questions, I reached Madison and Love Grove. By this time, there were two other police officers on the scene, one at each end of Love Grove Alley, which ran north and south. The officers were busy keeping onlookers from walking into the alley where the body of the victim was covered with a blanket.

One of the officers turned and said he had a call that the woman had jumped from the fourth-floor window of a woman's boarding house located near the corner. He asked if she was my first jumper. I thought he asked this because of my youthful appearance or the uniform still looking new. I answered and he told me to go give her a look. Walking down the alley toward the blanket-covered body, the thought struck me that her body was extremely close to the concrete alley. It did not look normal; just the average person lying down would protrude higher above the roadway. Another thing that struck me was that when I reached the covered body there was no blood seeping out from under the blanket. I knelt down beside her and held up the blanket not sure what to expect. The little old lady who appeared to be in her 80's was dressed neatly in a housedress, lying there as if she had decided to lie down and rest. The only injuries were a small amount of blood from both ears and her nose.

The officer walked up after the crowd had decided there was nothing to see and told me, based on information from the hotel manager, that the woman was despondent over the loss of her husband and that was apparently why she had jumped. I commented I had expected the body to be in much worse condition after hitting a concrete roadway from that height. He smiled back and told me I would find them in every physical condition imaginable, governed by what they hit on the way down. "You think this woman is in good shape? Pick up her arm," he said. I reached down and picked up her left arm, holding it away from her body. The little old, maybe ninety pound lady had turned into a large rag doll. Her arm bent at any point you held it. Evidently, no matter how well she looked lying there, the fall had broken every bone in her body.

While assigned to car 105, I had two jumper calls, one of which was on view. Doug Cash and I were southbound on Cathedral Street stopped at a traffic light. I was in the driver's seat at the time and noticed what looked like a blur out of the corner of my left eye, followed by a thud sound. The sight and sound drew my attention and I looked toward my left just in time to see a body parallel to a parked car bounce as high as the roof of this car and then settle back to the sidewalk. I turned on our roof emergency lights while Doug called for an ambulance. We both jumped from the car and ran over to the victim. One side of his head was crushed and it was evident that he was dead. Examination of the body revealed that he was casually dressed, but was not wearing shoes. He appeared to be in his fifties. Looking up, we saw an open fourth-floor window with its curtains gently waving in the light breeze. An ambulance responded and removed the victim's body to a nearby hospital, awaiting the medical examiner's wagon. Armed with his wallet, we entered the building he had apparently leaped from the Baltimore YMCA.

The manager gave us the victim's name. We learned he had checked in about a week ago and had been staying in a fourth-floor room overlooking Cathedral Street. After hearing our description, the manager was sure the victim was our man. The manager ushered us to the room and we gained entrance by means of a passkey. Across from the front door was the open window we had seen from the street, its curtains still blowing lightly in the night air. Beneath the window, as if placed there with thought, were the man's shoes. The single room was neat and clean and showed no signs of a disturbance. The door we entered was unmarked and showed no signs of forced entry.

On the night table was an open piece of paper with a pen. The man had written to his wife and daughter telling them that he had fought against alcoholism as best he could, but he knew it was a losing battle. A week ago, he had lost his job because of his problem and reached the end. A failure, he begged them to forgive and forget him signing, "Your loving husband and father," followed by his first name. A name and a person he no longer had faith in.

The other jumper call was to investigate a female body found in an alley. At the time, we were in car 105 on the dayshift while driving south on St. Paul Street from North Avenue. The call was for a hotel address located on Mt. Vernon Square. Down St. Paul to Biddle to Charles, we drove in the shadow of the Washington Monument. Reaching our destination, we saw a crowd of ten or fifteen people standing at the alley entrance.

An ambulance pulled to the curb on Charles with its lights still flashing and the crew both up the alleyway. As we walked into the alley, we observed them standing near the far side of a green metal dumpster with the large cover door open and dangling between the dumpster side and the building wall behind. On the far side of the dumpster stood the paramedics hovering over a woman clad in a coat and dress. My mind wandered back to my first jumper scene. That lady did not even appear injured until you realized the broken bones she had suffered as a result of the fall and impact. This woman made up for my first one and was more wrenching than I had thought jumpers would look. Blood and skull fragments were on the turnbuckle of the dumpster and on the pavement and street at the base of the dumpster. She had died before she had struck the ground. During the fall, her head struck the turnbuckle on the dumpster and the speed and weight of the falling body at impact tore half her head off.

Pronounced dead at the scene, we covered her and awaited the morgue wagon. The manager of the hotel established her identity and said she had lived there over a year. Her visitors were her children, who over the months came less frequently. The woman was an independent person who reportedly decided to live alone once she found out she was suffering from incurable cancer. Never complaining or showing any signs of deteriorating health, she must have decided she had enough suffering and that the quality of life she had enjoyed no longer existed. Her room was checked and she had left a farewell note to her grown children. Bad enough to suffer the sudden shock of losing a parent, but the closed casket at the viewing and the reason for it would also add to their deep sadness.

While in homicide, I received a call at 11:00 P.M. that a southwest unit was requesting us at the scene of a jumper on Edmondson Avenue, at the bridge just west of Poplar Grove Street. The nature of the call was for a jumper who had dived off the south side of the bridge into the small Gwynns Falls stream below after climbing onto the four foot retaining wall. Twenty minutes later, Tim and I were pulling to the curb in front of the marked unit parked with its emergency lights lit on the south side of the bridge. An ambulance was parked there also, but the paramedics were not to be seen.

On the Hilton Avenue side of the bridge were several radio cars with their lights on but unoccupied. A fire truck was leaving the scene as we arrived, probably dispatched in case of a recue situation, but after evaluating the situation indicated they were not needed.

The initial officer walked from his unit to us as we exited our car and started with an apology for calling us. Explaining the situation, he said he was westbound just short of driving onto the bridge when a man walking toward him started frantically waving his arms as if he was flagging down the police car. As the officer stopped his unit to see what the man wanted, the subject pointed directly at him. Then he jumped up on the four foot stone safety wall and without hesitation dove off the bridge as if he was diving into a swimming pool. The officer said he ran across to the point where the man leapt from, but because of the darkness and distance down to the stream he could not see the subject. He called in the situation as he climbed down the embankment to the water. He located the jumper in the rocky stream in about two feet of water face down. He carefully rolled him over expecting broken bones, but fearful he could drown if still alive.

"The guy looked up at me and told me he thought he had broken his right arm. Then he told me that his arm was the only part of his body that hurt. I had him lie still until the paramedics arrived. They came as well as the fire department and other police units. By the time I had found him, knew he had survived the leap and climbed back up to show those arriving where he was, you guys were here. The paramedics are treating him now down by the stream," the responding officer explained.

We climbed down the dark sloop, talked to the ambulance crew who were also amazed, and found out that the jumper was alert and talking. After their examination, it was determined the only injury he had suffered was a broken arm. They took him up the far sloop on a stretcher and left for the hospital and x-rays. The last conversation from the jumper was something to the effect that he could not even kill himself. Looking to the top of the bridge, it appeared a good forty to fifty feet to the roadway above.

What are the odds of someone surviving that, diving off a bridge and falling that far headfirst into what amounted at that point two foot of water in a rock-filled riverbed? Not only survive but also be able to complain about a broken arm minutes later. The hospital would treat him for whatever injuries and determine if he is on drugs and hold him over for a psychological evaluation because of his attempted suicide.

I've never thought of committing suicide myself, but after seeing the results of the impacts and knowing personally as I have mentioned before, that I have a fear of heights, jumping will never be my method should the thought ever cross my mind. Of course, with my phobia, the fall would scare me to death long before the landing.

Incompatible Friends

Two situations with Officer Tom Russell resulted in a pact between us. Although it was actually more of a joke between us, we kept the agreement. Tom was a congenial man, easy to get along with and dedicated to the job. We actually never worked as partners on the street, or later when we both became detectives.

Our first unplanned collaboration began when Tom was walking a foot post in uniform at the time and observed an altercation on Lanvale Street near Charles Street. Two men were fighting and one had drawn a small handgun from his back pocket as Tom rushed toward them. He reached the two before any shots could be fired and managed to grab the gun hand of the man. The gunman and Tom became involved in a wrestling match for the weapon when the other man stepped back fearing he was about to become a shooting victim. I was northbound on Charles Street at the time and for some unknown reason glanced in their direction. Seeing the situation, I stopped the car and ran toward the altercation. I joined Tom in his attempt to obtain control of the weapon by grabbing the man around the neck. We managed to take the .22 caliber revolver from the guy, and arrested him for possession of the weapon.

The second situation was when I was on routine patrol, with no new calls coming over the radio. I saw a man run into a row house with Tom running after him. Tom was up the front steps of the building in one bound. Again, I double parked the car and followed. When I entered the first-floor area, I observed Tom at the rear hall open door of the first-floor apartment with his gun drawn and pointed toward a man that proved later to be the tenant inside the open apartment.

Reaching Tom as I drew my gun, and looking toward the open apartment, I observed a man with a butcher knife in his right hand, holding it at his right side. The three of us stood about four feet apart: Tom and I in the apartment entranceway with our guns drawn and the man, who apparently lived there, holding a butcher knife. We were all close enough that if he raised his weapon, we would have to shoot to protect our selves. And at that close range, neither would miss.

The standoff had developed quickly. No one was quick to react; no need for sudden moves. He did not want to attack us and we did not want to shoot him. Naturally, the first conversation from us was for him to put the weapon down. He failed to comply, but never raised the knife from his side. During the standoff, we tried talking and asked what had caused the situation. He admitted that his marriage was on the rocks; he was working and trying to take care of the home while his wife was apparently running the streets, not even taking care of their two year old child.

He motioned toward the kitchen area slightly with his head and there was the toddler. The child had not been noticed to that point because he had been quiet and we were not about to take our eyes off of the suspect. We talked for a good while about the man surrendering without him being injured, but the difference came when we talked to him about being shot in front of his child. After long minutes that proved ineffective as far as talking him down, when his kid was mentioned and the fact that the child could witness his father taking a bullet, the man's eyes tiered up as he dropped the weapon and apologized. The confrontation ended with a man in despair over his marriage, but alive in order to participate in his child's future. After criminal charges and a mental evaluation, it would be his responsibility to work on his marriage.

Tom and I joked about these events. Together we always found ourselves in situations involving weapons and possible harm to either ourselves or suspects; that's why we never worked together. Just chance situations, but why tempt fate? Ironically, Tom and I ended up in Homicide Unit together, but on different shifts. We never forgot our agreement.

Over the years, I faced many situations with weapons and the incidents always worked out favorably. No one was injured, not any suspects or I. How lucky, a split second to lunge with a knife, or pull the trigger of a revolver in a fraction of a second, and a totally different result. A life-or-death decision made in a fraction of time; what a responsibility, a spit-second decision based on circumstance, situations and the state of minds of those involved.

Bank Call

Yes, we were a shotgun car because of the area banks in the Central District, one on North Avenue and the other on Maryland Ave. Several were also spread around the downtown area, mainly on Howard Street, which was the heart of Baltimore City retail shopping in the 1960's. The shotgun was not carried in a locked position between the driver and front-seat passenger; it was locked away, loaded with pumpkin ball shot, in a wooden box in the trunk of the car.

Our procedure was that the driver upon arrival at a bank call would unlock the trunk and open the shotgun box. His partner, who had been his passenger up until that point, would reach in and take out the shotgun. He was the one armed with it and would approach the bank ready to use it. But please forgive me; this is not a tale about arriving at a bank and having a dramatic television or novel-type shootout with the bad guys as they escaped the bank with money in hand and their guns blazing, only to be shot up by the responding police, wounded or killed with the survivors forced to surrender.

Although we responded to countless bank calls, hold-up men were never on the scene when we arrived and we were never faced with a potential shootout. Normally, bank alarms were false alarms, accidentally set off by employees. If the bank had been actually robbed, the hold-up men were usually gone minutes before we arrived. It's definitely true, real life isn't never-ending excitement. Seldom are calls serious. You may never fire your gun in your entire career as a police officer, but you have a good chance of developing a callus from writing reports. Generally, the excitement of shootings and gunfights is left to the movies and television, and it's what sells them. When police face such situations, the results are real and everlasting.

One thing always tickled me and remained in the back of my mind about these calls, especially those in the downtown area. At the time, the traffic police manned the corners of almost every downtown intersection. Most of them appeared overweight and all they did was blow their whistles, give directions to those who asked and, as far as I was concerned, call out to lunch at the most inappropriate times. I never saw one of them smaller in size than my one hundred and ninety pounds at the time. We would come screeching to a stop, siren wailing, grab the shotgun, the other take out his handgun, run into the bank and always beat the traffic cops, who directed us while we were speeding through the traffic in our marked cars. Often they never made an appearance inside of the bank. At the time, we did not have personal radios. They could not hear the bank alarms come over; they must have called out of service on the sound of the approaching sirens and squealing tires as we slid to a stop.

Well, this was not that type of call, but it appeared like a definite attempt at stealing money from a bank. Late afternoon on one Sunday shift, just coming out of the station on the 4-to-12, we received a call for a burglary alarm sounding from one of two drive-thru banking windows of the Maryland National Bank located at North Ave. and Maryland Ave. We were just off the floor from roll call, but luckily northbound on Charles St. at Mt. Royal Ave., blocks from the location. Cash and I arrived within minutes of the call, driving onto a rear lot just east of the two small drive-thru banking booths. No one was observed in the area and both buildings appeared secure. We both exited the radio car and checked the exteriors of both small buildings. All appeared normal until I reached a small window next to the entrance door leading to the office area of the drive-thru. The closed window was unlocked and opened just a crack. The open window allowed you to reach in and open the door by turning the knob. Apparently, no more than a light breeze had been enough to open the window and set off the alarm.

There were no pry marks on the window or door entrance points. Once inside we noticed no signs of any type of disturbance to the small office area. With all secure inside, we initially agreed that the window must have been blown open by a gust of wind and set off the alarm system. The safe appeared in a normal, closed condition, with no signs of tampering so neither of us tried its handle to see if it was open at that time. We would go over both buildings once the ADT man arrived. I called back in on radio and requested ADT to respond.

Within minutes, a young male representative driving a compact car marked "ADT" arrived and walked in wearing a shirt with his company logo. We explained our call and the condition in which we had found the drive thru. I commented that it could not have been a mistake for the teller to leave the window next to the door unlocked, leaving the interior accessible. She has to know to be conscientious when locking up at closing. I walked a few steps over to the small bank safe under the window counter that we had found open. Reached down, turned the door handle and the safe opened, while I was in the process of kiddingly saying, "Now watch this be open."

All of us were surprised when the safe opened and we saw piles of green paper in view. Both of us stayed in the company of the ADT man while he counted the contents of the safe, $24,000 in cash and $35.00 in change. Our report described the scene as we found it, the amount of money recovered from the open safe and the ADT rep's identification. We added that the teller on duty who left the drive-thru in the condition it was found should be considered a suspect in an attempted larceny. The report went to detectives after review.

When we hit day work almost two months later, we received a request for a follow-up report from those involved at the bank during their work hours. Wondering why the initial report had not been followed up sooner, we responded to the bank. The manager when interviewed seemed to be a little too nonchalant and advised that the employee was considered reliable and that the incident was not considered to be a problem of any magnitude.

We then interviewed the teller reportedly responsible for leaving the drive-thru in the condition we had discovered it. She advised that at the time she was preoccupied with her mother's illness and that her family concerns were responsible for her not locking the window and safe. The fact that she was so upset with the family illness crisis was her reasoning for her diverted attention. She expressed concern for her job, saying the matter was still under review at a higher level, but her responses to our questions and her general demeanor did not indicate that she was truly concerned over the matter. Both of us were even more convinced of our suspicions at this time.

We approached the manager again and asked if the state of the drive-thru when found raised any questions in his mind, and did he consider it a deliberate act on her part. He replied he considered her a loyal and faithful employee, and although the matter was up for review, he hoped she would weather the situation without being considered a suspect in such an act, or by being penalized for her mistake.

On our way out of the building, we were stopped by one of the indoor tellers. She motioned us toward her and said quickly, "I don't want to get involved, that girl, the outdoor teller and the manager date one another. I thought you guys should know that." After the comment, she turned and walked away as quickly as possible. We noted her name for the report. When she reached her teller window with her name plaque sitting on the counter outside her service window, she added that she should not be interviewed at work because she feared ramifications.

The supplement report was submitted and directed to the Property Division. The report identified all the players, the relationship between the manager and the teller, and the name of the teller who gave us that information. The case was no longer ours; whatever happened was not related back to us. Apparently, it never resulted in a court docket, or if it did, it was accepted without our testimony. The incident and our investigation at best represented a possible attempted theft with potential suspects if that could be proven, which would have been difficult without a confession. I often wonder if the manager and his girlfriend withstood the bank internal scrutiny and that of our detectives.

Living Conditions

———————————————◦∞◦————————————————

A t the time, we worked what could be considered the better residential area of the district when in radio car 105. Businesses, churches, theaters, restaurants and hotels located all along Charles Street from the Washington Monument north were among the finest. The homes and even the apartments were kept nice and furnished well. The homes to our east in the Greenmount Avenue area and to our west in the Druid Hill Avenue area, although both located in the Central were different stories. Because of the economic and social circumstances of the time, you could find yourself exposed to any condition imaginable when answering a call.

One of my first domestic calls was on McCulloh Street with one of my sergeants, when I was still a footman. He joined me as I walked toward the address of the call saying that he had been there several times and that I was in for a real experience and that I had to prepare myself for what I was about to see. He added: "Don't touch anything, and don't sit down. Keep your hat on and when you come out, take it off and shake it. Remember to brush your shoulders off, too, that will get rid of the red men." I answered I would while thinking, what the hell are red men? Then, in a deliberate tone of voice he said, "After your shift, go right home, get undressed on your porch; leave your clothes out there. Take a hot bath and get your uniform cleaned first thing in the morning after you retrieve it from the porch."

We reached the address and banged on the door. An elderly unkempt woman opened the door and said, "It's about time." The sergeant, who was an old salt, replied, "There's never a rush; you two fight all the time with or without us." She sighed in acknowledgement, stepped aside and allowed us to walk past her. The sergeant knew what he was talking about. The two of them, who had lived for years as common law, had fought every weekend for the past few years, to his knowledge. Sometimes they called the police more than once a weekend, always to settle disputes between the two of them.

The moment I walked in I noticed a foul odor in the house. Unkempt litter from either a cat or maybe a dog was causing the smell. The floors were dusty and dirty. Old newspapers were strown, on the floor as well as on pieces of furniture. As I entered the living room, I glanced back into the dining room and the kitchen behind it. The place was unbelievable, dust had settled everywhere, even on the ragged furniture, and the odor was so strong you wondered how they could live with it.

The domestic argument was settled almost as soon as we entered; both promised to calm down and treat one another better. Two false promises made from their previously known complaints. My thought, why don't they fight about the condition of the house?

There was another fight going on at the time, one we could not control or even have a say in. More roaches than you could count were running, clawing and standing on the coffee table. During a closer look at the living table, I observed what appeared to be little red bugs scurrying about the table intermingled with the roaches. It was the first time I had ever seen them things. You had to look closely to even see them. They were about the size of a pinpoint with multiple little legs on each side. Along with the place being crawling with these bugs, I noted cat excrement on the floor and in one corner of the room. The floor rug was almost unidentifiable, frayed and filthy. The sergeant nodded his head toward the door as if saying, "Let's get out of here." We told them not to call again and left as quickly as possible.

When we reached the street again, I asked, "What are those little red things I saw?" "They're mites. Get used to them. You will see them again in some of these houses," he said. The sergeant added, "We call them 'red men.' I don't know for sure how they develop, but they have their share of them. They say one way they come is from plants, but I didn't see any plants alive in there. I've reported those people to the health department several times, but nothing is ever done to my knowledge. One day, either or both will come down with some unknown disease if they keep living that way."

Upon arriving home from the shift, I did what the sergeant had suggested. My uniform was left on the back porch after walking straight through the house to get there. It was a raised porch area with no steps from the yard, or I would have gone directly to the porch, not taking the chance that some of those roach and red mites would get in the house. I had dusted my hat and shoulders when we left the call, but continued to think bugs were on me until I stripped and took a hot shower. The next morning, the first thing I did was a trip to the cleaners with my bagged uniform. That was my first time undressing on the porch because of unhealthy conditions I had been called to; the second such situation follows.

Working day work now in the car with Eicher, we received a call to supervise an eviction on Read Street between Charles St. and St. Paul St. When we arrived, there was a city crew with a large open-walled truck cleaning discarded furniture that looked intended for the dump from the front sidewalk of the address we had been called. One city worker advised that a crazy old lady that had been evicted from the second-floor apartment had threatened him about them taking the furniture.

We walked up to the second-floor apartment landing and entered through the open door into the first room of the apartment. The first room was relatively empty except for dust and a few newspapers crumpled on the floor. This must have been the room emptied of the furniture already on the street. The next room was a different story. We were shocked at what we saw; it was incredible, newspapers everywhere, piled to the ceiling in all directions. Piled so high you could not see the ceiling anywhere in the room and forget where the walls were located. The piles of newspaper's were so high the papers had collapsed near the ceiling forming a paper tunnel walkway through the room into the next, which was a kitchen area where the elderly woman was scurrying about whatever business she thought she had.

Before we stepped into the manmade tunnel, we looked at each other and shrugged. The newspapers were brimming with roaches; those near the top of the tunnel losing their footing were falling onto the floor of the paper cave. Ralph said what he must have been thinking, "Why hadn't the other tenants complained long before this?" Unfortunately, there was no other route to the woman. We walked through as quickly as we could, hunching our shoulders, trying to make smaller targets for our little brown friends. After reaching the woman and having a conversation with her, we decided two things: one, she was no threat to the workers downstairs, and two, she definitely needed help, because of her mental condition and that of the apartment she lived in. Her sister was coming to get her and would have her live with her. In the kitchen, the mess was different, food-crusted pots and pans cluttered about the stove and floor, the sink was filthy, and our newfound friends were running wild in there also.

On our way out, we had to walk, well, semi-run, the tunnel gauntlet again. Once outside, we explained that we would not stand by, because it was evident the job would take all day, but we would be alert for the call should they need help. We explained that they should call for another crew and truck for the mess upstairs, which they had decided to do before we made the suggestion. There was no way just one crew or truck would handle what appeared to be a full day's work. We both felt that the battle they would face with the roach population in that apartment would result in their defeat. Faced with cleaning out that apartment you would have to consider giving your notice and finding another job

The woman's sister drove up, as we had been told, identified her self and took charge of her bewildered sister, driving away with her. Their departure brought a great deal of relief to the city workers who had called us. We stomped around on the pavement for several minutes and checked for bugs before calling back in service. We removed our hats and a few roaches from them and our shoulders before getting back in the car. Ralph commented, "Watch, with everything else we have to put up with, now we get roaches in the car."

At the time, there was a carryout located beneath the eviction apartment on the first floor. The owner of the carryout was a nice guy, maybe he did not know about the critters that ran about in his business after closing, but we had to report the matter to the Health Department. Until that day, we occasionally bought our lunches at that storefront deli; needless to say, that marked our last time. We had responded to a call in an upscale neighborhood with a mentally impaired woman, or one with Alzheimer's disease, a tenant unable to attend to either herself or her apartment. The conditions we found were as bad as any we had ever seen.

District Operations

After five years in the car, I moved to what was then called operations in the central district. We worked plainclothes for two shifts, working the streets for any crimes observed: vice, larcenies, burglaries, street robberies, etc. On the 4-to-12 shift, we filled in high-crime areas in marked cars and uniform. There were five of us, and a sergeant who supervised. The following events, including the 1968 riots, occurred during my assignment to operations.

The Officer Huffman Shooting

O n October 3, 1967, we were working plainclothes in the operations division of the central in the area of Pratt Street when the dispatcher announced that two southern district police had been kidnapped at the scene of a commercial burglary, and later released. The suspect had subsequently commandeered a Sun cab and headed in the direction of Camden Yards railway station. He was described as a black male standing 5'8," twenty three to twenty five years of age, in possession of both the officers' guns and therefore considered dangerous.

Turning the unmarked car onto Pratt Street heading toward Camden Yards, we heard a series of rapid gunshots. The shots sounded as if they were west of us on Pratt Street. We observed a marked unit on the southeast corner of Pratt and Paca streets, pulled to the curb facing westbound about a block from our unit. As we reached the scene, Officer Huffman was out of the car standing near the open driver's door, holding the roof of his radio car for balance, bleeding from an apparent gunshot wound to the right side of his face. The suspect was lying on the pavement near the rear of the car on his back suffering from several gunshot wounds to his chest area in a semi-conscious state.

It was nearly midnight and the area, which was slated for urban renewal, was isolated except for the rapidly growing police presence. Within minutes, a cruising patrol reached the scene and transported Officer Huffman to University Hospital. The suspect was taken there shortly after by ambulance.

As Officer Huffman was being taken away, an unidentified man walked up and asked, "What the hell happened? Is the cop OK?" Before I answered, he said," I would not have your job for a million dollars." I guess partly because of the situation with Huffman being a friend, and partly because such times prompted the general public to appreciate us, I answered by telling him to go about his business or I would lock him up. The wrong response I know, he was probably sincere in his concern, but it seemed as if the only time the general public realized the risks we take were in moments like this.

I had worked with Huffman before my assignment to 105 on another shift during loan outs. and found him to be personality plus, always polite, jovial and always willing to perform his job. Now, as the cruiser pulled off, I wondered although he was on his feet, conscious and responsive, would he actually survive and if so would he ever be able to see again? He was out looking for the man the southern dispatcher described and he had found him.

The following events led up to the Huffman shooting.

Officer John Toronto was a rookie cop recently assigned to the southern. His partner for the 4-to-12 shift was Harvey Andrews, a sixteen year veteran of the department at the time. Their patrol area included the area of Patapsco Avenue and Ritchie Highway; previously, they had received two minor calls and had cleared both without any problems or reason to arrest

Toronto was anxious to learn the job and to prove his worth. He felt that the marked patrol car assignment was a quick way to gain experience with all the various types of calls they would answer; it would definitely expand his knowledge. Handling call after call and learning the ways they were resolved was a faster way to learn the various situations the job would present. Walking a beat and hoping to run up on problems that required police presence and solutions certainly would not help him learn as quickly as multiple dispatched radio calls

Riding through the mostly residential areas on their post, which was a middle to lower class neighborhood. Toronto answered what Andrews considered a mundane call. The dispatcher called their car number and advised that they had an alarm off at the Patapsco Diner and gave the address. Toronto thought at first perhaps it could be a real burglary call. Andrews shrugged and said, "It's nothing, kid. These alarms go off all the time; wind, faulty systems, rain, unlocked doors and windows you name it. Don't get excited on me, it's not a burglar. Some of these places have alarms that go off every time it rains."

Andrews switched on the dome lights but did not use the siren. The lights allowed the emergency vehicle to cut through traffic and arrive at the diner quickly. The front of the lot was empty and the diner's lights were out, with no signs of life from within. Apparently their employees had called it a night. Toronto, who had actually hoped the call would be more than an alarm sounding, felt the anxiousness leave as he looked toward the entrance door and the closed appearance of the darkened diner.

They walked across the empty parking lot that was set well back off the street. As they both exited the marked car, Toronto had drawn his service revolver. Andrews looked with a frown at what he thought was the overzealous young officer and told him, "No need for that. I told you ninety nine percent of these alarm calls are nothing. God knows if you will ever have to draw your gun." Toronto complied by holstering his revolver. They both walked to the front door and up the short number of stairs leading to the entrance. Neither seeing signs of forced entry, Andrews reached for the door handle and found the door to be unlocked. The veteran commented, "See, the alarm's off because they forgot to lock the door, nothing to it."

Just as Andrews pushed open the door, a young man stepped in front of the two officers with a gun in his hand. He said he would shoot both of them if they attempted to draw their guns and beckoned them both inside, motioning with his free hand. Once inside, he ordered both to turn around and remove their guns from their holsters with their opposite hands. At this point Toronto thought, "My first mistake on the job and it may be my last." The only comforting thought was that the assailant had taken time to disarm them rather than shoot first. Still, there was little solace in that thought. He could shoot both of them at anytime he wanted.

They both complied when they were told to turn around. With

their backs turned to the suspect, Toronto waited to hear the shots; they didn't come. Instead, the burglar calmly stated, "I don't need all this. Do as I say and no one will get hurt, but know I'm not going to jail for this." Both officers came to the same conclusion: better to cooperate under the circumstances. He allowed them to turn around and they both got a good look at the man for the first time; the man who was now holding them captive and now had control over their lives was a young man of about twenty three or so years old, and appeared to be about 5'8" in height. It looked as though he was in a western movie, one gun in each hand and one now stuffed in his belt.

What really impressed Toronto, and also sparked a feeling of fear, was that their captor did not appear frightened at all; that caused him to feel less secure in their situation. This guy may have fallen into a botched burglary, but he was not afraid of the fact that he had found himself in charge of the situation. He had not panicked; he was calm and cool. You could almost see the wheels turning, what's the next move, how do I get out of this? All the while, this guy stood there thinking Toronto noticed that he was holding both guns steady in his hands, apparently not shaken by the situation deliberately planning his next move. Both were a second away from him pulling both triggers at point-blank range, if that thought was decided. Was he thinking shoot them both and run, or, what would be the most reasonable move for him in this predicament?

While the young man weighed the situation, both policemen attempted to talk him down, explaining that nothing bad had happened yet, no one hurt, just a do nothing burglary, let them go, he would probably beat the charge. Toronto under the circumstance even offered to let him get away, anything that would save their lives. The suspect looked for a minute as if he was considering their suggestions, but then turned with resolve in his face and said, "Too late. This isn't what I wanted, but it's what I got. Let's take a ride. Maybe I can figure this mess out." The burglar now turned gunman and kidnapper had made up his mind as to what he was going to do, but what was going to happen to them? "Act as if everything is alright as we go to your car. I'll get in the back," the gunman stated in a calm, controlled voice. Toronto thought to himself as he turned back for the diner's door with Andrews at his shoulder and the loaded revolvers at their backs: This is scary; this guy has self control and is confident. He might just do anything the situation calls for. Any move on our part could get us both shot.

They complied with his order and afterward were told to drive around in their normal patrol area, with the gunman seated behind them in the back seat. Andrews at the wheel and Toronto in the shotgun seat were ordered not to talk again; the suspect still held the advantage. He was seated in a position that he could shoot either if they attempted to react or refused his commands. After about ten minutes of relative silence, except for directing some of the patrol car turns, the suspect announced that he wanted to return to the diner. The police questioned why, but were promptly answered: "Just do as you're told. Shut up and drive, no more talking."

Upon arrival at the diner, he ordered Toronto to go and get the cash register from inside, while he guarded Andrews in the car. There was some questioning about the cash register; did he want the register or the money from it? The guy responded by saying, "I could not get it open. Bring the whole thing. Get me the register. I'm watching you from here. In and out, or I'll shoot this guy." Toronto came out with the register after looking about the counter hurriedly for some sort of weapon but not having found any. Since he was being watched from the radio car and told not to get out of sight, slipping away to the kitchen in order to get a knife wasn't possible.

His prayer to obtain any type of weapon would be left unanswered. As he walked back to the car, Toronto thought who runs a business and doesn't have a gun or weapon under the counter? Maybe that was where the burglar's gun initially came from; he had found it before they arrived on the call.

Once again, the three of them drove around the officers' assigned post at the request of their kidnapper; twenty to twenty five minutes passed. The dispatcher had called several times about their assigned call, but they had been told not to touch the radio for anything. With no response from the officers and no additional backup request, the dispatcher had to assume they were still out on the call and all was well.

The gunman suddenly yelled for them to stop the car, tugged the cash register into his arms from the other side of the back seat, and exited the police car. He looked back into the car and told both of the officers to get out. Both complied, with Toronto coming around from the street too the curbside of the car. Their captor looked at them and said: "It's been real. Turn and run up the street or I'll have to shoot you." They looked at each other without a word, turned almost at the same time and ran; both expecting gunshots to ring out As they broke into a run, they looked over their shoulders and observed the man getting into a sun cab, stuffing the cash register in the back seat. Cab number 257 headed north on Charles Street.

Both officers running south not far from the southern station house, ran as quickly as they could with the realization they both had survived an encounter they should not have. When they reached the district and bust through the doors, both were exhausted from their run and filled with emotion from their frightening experience. They detailed their captor's description, manner, method, time and direction of escape, which was immediately patched in to communications.

Afterward, Toronto had time to reflect as he sat there with an empty holster. The thoughts flashed through his mind so fast he could not dwell on any one of them; too many thoughts, with two that stood out: he had survived a life threatening experience and never in a hundred years would he expect a call or situation to be routine.

Officers Huffman and Raziwitz heard the dispatch and were in the area of Camden Yards, manning a central patrol unit. Huffman, who was driving, thought better of responding to the railroad area, knowing that many units would respond there on the call information just because the dispatcher gave Camden Yards as the area in which the cab was headed. They had just come off a routine uneventful domestic call on Eutaw Street and were presently on Pratt Street, blocks east of Camden Yards. They were driving slowly and checking address fronts of commercial buildings that were abandoned and in the process of being torn down for redevelopment. Using their spotlight to detect any movement and to check darkened areas, they pulled slowly up to the southeast corner of Paca and Pratt streets. From behind the rubble of an old gas station located on that corner walked a young man headed directly toward their car.

Officer Huffman noticed as the young man approached the uniformed officers in their marked car that he fit the description of the police kidnapper, and that the handle of a revolver was protruding from a front pants pocket. He turned to his partner and said, "This is the guy; he's got a gun." Raziwitz removed his gun from its holster. Huffman grabbed the door handle with his left hand and unbuckled his holster. The man walked up to Huffman before he could get out of the car and asked, "Do you officers know where I can get a cab?" Before Officer Huffman could answer, the man stepped back toward the back door on Huffman's side of the car out of sight. Huffman realizing this reached for his gun. As he was pulling it from the holster, a bullet struck him in the side of the face and he returned the gunfire blindly in the direction he had last seen the suspect move. Officer Huffman shot out the back window of the radio car firing all six rounds, hitting the suspect three times in the chest area, once in the elbow and once in the wrist. The other bullet lodged in the rear seat of the patrol car.

Officer Huffman got out of the car, placed his hat on his head, disarmed the suspect, who was in no condition to start shooting again, and called in a Signal 13 an "assist an officer" call. He was transported to University Hospital for a gunshot wound to his right temple area. After surgery, he learned he had lost the sight in his right eye. Joe, almost fatally shot, never lost consciousness or his mental capacities. He remained alert and aware at the scene and in the hospital.

Officer Joseph Huffman married and the father of three teenage children at the time had come to the end of his six-and-one-half year tour of duty. Blinded during this shooting, he was medically pensioned and received a guide dog and training in its use from the city. Joseph Huffman later lost his vision all together due to his injuries. No one can imagine what a man blinded at the age of forty must have gone through mentally and emotionally during the remainder of his life, not only him, but his entire family.

The suspect was also transported to University Hospital, where he died as a result of the described gunshot wounds, actually hours into the next morning. Naturally, as is often the case, he had an extensive arrest record prior to this burglary kidnapping. That's all you hear. Most of those who commit crimes, assaults, murders, robberies, should not have ever been on the streets to do so. Bleeding-heart liberals are responsible for much more harm and problems because of their misguided concepts. Their solution of putting people back on the street seldom invites their intended rehabilitation and good citizenship.

A subsequent investigation indicated that Officer Huffman had been shot in the right temple accidentally by his partner who had attempted to fire at the gunman from his seated position next to Officer Huffman at the time. A chaotic situation, three armed men at point-blank range, with the position advantage to the suspect, all firing desperately thinking they would be killed at any second.

The rookie involved in the kidnapping went on to become a detective assigned to the homicide and later made lieutenant, retiring from the uniform division. He had learned one of the most valuable lessons in police work, almost having fatal results at a point early in his career. Perhaps before any other police had time even to tell him, never except any contact or situation with the public as routine. Always expect the worst of every situation. Always be prepared for the worst. The one time you let your guard down, that's the instant you get hurt or killed. A hundred domestics, car stops, assaults, etc., it only takes one situation when you are not alert and prepared.

Opportunists

———◦◦◦———

J ust to show you how crime takes place based on the opportunity, time and place, I wanted to share this next incident.

In operations we worked plainclothes day work. At the time, four of us were in the Bolton Hill area watching a male subject walking close to the street curb, eyeing each parked car he passed for its contents, usually not even turning his head in the direction of the car, just lowering his head and turning his eyes so as not to attract attention. This went on for about an hour. He must have checked out a hundred cars. He was so deliberate we had time through the use of handheld radios to position ourselves in four directions around him should he break into a car of his choice. He never did. Honestly, we watched him for an hour.

Tired of the surveillance we began, we thought he would never find a car with objects in sight worth taking. He walked around a corner of Lanvale Street and turned north on Bolton Street, and no sooner than I lost sight of him, I heard a woman scream. The young lady just had her purse snatched. One of our guys that saw it shouted over the radio, "That bastard hit a purse. He's running north on Bolton!" The opportunity had presented itself, this thief, who wanted to break into a car, had accidently found a more desirable victim and opportunity.

The race was on. With purse in hand, he ran north toward North Avenue. The youth was finally run down near Park and North Avenues in a small park area just southeast of the intersection. The woman who had her purse snatched had it returned and was thankfully unharmed. Quite often, physically pulling the purse from the female victim throws them to the concrete resulting in injury. It was even more worrisome when elderly woman would be assaulted and knocked down, since they were more likely to suffer serious injuries such as broken bones.

The problem that existed for the Bolton Hill area and still does is that it has opportunists walking into the area from surrounding bad neighborhoods. These opportunists see an affluent target and are geared to any crime that could present itself and increase their buying power for their drug usage or personal needs. Items from cars or houses or an occasional victim on the street for their purses, wallets or valuables are more than likely

This kid and those like him are predators. They will commit any type of theft or assault that presents itself in a situation in which they feel safe to commit the crime. They will commit property crimes such as burglaries, larcenies from automobiles, and purse snatches, which are technically assaults and robberies. Those who have graduated from those crimes rob stores and pedestrians at gunpoint. Among those hold-up artists are those that would just as well shoot you in the process, or even afterward for no apparent reason.

I know that the job we did exposed us to these situations daily, but often we saw people become victims because of their faith in their fellow man. It's human nature. If you are fortunate enough to be raised without being a victim of a crime, or knowing anyone that was you have a tendency to accept people at face value. You think others have the same morality. Work at not being so naive, predators are not. They seize the moment. The story below is a perfect example of trust combined with faith in his fellow man.

We received a call for an auto larceny in Bolton Hill. The parking spot for the vehicle was in the rear of the home, across from a small park area. The owner of the car was a well-educated professional person who just could not conceive of anyone breaking into his expensive vehicle. While looking at the damaged window on the car and taking his information for the loss report, he turned to me and said, "Whoever did this was trespassing. Look, there's the posted sign; he's not allowed in here." Like that sign should have kept the thief out. I smiled and said nothing. Perhaps that was the naive answer to all our problems: just post signs everywhere, that would surely ward off the bad guys.

Vice

———⊱•◦•⊰———

While in Operations, one of our details was related to district vice work. Once a year, usually during the summer months, we were used to make vice arrests in the various strip clubs located on "The Block" and to the west along Baltimore Street. One year, Officer Joe Ballista and I were working the club detail making arrests for solicitation from the girls at the various clubs. We had been successful for about a week and a half.

Club after club, managers and owners were looking for two new faces; two guys both over 6' plus and in their mid-twenties, our descriptions. My wife happened to be a member of a cancer fund organization in northwest Baltimore at the time, and was offered one hundred dollars for a photograph of me by a co-member, who was the wife of a strip club owner. Naturally, she refused and told the woman I did not even work plainclothes. If this woman was asking for a photo of me at a club meeting in Reisterstown, somebody had to think I was one of the two undercover cops. We were sure that our run on club girls was at an end.

Thinking of ways to get over on the club personnel, we decided to use my brother-in-law's vehicle as a way to partially hide our identities. Jim, my brother-in-law, was in the marines and presently living in California. He had come to Maryland for training in a nearby state and to visit with us before reporting for training. I borrowed his new mustang at the time with California plates, and Officer Ballista and I drove to one of the clubs that had opened west of The Block, but still on Baltimore Street near Paca Street. We parked in a no-parking zone in front of the club and asked the doorman if it would be all right to park there. He glanced at the out-of-state plate and said it would be fine there; he would watch it for us and get us if there was any problem.

While the doorman watched our car, we separated as we entered so as not to be noticed as being together. We sat on opposite sides of the oval bar so that we could see each other clearly. We had a pre-arranged signal should either of us make a case. I sat at the bar, and as usual was approached immediately by one of the club girls. Apparently, no one had realized we were together. No moves were made by the manager at the door or the bartender to warn the girls. Another girl had seated herself next to Joe; smiling, she engaged him in conversation. As the girl sat down next to me, I ordered both of us a drink, after asking her what she wanted. She immediately reached around my waist, feeling my right side with her right hand, and pressing her elbow against my back. By doing this she had checked to see if I was carrying a gun and had probably reassured her self that I was not a cop. She had just patted me down for a weapon; she smiled and relaxed, finding confidence in an unarmed customer, hopefully with money to spend.

We never carried guns in this type of work and it made me wonder why they still kept checking. The club owners and managers know we never carried. While she thought over whether I was a potential trick and if she should go into her soliciting mode, I relaxed and told her what little I knew from Jimmy's real life. I was a California resident, in. town visiting my sister, and out-of-state training with the marines. Before long, while I watched the stripper on stage and chatted with the one seated next to me, my new girlfriend suggested that for fifty dollars plus the cost of a champagne bottle I could receive oral sex in one of the darkened rear booths. I continued talking as if I was weighing the suggestion and gave Joe the pre-arranged signal that I had her. I tugged at my right ear giving him the signal; he smiled back and gave none, meaning he was not ready yet. Joe was successful also, but it took several tugs at my ear, while the girl with me wondered why I wasn't taking her up on her offer. My excuse was that I wanted to finish my drink, which I was forced to sip.

Officer Ballista gave the signal, stood and announced to his female partner that she was under arrest and identified himself as police officer, as he displayed his badge. I reached for my badge as I stood. The girls acted surprised and then concerned and upset. The manager realized that both girls were under arrest and reacted by saying, "You dumb bitches; we have told you and told you these guys were coming." The club managers and personnel knew not to get involved at this point. Any resistance to an arrest on their premises meant the liquor board would review their license, normally resulting in suspension or fines. The manager accepted their arrests with a few more choice words directed at the girls. I'm sure both were more concerned with losing their jobs than the arrest. After all, they had known our descriptions and still had gotten caught after weeks of us being on the street.

The girls, one almost in tears, insisted that they could not go to jail dressed the way they were. The club manager knew it was our procedure to accompany them while they changed and watch them for our own protection. He said nothing as we agreed they could change and as we walked with them back to their dressing room. All of a sudden, modesty from strippers who danced nude on stage in front of strangers for a living, and offered sexual favors for money, give me a break. The arrests went off without a hitch. As usual, the girls had been released on bond before the paperwork was completed and were probably back dancing, and perhaps slightly gun shy to solicit anyone before we were even finished. The various bondsmen were usually in route to the station before we finished the paper work; notified by the club manager they had been busted.

Another vice situation presented itself one evening when I walked from the station onto the nearby City Hall Plaza, at Holiday and Fayette streets, just two blocks from both Headquarters and the Central District. Again, we were in plainclothes and alert for any violations. I reached the plaza on the west end and sat down on a small retaining wall facing Baltimore's City Hall.

A station wagon with one occupant turned from Fayette Street north onto Holliday Street in front of City Hall and stopped in front of me. As the passenger's window went down, a man leaned over toward the open window and asked, "Do you want a ride, some company?" At that point, we were about twenty five feet apart, him in the car and I still seated on the three-foot wall. I was holding a walkie-talkie in my right hand, wrapped in a pint liquor bag. The talkie was not even thoughtfully concealed. I thought, doesn't he realize I'm a cop? I replied, "I'm not interested," and turned away from our brief conversation. The man shrugged and drove off. I dismissed him, thinking it had finally dawned on him that I was a police. But, no, a few minutes later the same man drove by again. On what would have been his third drive-by, he stopped and said, "Come on, you want to." This guy was either in heat or just stupid. I replied, "I'm a cop, and this bag contains a radio. Get the hell out of here." He drove off again shaking his head as if he did not believe me. Ten minutes passed and I did not see him or the car in the area again.

Convinced that I had scared him off, I walked to the southwest corner of the intersection to take a leak at what was then a hotel combination bar; it was later demolished and became the site of the old city employees' credit union. I walked into the downstairs men's room and approached a urinal. As I stood over the urinal, relieving myself, the man from the station wagon slipped beside me. While staring down at me doing my business, the stalker said, "Come on, let's have sex anyway. Anything you want, me on you, you on me." Well, how many chances to get away do you get? I had, had enough of this poor bastard. If he did not know a cop when one announced himself to him, he was bound to go to jail sooner or later, and he had certainly gone out of his way working hard at it all evening.

I thought of the station wagon as I walked the poor soul to the nearby station house for booking. He must be a family man, because of his ride, and was certainly new at trying to pick up young men and boys. After this booking for solicitation, his overpowering desire for men would definitely become known to those he cared about and loved. What far-reaching ramifications in his life, both personal and business, would this cause? How many years had he attempted to hide such desires? Now quiet and softly sobbing as we walked, he must have realized his plight and its implications. On the positive side, he was perhaps glad that he would finally be out in the open, not having to hide and lie any longer, but definitely concerned about the effects of his newly exposed preference on his former life.

The '68 Riots

———————◦◦◦◦◦———————

The assassination of Dr. Martin Luther King Jr., the great civil rights crusader, occurred in Memphis, Tennessee on April 4, 1968 while he stood on the balcony of the Lorraine Motel, prepared to lead a peaceful march in support of striking sanitation workers. The loss of this amazing man led to major riots and turmoil in many of our large cities. Many prayed and consoled one another over the horrendous loss of this non-violent leader. Others took to the streets and out of their profound feeling of loss, or the opportunity that masses on the streets afford looted and burned their respective cities.

Our society functions in a mysterious way. It seems to have more than a tendency to take the lives and personal hopes of those who appear to want to make positive improvements in our nation. At the same time it nurtures and respects those who fall short and are self serving. Perhaps that's why we live in times without true heroes and accomplishments.

We were trained for the riots, which broke out that year. Meeting only sparingly, two days weekly, hours each day, the training took place at a former police boys club, an abandoned building located at Pratt and Calhoun streets. The operation units of each district were chosen for this assignment. For the most part, we learned the use of riot sticks in crowd control, and formations used to control and divide crowds.

We spent a week of twelve hour shifts trying to restore order to the streets once the riots started. The riots were a strange period in my life, and probably for every other officer that was involved. We spent twelve hours on and twelve hours off. My children, both boys, were babies at the time, one a newborn and one three years old. I did consider the possibilities of being injured, with the sights and sounds and situations we found ourselves in on the streets during that time.

I lived within walking distance of one of the district stations where buses continually brought people that had been arrested. My neighbors saw only that aspect of the riots and several commented that they would have liked to be me. I never considered any aspect of the riots to be enjoyable, and considered given them my uniform.

The whole concept of the city in which you had grown up in being looted and burned left me with a strange, eerie feeling. It was not as deadly as an actual war, but it felt like one, and certainly looked the part. My town looted and burning, an American city, a hard concept to accept, a picture of destruction and rioting. At the time, I would have gladly changed places with any of my neighbors. I saw the commercial thefts, the fires, the destruction, the injuries, the disruptive crowds, and heard of the deaths when stores and properties were set afire.

Most people knew that Martin Luther King's death was an excuse for the riots and I saw firsthand that the results only left the poor that much worse off. Prior to the riots in Baltimore, we scrambled to catch up after seeing the riots in California. District riot teams were developed and formed. I was an acting sergeant in the Central District Riot Squad that only consisted of the following patrolmen: Douglas Cash, Dick Ellwood, Joseph Ballista, Dave Bryant and I. We learned about formations to disperse crowds, sniper techniques and the use of riot equipment.

The first signs I personally saw of the developing Baltimore riots was at Fayette Street and Central Avenue when a group of five youths ran out of a corner store. Radio cars with their emergency lights sped about the area. People on the street started running from one business to another as if window shopping, frantically looking for buys, but they were looking for objects to throw through the windows. As the glass fronts of businesses shattered, people pushed and shoved one another to get at the window merchandise and gain entrance to the businesses.

Watching the scene, you could actually see it escalate within minutes. I was going to visit my mother on the east side at the time. The kids were in my private car with my wife when I told them it had started. I drove them back to our home and left for the district as soon as I could pull the uniform on.

All our advanced training did not come into play. Once at the district, everything was in confusion. Men standing around, waiting and looking for assignments, no supervisors were available, and worse, no transportation. Waiting was not in our vocabulary; we actually stole a meter maid's car from the lot north of our station and crammed the five of us in the small white compact. Hearing on the radio that a command center had formed on Gay Street where the riot had started, we drove there and fell in line for calls. One of the officers in line needed relief so we took his marked blue and white and had him return the meter maid car, not mentioning to him that we had stolen the car initially.

We awaited our first call, which was a reported break-in at Mondawmin Mall, some two miles or more away in another district. By the time we reached the call location, all was quiet and secure. The calls for service were dispatched to designated radio cars and to the district units at the same time. Apparently a car in the area of Mondawmin Mall beat us to the scene, handled the call and left. No break-in had occurred, at least not at that time.

Baltimore was ablaze. Fires and smoke like a dense fog hung over the city. As night fell, nothing but the sounds of sirens blaring, people running and glass breaking filled the dark streets. People loaded with merchandise looted from the stores ran and sometimes staggered under the weight of their newfound gifts. Broken glass from the stores shined on the sidewalks under the streetlights and caused some of those running to lose their feet.

For a week, we worked twelve hour shifts, from midnight to noon. I had mixed emotions seeing my hometown in this turbulent state; it was an unreal experience. A curfew was instituted, and after midnight, the streets were quiet. We took advantage of the time between calls to rest. On the first night, we parked in a German beer garden up on Cathedral Street because it was surrounded by a high stone wall, which afforded security. Having only one entrance, it was easy to guard. It's strange what you remember during chaotic moments. We posted a designated guard from our group, while the others tried to rest. Two hours later, after we had previously agreed to one-hour shifts, he still stood guard over us. Asked why he had not requested someone to relieve him, he replied, "I'm too scared to get any rest."

The next day, we chased calls all over the district; answering fires, disturbances, disorderly crowds, burglaries, sniper call's, assaults, etc. These calls all started at daybreak and lasted continually until an imposed curfew at night. One of the calls was at a bar located at Greenmount Avenue and Biddle Street. When we reached the location, a group of twenty or so people began throwing cans of full beer at us. It was like getting hit with a brick; fortunately, no one was injured. As we exited the car, one of the guys asked what we should do. I answered, "Take your guns out; all of you do it at the same time." Once the guns were drawn, the crowd ran back into the bar and out the other street entrance. We occupied the bar and threw cans of full beer at those in the neighborhood who tried to enter.

After brief control of the premises, it was back to the streets and the mobs. The crowd numbers were so large we could not contain them. At one point, we watched the crowd set fire to a store as we pulled up. We called the fire department and cleared the intersection for their trucks, forcing those on the street into vestibules, whether they lived at those addresses or not.

Even among all this racially charged upheaval, I managed to experience a few light-hearted moments, including the following. We pulled up at 22nd Street and Barkley and observed ten or fifteen looters in a corner grocery store. One of our guys chased one of the looters as he left the store, weaving in and out around parked cars on the same block. All the while, the looter managing to throw items he had taken from the store out of his pockets. Initially, he ran away from us and then back toward us several times, with the officer just out of reach, running in and out of parked cars on the street. With the other looters disappearing, the group of us stood and watched the foot race with great interest. Some were talking about betting on whether the looter would make good on his escape. Before any actual bets could be placed, the chase was over. When the looter had successfully emptied his pockets, he abruptly stopped running and allowed the officer to catch him, proudly announcing while he pulled his pockets inside out, "There, you have nothing on me."

We all broke out laughing, even the one trying to chase him down. Truthfully, it was so funny at the time that we let him go. A few items from a corner store for the brief period of entertainment that the chase and his response caused at its conclusion were worth it. Arrests had to be considered. Was the event worth being out of service to book the subject or was it better to stay on the street and try and stop the looting and the destruction of property? The arrest lines were two and three abreast and circled the central district, which occupied an entire square block. In order to affect arrest, we had to drop a man off with each person arrested, depleting our manpower and our potential safety. We had decided on felony arrest only.

One of the details that we had during the riots was at the civic center downtown, which was used as a makeshift jail. Upward of a thousand people were there, bused in after their arrest, mainly for curfew violations. I was on one of the floors with a shotgun, with one other unknown officer. About two hundred arrestees were restrained by a rope strung around pillars, separating two police from all those arrested. We told them if anyone came over the rope, they would be shot. Three hundred or so against two made for an unbelievably trying night. At one point, an unknown male entered with a tray of sandwiches, which naturally aroused the hungry crowd. For no reason whatsoever, once the man had their attention, he threw the sandwiches off the large platter into the crowd and called the group "animals." I thought that would do it; the crowd rushed forward yelling obscenities, pushing against the rope. One ducked under the rope to my right. Seeing just the motion from the corner of my eye, I turned and pointed the shotgun at him. Thankfully, he did not keep coming. Still, in his slumped position from ducking under the rope, he realized I had swung toward him with the shotgun aimed. He backed under the rope and apologized. You had no odds, only one shot if you had to take it. It's always amazed me that during that entire shift we were never overpowered. It was that old saying you sometimes heard in movies when there was one individual against a group, "Which one of you want to be first?" The answer after the question is thought over is, "No one." Thankfully, the theory prevailed.

The State Police and the National Guard had been called in at the beginning of the riots. Neither group was used to policing in the big city. They were mainly used for securing and guarding our commercial area, which meant they were detailed to Howard Street mainly and armed with rifles. The State Police could not believe the force we used, and the National Guard was made of essentially citizen soldiers carrying weapons that were by order unloaded. One busload of State Troopers arrived at the 5th Regiment Armory, which was their staging area, and actually ran inside. We imagined that after seeing the sights coming in town during their ride, they were more than anxious to find safe shelter.

Another notable incident from that time occurred on the 800 block of Whitelock Street, a commercial area between Linden Avenue and Brookfield Avenue, when we were sent there on a call for crowd control. The small commercial area was just two blocks north of where I was raised. As we pulled onto the block on Whitelock Street, I was looking at a store where I played pinball machines in my teen years. People in the area had looted the stores and massed on the streets, refusing to disband. Shortly after we arrived, a group of paratroopers backed us up. A lieutenant, who was only about 5'6" and maybe 160 lbs. soaking wet, walked over to me and asked what was going on. He was told that we just didn't have enough men to handle the crowd and the bottle throwing. He replied, "We just came back to this country from Vietnam. This shit is not going to happen in my country. We did not fight and die for this." He walked away, yelled some orders to his men, supervised them while they set up their weapons and called to the crowd: "This is a .50 caliber machine gun and if you don't get off the G.D. street in two minutes, I'm going to take it back. I'll cut everyone of you, mother and child, in half." He sternly yelled it into a megaphone with a callous look on his face; I thought he meant what he said, and so did the crowd.

Needless to say, only the police and the paratroopers remained on the street after two minutes. We left the lieutenant and his men well in charge of the situation. The sandbagged machine gun faced east on the long east-west street, with men armed with rifles taking cover on each side of the street. At the time, there was no question in my mind who had taken control of that situation. As we drove from the scene, I thought back on the lieutenant and his men just returning home from a war where I'm sure they saw and fought through sights we could not imagine or expect. Some of them had been wounded and killed, just for these to come home to civil chaos afterwards. How much restraint could they be expected to show? If I were the people on that block, I would think twice before I came out on the street and started trouble again.

With the civil disorder, riots and the emergence of the Black Panthers around the country, as well as the hippie movement it became popular to label police as "PIG'S." The animal was considered a filthy farm creature that wallowed in mud and its own waste; now many thought it was a suitable term for describing police. It always pleased me how police turned that word Pig's around; it became an acronym standing for Pride, Integrity and Guts as far as police were concerned. They proudly wore pins and tie tacks with images of the animal. A term intended to be used as an insult toward police; PIG'S actually ended up bolstering our morale.

The riots ended as quickly as they had started. The damage was unbelievable, the cost and destruction yet to be recovered from. I know it impacted me; it was my town I had seen burnt and looted. It was an incredible scene like newsreels from a distant country, with armed military troops and police trying to establish peace and order. Areas that were once residential homes were run down, burnt out or rotten; abandoned empty shells distend to be bulldozed, empty, undeveloped lots.

All of the chaos started on April 6, 1968, and lasted until April 14, 1968. Damage estimates in 1968 were placed at $12 million. Today, that figure would exceed $77.5 million. During the riots, there were 5,500 arrests, 3,488 curfew violations, 955 burglaries, 665 lootings, 391 assaults and 5 arsons.

Thousands of Army National Guard, and returning paratroopers and five hundred State Police helped the city police to quell the riot. Personally, I don't think the city ever recovered. Many of the homes were lost and many of the commercial establishments never reopened, especially the small, corner stores in neighborhoods. The owners of these stores had known their area people and allowed credit to those they trusted and those who needed it. Neighborhoods were forever changed, going from functional communities to rundown blocks of decaying housing and eventually in many cases excavated rumble.

2015 A Year of Civil Unrest

D uring the writing of this book, perhaps you have noticed that I have not made a point of referring to the race of the individuals involved in the different events and stories I have depicted. It was done deliberately, not because I wanted to be politically correct, but because I wanted to be fair. The people portrayed or mentioned in these pages were victims, witnesses, suspects, officers, detectives, attorneys, judges, pathologists and fire department personnel. All dedicated to the enforcement of the law at several different levels of the judicial chain, not segregated by their race, age, color, sex, backgrounds, ethnicity, or financial status nor are violators of the law

Bad people involved in criminal activity are arrested, charged and prosecuted for their crimes. They are not arrested because of their color, background, ethnicity, financial status or age. They are arrested and charged with the crime they are responsible for and have the opportunity to be tried by a jury of their peers for the act committed. These people are criminals, not arrested for any of the previously mentioned reasons we have heard over and over for years as excuses for their lawlessness, but because they have broken the law, violators, black, white, red, yellow, male or female, young or old are charged. It is that easy to figure out, "They're bad people." Not the one who makes a mistake in his youth, or the one that finds one or two charges in a lifetime against him, but those who knowingly break the law and have no respect for it.

Recently, events around our country have reached such misdirection that I feel that these occurrences have to be addressed: the disregard for law and order and what appears as a concerted effort to undermine the authority of police officers in the performance of their duties.

Ferguson, Mo.

A large youthful male accompanied by another enters a local store in Ferguson and takes cigars from behind the counter without paying. Soon after, he is approached by the store operator, who he pushes out of the way to leave. Outside he turns, re-enters the store and pushes the man a second time. Minutes later, he is reportedly walking in the roadway, stopped and investigated by a policeman on patrol. An altercation ensues; the policeman suffers facial injuries and reportedly fires his revolver several times at the youth. The male dies at the scene. Another youth who was at the store with the victim witnesses the shooting and indicates that his friend was surrendering to the officer at the time of the shooting and had raised both hands over his head to indicate he was giving up.

The symbolic hands-over-the-head represents a shooting of an innocent non-combative victim by the police. Tensions mount in the community over the shooting. First demonstrations in the street lead to marches, protest signs; police cars turned over and fire bombs. Escalation of the situation leads to shots fired and police response. Next, commercial buildings are broken into, looted and burned. Riots continue not only there but also in numerous cities around the country protesting the Ferguson matter.

Al Sharpton rallies the crowd in Ferguson. A grand jury is empanelled and the facts of the investigation are submitted for possible criminal charges against the officer for his action. The grand jury fails to indict him. Eric Holder, the attorney general of the United States, comes personally to Ferguson and declares an investigation into the local police department and the findings of the grand jury.

The medical examiner rules the case a justifiable homicide by shooting, and indicates that the autopsy revealed that the subject was not holding his arms up in surrender when he was shot. The friend of the victim at the scene of the shooting admits the victim was not surrendering when shot with his hands up. The hands-up symbol continues to be used in demonstrations, marches and protest around the country. Members of a pro football team recently entered the field with their hands raised, although the hands-up surrender has been disproven. Public outcries are heard because the police have and use military type vehicles during crowd disturbances. This equipment is for their protection during riot control and armed standoffs, furnished through the U.S. government.

During the investigation, the news media identifies the officer by name and address. The involved officer resigns from the Ferguson Police Department weeks after his exoneration. He loses his livelihood after being found innocent of wrongdoing, forced out by illegal protest and unfounded allegations and anonymous threats. Could this be justified in any other occupation?

New York, N.Y.

A large man stands outside of a commercial store selling single cigarettes. The store manager calls the police for the violation of the law. Several police arrive and approach the man selling on the street. One of the officers puts the subject in a chokehold to restrain him while he keeps other officers from grabbing him with a pawing action. The man is eventually subdued by the officers and thrown to the ground during the arrest, all the while saying he cannot breathe. Shortly after the arrest, the man dies.

Again, protests over the occurrence. Marches and sit-ins spread from New York nationwide. Traffic and pedestrian right of ways are blocked in protest. Police are assaulted when a bridge is blocked. The mayor of the city allows marches without permits and orders the police to standby. One such march results in the marchers yelling, "What do we want? When do we want it? Now: dead police." The mayor states that his biracial son has been told how to act if confronted by the mayor's own police department.

Days after the march calling for police deaths, two minority officers, Rafael Ramos and Wenjian Liu, are shot to death seated in their patrol car. There is always someone ready and willing to take up the cause.

That is why we cannot yell fire in a crowded theater. First of all, if you are protesting in a group march for whatever reason, you have to consider what ramifications a call for police deaths could and did have. If it is not rational, don't participate. Also, who, why and what are the real intentions behind such a march? Do your homework. Just because you have a good and valid intent does not mean that everyone does.

There are no marches, demonstrations, protests or racial allegations regarding the assassination of two police officers. Al Sharpton rallies the crowd in New York, takes an active part in marches. The mayor fails to back the police, who turn their backs on him at the funerals of the two officers. Another grand jury fails to indict the police officer in the death of the cigarette street salesman. Autopsy reveals no crushed vertebra to the neck area, and states that existing health complications contributed to the man's death.

Both Ferguson and New York became examples of police brutality and racism. The police are reportedly killing blacks as if they were targeted. Neither of these cases represents racial bias or show deliberate intent to harm. Race is not a factor in either.

As mentioned, Al Sharpton, who has a history of false allegations while fomenting racial conflict, appeared at both locations. He creates headlines and contention, and left a wake of destruction in Ferguson and a march in New York that may have indirectly caused the death of two police officers. All the while he is a frequent visitor at the White House and named as a racial advisor to the president while having an exorbitant debt in back taxes owed to the IRS.

Eric Holder quickly initiates an investigation into both involved grand-jury findings, and an investigation into possible racial bias on the part of the police departments. This is the same Eric Holder who did not indict Black Panthers for disrupting a polling place in a past election. He is the same Eric Holder held in contempt by Congress regarding the "Fast and Furious" ATF case because he failed to comply by turning over requested records.

For what reason does what appears to be a concerted effort against the police exist? I'm old enough to see during my lifetime the enormous change in race relations that has taken place. Born in the city in the

1940's, I went from "don't trust the blacks" preached by the adults to working in the neighbor pharmacy with them, playing sports and going to school with them. Long before my life in the police department depended on them, I realized that people are individuals not colors.

Baltimore, Md.

On April 12, 2015 a subject by the name of Freddie Gray is arrested on weapons charges. The arrest took place at 8:53 A.M. At 9:24 A.M. an ambulance is called for him and he is transported to the University of Maryland Shock Trauma suffering from a severe spinal injury. Mr. Gray dies on April 19th. On April 27, 2015 police are in force in the area of Mondawmin Mall as a result of internet conversations inspiring youths to meet at the mall and "Purge" around 3:00 P.M. Purge is taken from a movie that advocated one day of crime being made legal. The youths gather and confront the police who remain in lines and attempt to control the areas in which the youths are demonstrating. The youthful crowd grows in number and they throw bottles and rocks at the police. Police hold their ranks and actually fall back under the threat from the thrown objects. At one point the disorderly crowd now made up of youths and adults loot and then burn a CVS Drug Store located at Pennsylvania and North Avenues while a police line can be seen in the same news media shot. This is the beginning of looting, and the burning of property and vehicles throughout the city and our first riot since 1968. The Nation Guard and State Police as well as numerous State law enforcement agencies are called in and our curfew is placed on the city to stem the violence.

Obviously our Mayor Stephanie Rawlings Blake and our Police Commissioner Anthony Batts where both aware of the pending "Purge" request and took steps to prevent it based on the fact that a large contingency of police where placed in the area of the mall prior to school dismissal. Just as obvious was that police officers where ordered to stand their ground and not take any action against witnessed violations of the law. Police whose lives where in jeopardy from the objects being thrown at them were ordered to risk injury while they watched civil unrest lead to looting and arson.

The mayor takes three hours after the riot starts before contact with the governor is made about the ongoing situation. Governor Hogan promptly declares a state of emergency and calls in the National Guard. One hundred and thirteen police are injured during the riot, countless neighborhood stores are burned and looted, some of which never to reopen and millions of dollars in damages are estimated. Again as in the past rioting neighborhood people loss their convenient access to shopping, face curfew restrictions and transportation problems while city functions are canceled throughout the duration.

Our school system administrators decide that no action will be taken against students identified as participates in the disorders. The mayor declares that no charges be brought against those arrested for curfew violations. The arrest was enough. I ask you, Do either of these steps, not punishing the students, or letting the curfew violators go, do anything in the way of preventing another disturbance.

Commissioner Batts you should be ashamed of yourself. You have the courage to except the salary for the position but not the backbone of any one of your police officers. They showed their loyalty to the department by obeying an unlawful order, stand down and watch violations of the law. Since politically you are the low man on the totem pool, why didn't you stand up first of all for the law and then for the safety of your men? Were the politics more important than to safeguard your men and woman and the security of your city you swore to protect?

Then states Attorney Marilyn Mosby steps up and declares that the cause of death of Mr. Gray has been ruled a homicide and as result she will bring charges against six police officers involved in the arrest of Freddie Gray. Standing on the steps of the courthouse she announced multiple criminal charges against all six Baltimore City Police Officers ranging from felonies, to misdemeanors. Adding, "I feel your pain." meaning the pain of those seeking justice in this case. National news media outlets almost immediately debate the ability to prove these charges. The states case will have to establish intent and personal knowledge in order to convict.

Mayor Blake requests the involvement of the federal government in a review of her own Baltimore City Police policies and procedures. United States Attorney General Loretta Lynch advises that the Department of

Justice will investigate the police department concerning civil rights violations. The Federal Government now three for three interjects itself. Where is their involvement when police are killed and injured? Commissioner Batts is in favor of the review and because of his stand down order maybe responsible for the various police action justifications and resulting officers being shot throughout the county.

Is this politics as usual? Pass the buck; don't address the real problems, let's put on a show until they forget. Or is it a way to seek more federal control over local police jurisdictions. The Federal Government which has interjected itself or by request in Ferguson, New York, and Baltimore may well find situations that they find illegal or violations of civil rights which they could move federally by law to rectify. The first steps in dictating to state law enforcement. Since President Obama has decided that military equipment used by local police should be limited because its misuse could cause severe injuries to the public and represent military power. Never mind the safety of the police in riot conditions. Another finding by an impaneled group by the President suggested softer looking uniforms to placate the differences between the public and police. Neither addresses the problems that exist.

In 2008 then former Senator Barak Obama suggested the formation of a Civilian National Security Police Force funded as well as our military. This concept not well publicized or accepted is apparently being put into place at the federal level. Presently forty government agencies constitute a one hundred and twenty thousand manned group representing such agencies as: The Library of Congress, The Federal Reserve Board, The Environmental Protection Agency, and Home Land Security which is reasonable. Some of those agency employee's have the right to carry weapons, have arrest powers, and in some cases have riot equipment and training. This is just another thought to consider when pondering Federal involvement in local law enforcement activity and disturbances. We now find local agencies expected to explain each and every involvement in assaults and shootings to the media and the public. Will these situations lead to the Attorney Generals investigations mandating rules and regulations through federally passed laws on all of the nation's law enforcement agencies?

I was a police officer as I have stated during the riots of 1968 at which time I witnessed the city that I was born and raised looted and all but burnt to the ground. The positive things not seen then where: Neighborhood people cleaning the streets at Pennsylvania and North, marches for peace by the different ministries, community people turning their backs to the police to protect them from the crowds, a mother physically handling her child to get him off the street and out of the disorderly crowd, and the town meetings held to bring peace and develop environmental, economic and educational prosperity to the communities effected. Its not Ferguson, New York or Baltimore it's all of our country. The monies meant to fund projects in poor communities continue to be allotted but miss managed, diverted, stolen, what ever. In order to change the plight of these areas and the people who live in them there must bring a return to the things and beliefs that made this country strong. Self respect and reliance is necessary. From the strong family dedicated to see their children make good in life, to the community ties that strengthen and grow neighborhood economies. The election of community leaders who are dedicated to redevelopment and watch dogs over the projects and monies promised. Elect and re-elect leaders on accomplishments not promises. The beginning of the community is in the home, having a child is not the end of a parent's responsibility it's the beginning. Teach your children to develop respect for others and a desire to accomplish their desires. Never let them not learn from life or education and preach to them they can obtain anything they set their sights on. Education and poverty do not go together. You can not settle for the status quo and expect more. Hundreds have come out of the same circumstances because of their desire, instill that in yours. Forty seven years since the sixty eight riots and Baltimore's population has fallen by nearly three hundred thousand people, we have lost businesses jobs and services. The school system is terrible and the neighborhoods continue to decline, but we can boost that we are the heroin capital of the country. Police are not perfect and like any other occupation some should be weeded out. They should be fired when necessary and legally charged for criminal acts committed. But do you really think police are the problem?

Baltimore's 2015 riot and its ramifications were terribly handled by our local elected officials, the mayor, the police commissioner and the states attorney. The mayors order to restrain the police, the police commissioner for obeying the request that hindered the sworn protection of life and property, including his own officers. The states attorney who quickly and questionably over charges the officers involved in the Grey death. After the fact the children identified as involved will not be punished by the school board for their misdeeds. Those arrested for curfew violations will have the charges dismissed. Personally allowing the riot to start, allowing injury to police along with theft and destruction of property as well as the get out of responsibility card to those involved in the illegal acts does nothing but advertize that another such incident has no ramifications.

Maybe all that Ferguson and New York and Baltimore represent is an effort to divide and conquer, rich against poor, black against white, and right against wrong, who knows, or maybe it's the old game of taking your mind off of the serious problems we face. I hope it's that simple. Looting takes place in Ferguson and to a smaller extent in other cities around the country using the events in Ferguson as an excuse. I first recall hearing the word "looting" during the 1968 riots that spread from coast to coast throughout some of our major cities reportedly in protest to the assassination of Dr. Martin Luther King Jr., who during his lifetime advocated social equality through peaceful means. The greatest racial divide healer of our times, he would have never advocated violence and destruction. The looting resulted in property theft and destruction, loss of commercial and private businesses and livelihoods, shootings, arson and lives. Entire neighborhoods in several major cities never recovered; some remain with blighted housing and lots of rubble. The hundreds and thousands who took to the streets at the time and committed these criminal acts did so for personal gain, not to show respect or to honor Reverend King.

Looting comprises criminal acts such as theft, burglary, property destruction, vandalism, and in some cases arson, and curfew violations. All of these crimes are criminal offenses and have terms if one is convicted of years in prison. When such acts are committed, every tool available should be used to identify those involved, bring them to justice and charge them with the proper violations. After such acts as looting and rioting, business and street cameras should be used to identify involved subjects responsible for such crimes and have them face years of incarceration for their crimes. If you risk years behind bars, it's only natural you would stop and think before committing the crimes. Ever notice that usually the arrested subjects in criminal acts have extensive prior arrest records and frequently are career criminals who should not have been on the street to commit the crime in the first place? They represent another example of lenient sentencing.

Back to the topic of this chapter: "If NOT the police, then who?" is the question. Trained, dedicated officer's serving around the clock: those fearlessly responding to any situation for your protection and the preservation of a normal society, or the alternative throughout other parts of the world. The only other option appears to be government use of military control. Remember the complaints of heavy armored men and equipment. Do you prefer your streets patrolled by armed solder's asking for your identification papers when you walk to the store? Not America's dream for the past or the future.

There is a book published containing the history of the Baltimore Police Department, showing its evolution from 1797 until 1997. In this book there is a section dedicated to those who have given their lives in the line of duty. I served from June of 1962 until June of 1987. In those twenty five years alone, thirty three sworn personnel were killed.

The National Law Enforcement Memorial in Washington, D.C. has the names of 20,267 federal, state and local officers dating from 1779 who have made the ultimate sacrifice during the performance of their duties and responsibilities. Less than three days pass without an officer's death.

Even against these staggering statistics, the lasting effects of situations and pressures no others witness, the threat of bodily harm, the job and domestic stresses placed on them, they continue to try every minute of the day to keep you safe.

Limited Injuries & 'A Secret Club'

During my patrol and operations experience, I suffered the only two injuries in my police career. My first finger on my left hand was shattered during an altercation at the Famous Ball Room on Charles Street. A large fight broke out over the theft of a security guard's revolver. I was treated at Mercy Hospital initially and then at Headquarters' Medical Section. Initially, I was advised that I would never use the finger again, but I fully recovered from the injury and did not even develop arthritis in the finger as I have aged.

The second career-related injury was a dog bite during a high school basketball game. I was off duty at the time at the civic center for my former high school basketball championship game. Polytechnic played our archrivals, City College, A riot broke out during halftime and I ended up being bit by a police K-9 dog while I was in plainclothes trying to separate kids who were throwing punches at one another. I was already leery of strange dogs having been bitten once as a kid. I was so frightened by the dog grabbing my hand that I wrenched my hand away, without a puncture wound, and drew my revolver. If the dog had attacked again, I would have shot it. The officer handling the dog pulled him back and looked at me as if he did not believe my actions. My badge was pinned on my coat so he knew I was a policeman, and as he pulled the dog back on his leash he looked quizzically at me. I recovered without any problems from the scratches, not requiring any stitches. I'll never forget the K-9 sergeant at the hospital while I was being treated telling me that I could not have assaulted his dog to get away from the bite because the dog was departmental property. I commented back, "So am I, if that dog had a grip on my hand and was tearing it apart, I would have shot him without thinking about it."

The police department was closed to the public, almost a secret club, and a society within itself. Only other police understood the stresses and responsibilities of the job. Police tend to associate with one another for acceptance and understanding. Only other police had been through similar circumstances and understood their plight. They risked their lives on daily calls, could be reviewed for whatever actions they took with only seconds to decide their responses, and faced criminal as well as departmental actions when they made wrong decisions. Because of the exclusiveness of their job, they tended to drink party and hang out with their own while off duty.

Too much of anything has been proven to be unhealthy. Even after my career, I found the same shift group from one of the districts seated at a retirement meeting. I smiled recalling the lasting commitment of police to one another, like a closed club with only members who could relate to their own. To escape the pitfalls of this "club," I found an outlet in organized fast-pitch softball. I first played in a police league my first year in the central district and then in citywide unlimited leagues for the duration of my police career. Little did my fellow players know that softball was not only a game that I loved but it was a release from the job and the tensions that it caused?

Homicide

I came to the detective unit promptly after passing the test and interview. I still recall the worst answer I gave to questioning by several unit captains at my interview. In response to the question "Can you type," I answered, "I would have to take typing lessons because I would have to learn." The response from the captain of the Homicide Unit: "You won't have time to learn." I thought that answer sealed my fate; the only unit I wanted was homicide. After the interview, I heard several units were interested so I considered it would be one of them, but not the one I wanted.

Two weeks later, I was assigned to homicide and the captain's words proved to be true. Almost every day at work meant a new case, while trying to find time to handle the ones from the days before. Each day at work was exciting and every day was different. No two cases were the same; even domestics were different from one another because they involved different personalities and circumstances. I approached my job like I had during patrol, nothing seen or heard was taken home to be dwelled on or cause concern.

Man's inhumanity toward his fellow man did exist. Some people in society were more than willing to harm anyone without provocation. If this obvious fact did not exist, there would be no need for police, the law or the court systems. You can be in the wrong place at the wrong time and be killed or injured without provocation by those who think nothing of their actions, it's a fact.

One of my first homicides on the street as a rookie involved an argument over the wrong song played in a bar jukebox. Drinking, an argument and the five cents used to play the mistaken tune at the time caused the shooting that led to the victim's death.

Initially, even with my background and time on the job, I found once I was assigned to homicide I was impressed with the ability of those detectives as well as their hard work and ethics. But now after eight years and between ninety to one hundred cases under my belt, my self confidence was as high as anyone in the unit, watching and learning from those I realized were professionals. The hours were ridiculous, often twelve to sixteen hours a shift, although each shift was scheduled for eight hours. Even a domestic murder took eight hours of work with processing the scene, the survivor's confession and reports. Calls never came in at the beginning of the shifts, usually the phone calls came one or two hours before the shift was to end.

In regards to that, I recall two situations where the hours just wore on. The first, a bar shooting in which the witness hid from us for several weeks afterward having left the scene before our arrival but still named to us. I had just gotten home from a fourteen hour day. I hit the bed exhausted, literally rolled over and answered the ringing phone to hear that my witness had been located and awaited my interview at the homicide office. I got up, dressed and drove back thirty miles to an office I had just left. When I arrived, I found the witness drunk, which had not been mentioned before. I got us coffees, one for him to straighten up and one to keep me awake during the interview. I waited until he could comprehend my questioning and then we started.

The second indication of how much time we spent at work was a policy implemented by the State's Attorney's Office. They arranged sleeping cots in the courthouse for those detectives having come from work to be able to sleep before their testimony in cases. On one occasion, that policy was greatly appreciated. Working the 4-to-12 shift, I finished up a fresh case at 8 A.M. and reported to court at 9 A.M., testified and was put on standby to be recalled by the court, I left at 3 P.M., returning to the office for my next shift.

The average detective with his overtime made captain's or

lieutenant's salary and for the same reason avoided promotional tests. To be promoted at the time meant reassignment back to uniform patrol as a sergeant and a definite loss in pay, with no guarantee that you would ever return to detectives. The possibility of staying in homicide at the time if promoted was small; never being in the detective bureau again was conceivably larger. Usually, the unit stayed fully staffed with supervisors.

The homicide investigators numbered fifty detectives at the time. They worked the same three shifts as the districts, but rotated more frequently. Their leave system rotated days; subsequently, often partners were off at the same time. The unit was responsible for handling all VIP threats, serious assaults that could result in death, and obviously homicides, with only five or six people working on each shift.

Often our sergeants and lieutenants helped with statements and interviews on new cases knowing the necessity. My first lieutenant was "Pots" Callahan, a large, rather loud, take-charge man who would bark orders as if he was angry, but was tireless in his dedication to solve cases as well as in his support of his men. He really did not mean anything by his bark. My first partner was Det. John Wagner, an ex-marine who was from the suburbs of Baltimore's east side. He still had that marine attitude but through his spit and polish attitude had the fortitude of a dogged investigator. He and Lt. Callahan were closer than just a working relationship; they became friends, probably because they were so much alike. John frequently was the acting sergeant for the squad. When promoted, he left the unit and went on to achieve the rank of Major.

My second partner was Timothy Timmons, a partnership that lasted for years. Our leave schedule of rotating days frequently kept us apart, with one working and the other off half of the time. The detective working would catch new cases and would either work them alone or fill their partner in for joint investigations. Therefore, frequently I did not work directly with Timmons, who I considered the best partner I had ever had. Tim enjoyed writing the necessary warrants and I wrote most of the investigative reports, while we both were willing to work extended hours without complaining. We looked after each other job-wise and personally, a necessity for good partnerships.

The work was demanding and long hours expected. Even a domestic murder, with a smoking gun and a confession at the scene, took eight hours with the investigation and the necessary reports. Other cases such as robberies with employee victims took longer at the scene, especially the initial investigations. These were hold ups at corner groceries, street robberies, or muggings of cab drivers that resulted in the owners and or employees being shot or seriously injured. All of the detectives caught overtime frequently more often than not.

When I left homicide, it was one of the most heart-wrenching decisions of my life and certainly of my career. I loved the work and the men and women I worked with. I've previously mentioned how each and every one of them was a professional, experienced and meticulous. The supervisors were our equal and worked tirelessly hand in hand with us. At the time, we were one of the best homicide units in the country. Surrounding police jurisdictions frequently asked for our assistance. In the 1970's, we had a clearance rate always in the ninety percentile. An unheard of clearance rate for today, accomplished with none of the modern scientific tools. This was done by a group of fifty detectives and their supervisors on around-the-clock shifts.

I know each generation of police, like in each family generation produces outstanding and dedicated people, and I'm positive they serve the public today as we did in our era. Helping their cause are tools not available to us at the time: DNA analysis from skin tissue, blood, saliva, semen, and/or hair collected at the scene; extensive computer database searches for information pertaining to premeditation in murder cases, incriminating email communications, etc.; and the Automatic Fingerprint Identification System, which allows national fingerprint database analysis. There are also criminal profilers now available who psychoanalyze violent criminal and sex offenders and can be quite helpful in missing persons' cases. Most of these technologies, techniques and fields of criminology were in their infancy in my time, but now they contribute greatly to modern case analysis and law enforcement overall.

Printed and framed, hanging in the 6th floor offices of the Baltimore City Police Department Homicide Unit at 601 E. Fayette Street at the time I was reassigned was the following:

The Homicide Investigation

No greater honor will ever be
Bestowed on an officer or more
Profound duty imposed on him
When he is entrusted with
The investigation of the death of
a human being.
It is his duty to find the facts
Regardless of the color or creed,
Without prejudice, and to let
No power on earth deter him
From presenting these facts to the
Court without regards to personality.

Author Unknown

This poem was a summation of our duty and responsibility as detectives in this unit. Posted for all to see, it was closely read and adhered to by everyone assigned

The Spicer Homicide

After the initial information was received and it was learned that the victim had some notoriety, more than the usual two-man team of detectives were dispatched to the scene located in Druid Hill Park. I was a rookie investigator, under the wing of everyone in the office and more than willing to learn. I was more than anxious to respond on what I considered my first opportunity to prove myself. Initially, I was assigned to then Sgt. Dick Francis and Det. Melvin Diggs of the robbery unit had combined with homicide for the investigation.

My first homicide investigation was that of a reporter named Harold Spicer, shot to death while seated in his vehicle in Druid Hill Park on January 14, 1971. He was parked near the Echo House at the time of the shooting, on a road that encompassed the park reservoir, the same park that had been my playground as a youth, having lived just blocks south of the park. My friends and I often frequented the park's zoo, built paths and rooms in the bamboo jungles hidden from sight from those who passed by, and played baseball and football on the park's fields as well as swam at the park's municipal pool in the summer. It was an easy walk from North and Linden Avenues.

When I reached the location of the shooting, I realized I had often played "red line" in the woods just off Reservoir Drive on the hill south of the "Echo House," not far from where the victim was found. I used to deliberately run into a patch of poison ivy located on the south hillside so those on the other team would not follow. At the time, I was not allergic to anything; now it's become a different story. After the age of thirty, all I had to do was look at poison ivy or oak and I would have it. The park was always a convenient location for near bye city kids to play. What with all the concrete and restrictive areas of the city, park locations where at a premium? We felt privileged to have the park to use. How ironic, once a childhood playground was now the scene of my first high-priority homicide investigation. Not that I thought my park experience at the time would contribute to the case's solution, but it is strange how things turn in life.

The reservoir is located at the southern entrance to the park and has a wide paved road surrounding its entire perimeter, roughly a mile and a half around. A single round two story water fountain is located on the west end of the oval reservoir. The multi-colored, lighted fountain has been in use on occasion and dark during other periods. The entire area around the reservoir, which we referred to as a lake, was treeless and made for beautiful scenery. Because it was so open, it would have afforded a view of the victim's car and the shooter at the time of the crime.

The Echo House, as the locals called it, is located on the southeast front corner of the wide road that surrounds the reservoir. It is a light grayish, stone, round building just over two stories high. Initially, it functioned as a pumping station for the reservoir but had long been taken out of service, replaced by a modern pumping station located on the hillside area to the south. The building resembled a castle in its architecture and appearance. Its top has a rampart wall, which on that day overlooked the victim's car some one hundred feet north parked on the reservoir road overlooking the JFX. The vehicle was found in a parked position pulled to the right of the drive facing north. From atop the road you could relax in your car and overlook the traffic north and south on the Jones Falls Expressway, watch traffic over the 28th Street Bridge headed east, and see the towers of the John Hopkins University about a mile further to the northeast.

It was a peaceful place to park and relax. The reservoir area was a scenic setting with sociable, yet infrequent walkers or runners circling the reservoir. Not many people to disturb you or your morning paper with coffee, but near enough to downtown and the rest of the city to respond to most news story locations if any breaking news was reported over his radio. We didn't know how often Spicer found time to frequent this location, but at the time, the serenity and beautiful view with the autumn leaves gone from the bare trees of January and the crisp smell of the cold air added to his relaxed solitude. Little did he know or have reason to suspect that he would never enjoy this favorite parking spot again.

Harold Spicer's death occurred on a winter morning while he sat defenseless parked in his automobile, unaware of the pending danger, relaxed, contemplating his next News American assignment. The shooting occurred at relatively close range as the shooter had approached Spicer's vehicle and fired at him from within a few feet while the newsman was seated in his car. The victim would not have had time to react to the situation and may not have even seen his assailant if the suspect had approached from behind the driver's seated position.

Seconds after the shooting, Harold Spicer managed to radio into his city desk with the last frantic seconds for help, "Help me, help me, I'm being shot." Those were his last words. As a result of his call for help, he was found minutes later by a co-worker, a Mr. Howard, who was in the area and had monitored Spicer's call for help. He attempted to revive Spicer to no avail after finding him sloped in the front seat of his vehicle suffering from apparent gunshot wounds to his head and left wrist. Howard's attempts at resuscitation proved fruitless and within minutes he announced on his car radio that he felt no pulse. Harold Spicer at the time was a fifty two year-old, award winning newsman. He was transported to Maryland General Hospital and pronounced dead shortly after 10:00 A.M.

According to Dr. Peter Lipkovic of the Medical Examiner's Office, his autopsy revealed that Spicer had been shot twice; once in the left arm and left wrist, which was a shot through the driver's window that hit and shattered the glass before striking Spicer. The second bullet fired was from a distance of approximately three feet, striking the victim in the head. Death was within minutes. The fatal shot struck him just in front of the left ear. Despite not recovering it, the murder weapon was determined to be a .38 caliber handgun through ballistic analysis of the spent projectiles recovered. Cause of death was ruled homicide.

The scene consisted primarily of the victim and his vehicle, which were photographed from every possible angle, with Spicer fingerprinted before the body's removal. Numerous individuals who frequented the park area and its road around the reservoir were located and interviewed during the processing and afterwards as they became known to the investigators. Most of those interviewed were elderly walkers or runners of various ages; some identified by others who knew them from frequenting the park and from having seen them around the time of the shooting exercising on the reservoir road. All any of them recalled was a man seated in his car as they passed by. One point that would later become an important issue in the investigation was that Harold Spicer's vehicle resembled that of one of our own unmarked cars.

A co-worker of Spicer's confirmed that Spicer often emulated police officers, even driving a car that looked like a detective cruiser, as did the car Spicer was found in. Spicer often kidded that the look of his car allowed him access to crime scenes when he pulled up on them

During the first-day interviews a young man who identified himself as Elmer Robinson at the scene, who appeared no more than an apparent onlooker was questioned. Elmer was interviewed by one of the uniformed officers. During his interview, he indicated that he had seen the man seated in the car when he and a friend drove through the park that morning after work. Nothing appeared out of the ordinary at the time they drove by. The man was seated on the driver's side of the car, he appeared normal and the driver's window was intact. After telling his story to the officer, he was asked to submit to an antimony and barium test, a gun residue examination to determine if a person had fired a gun recently Robinson readily agreed to submit to the test. Later, treasury chemists would testify that large amounts of both of these substances were found on Elmer Robinson's hands at the time he was tested.

The day after the homicide of Harold Spicer, I was part of a team of detectives from both robbery and homicide, as well as uniformed personnel from the northern district, that did an area search of the hill just to the right of where the shooting occurred. To me, this steep hill was known as Seven Pines because as youths we slid down the steep hill from Reservoir Drive toward the JFX and into the seven large pine trees at its base. We had to avoid hitting the pines while riding pieces of cardboard like sleds. Those trees were now a thing of the past, casualties of the construction work for the JFX Expressway.

It was a cold, windy day and the hill's angle resulted in a treacherous search which attempted to cover every square inch We walked at arm's length slowly in a straight line across the hill from top to bottom, looking for any item or article that might relate to the shooting. Not exactly what I expected homicide work to be, but I had to pay my dues and this was a job for the new guy, though, even the more experienced detectives also took part. Not a footprint, a weapon, an article that might be considered evidence, nothing to help; at least this possibility had been covered and ruled out. When we were walking the hill high above Falls Way Expressway, I wondered during the search how many southbound cars had passed exactly at the time of the shooting and had the occupants looked up into the park? How many could have been potential witnesses? Or would they even realize what they were witnessing from that distance and speed? That possibility was also covered. The newspapers put out a plea for anyone in the area with information about the shooting to contact the police and listed our phone number. Unfortunately, we had no resulting calls.

The second aspect of the case that I was involved in was a timed route run from the scene of the crime in Druid Hill Park to Elmer Robinson's job on the east side of the city. That run taken and timed by Detective Wagner and I proved to be important in establishing that Elmer Robinson had ample time to leave his place of employment and be in Druid Hill Park at the time of the Spicer shooting. We would testify to that aspect of the investigation in court.

Over the next few weeks, a circumstantial case was developed against Robinson with only the positive firearms discharge test being the most solid evidence in the case Robinson would attempt to justify that test result by saying the gunshot residue was a result of him working on his car around the same time period. No fingerprints establishing Elmer Robinson's involvement were found at the scene, although we did not think we would find any unless the suspect touched any personal property belonging to Spicer or the vehicle itself during the shooting.

Fingerprints were doubtful with the coroner's findings that the shooter was outside of the vehicle at the time shots were fired. It was reasonable that the assailant had not touched or entered the vehicle at any point during the shooting. The victim's wallet, watch and money were all found on the body, and the clothing of the victim appeared undisturbed. But if robbery was not the reason for Spicer's shooting, what had been?

During the investigation, it was learned that within ten minutes of the shooting in the park, Elmer Robinson walked into a ladies hair shop on 36th Street and told his mother, who was employed there, that a policeman had been shot in Druid Hill Park. Several of the shop's employees were established as witnesses to Elmer's statement. The news of the shooting had not been on any public radio prior to that time. It was reasonable to assume that it was a policeman that had been shot because the victim's car resembled that of a plainclothes car used by detectives. How could Elmer Robinson know at that early point in time that the man sitting in what looked like a police cruiser had been shot?

Another thing that destroyed Robinson's credibility was that he stated after he and a friend from work drove through the park area, he went to his girlfriend's home and stayed there for a while with her parents. This statement conflicted with the time he was seen by employees of the hair shop telling his mother and them about the shooting in Druid Hill Park. The co-worker he initially said he was driving with in the park on the morning of the murder denied being with Robinson in the park at any time that morning or having driven him home from work that day.

At the beginning of the trial, State's Attorney Leslie Gladstone admitted to a circumstantial case, neither having established motive or having recovered the weapon used in the murder. But he knew he had witnesses to support his case and destroy aspects of Robinson's defense. After testimony was received about the appearance of Spicer's car and its resemblance to that of a police cruiser, he introduced employees of the hair shop who testified that Elmer had entered their shop within minutes of the shooting and told them about the policeman in Druid Hill being shot. He then introduced records from all of the various television, radio and newspaper programming establishing that Robinson was talking about the shooting before it had been broadcast on any media. His statement about being in the park earlier with his co-worker was disputed in open court by the worker who denied being in the park with Robinson that day or with him at all.

Robinson's defense put his girlfriend, who at the time was his fiancée, on the stand as well as his girlfriend's sister and her father. All testified that at the time of the Spicer shooting, Elmer Robinson was seated in their living room with them on Falls Road, about one-half mile from the scene. At the conclusion of their testimony, Leslie Gladstone called all three, "liars." Their timeline conflicted with Elmer's own statement to the police during his initial contact with them, particularly the timing as to when he had entered the hair shop telling the employees about the shooting.

Our timed run from his work to the park allowed him ample time to get to the scene of the crime. Most or almost all of his defense testimony had been discredited; even his own witnesses had failed to help his cause. The neutron activation testimony by the two treasury chemists sealed his fate. The chemist using an electron microscope equipped with an energy dispersive x-ray spectroscopy detector were able to determine the amounts of lead, antimony and barium found on the sample swabs taken from Robinson's hands, the residue elements left on a person's hand after firing a handgun.

Physical evidence of Elmer Robinson's involvement in the shooting of Spicer was established. What was a circumstantial case at its start was the strongest circumstantial case I have ever seen at its conclusion. Robinson's own witnesses discredited him. After eight days of trial testimony, Judge Albert Menchine sentenced Elmer Robinson to twenty years in prison for the murder of Harold Spicer. The only conceivable motive for this act, because only the perpetrator knew his reasoning, was that Robinson thought Harold Spicer was a policeman at the time of the shooting, and because it occurred in an isolated area, he thought he could get away with the killing.

In mid October of 1977, Elmer Robinson won a retrial through his attorney and a change of venue to Oakland, Maryland; a small conservative town surrounded by acres of rural land, just miles from one of Maryland's resort spots, Deep Creek Lake frequented in the winter for snow skiing at The Wisp and in the summer for the lake's boating and water skiing.

My first thought when I heard of the retrial and its new location was why? I realized the defense would want the trial moved from the city because the victim was a well-known city news reporter and they feared a prejudiced jury. But Oakland, those people slept with their doors unlocked, respected the law, everyone's rights, and had little to do with part one crime in their community, they probably had not had a murder case in years. They were not the kind of people to have mercy on this previously convicted murder.

When I received notice of the retrial, I realized that I was the only representative of the homicide unit remaining in that office. Six years ago, I was a rookie on this case; now I was not only the senior detective on the case, I was the only one left from the initial investigation and the court trial still in the unit. I spent a week in review of the case with several of the days needed to locate and advise potential witnesses from the initial case. I made a formal request that I be issued a car for transportation and that my partner, Timmons, although not involved in the first trial of Robinson, be permitted to assist me in case preparation and handling the witness accommodations and re-interviews for trial preparations at Deep Creek Lake, where all were lodged at the Wisp.

The case was to be prosecuted by the Garrett County State's Attorney's Office. I was assisted by one of their investigators at the time, Bill Ferry. He was a congenial man with a slight southern accent that added to his slow and deliberate tone. His likeable, easygoing personality made him easy to befriend almost immediately. In his years with the local state police department and with investigative assignment with the State's Attorney's Office, he had well learned his trade. He was more than a liaison for the trial, helpful at every step, he was also fascinating. This man from a small-town jurisdiction was well versed from his present and past occupations. We sat one night and he rattled laws and regulations pertaining to everything imaginable, from truck weights on the highways to criminal investigations involving homicide and other Part 1 violations.

The trial lasted four days. My only responsibility during the actual retrial was to answer the phone when it rang for the next witness testimony and see that they were delivered to the courthouse immediately. My original testimony about the timeline routes of Elmer too and from work were accepted into the court record without my testimony. To be truthful, Timmy and I handled some of the calls for the witnesses from the comfort of poolside at our hotel. At the end of the trial, Elmer Robinson was found guilty for the second time and recommitted to prison. The word we received was that the jury could not conceive of such a heinous deliberate act. This quiet, God-fearing community and its people could not imagine such an act and definitely could not abide with what they comprehended as a needless death. The murders that had become almost a daily occurrence for us in Baltimore were interpreted as terrible senseless acts and the taking of a human life could not be excepted. This trial was another example why the inhabitants of small-town Oakland would never move to the big city.

On a different note, really not related to the retrial except by the date, I loved baseball. Reggie Jackson, coming off a physical fight with his manager Billie Martin, in Boston on October 18, 1977 at the end of the Robinson retrial, hit three home runs in one World Series game against the Los Angeles Dodgers. Jackson became the second man in baseball history to accomplish that feat. Other than Reggie, the first player to do the same was Babe, aka George Herman Ruth.

Having been a rookie detective at the time of this case, I accepted my minor roles; the area search, which proved fruitless, and the timeline run, which aided in the investigation My small part in these activities certainly did not excite me, but I was totally impressed with the solid work displayed in bringing the case to a successful conclusion. Like anyone in a new job, I was anxious to prove myself; surrounded by talented detectives, I so wanted to be one of them. To solve my own assigned cases, that day would come soon enough, and often.

The Lombard Street Sniper

O n April 16, 1976, it was a warm, clear, late afternoon with the temperature reaching in excess of ninety degrees, the type of conditions that would ensure we would be busy. I was seated in the Homicide office when the phone rang. Little did I know it would prove to be the worse call I would ever have.

At about 6:00 P.M. a call came in from someone who sounded like a young white male. His voice was controlled and he spoke in a calm, collected manner. The caller started by saying, "When it starts to get dark, at dusk I am going to shoot anyone I see on the streets." Automatically, I asked his name and address before even asking why he intended the shooting. He responded that he had not called to give himself up, or supply information to help us; he had called so we would know what he was going to do, not because he wanted to identify himself and surrender. He stated that by shooting randomly, he would force the police to kill him. Asked why he had come to this point, he indicated his girlfriend had jilted him, and his family and friends had let him down. Adding to his despair, he could not find a job. Within minutes of the call, I motioned to Timmons to pick up on another phone. He immediately did so, cuffing the phone as he began to listen. I attempted to talk the caller down.

During the call, he indicated again that he had lost his girlfriend and had no job prospects. He was told that he could always find another girlfriend. Years from now, he would not even recall this one's name and not even consider the pain he felt for her now over the breakup. This plan of his was ridiculous. He stated that his family did not understand him; I countered with saying that being someone at his stage of life that was very normal, everyone felt that way at one time or the other. He would come to realize that family would always be there for him and always care about him but not until he grew up and realized it. How much would he hurt them with what he wanted to do? A job was just another application away and may well prove to be what he was looking for. He calmly replied that I did not understand all the things that were wrong, but he wanted to prove to everyone that he could do what he said he would. That he was brave enough to do it. The neighborhood and everyone in it would know that he was brave enough to do this.

Although I tried everything I could think to say, the caller was steadfast in his intent and avoidance to identify him self. During the call, that lasted about ten minutes, he casually dismissed all attempts at identifying himself, his address, his neighborhood, his girlfriend or any of his friends. Anything that would help us identify him and his location was calmly withheld. Sometimes he hesitated before he answered, realizing I was trying to draw out information. Occasionally, he would indicate that he understood what I was trying to do; he was not mad because he knew it was my job. "I only called because I wanted you to know what I was going to do," he said, making his point again. During the conversation, he stated that he had all kinds of weapons: rifles, handguns and shotguns. He had been trained in the National Guard and was a good marksman.

As I spoke with him, I was attempting to get two things: his identity and his location. I heard both the sounds of passing pedestrian foot traffic and that of moving vehicles in the background. He was obviously using an outside street phone at the time. I had established that he was somewhere near Carroll Park, which was on the west side of the city. When asked if he knew where the park was? He replied, "Not far, I've played ball a lot of times there." To keep him talking, I said that my grandfather worked at the transit car barn there at the park, on the corner of Washington Boulevard and Monroe Street. I then offered to meet him in Carroll Park to discuss his problems and help him out. He stated that I seemed to be all right, but he couldn't do that because he would be too exposed out in the open. He stated, "I am well-fortified where I am; you will not get me easily." After repeated pleas with him not to shoot anyone, especially innocents just walking on the street, he said, "They have to know that I'm serious and that I will do it. They'll remember me. Goodbye. You will know who I am at dusk when I start shooting."

The caller's deliberate conversation and demeanor, and the steadfast intent in his voice while questioned, convinced me, after the call Tim agreed. Of all the odd calls received over the years, this one was convincingly real. The caller definitely sounded intent on carrying out his threat. He was going to do what he had stated. He had calmly discussed every aspect of his plan: the weapons, the secure position, the reasoning behind his acts, and the shooting of innocents to reach his desired death by police officer.

I immediately made two phone calls. The first call I made was to communications, advising them of the phone call and that I thought it was credible. I thought the subject was in the west part of town because of the amount of background noise from passersby on foot and also from vehicular traffic. This indicated he had used an outside phone, and I thought he was near Carroll Park. From the sound of the caller's voice, I described him as a young white male. At the time, public phones were mounted on walls usually outside of commercial businesses. They afforded little privacy and were open to surrounding street noise

Knowing about a seafood carryout at Monroe and Pratt that was always busy, I thought maybe that was the location he had called from because of the amount of background noise, and its proximate distance from Carroll Park. I guessed he was in that area. Not knowing at the time, I would prove to be only one-half mile from the caller's true location.

Next, I called my shift lieutenant, who was off duty and home I shared the caller's information and advised him I was convinced that the caller intended to carry out his threats, starting at dusk. I told the lieutenant that I had notified communications with all the information available. Lt. Steven Tabling advised that he was on his way into the office and hung up the phone. The next time I would see him would be at the scene in the 1300 block of West Lombard Street in front of the home of the Lombard Street Sniper, as he later became known. The shooter, and previous caller, identified later as John Earl Williams, would eventually surrender to him, running down the front steps of 1303 W. Lombard Street into the lieutenant's arms, sheltered from his deeds.

About fifteen minutes later, an off-duty detective, Nick Giangrosso, called into the office. He was and remains a good friend. The purpose of his call was to invite Timmons and my self over to the west side area bar he was at after we got off. I told him of the caller and advised him that I thought he was going to carry out his threats. Both Timmons and I were on the line telling him if he heard shots that he should be careful. I thought he was in the area of the caller from his location. Nick indeed heard the shots; what sounded like a war erupted blocks from the tavern he was at. He responded off duty to the sound of the shots. He arrived at the scene and witnessed several officers pinned down by gunfire in the intersection of Lombard and Carey streets. Nick commandeered a van and used it while under gunfire to rescue a wounded officer from the hail of bullets being fired into the intersection at the time. Afterward, he voluntarily returned to the office and assisted with the investigation, although off duty.

Just at dusk, communications called and advised that marked police units were receiving gunfire at and near the intersection of Lombard and Carey. The first call came in from a tactical unit, which ironically had been redeployed in the area in response to the caller's threats. The shooter had started firing unannounced at will at the police unit and had control of the immediate intersection of Lombard and Carey Streets, firing initially from his third-floor front bedroom windows at 1303 W. Lombard Street. He had, as he had stated in his call, a well-fortified position stocked with the weapons he had previously described and plenty of ammunition for them. Not only did he do exactly what he had promised, but was also a frightening skilled marksman.

At the sound of the first shots, two females who had been seated on the front steps of 1303 W. Lombard jumped from the steps and ran to the corner store for protection. Had Williams leaned out of his third-floor window and seen them seated on the steps below, they could have been his first shooting victims. The east wall of the neighboring store at 1301 Lombard Street where they ran was an outside wall phone at the intersection with Carey Street; which in all probability was the phone the shooter had used to call our office.

Police units from the southwest, southern, western districts as well as tactical units responded to the scene, entering a hail of gunfire from both the suspect and police returning fire. Several off-duty police officers responded from their area homes and in turn became involved in the gun battle. Based on the lack of communication, the excitement, and the yet to be established location of the shooter, initially several responding units became pinned down in the intersection of Lombard and Carey. They found themselves under direct fire from a capable sniper in a strategist position. Because the sniper's shooting platform overlooking everyone from the third floor, many of the officers were trapped in the intersection until their fellow officers could neutralize the sniper. What sounded like a war followed for the next twenty minutes?

Upon being advised by communications that shooting had erupted at Carey and Lombard Streets, Timmons and I drove to Baltimore and Carey at the command post. We worked our way to a position on the northwest corner of the assaulted intersection and realized like others we had given the suspect better targets of us than we had of him. I will always remember Timmons saying with a smile as we hugged the wall and looked for a clear shot on the suspect, "Let's meet him in Carroll Park and talk him out of this; one day, you will get us shot." I looked across the street and saw the wall phone and thought, that's from were this bastard called us. I thought it was from Pratt and Monroe. I cursed the thought, why couldn't I have been right?

Repeated gunfire from the suspect was returned by countless numbers of police officers firing back with their handguns and shotguns from every point possible that would afford them any protective cover and an eye view of the target. A harried command post was set up at Carey and Baltimore streets. Tactical shooters ran down the street zigzagging, attempting to avoid the ricocheted bullets coming north on Carey. Some policemen took up positions on the roof of a firehouse just north of the intersection turned shooting scene, on Carey's east side of the street. This gave them a vantage point to fire directly across at the subject. But armed with only shotguns, they did not have effective firepower for their target, and requested rifles or shotguns with pumpkin shot at that location.

Pinned in the intersection were several police officers, some of which were wounded to various degrees. Officers risk their own lives trying these very same rescues. During the same time period, other officers attempted to enter the rear of 1303 Lombard Street. The department would suffer the highest number of killed and wounded personnel ever at a single confrontation. The officers attempting to gain entry in the rear of the suspect's address had a shotgun fired at them by the suspect from a rear window, causing injuries to several of them. At one point during the continuous gun battle, an officer who had positioned himself across the street in a vacant house observed the suspect at the third-floor front window. He radioed communications and advised he saw the suspect and requested a rifle for the shot.

Just prior to his surrender, the suspect moved to and fired from a second-floor front window. I lack the ability to describe the scene. I had never served in the military, but this was a firefight by anyone's definition, comparable with any you would see in actual combat situations I thought. So many rounds of ammunition were being fired at the same time, the gunfire sounded like a continuous roar.

The shooting from the suspect slowed and finally there was a lull on his part. The first thought I had was that he had been hit, wounded to the point that he could not fire, but what if that had not happened. Was he waiting just for someone to give up their cover so he could shoot them? While I guess everyone was considering the safest way to attack his position, it was actually over.

In the end, Williams reneged on one of his many promises: he did not want a death by police. He had fired from at least three points in his house at police, the third and second floor fronts and rear windows into the yard. When he stopped firing, he had gone to the secure basement, which had cinder block concrete front basement windows, and a hurriedly rigged phone line. The basement had been made a secure position to place a phone call from. He called communications and after convincing the officer that he was the one responsible for the shooting, advised he wished to surrender. He was told to come out the front door, unarmed, with his hands up. Communications broadcast to those officers at the scene for them to hold their fire; that the suspect was going to surrender.

Within minutes of his conversation with our dispatcher, Williams appeared at the front door, ran down the steps to the arms of Lt. Tabling with his hands on his head and surrendered. It seemed that the sniper shooting that started with shots fired at a police car had ended as quickly as it had began, minutes after the last shot fired by Williams. Hundreds of rounds of ammunition had been fired in his direction during the ordeal; it seemed unbelievable that he had not received the slightest gunshot wound. I was struck that this unkempt, skinny, insignificant looking nothing of a human being had inflicted so much pain and suffering on others, had survived without a scratch.

Now, Williams was reduced to what he truly was: a sniffling young coward who fired on innocent unsuspecting officers, who all became unknowing heroes as a result of their responses. Some of whom along with their families would suffer a lifetime of heartfelt tragedy as a result of his actions.

After Williams' arrest, Tim and I entered 1303 Lombard Street and walked up the steps to the third-floor front bedroom. The house still smelled of gunpowder. The first thing I noticed going up the third floor stairs was that you could actually see the movement of a crime lab technician in the bedroom through the south wall as we climbed the stairway; there were that many bullet holes in the wall from the shots that had been fired at Williams. They had entered the room from the front windows and come through the wall behind. On the bed, centered between the windows, were some of the weapons used in Williams' assault along with live and spent ammunition on the bed and floor. That one area, the third-floor front bedroom, revealed over seven hundred pieces of evidence: long rifles, shotguns and rifles, ammunition spent as well as live rounds, and the hundreds of bullet holes in the room's walls.

The exterior brick wall of the house was pock marked from the roof area down to the second floor area where bullets had hit and chipped pieces from the brick. The glass was gone from the third-floor windows and the wooden window frames were all but shot away from bullets hitting them. Again, with all this concentrated gunfire how did Williams survive, much less not even been wounded? The house was such a large crime scene that areas of it were assigned to different detectives and crime lab units. I had a chance to look in the basement area and was convinced that Williams had prepared this area as a safe house to make his call for surrender. The front windows were cinder blocked with only a small opening about four inches high and eight inches wide in each. The phone was jury rigged in the middle of the basement. Even looking in through the narrow windows, Williams would have been hard to locate while standing using the phone.

The Lombard Street sniper started firing at 18:59:10 hours, 6:59 P.M. and 10 seconds, at a passing tactical unit on Good Friday, April 16, 1976. The gun battle lasted until 7:47 P.M. at which time Williams identified himself on the phone to police communications and announced to them that he wanted to surrender. He was advised that no one would shoot him; he should come out the front door, with his hands up, leaving his weapons behind. In that period of time, so many lives were changed forever.

Six police officers had been victims of the shooting spree: Officer Jimmy Holcomb of the western district had died from a gunshot wound of the neck and shoulder area. He was a decorated marine and a Vietnam veteran, the father of three, and the loving husband of Angela Holcomb. Officer Holcomb had been lost to his loving wife, children and friends forever.

Officer Jimmy Brennnan was wounded in the left side and the right shoulder, rescued from the intersection by Detective Nickolas Giangrosso, who commandeered a van and under gunfire accomplished a daring rescue of Officer Brennan. Nick was not injured. Detective Arthur Kennel suffered shotgun pellet wounds of the face and eye when he attempted to gain entrance to 1303 Lombard Street from the rear yard. Officer Neal Splain also received shotgun wounds to his face as did Officer Calvin Menchen. Officer Roland Miller received shotgun wounds to his left arm.

As a result of their injuries and the traumatic experiences of that evening, Officer Brennan returned to duty recovered from a fractured elbow, leaving him with partial use of his arm. Considering his possibilities for advancement, he retired. Unemployed, he returned to his home state of Maine. Art Kennel lost sight in one eye and afterward returned to work for a brief period and then retired. He became an insurance adjuster in Towson, Md. Officers Neil Spain and Calvin Menchen remained on the job. So many lives were impacted by one person, theirs, their wife's, children, and relatives; that day would never be forgotten by those individuals involved or by the department.

Everyone, the off-duty police who responded to the sound of shots fired, those taking immediate fire and those who responded to help apprehend the assailant and attempted to pull those injured to safety while under fire. Everyone there was a hero and should be proud of their individual actions. The average man ducks then runs and hides at the sound of gunfire; police run to the sound to prevent further injuries and they unselfishly risk their lives for others. The job takes a special type of person.

At the time of the Lombard Street shooting only one tactical team had been trained to respond and properly handle this or similar situations. Lombard Street exposed the department to several glaring facts: the lack of organized communications, responding before determining the location properly, inadequate weaponry, inadequate protection for the involved officers, a established plan for the extraction of wounded officers and or civilians, and organized decisive decisions. The QRT, or Quick Response Team, was still developing at the time. It consisted of one team training on their own time, buying some of the necessary equipment out of pocket. The initial training had just begun. Procedures regarding the proper solution of situations such as snipers, barricades and hostage situations were just being instituted. Training procedures were drawn from other departments and from the military, but to date Lombard Street was our first live experience and led to many training advances, procedures and equipment in the handling of such calls. The general order for tactical training had been signed, but not implemented. This fortified barricade shooting brought about most of the standard procedures now used to evaluate situations and protect the officers involved.

After his surrender, John Earl Williams was transported to the homicide office and there gave a statement to Sgt. Buzzuro. The statement was close to the same information he had given at the time of his call into the office prior to the shooting rampage. Discovered in his jail cell prior to his court appearance was a transcribed tape by John Earl Williams describing his life.

"He expressed that he was a loner and misunderstood. His mother left, not explained why, and he advised that he never knew his father, not explained. A good stepfather lost his children to what he referred to as the system. He dropped out of school for the service. No military information. Fell in love with a girl named Joyce. They were on and off several times, breaking up over another boy in Joyce's life. "I wanted to die over it, so I started planning it on either the 3rd or 4th of the month. I wanted to show Lombard Street they couldn't just run over me. I started planning the biggest shootout they would ever see. I had all the guns and ammo I would need. I had it all set up and planned to the max. I told Ronnie, a friend, we had all the firepower we would need. I did have it all .300 mag. two.30/03 pumps, one.30/30 winchester, one.8 mm magnum, one.44 magnum, one.357 magnum, two 12-gauge shotguns and two.22 auto magnum, as well as one.30 mm carbine with a.30 round clip magazine, and 1,500 rounds of ammunition. Ronnie freaked out when he realized I was serious and said I was crazy and left. I had already taken seven hits of acid and sniffed glue earlier that day. I picked up my 12-gauge shotgun and shot my windows out. Just as soon as the glass hit the ground, the police came down Carey Street and rolled onto Lombard. He jumped out and shot at me. I didn't want the police to get into it, but guessed he wouldn't just stand there and let me shoot. After he fired all his rounds, he just stood there so I shot at him. Then I picked up the .30 magazine and shot his motor up. He called for backup and the next thing I knew, police were all over the place. I really wanted to stop shooting but something told me to keep shooting, it was getting to be fun. Police ran everywhere; it was like the movies or television. The television man said four police were hit. I never knew I hit any police. Now I was coming to my head, we shot back and forth for a while, my ammunition was low. If the police knew that, they would have never let me out. This was the biggest thing Lombard Street had ever seen."

"I was just setting there thinking what to do next. I felt good about everyone who had ever known me. I was not someone to run over now. I felt high still, and fell down once or twice, then I made it down to the phone and called the police. I told him I wanted to surrender. They were told when I came out not to shoot. They took me downtown and then to jail. I spent some time at CTP Hospital (probable evaluation). I think I'm going to jail for a long time. I liked the Army. I liked to play the war games until they put me out, then I joined the National Guard, I guess they will put me out soon."

Assistant State's Attorney (ASA) Stephen Tully tried the case with testimony from Officers Joseph Gilpin, Steve Coleburn Jr., Burchard Schwabline, Alan E. Small, Thomas Reagan, Neil Miller, Glen Hauze, James Brennan and Dave Williams regarding the scene and the events that had occurred. Det. Arthur Kennell, Det. Sgt. Buzzuro and I also testified. A model of the scene was introduced, built by members of the police department, showing an overview of the scene and Williams firing positions, the general area, and the positions of the police officers during the barrage, along with area addresses and landmarks that related to the confrontation.

After the reading of Williams' tape recording reduced to writing, I was more at ease with myself. Whenever I think of Lombard Street, naturally I wished I could have done more, if I could have only identified him. Ideally, I wish I could have talked Williams into identifying himself and where he was calling from; that information may have prevented the entire occurrence from ever happening and definitely altered the outcome. But after talking with him before his actions over the phone and reading his later account of the shooting with his steadfast attitude toward harming police and/or the public, I realize few could have talked him into not acting out what he thought would make his trivial existence important.

Still, it bothers you; the last thing you want on the job is for another police officer to be killed or injured. It haunts you somehow, someway, could you have prevented it? What were the right words to talk him down, the right buttons to push; were there any?

The testimony at Williams' trial was more of a tribute to those policemen fired on, lost life, were injured and who had survived the ordeal. With the physical aspects of the barricade situation and the apparent premeditation on his part, Williams had little to no defense for his actions. John Earl Williams was convicted of first-degree murder and of assault by shooting with the intent to murder the other officers who were injured during the shooting spree. He was sentenced to life plus sixty years. His first parole hearing was postponed because of the public's outcry against his possible release. Williams, who wanted everyone to remember him, is now forgotten to everyone, unfortunately, except by those whose he directly affected forever, the police and their families. They think more of Williams well-deserved fate than the people of Lombard Street he wanted to impress.

Williams, who wanted respect and standing regarding his community and friends, along with a relationship with one particular girlfriend, accomplished none of those things; he is jailed and forgotten instead. The house he fortified himself in is now restored to its normal condition, the neighborhood changed; those who lived there at the time moved, the shooting forgotten by the pubic. Many of those who fought there had their lives altered by the events and injuries that occurred that evening. Forever changed were the lives of those wounded? The worst result of all regarding the sniper's shooting spree: the loss of a beloved husband, father and patrolman from his family and friends. This horrendous act changed so many lives in countless directions and in various unknown ways, and brought to light the shortcomings of the department with regards to its preparedness for such horrible acts.

One Bad Decision

I t was the third of three strip clubs he had frequented that night. He would be taking to the streets shortly in search of a prostitute to solicit. He had spent two hours nursing beers and watching topless young women flaunt their desirable bodies in front of him on stage dancing suggestively and taunting him with sexual promises to be performed at the rear booths of the club when seated with him. Watching the girls, combined with the alcohol he had consumed, peaked his arousal. Although he was tempted to accept their offers, he was a rather conservative person and thought better of the situation, not wanting to be embarrassed if caught in such a situation.

Becoming more aroused as he watched the scantily clad girls, he had decided that his best opportunity to satisfy his sexual desires was on the street with a quick agreement with a hooker and a discreet hotel romp. Much more to his liking, he would be satisfied and no one would know his business. Although the thought seemed to occupy his mind, the idea of actually carrying out his newly conceived plan was not as positive to him. He had never tried to pick up anyone before and had second thoughts about doing it. Yes, he was a young man in his twenties, with a nice appearance, looked and dressed cleanly and could carry a conversation, He looked in his mind like the average "John," but this was different, his first attempt at such a thing. While these somewhat rational thoughts filled his head, the drinks and semi-nude women bolstered his sexual thoughts; he decided that was what he would do.

All he could do if he failed was strikeout. Why not try? Leave the bar, find a clean prostitute and get laid.

He left the club and walked the area streets, taking in the sights and sounds while looking for a sexual partner. The bright lights of the clubs, one after the other, the doormen barking their "come on in" lines, sometimes actually grabbing him in their attempts to get a customer, the cars slowing to watch the action on the streets and view the semi-nude signs on the club marquise, the slow walking sometimes staggering ex-customers coming out of bars trying to find their misplaced cars.

This was always a strange and perhaps a boggling scene for some, but rather a constant one for this area: the brightly lit clubs advertising their wares, signs so colorful they blended into one another, causing reds and yellows to have a greenish tint; they all but advertised sex for sale, prostitutes soliciting on the street corners, girls dressed provocatively coming and going from the clubs either starting on or finishing their shifts; and drivers causing traffic problems while they drifted slowly in their cars to witness the street events, while mingling with more marked police cars than they probably realized.

The uniformed police were not there for the activity on The Block, as locals called it; no, they were home. Not because of The Block and its world-famous activity, no, because the next block east housed the Central District Police Station, followed by the Police Headquarters Truly making for strange neighbors to say the least. The blocks of ill repute stopped and the authority for enforcing the laws began. Right next door in the backyard of those club owners, girls, prostitutes, pimps and Johns breaking various laws were the police.

For that reason and the fact that this new project was quite an undertaking for him, our nervous John had to be careful not to be arrested on the street while he attempted his solicitation. Did the cops have plainclothes females and men on the street watching for the likes of him? Did they have attractive female undercover police acting as prostitutes working in the area? He personally had heard or read of such arrests, but they seemed far and few between. But if he was thinking along these lines, it could happen. Such things had to be considered, but his desire to have sex overwhelmed his worries of arrest. He was still drunk enough to muster up the courage to carry out his plan. He must have walked up and down the street several times and even ventured onto the side streets in the area. Often during his wandering, he was approached by more than one working girl that solicited him, but for whatever reason his inner self told him not to commit.

Just when his slight high from the beer started to wear off, and he was beginning to reconsider the whole thing, he noticed an interesting possibility standing near Gay Street on the southeast corner at Baltimore Street. She was in her twenties with a slim build, and dressed to be noticed but not bad looking. As he approached from about a half block away, he noticed that she would approach cars stopped for the light, lean down and talk with the male drivers. Her looks and her actions convinced him that she was a hooker and reassured him that she would be approachable. He had watched her for about five minutes now before he tried. There had been no takers from the show passing cars. As he walked faster toward her, he realized his pace quickened to reach her before anyone else did. There were no uniformed police around and the street block was clear of pedestrians at the moment, nothing to prevent his approach. The lighting from the nearby clubs made her look even better. Why not take a chance? She looked attractive enough even up close. He walked up to her and naturally she greeted him with a smile. He, in turn, smiled at her and started a conversation. "What's up, nice night," he said, feeling foolish as soon as the words left his lips. What the hell, first time, he didn't know what to say, he thought. She's streetwise, she will carry the conversation and not waste any time in seeing if I'm interested.

The girl, who was prettier than most he had seen that night, laughed and told him to relax. Evidently, his nervousness was apparent. She helped him relax immediately by asking, "Are you out for some fun?" He smiled back and replied, "Sure, I am, you?" Feeling more confident, he suggested what he had in mind and if she would accompany him to an area hotel. She smiled again, told him the price and said, "Sure, Hon, if that price is alright with you, you're talking hours instead of minutes of my time." She relaxed, hugged him and said, "Let's go." The rule had been met, prostitutes and lawyers insisted on their money either paid upfront or no deal, always referring to it as "Rule One"; that in itself tells you something, no money first, nothing follows. He had accidentally solicited her. She had felt for any weapon when she hugged him and knew in her mind that this John was all right.

They passed the time making small talk as they walked to his car just over a block from where they had met. She walked close to him but not arm in arm; the local plainclothes cops may have recognized her and followed, thinking she was about to perform oral sex in this guy's parked car or dark doorway. She did not want to be seen with what looked like a new trick for that reason, and because other jealous hookers might try and steal her mark. The conversation centered on things like their ages, areas they lived in, his job, etc. Of course, his thoughts were elsewhere. Her answers were probably not truthful anyway. Although he seemed to be telling the truth about questions asked of him, he could not think fast enough to lie about everything asked.

When they reached his car, she slid in on the front passenger's side and immediately grabbed his crotch area as he sat behind the wheel. She suggested some alcohol before they got to the hotel because it would be cheaper if bought beforehand. Actually, there would be less hotel employees to identify her with this guy. He agreed and drove around until he found a liquor store over on Eutaw Street, buying a pint of whisky for her and a six-pack of beer for himself. When he got back in the car, she continued to market her wears; she reached over and placed his free hand on her breast and then her thigh. Excited again, he could hardly wait

He decided on a downtown hotel and asked if it was all right. She said, "Sure," probably thinking she had hooked into a rich winner. The hotel was much more impressive than she was used to. She turned to him and planted a wet kiss on his lips as they pulled to the curb. She smiled broadly and pulling him close to her said, "I'll give you a night you will never forget." Little did he realize that would be one of the most honest and meaningful statements between them. This night would impact the rest of his life, changing it forever. But at the time he could only think about having her. As they pulled to a stop, she agreed with his selection of hotels, thinking "This is a decent place; the cops won't mess with us up here."

They walked toward the front entrance of the hotel and she suggested that they enter separately. She would wait in the lounge area for him while he registered. She added, "Don't use your real name. You do have cash, right?" He signed in at the front desk for an upper-floor room and thought in his own mind that neither of the desk attendants had even looked at her when she came in and nonchalantly walked away from the desk toward the hotel bar. Reaching one of the elevators, they reunited and kissed and groped each other as they rode to their floor.

Once in the room, she set about her plan, opened the whiskey and insisted he drink. Perhaps her scheme would be real easy, get him drunk, get his money and forget about any sex. They drank and drank, fell onto the bed in each other's arms and fondled one another as they laughed and explored each other's bodies. All the while, she talked sex and allowed his roaming hands to touch her anywhere he desired. The night with this guy was playing out exactly as she had planned; as the hour wore on, he got drunker and drunker. It was going to work out fine for her. His thoughts were fading from his intended purpose, as they wallowed on the bed drinking. Suddenly, he realized he was in a semi-conscious state from the alcohol. He found himself too far along to fight it. Leaning back and closing his eyes to the room spinning around him, he thought he would relax for just a minute. He must have fallen off to sleep at some point. He stirred feeling a slight movement next to him, but it did not immediately register. The touch he had felt was mixed with him trying to realize how long he had nodded off. He smiled drunkenly and remained enjoying the comfort of the bed with his eyes closed.

Sometime shortly thereafter, he heard the room door open. The sound shocked him back to semi-consciousness. He opened his eyes, braced himself up in bed on both elbows and watched as the nice-looking prostitute, now dressed again, smiled at him and closed the door behind her as she entered the hotel hallway. Instantly, he processed the image. Now alert and awake, it registered. "That bitch," the John grumbled. He looked toward the chair near the bed where his pants were only to see them lying on the floor instead and noticed his pockets turned out. Glancing at a dresser near the door, he saw his open wallet lying on top of it. Leaping from the bed, he staggered slightly while half running to the room door. He jerked the door open and looked with anger down an empty hallway.

He turned back into the room and frantically glanced about for the phone. The blurred numbers and the small plaque with writing on the face of the phone revealed the desk number. He franticly called the front desk, yelling into the phone, "I've been robbed, a girl in her twenties, dressed like a hooker, stop her, she robbed me, the bitch, get her. I'll call you back." Slamming the phone on its cradle, he staggered slightly from his drink on the table and cursed the whore. After about five minutes of thinking about what had just happened, and getting madder by the minute, he called the front desk back and in a rage yelled for a response to his question, "Tell me, did you catch that bitch?" They realized from the room-number phone it was him, interrupted his heated questioning and apologized in a sincere voice that they had not been able to stop the woman he had described, not finding her anywhere on the hotel premises. He did not know, but in all probability the hotel employees did not even look for her; they were taught not to bring any type of bad publicity on the hotel. Obviously, this was exactly that sort of situation; they did not want a prostitute linked to their hotel for being arrested for robbing a guest. When he hung up the phone, he was angry, upset at the events that had transpired and disgusted with him self for falling into her trap, no he was downright mad that she had robbed him and no one stopped her from leaving.

The second call ended abruptly after the desk announced that they were unsuccessful in stopping her. He was so mad he could not think. He had been jobbed by a street whore; taken advantage of, robbed and no one wanted to help. Thinking that the hotel management did not even try to catch her, how could they not see and stop her? What to do to get even?

In a mixture of rage and foolishness, he had conceived a plan to get even. He gathered his belongings, dressed quickly, grabbed his wallet from the dresser, hurried to the room door, turned out the light at the wall switch and looked back as he entered the hall and closed the door on the now burning bed. By this time, the room had a glow all its own.

As he ran down the empty hall, he thought, "At least this would spite the lackadaisical management; he would get even with them. Get even with somebody." He got off of one of the elevators on the second floor, noticed an exit sign, ran down the flight of stairs and exited the hotel by one of the side-street exits.

Minutes later, the hotel's fire alarm system sounded and indicated there was a fire in the hotel on the jilted John's room-level, the front-desk called in the fire alarm as well. When "The Steadman Station," which was just a block away, received the alarm and drove out of their firehouse, flames were visible coming from the hotel's upper-floor windows. With the fire station only a block away, one of the firemen laughed to him self and said, "We could just run over to this one, except for the equipment."

Unfortunately, while they were responding, one of the hotel employees went up to search out the location of the fire and determine its extent. As he ran down the hall, he noticed smoke coming from under one of the room doors. Reaching the room, and not knowing that it was now totally engulfed in flames, he unlocked the door, opened it and was immediately knocked backward by the heated back-draft of fire, the pressure created when air is suddenly added to the fire. The responding fireman found him lying in the hall at the base of the open room door. Initially, he was thought to be unconscious and badly burned, suffering from smoke inhalation. But attempts to revive him failed and he was pronounced dead from smoke inhalation and shock from his burns at the scene.

Our office received the call and I responded alone. The crime lab processed the scene; the fire destroyed the room and its contents. The exit doors were swabbed for prints and the video footage from the exit cameras was retrieved and reviewed. However, neither the prostitute nor suspect was clearly identified on the recordings. The room fire destroyed the possibility of fingerprints. Using her street smarts, the prostitute had covered her face with both arms and pushed the hotel bar door open with her hip. Probably she used this method of exiting from her past hotel visits. Only her dress, hair color and race were identifiable to us two of which, hair and dress, would change immediately for her own protection. The suspect had left via another exit door, with his head down, not allowing for a glimpse of his face, he to had pushed the bar door open with his weight. Interviews of the hotel management as far as the subjects' descriptions were concerned came out fragmented and distorted. One of the front desk clerks at the time the man entered and signed in as "Mr. Rawlings" said he was an artist and if we used artist conceptions, he was sure he could recreate the man's likeness in a drawing.

Two days later, I had him respond to our office to meet Jim Joyner, the artist we used in reconstructive drawings. Ironically, I had known Jim from years before up on my foot post. He was quite a talent and had philanthropists back his work at times. Jim did dollar sketches on the boardwalk at Ocean City, and looked and acted like a hippie every day of his life. But the skilled artist was really a nice person and would help police anytime, night or day. The clerk and him sat down to work and within an hour had a rendering of what our suspect looked like, at least what our clerk witness thought he did. We disseminated the likeness drawing of the suspect to all of the surrounding counties and hoped it would have positive results. It was all we had. The districts were advised of the case and the drawing was given to them.

The prostitute had changed her appearance by now, if still risking going on the street, and perhaps had even left town if she knew of the hotel fire and death linked to her trick. Vice units in the district's had no information. She was not talking about the matter.

Being the one actually responsible for the fire, the fleeing suspect had already made up his mind not to give himself up. Why should he? It had been days and no one had knocked on his door; his fear of arrest was turning to a self-confident feeling that he wasn't going to get caught. His only problem was with his own conscience, having to live with the fact that he had accidentally caused the death of someone. But we did not know this was a problem for him; we were looking as far as we knew for the average son of a bitch that just didn't consider anyone or anybody else. Someone who would set fire to the hotel and not care if it burnt to the ground with countless lives lost in the process.

Not that this has anything to do with the case, but an ironic occurrence happened when Rescue One, housed at the Steadman Station, responded on the fire alarm at the hotel. One of the firefighters was Robert Wagner, a personal friend since we were sixteen years of age. We met when the two girls we later married were school friends. The four of us have remained friends all these years, almost too many to count, fifty six years to be exact. Bob was a dedicated third generation firefighter and worked thirty six years on the job, even after a line-of-duty heart attack. Lifelong friends, one dedicated to saving lives from threatening fires, gases, explosions and automobile accidents; the other spending then eight years working at solving murders in the names of the victims for their families. We met on only one case over the years, both practicing our respective professions, and it just so happened to be this one.

Two or three weeks passed, and still no information as to the identity or location of either the involved prostitute or the suspect. Finally the phone rang in regards to this investigation. The voice on the other end identified himself as a rookie police officer in Howard County. He was calling because he had arrested a man for disorderly conduct in a bar disturbance and felt that the subject looked like the wanted suspect in our drawing. During our conversation, he was asked about the physical description of the suspect and he answered by saying it also fit. I advised I would be right out and interview the subject about this crime.

Tim was off that night, and since I was the only one assigned to the case, I rode out to the county alone and met with the officer who had called. He stated that he had not mentioned the look-a-like resemblance to our drawing to the arrested man. After the arrest, the subject was well mannered and compliant. Once I had gained the arrested man's information from the officer, and the vitals regarding his recent arrest it was time to talk to the man directly.

I sat in the interview room alone waiting for him to enter. The door opened and in came a man who indeed fit the physical description as well as general appearance of the man in our drawing of the suspect. After sitting, he did not show any reaction to me telling him I was from Baltimore, but shifted nervously in his chair when I mentioned I was a homicide detective and that I wanted to talk to him about another crime. As a matter of fact, his nervous reaction continued as he quickly replied, "If I can help," but he did not sound self-confident in his statement.

I discussed the known aspects of the case, a man and prostitute rented a room at the hotel. The man was apparently rolled by the prostitute, who then left the building. The room was torched. An employee responded to the room fire and he was killed. The suspect responded by saying, "I don't know anything that could help you. I know nothing about the incident." I told him I wasn't there by accident, "You fit the description physically, and facially you match the drawing created by one of the witnesses. I think you did it." That's when it happened and it convinced me that he was our man. He tried looking nonchalantly at me and answered calmly, "It wasn't me,"

No one reacts casually to being accused of murder. If innocent, you protest; if guilty, you tell me how it could not be you, you insist or even rant and rave about your innocence, and usually donate your whereabouts at the time of the crime, which come to think about it is a difficult thing to do. Think back several days or weeks ago and be able to remember what and where you were. Every time some suspect does that I think they are lying. He did neither, he was my man. The county rookie was going to make one hell of a police officer. I told the suspect I thought he was responsible and that I would show his county mug shot to the clerks and the prostitute, and afterward would be back to charge him with the crimes. Still composed, he replied, "I did not do it." I replied that the fire was not deliberately set to harm anyone, it was an accident that anyone got hurt, and that it would be better for him to tell me the truth about what happened that night than to wait until witnesses identify him. "Hold out until you are identified and you look guilty," I advised. After a conversation of about thirty minutes dealing with the crime, mixed with some lighthearted talk, I left and he went back to his cell. The crime did not constitute a first-degree charge of murder, but still the now prime suspect in the case was unwilling to admit to manslaughter. My conversation with him led me to believe that in general he was a decent individual, not the hardened type we were used to dealing with. This guy made a mistake, he realized it, and was trying to conceal his guilt more because of fear than anything else. In the long run, he would confess when his conscience got the best of him, if he did not take a lawyers advice.

Two days later, I met him in the same interview room and opened the interrogation, advising him of his rights and telling him he had been, indeed, identified by the prostitute as the man she was with in the room that later was set afire at the hotel. He signed his rights form and agreed to talk further, still not having considered a lawyer's representation. Efforts to show the young desk clerk his mug shot had failed; he had left the state for college. It would take days, maybe longer, to locate him and make arrangements for him to view the mug shots. Of course, I was lying about the hooker identifying him when I told him she had looked at the photo. I still didn't know who or where she was. But that one little lie was all it took.

The man, who fit the description facially, based on the artist drawing, dropped his head to his chest and stated, "You're right, I did not mean to hurt anyone with the fire. I was just so pissed that the whore stole from me and got away. I acted out of rage at the time. I didn't think anyone would get hurt or die, I never thought about anything like this would happen." His admission led to a full statement, all of the previous information describing the facts of this case was related in that statement. At the conclusion, after his return to the lockup, I was ready to accept that the accidental death of the hotel employee was the result of one bad decision on the part of the suspect, and one on the part of the worker who opened the room door before he considered any fire safety precautions. If only our suspect would have controlled his anger, calmly left the hotel and never considered the fire.

The case was later tried and a statement of facts accepted by the court on behalf of the defendant, who pled guilty. The arson homicide count was reduced to a manslaughter charge. As in his statement, a foolish reaction without regard to its ramifications had cost an innocent person their life. During the trial, it came out that in truth I had never located the prostitute in this case. Nevertheless, the subject's confession contained the facts that led to his conviction. I know my falsely saying that the prostitute had identified him would convince and result in his confession.

As the subject was led from the courtroom, he turned and said, "You lied to me; I'll kill you for that." I looked back at him and said, "The man died as a result of an accident, you did not kill anyone deliberately. You don't want to kill me or anyone else it's truly not in you." Ironically, once I had his home address, I realized that I drove past the house daily on my way home from work. I find myself wondering, is his family still there and whether or not had the one big mistake of his life ruined it forever?

Regrettably Robert (Bob) Wagner passed away this March as a result of a massage stroke. A Baltimore City Fireman, for over thirty years he was a fine fire fighter and a far better person. His wife Joyce and children have been friends for nearly sixty years. Never a bad word between us and more enjoyable times than can be remembered, he will be greatly missed and fondly remembered. He and Robert Schaffer are the brothers I never had.

Serial Killer

———————◦◦◦◦———————

Mel woke with a feeling of anticipation recalling the reason for his mid day nap. His live-in girlfriend of near two years had a lunch waiting. He ate hurriedly and told her he would be back before nightfall meaning hours before he would have to return to work. It was mid summer and darkness started shortly after 8:30 P.M. As he jumped behind the driver's seat he smiled to himself. This was the start of one of his favorite things. He was off by himself to root through who knew how many vacant homes for what ever he considered of value. The area of abandoned properties lie less than three quarters of a mile from his apartment and could render valuable or either desirable items. He could not explain it to himself but the idea of being alone searching through these properties brought about a real since of peace. It was like being a child again and the anticipation of finding items worth keeping some how fascinated him. People who were evicted or just moved because the area was blighted left all sores of things behind. He had found good clothing still hanging in abandoned closets, dishes still on kitchen shelves, and silverware in the cabinet drawers, along with various work tools in the basement make shift work shops. Among his favorite finds up until now were thirty three copper colored tokens used at one time for the Baltimore Transit Co. fares. The other where World War II pressed dime sized red cardboard food tokens. Both of these items are rare and it made him proud that he possessed them. No body else had things like this.

172

The area to be searched now reached for about a mile along an area the city had decided to turn into an inner-city expressway. It ran east and west across the west side of Franklin Street for about a mile. Initially that corridor and the row houses on both sides of the street were condemned or purchased by the city to widen the two lanes that would run the route in both directions. With the closing and division of the neighborhood because of the construction time as well as the loss of area small stores and the traffic disruption blocks surrounding this project also fell victim to the development. Those row houses already in disrepair and occupied by the poor now fled for neighborhoods more suitable. The city boarded the properties as they were vacated and the area became a ghost town. The area was now frequented by drunks and homeless squatters.

He pulled his car to stop in a deserted block which dead ended at the street intersection due to completed construction that no longer allowed a through street. Another problem caused by the new roadways that may have added to the exodus of the former residents. Locking his car and carrying a hammer to assist him in his hunts, and as a weapon for protection he looked up and down the street for any properties that had been broken into. When vacant the city had used plywood to board up the floor doors and windows, both front and rear, to keep down vandalism and possible fires from being accidentally or deliberately set. His thought was if they were broken into anything of value was gone, those addresses were not worth messing with. Walking to the rear though an alleyway between two row houses he decided to enter the one on the right. Using the hammer he pried the ply from the door and entered the kitchen area. After about twenty minutes going from room to room on both floors and finding nothing of value he thought he would try the basement. While looking down in the basement he heard a noise coming from the upstairs kitchen area. First like someone walking and then he heard two people talking. Armed with his hammer in his right hand Mel walked quietly up the basement stairs and rushed into the room. Two men surprised by his sudden appearance first appeared startled but then turned demanding an answer as to what he was doing in the neighborhood? Mel with hammer in hand stated he was just looking for things left behind. He did not want any trouble. The two glanced at the hammer then at Mel and thought better about the situation. Mel walked out the back without a word.

Walking back to his car he considered the situation he had just found himself in. Of course such confrontations where expected under the circumstances and would occur from time to time. But he had not considered all the aspects. Alone in and abandoned property with strangers it could happen. He could have raised the hammer twice and afterwards finished them. They were either drunks or vagrants, no one to miss them, no one to witness what he did. Nail up the back door and they would not be found for weeks if even then. They could be skeletons before they were found with no work or no real effort on his part. As he reached his car and turned the ignition he glanced back at the vacant block and smiled as he thought: "I've gotten away with it before, it is something to consider, but it's not my thing, I have nothing against those guys."

Timmons was on leave that night. I was up, meaning I would get the next call for service that came in. I was working with Bob Jansen, recently reassigned to the unit from burglary, where he had been a detective for years, but considered a rookie homicide detective due to his short tenure in the unit and his lack of case experience.

Most of the other detectives were busy catching up with various reports and those that were free were watching television; all were expecting a busy night. A few brought up the Thanksgiving Day killing; a homicide that was remarkable in its own right and probably would never be forgotten.

When the detectives responded on the call, they found that a son had killed his father in front of the entire family at the Thanksgiving Day table. An argument between the two over which one would get the wishbone broke out during the carving of the turkey. The son wrestled the carving knife from the father and during the ensuing struggle stabbed his father in the chest, killing him at the family table in his own home, on what is normally a quiet, joyous holiday reserved for family and friends.

At the climax of the Thanksgiving Day story, one of the phone lines into the office rang and I answered. An excited female caller indicated that a man she was acquainted with for years had attempted to sexually assault her ten year-old daughter, breaking the front-door lock of her home and chasing her daughter across the first floor and into the bathroom where she escaped behind the locked door. The mother stated that she was not home at the time and her daughter was home alone. The child's quick thinking, running into the bathroom and locking the door, was the only thing that had saved her, the mother thought, from being sexually assaulted and possibly worse.

The caller advised that the man had been arrested by a uniformed police officer assigned to the southern district on an assault warrant she had taken out for him. When the first officer responded to the call from neighbors, he advised that a warrant should be obtained; the suspect, Melvin, had run off by then. But she got the warrant and he was arrested today. He had broken into their house two days ago. She added that neighbors had seen Lemons break in the door. The woman readily identified herself and her daughter.

When asked the identity of the man who had broken into their home and attempted to assault her, the daughter stated, "He is my mother's boyfriend, Melvin Lemons." She willingly stated that she had known Mr. Lemons for years and not questioned his sanity or his ability to properly conduct himself around her family prior to this incident. He was a live-in boyfriend of her mother, Evelyn Carnes. They lived just a few blocks away in his apartment. Up until this point, she felt that Lemons was just strange by nature. He was quiet and seemed to be a loner, content in spending time alone without any close friends. Her mother had stated he enjoyed rummaging through abandoned buildings for junk. His only friend and companion was her mother.

The assault had brought back to the mother's mind many of his strange statements and actions. In the past, she knew him to draw depictions of nude women being stabbed and mutilated with various weapons; some of the pictures showed dismemberment of their limbs and deaths by decapitation. She stated that she had known this subject for over five years. He was generally a quiet man and his only drug involvement to her knowledge was the occasional use of marijuana, and moderate drinking. The other similar incident was with another family member, also a female child. Lemons had taken her years ago to one of the bus stations and attempted to leave the state with her without parental permission. The child was her sister's daughter. The child would have been around the same age of her daughter at the time. The family involved decided for the sake of their mother that it would be dismissed as a harmless incident and they would not press criminal charges, it had happened years ago.

Now that her daughter had been assaulted by him, in what was the second such incident, she felt he was capable of the acts he depicted in his drawings and definitely had some type of fetish with regards to female children. She gave hers and sister's full name and address, as well as that of her mother's. With the information gathered, the caller was assured that the matter would be looked into.

Perplexed by the call, I had to decide the legitimacy of the caller and whether the information was sound enough to further investigate. Was the caller trying to implicate the arrested subject, Mr. Lemons, because of her anger over some family dispute that had festered, or were her motherly instincts true about Melvin Lemons? Another possibility presented itself to him with the talk of dismemberment and decapitation, was the caller herself stable? Was her sanity in question, or was she distraught over her daughter's assault? Was she calling with truthful information, or should her mental health be questioned? Naturally, she sounded excited during the call, but was the excitement that of a rational person?

It was not odd for detectives to receive numerous similarly psychotic-sounding calls, including ones involving unfounded bodies being dismembered. Who shot President Kennedy, why Jack Ruby was really killed, calls lacking credibility? Calls from those established as having mental problems by their conversations and police records, such as a lady who frequently called advising she placed tin foil in her hair to allow radio reception from aliens.

Yet the caller sounded intelligent and truly concerned even through her excitement. Having the name of the caller, her mother and that of Mr. Lemons, with their addresses, I checked them through central records and determined that neither the daughter nor mother had records of arrest in Baltimore City. This established a little more credibility as far as the caller was concerned, and helped to rule out instability on her part. Lemons' criminal record did not substantiate violent criminal activity on his part in the past. It indicated a handful of misdemeanor arrests, nothing to indicate the horrendous crimes that the caller was accusing him of. Because we were free of calls and we had time, I decided to investigate the caller's complaint and subsequent information further.

Officer John Young was determined to have been the initial officer on the call. Upon his arrival at the scene, hearing the facts and knowing that the named suspect, Melvin Lemons, had fled, he advised the mother of the victim to obtain a warrant for Lemons the next morning at the southern. She complied and on January 13, 1979, a warrant was issued and served. Lemons was charged on the warrant and held at Baltimore City Jail on charges of burglary and assault, with bail pending, having forced his way into the home and attempting to assault the ten year old girl based on her information. Ironically, I personally knew Officer Young. Young had been in homicide prior to his assignment to the southern district. During our conversation, I advised him of the conversation with the mother of the child.

Young did not believe the subject to be capable of such violence; although he admitted that since the assault on the child had not actually occurred, perhaps that aspect of Lemons' nature could not be judged. The suspect was small in stature, mild and meek, and talked low. He did not give the appearance of a man who would resort to violence or assaults; his physical size and appearance would not intimidate anyone. When arrested, he did not offer any resistance, but gave no reason for his actions when questioned. Officer Young was advised of the caller's information and that it would be followed up by a personal interview of the grandmother, Evelyn Carnes, possibly on this shift if other calls for service did not interfere. He would be kept advised of our investigation regarding her interview.

I turned to Bob Jansen and said, "Let's take a ride." Without an answer, Bob jumped to his feet, grabbed his dress coat and followed me out the door while pulling on his coat. As we walked down the hall to the floor elevator, I explained the caller's information to Bob. I added that although I had confirmed the arrest of Melvin Lemons, I had not made a decision on whether or not the information would lead to anything at all. "Anyway, this will give you some experience," I said to Bob.

We got an unmarked cruiser from the headquarters motor pool and headed about two miles west to the address of Ms. Carnes. I discussed the information I had obtained with Bob during the drive to fill him in. During the ride, I mentioned the odd calls that came into homicide and advised that the possibility existed that this would be resolved just by discussing the information with Ms. Carnes. It was about 9:45 P.M. She would probably be awake considering the events of the day if she was not at her daughter's, the caller. That would be the second place to check if necessary, and allow for interviews of both if she were there. The mother for a second time to confirm her information.

As we drove across town after I had explained the reason for our trip, I started thinking to myself about my city. Baltimore was becoming a small town, from about 1 million people in the past to about 800,000 people at present. Everyone who could was moving to the surrounding counties, just like the flight taking place in most of the major cities on the east coast. They left the city with its problems of high crime, poor education and services, mounting taxes and expenses, fleeing to an area where their lives were less complicated by problems and less concerned with the everyday strife that plagued city dwellers. Regarding the escalating crime rate, those that had nothing were stealing from those that had, and killing or injuring them more often than in the past. It was a relatively small city with a high crime rate. Most of the nightlife carried on just outside of the city limits, except for small neighborhood bars. The town died after dark set in, the streets were devoid of the law abiding out of fear, and those on the streets were scoring drugs, or out to break in cars and houses, or commit random crimes that presented themselves, or break the law in whatever manner it took to obtain money for their daily drug habits. Stolen merchandize was sold for pennies on the dollar, but those pennies added up to drug buying power

Like other cities that had gone though lawlessness, immorality and poverty, Baltimore was on the verge of a definite decline. Gone were the nice, clean, ethnic neighborhoods like the Greek, Polish and Italian neighborhoods with their painted screens on the windows of east side homes. Washed marble front steps and clean swept sidewalks and gutters were becoming things of the past. Pride in their homes, which they worked for and kept in good repair, was on the downturn as were entire neighborhoods. Once those proud elderly people died off and their relatives tired of keeping up the properties, with renters who did everything to destroy their surroundings, it was over for the once proud communities.

The tax base was dwindling and the city services suffered. As I thought this, we drove past a known drug corner and watched fifteen or more young, black adults and teenagers scurry from the corner. They had seen the police cruiser coming and, thinking it was narcotics cops, vacated the corner, if only for a matter of minutes until they thought the coast was clear.

On one of my cases, a youth of fifteen shot another boy and was apprehended running from the scene, throwing the gun he used in an alley trash can in one of the yards he passed. His actions were observed by a uniformed police officer giving chase and the weapon was recovered almost before the ringing sound of it hitting the tin garbage can had stopped. When interviewed about killing the boy, he made the statement, "I did it for the promised territory," meaning he did it to take over the victim's area to sell drugs. The youth added, "What else is there? This way, I would have gotten money, cars and women, and be dead by the time I am thirty." A fifteen year-old child had weighed his options and decided on the path he would take in life. It was a promise of a far better life than their poor home life and lack of education would ever bring. These were street youth with no visible escape from what they were born into except what was offered through drug money. They had not lived long enough a life to fear death, or to realize how important life was. The sad and scary reality was with every passing day, there were more kids believing this was the only way out. Personally, I was always more fearful of a youth with a gun than a man with one. The man, if he hesitated using the weapon, was thinking over the ramifications of his actions. The youth had no fear of death, which is a natural human tendency at a young age, and probably having never contemplated death, would not consider his actions

On another case, I spoke with the owner of a funeral home on McCulloh Street after the death of another young black man involved in selling drugs. He stated, "My business is in a sad state of affairs. I stay open serving young gangsters, burying their fellow gang members and handling the funeral arrangements. They come in here and ask for the most expensive arrangements that can be afforded them, and pay with ones, fives and ten dollar bills. Most of them are mourning personal friends that have died in their teens. I beg them to stop, but they never do. Often, one or two funerals later I am burying the boy that had just paid for his friend's funeral."

Drugs were taking over the streets and it was turning a major portion of the black population into street thugs or addicts. Either they sold drugs, bought drugs, or both. The money to support their habits had to be found daily, no matter how. No longer were there just a few bad guys in a neighborhood, like when I grew up, strong-arming those they dealt with, running prostitution or gambling houses, or numbers. Now there were gangs or groups of youths high on drugs that would attack anyone for their money, and their numbers had increased tenfold from just a few years ago. I remember the time growing up when you could sleep on hot nights on your front steps knowing no one would disturb you; now we had cases where they broke down locked doors to get at the victims, and frequently harmed the occupants. True often, these home invasions were drug related, either break-ins to shoot business foes or to rob them of their drugs and money, but it also represented another crime method.

The age for those involved continually got younger; even a ten year-old was arrested for selling narcotics in front of a high rise. He stated that he "was hired by a man named 'Boo,' and told not to mess up his drugs or money." Naturally, this boy was frightened and very cooperative during his interview, but only knew "Boo" by that street name and description. Finding a new way to remain anonymous, the dealers used this method to help hide their identity and still work at their trade while paying less for workers.

I realized we caught more and more drug-related cases, but working in homicide was far easier than working in narcotics. Our involvement was usually at the fatal end caused by drug usage, robberies or territorial shootings. Our victims were killed over territorial wars, or nonpayment for drugs, or by hotshot deaths. We did not have the daily battle over controlling usage and those who were involved in the manufacture and sale. But unfortunately, the victims of this hideous drug usage were younger and younger, kids killing kids. They were coming from broken and poor homes in which they were neglected, locked out because their parents were doing drugs themselves or laying up with anybody; dropping out of school because no one cared if they went or not, and taught to survive by whatever means necessary. What chance did they have? Instead of a few bad actors in a neighborhood, we were breeding entire neighborhoods of bad guys, and still are.

As we neared our destination, I recalled the case to date that had affected me the most. It had occurred in this area not far from the address to which we were headed. Timmons and I were working the midnight shift, 11:30 P.M. to 8:00 A.M. We had dealt with a shooting homicide around 2 A.M. and were driving to the southwest district to obtain a warrant for the person identified as responsible. Another call came in for a homicide on Ramsey Street and another unit picked it up on what was now the day shift. It was about 8:30 A.M. at the time. We continued on to obtain the warrant for the subject who had fled the scene of the shooting but had forgotten in his haste that others at the scene who witnessed the shooting could identify him. After obtaining the warrant, about one hour later, we decided to drive over and see what the day shift had caught.

When we arrived at the Ramsey Street address, we were directed to the second floor by what appeared to be an angry, young uniformed officer. Without conversation and with a disgusted look on his face, he just pointed us in the right direction, up the stairs to the scene. We walked into the second-floor apartment and observed a sight that would stick in my mind for life: Lying in their cribs were two babies, dressed only in their diapers, probably twins about 18 months old, with both of their arms bent at the elbows, hands raised above their heads as if in a surrendering position, as if they were old enough to give up. Both had been stabbed multiple times in their small chests, both helplessly and innocently dead. Both babies were lying in pools of blood soaking into the white bedding under their small bodies. The first thing out of our mouths was, "Who did this!"

Det. John Kurini, who had caught the case, said, "The father, he was high on PCP, shot his wife in the leg and stabbed his two babies." The next question was one that I think every cop on the scene had asked, "Where is he at!" John replied, "Afterward, that son of a bitch shot himself. He's dead. He's in the next room, blew what little brains he had left out." Everyone at that scene must have thought, he had better be dead.

I never dreamed of this case, I never dreamed about any of them, but once in a while my thoughts turned to that call and those little defenseless infants. Hardly old enough to speak, their only misfortune in life was being born to a drug-addicted father. You learned quickly whether seeing dead people affected you one way or the other when you were in uniform, long before the day you decided to join the detective bureau. But it must be the parental instinct in you when it comes to children. To see dead children, however they met their fate, left an empty feeling in the pit of your stomach every time with your mind asking the same old question, why? Children are innocent, harmless and defenseless victims. If they didn't want to raise them, give them to one of the countless who cannot have their own but would commit their life raising a child to adulthood.

Another youth killed handled by other detectives, was when an eight year-old was reported missing. The child was the son of a man separated from his wife who had joint custody of the child The father and son walked away from the mother's address on a hot summer's day with her permission. After the child was missing that evening and the father located, he indicated that all went well and he said his goodbyes in the same block as the mother's house around 8:OO P.M. the same night. He stated that he did not drop him directly at the door because he did not want to deal with his wife. None of the neighbors saw him drop off the child, and his wife was positive he had harmed the child.

Abuse was the reason they had separated. The husband was brought in and interrogated as a suspect and finally agreed to show the detectives where his son was. Several of us accompanied them to the area because it was wooded and might require a search.

We arrived in the small wooded area just east of Baltimore City and followed the man around as he looked for his son. After a few minutes, we walked up on the body of the child. His skull was partially crushed and a bloody rock near the head had been the weapon. The man walked up to the remains of his son, shrugged and pointed to the body and said, "There he is," as indifferent as he could be, as if he just discovered a dead animal. Once back at the office, the man stated he had killed the boy, not because of the separation with his wife but because they argued and his son wouldn't listen to him.

Baltimore was made up of block after block of two or three story, brick and stone row homes. Much like in other large cities, many of these homes had been turned into apartments on each floor by fleeing owners. Bob and I arrived at the Carnes home and rang the doorbell twice. Soon after, a second-floor apartment light came on, telling us that someone was there. A quick thought passed as I remembered we were within blocks of H.L. Mencken's home. He was a great journalist, essayist, magazine editor, satirist and critic on American life. He died in 1956 in our city. Now the neighborhood had deteriorated to such a point that such a man as Mencken could be a target of a street robbery if still living in the area, and perhaps worse, one of its victims. Now, two detectives were trying to determine if we had nothing, a mental case or a murderer. Lemons, ironically, worked as the night watchman at the same cemetery where my relatives are buried.

The electric door lock released and we entered the dwelling. Usually each floor of these types of apartments was separated at each landing by fire doors, used for protection should the building catch on fire. We reached the second-floor fire door and opened it, surprised by how clean the inside landing was to that point. Walking to a door marked number two, Bob knocked, announcing that we were police officers. A woman answered from inside, opened the door and identified herself when asked as Ms. Carnes. She did not seem surprised that we were there and said, "I knew it's about Melvin's arrest. Why did you have to come here?" Bob stated, "We wanted to talk to you about other information we had received." She seemed cooperative and readily admitted that she was aware of the attempted assault on one of her grandchildren and that her live-in boyfriend of over five years had been arrested for the crime.

Ms. Helen Carnes appeared to be about fifty years old at the time, 5'4" and with a slender build. She was dressed in a clean, flower-print housedress, and her efficiency apartment was above average in appearance considering those that the detectives had been in previously in the area on other calls. She seemingly was not well educated; she spoke slowly as if fishing for the proper responses, and mispronounced some of her words. When questioned about Mr. Lemons' arrest and if there were any other similar incidents, she was initially defensive and appeared almost motherly in her attitude toward her boyfriend. Her conversation frequently included comments defending him, such as what a kind and gentle man he was. We quickly got the impression that she was not only defensive about him, but she cared deeply for the man.

Finally, she relaxed and accepted the fact that we were there on another matter and for information gathering regarding what her daughter had told us. We told her we had talked over the phone with her daughter about the assault on her granddaughter. She seemed to appear slightly relieved as if she wanted to be truthful with us. I think that deep down she had realized the importance of being truthful and that it was twofold. Now that Lemons had been arrested, and with the statement that she had already talked to her daughter, it was easier for her to discuss the matters her daughter had already told us. Her only previous hesitation was in the fact that she did not realize what her daughter had told us. First, she freely stated that she was the mother of a large family, ten to be exact, three of which lived within a block of one another, including the mother and victim with her family.

Perhaps making her a little more apprehensive to talk, we stated that we knew other things about Melvin and that was why we wanted to talk to her. She thought about what we had said for several minutes, as if making a decision on whether to tell us the truth, and then replied, "I'm not going to lie about anything to you. My daughter has already told you what she knew, and she told you because of this misunderstanding with my granddaughter and Melvin." When asked, she admitted that on occasion Melvin did act strangely; that some people would consider him weird, but that she loved him, and in his defense he was a good man, worked hard and provided.

Then apparently satisfied in her mind that we knew much of what she was going to tell us about Melvin stated: "On one occasion, while employed as a night watchman, Melvin had brought home a mummified hand of an infant from one of the vaults at the cemetery. He said that the hand dated back to the Civil War period. Afterward, he stated that he had nightmares about the hand and ended up returning it to the vault. He frequently referred to this incident as, 'The Little Ghost,' distinguishing it from what he called 'The Big Ghost,' instead of calling those children or adults."

This information was new to us, but we allowed her to continue uninterrupted. She furnished information that Melvin worked as a night watchman at a named cemetery and that on another occasion he came home with white powder on him and smelling of a corpse. He had told her that he had dug up the body of a female who was buried that day and laid in the coffin with her. Ironically, that burial date was within days of the birthday of Detective Bob Jansen.

When asked about the abduction of the other grandchild a while ago, Ms. Carnes related that incident was about three years earlier. Melvin had taken another one of her granddaughters against her will supposedly, and was stopped by the police on the complaint at one of the two bus stations in town with the child. It was either the Greyhound or Trail Way bus stations; she did not know which. The family dropped what would have resulted in charges and had him released as a misunderstanding. Helen had pleaded with her other daughter, mother of that child, not to press charges at the time because of her own relationship with Melvin. Later, Melvin would say to her in a casual conversation, "If we would have gotten on that bus, you or yours would have never seen that child again." At the time, although frightened by the comment, she did not pursue the statement further with him, not taking the words as an intended threat at the time, thinking he was kidding. Even if that second assault had occurred and Melvin had been arrested, she had convinced herself that perhaps he was mentally ill. Still, her conversation indicated she was trying to stand by him. She thought over her last comment and said, "No, he's not crazy. He drinks and does marijuana a lot, but he is a good provider."

When asked about his artwork, she acknowledged that we must have been told already about it. As she reached into a dresser top drawer and removed some of his drawings to show us, she attempted to explain them to us as Melvin had explained them to her. These drawings depicted nude men and women, female decapitations, and dismemberments of human beings, both sexes. Melvin was not an artist by any stretch, but the drawings were done well enough to depict graphic and violent torture and murder scenes. Viewing the drawings, it was obvious that the artist enjoyed displaying his work and liked the amount of portrayed violence. The drawings gave the express intent that the artist hated women. They depicted vivid scenes of depravity. They were so forceful that for the first time since the initial call by the daughter about the assault on the child, it was reasonable to believe that Melvin Lemons could be responsible for the accusations being made against him.

Looking at these pictures, you could feel the artist's anger and his intense dislike toward women. At that point, I thought that there was something to the information. If Lemons was not criminally responsible for his actions, then at least his mental status was highly questionable, and he may have had intent to harm either or both of his girlfriend's grandchildren.

After sharing what she thought was enough to show us, Helen casually went on to discuss their lovemaking when asked, and volunteered information about what she called the "Book of Deaths." One night when they were in bed making love, Lemons bit her right wrist and drew blood. He stopped the lovemaking and sucked at the wound, drinking the blood oozing from the bite. Forgetting about the lovemaking, he physically stopped to suck the blood. Afterward, he declared laughing, "Who knows, maybe I'm a vampire? That was really good."

The "Book of Deaths" was described as being the registry book that was used at his mother's funeral. Over the years Helen and Lemons had been together, Lemons claimed he had killed three women before 1973. He still had his mother's registry and stated he had named some of his victims in it That he had killed before, drawing his victims in his sketches. He had told her that he lured the victims to his apartment, beat them to death and disposed of their bodies by dismembering them and throwing the parts away. She continued to speak of him protectively, saying that he was loving in their relationship and probably just delusional at the time because of the drugs and alcohol, saying she did not believe he was capable of such things. Some of these items could have assisted us; the drawings and the registration book were not removed from the home at that time. They were the property of Melvin Lemons and not legally taken without being obtained through a warrant or with his permission. If later used as evidence in a court of law, they would have been inadmissible because they had been illegally seized. And a warrant had to be justified by more than the hearsay evidence gathered at that point.

At the conclusion of our interview, we both walked down the steps and out of the rental deeply involved in a conversation about the information we had just obtained. Our talk with Ms. Carnes left us with more questions. Could this woman know so many strange things about the man she lived with and not only stay with him, but defend him after he had proven to her over and over that he was at the very least unstable? His admitted and witnessed actions were enough in themselves for a normal person to question her own safety and that of members of her own family. Was she possibly as deranged as she made Lemons out to be? Or if any of this information proved to be true, was she involved with him in the commission of some of these acts she and her daughter had accused him of? Or, as she appeared during the interview, had she readily accepted him out of her love for him and willing to overlook what she considered odd actions caused by alcohol and drugs that, if taken at face value, could destroy their relationship? Questions we would eventually answer.

As we drove from the apartment, both of us were bothered by what we had heard, with the obvious feeling that we did have further reason to investigate. We agreed that the easiest way to proceed was to determine if the information about the grave desecration was correct, and that would require an inquiry at the cemetery. If that information proved to be correct, it would allow us to open a full investigation into the other reported crimes and hopefully constitute probable cause to seize the articles at his apartment.

Initially, to proceed further, we just had to confirm the date of the possible grave desecration at the cemetery from the information obtained from Ms. Carnes. Was a body interned on that date at the cemetery? If a female was interned on that date, was the grave desecrated? Our first steps: verify the burial of a female on that date, exhume the body, confirm the grave was desecrated, and get the results of an autopsy if possible.

Working 4-to-12, we both reported to the office prior to our shift and requested a meeting with Captain Joseph DiCarlo in order to discuss the information received about Lemons. After listening to the macabre story, DiCarlo concluded as we had that presently there was no probable cause to even believe at this point that Lemons was responsible for any of the described acts. Direct or circumstantial evidence would have to be pursued should the allegations against Lemons be proven. It was agreed to by the captain that the cemetery investigation was the quickest and easiest way to make that determination. He readily agreed that the cemetery information should be followed up, and replied, "Do it. Don't spend too much time on this. Substantiate and investigate or put it to bed." I'm sure his thoughts turned to the possibility of three more murders to be investigated, not only old occurrences but if true difficult to prove.

It was agreed that the easiest method to determine if Ms. Carnes' information was correct to check at the cemetery where Lemons was employed, Bob and I set about the task. It would be easy enough to confirm by their records if a female burial had taken place on the date given. Was Lemons working there on the indicated date, and was a female buried then? Was he the only night watchman there? If he was alone during his shifts, surely he had the time and opportunity to do what he had reportedly told Helen. If he worked solo on the night shift, he would have had the run of the entire facility, possibly including the office records. The records would allow him to check on the recently buried, as well as the plot number of their internment. More questions we had to answer.

With the date of the burial being remembered easily because it was the birth date of Det. Jansen, a call was placed to the cemetery asking for the director or person in charge. A Mr. Whitehead was located; he came on the line and our investigative information concerning his cemetery was explained to him. Mr. Whitehead advised that it would take hours to check their records and that he would call back with the information he developed. He sounded apprehensive, naturally because his interest lye with protecting the cemetery and its image. During our conversation with him, Mr. Whitehead did acknowledge that a person by the name of Melvin Lemons was employed there. Two and a half hours later, Whitehead returned our call and verified that a female had indeed been buried on the date in question. We advised that we would obtain a writ to exhume the body buried that date, which took five days through the States Attorney's Office and Judge Pierce. By now, even our captain who had complained about the time we were devoting to this case was interested and wondered aloud where the case would lead.

The ride to the cemetery took place on the sixth day. The cemetery was located just inside the Baltimore City limits. It was large and established, well kept as all are, and dated from before the Civil War. Recalling the information about the mummified infant's hand, another bit of information that had been given to us by Ms. Carnes. We had changed shifts to day work, to work on this aspect of the investigation regarding the grave information. We obtained permission to investigate the cemetery issue after our call to Mr. Whitehead had confirmed the burial on the date received Lemons had worked there at the time. No longer was the captain indifferent about the investigation now that there was a bit of confirmation from the cemetery authorities, although he was still apprehensive to add potential murders to the official count. We had the writ in hand after a formal report to the judge explaining everything learned to date: the information from the caller, the Lemons arrest on those charges, the interview of Ms. Carnes and Mr. Whitehead's information.

At this point, neither of us realized that we were starting an investigation that would prove to be the strangest case we had ever worked. The thought was still there that the principal in our case probably needed no more than the attention of a psychiatrist. How could anyone have done the things attributed to Lemons? And how could Helen Carnes accept the things Lemons told her, or his actions around her, and not report him to the police or think that he did not need help?

Leaving the headquarters garage, we stopped and picked up ASA Michael Gloshakow and then Dr. Ann Dixon, one of the state's medical examiners, from their respective offices. During our twenty minute ride to the cemetery, we engaged in conversation with Mike and Ann about the strange case and our beliefs as to the credibility of those involved to date. Ironically, the ride almost took us past the apartment shared by Lemons and Carnes. Perhaps all four realized they were taking a ride that in all probability they would never repeat, not in the careers of three of them at least; working cases, not one of them had ever exhumed a body. Normally, only Ann Dixon because of her occupation could have. But even after years in the Medical Examiner's Office with her varied and multiple investigations to date had not been involved in any exhumations. She was being driven to her first one.

Upon our arrival at the cemetery, we entered the north entrance of the stately complex. The grounds themselves were spacious, well kept and accessible from two entrances, one on the north another on the south, and contained beautiful marble tombstones in rows, along with small, aged, dark stone mausoleums. We identified ourselves to a female office secretary behind a desk, asking for the director, Mr. Whitehead. The secretary reacted by standing and walking to an inner office in which a man seated at a desk was visible to us. Mr. Whitehead appeared in a dark colored, expensive suit, wearing an appropriate, matching black tie and shoes. Dressed exactly the way we expected befitting his occupation, his clothing was conservative and he could be envisioned consoling the recently bereaved. My first thought was that it was a Brooks Brothers Suit, or perhaps a Jos. Banks. He greeted us with a hesitant smile and started the conversation directly concerning the matter at hand, almost before we could introduce Ann and Michael indicating their respective occupations and why they had accompanied us.

Naturally, his initial concern was with exposure to the media should our suspicion be correct. His concern was in protecting the interest of the cemetery. Gloshakow assured him that neither the State's Attorney's Office or the Police Department was interested in any bad publicity befalling the cemetery, and the last thing we wanted to do was release the matter to the papers. Whitehead appeared to be relieved and made a call for the head groundskeeper to meet us with a probe at the indicated gravesite, knowing deep down that he had to comply with the writ we presented him.

Mr. Whitehead drove to the site location with the four of us in our vehicle. He explained again that Lemons was a night watchman, worked that night on the date the lady was buried, and would have the run of the whole operation and could have desecrated graves and tombs without anyone's knowledge. Lemons had been employed for the past three years, up to his present arrest, naturally, not reporting since. As we had heard before from Carnes and Officer Young, the cemetery head commented that Lemons was a mild mannered, quiet, apparently considerate man, adding that he had no work problems as far as Mr. Whitehead's research of employment records revealed.

Upon arrival at the site, a man who identified himself as Ted walked up as we exited our car and approached the gravesite in question. Ted was the chief groundskeeper, confirmed by Mr. Whitehead. He was a burly man, about fifty years of age, and stood about 6'0" tall. His full face was slightly tanned; apparently from his outside work, probably what you call a farmer's tan. He was dressed in worn dungarees and a faded, long-sleeve sweatshirt with "MARYLAND" printed on the front. Ted had stood by the site with the requested probe. The probe was an iron tee shape, the handle about three feet across and the length of about eight feet; the iron probe itself was about a half inch round. It appeared to have been handmade of one-half inch rounded steel soldered into welded into its shape.

Ted probed an area above the gravesite and announced that the grave was sound. Mr. Whitehead turned to Ted and gave him a disgusted look and pointed to the area he wanted probed. In turn, Ted did as directed, but reluctantly. Obviously, Mr. Whitehead had decided to cooperate and knew more about the business than just being the administrator in the front office. Ted complied and probed the spot indicated by Mr. Whitehead, again reluctant in his slow, deliberate motions. He was probably feeling loyalty for his position, and mixed emotions about finding problems and bringing discredit to the cemetery. But he complied. This time, the probe went further into the ground than it had during the first attempt.

Mr. Whitehead turned to us and stated, "We will dig it up; it has been disturbed." Ted pulled the probe from the ground and stepped back, still with a concerned look on his face. We had to wait a few minutes before additional workers responded with shovels in hand, called to the location by Ted on his walkie-talkie. The grave was only three feet below the surface; the lady in question had been buried above the grave of her husband, who had died some years before. The grave was excavated carefully and promptly by experienced burial personnel.

Once the grave revealed the coffin, we observed the top portion of the coffin covered with a piece of half-inch plywood. The top lid of the coffin, open at the time of viewing so the upper body is displayed had been torn off and was lying inside the coffin over the remains. The plywood was removed, as was the coffin lid, after the crime lab responded and the technician photographed the scene. The remains of a female lay in a fetal position within the coffin; no jewelry was noted on the remains. The skeletal remains appeared dressed in a light blue now tattered dress, dingy and deteriorated from the elements. The remains were not exhumed by the medical examiner after the overall scene was processed, photographed and the remains examined. Once examined by the medical examiner, the possibility of a sexual assault could not be determined because of the body's condition, exhumation was ruled out. The remains had deteriorated into a skeletal state, and a sexual assault, if having occurred, could not be determined.

After our investigation at the scene, we drove Mr. Whitehead back to his office and assured him that we would keep the exhumation occurrence and results from the newspapers. Obviously, Lemons had the run of the cemetery at night and had committed the grave desecration and probably crypt entries as he had confessed to Carnes. Mr. Whitehead advised that he would use Lemons arrest as a reason for his dismissal from his job should Lemons make bail on the charges he was presently arrested on; and that he would notify the family relatives as to the grave disturbance and the cemetery would rectify the damages.

When asked about the possibility of crypts having been disturbed by Lemons, Mr. Whitehead replied, "He did this, who knows what else? Truthfully, over the years we have had several incidents, usually youths in the graveyard at night breaking into the crypts, turning over tombstones, defacing them. It would be hard to prove if he had, or someone else could be responsible for the vandalism, unless he confessed to you guys."

Several days later, we were advised that since the statute of limitations had come and gone, we would not be able to charge Lemons with the grave desecration even if he would confess and that we did not have any physical evidence that the body had been assaulted should he admit to that. But having proved that the grave had been desecrated, we could gauge his truthfulness against our verification of damage at the cemetery. Ms. Carnes had not indicated any theft from the grave and therefore any charges of larceny did not exist. At least Mr. Whitehead was relieved to hear that the media would not report on the court charges of grave desecration at a later date.

We still had not had time to substantiate the reported murders or any chargeable crime. The next order of business was to notify the next of kin about the grave desecration and our subsequent exhumation of the body for what we thought initially would be an examination, within a reasonable time frame. The cemetery would readily do so to cover the situation they found themselves in, and our acknowledgement of why we were involved would satisfy the relatives.

Bob was off on the day I drove to Silver Spring, Maryland, to notify a Mrs. Taylor about the grave desecration; she was the daughter of the woman whose body was dug up by Lemons. I took the drive solo, which took about an hour, all the while thinking how I would break the news to Mrs. Taylor. I had told numerous people bad news while on the job, naturally relatives of homicide victims, but grave desecration was another matter. Not only did it present an uncomfortable and difficult situation but also meant detailing a terrible act

When I first went to homicide, I thought telling the next of kin that a son or daughter was killed would be a hard thing to do. I worried about it, but quickly learned that if it was street violence leading to the majority of the murders, the parents and friends frequently expected it to happen. How could anyone expect their relative having been physically dug up and possibly assaulted after their death? It seemed to me even a more heinous crime than murder. Since the autopsy could not determine an assault had occurred during the desecration, I decided not to discuss the possibility if not questioned by the relatives.

The inside of the D.C. beltway at Silver Springs is basically commercial. Above the beltway, the commercial buildings give way to a semi-rural area with individual dwellings, but still plagued with the almost-constant Washington traffic. This was the area in which the Taylor family lived. It was far enough from Baltimore and the burial site at the cemetery that it was assumed that at the time of the burial, Mrs. Taylor probably lived in the Baltimore area and afterward moved to her present address finding a nicer home for their family, or perhaps out of job necessity. I pulled up to her single ranch-style home located on a quiet shady, well-kept street, exiting my car and walked to the door.

Ringing the doorbell, I was greeted by a woman in her late thirties, who looked at my extended hand holding the badge, stepped aside and extended her right hand as a greeting to enter her home. A small female child about three years old scampered from the living room as I entered, running into an adjacent dining area. At her age, the stranger at the door apparently frightened her.

After entering, I observed a man about the same age as Mrs. Taylor seated on the couch in the living room. He was introduced as her husband, Richard Taylor. As tactfully as possible, I explained why I was there, starting with the initial call that furnished us the information, without any details in regards to the sexual allegation that had started the investigation. I concluded with why her mother's exhumation had taken place and why it was part of what was now an ongoing matter.

Both of the Taylors seemed much more understanding than I had expected; perhaps they were shocked, taken by surprise, and had not thought of the ramifications of such an act. Or they were such decent people having not been exposed themselves to such things they would not even consider the possibility. Mrs. Taylor confirmed that because of her mother's wishes, she was buried without any jewelry whatsoever. She explained, "My mother always said it was a waste. 'Keep the nice things for those who could use it, for the living to enjoy.'" They were advised that the mother's body had not suffered any assault, which although a possibility would never be proven, and definitely not worth mentioning. Why burden them with such a possibility.

The meeting with the Taylors lasted about twenty five minutes, with me answering all of their questions as best as I possibly could. It went as stated, much better than initially expected. I left the address with a certain feeling of self relief, feeling that the notification had gone well even if the Taylors had not had time to consider all of the aspects connected with the desecration. I was glad that they had not and hoped they would not call with lingering questions. As time passed, thankfully, they did not.

With the results from our experience at the cemetery, it was time to investigate the rest of the information given to us from Ms. Carnes and her daughter. In as much as the cemetery information was proven, could it be possible that we had Baltimore's first serial killer?

The next step in this case would be the interview of Lemons himself in order to obtain additional information pertaining to the presently supposed victims and to get a read on his personality. We wanted to see this individual in person and study his mannerisms and responses under questioning. After the findings to date, it was time to talk to the suspect in the case. We obtained a writ for Lemons, drew an unmarked car and proceeded to the Baltimore City Jail where he was still housed, having failed to make bail on the child's assault. At least to date, Ms. Carnes had failed in her efforts to have her daughter and granddaughter drop the charges that he was being held on, and apparently she had not been able to raise the money for his bail. We were convinced that no matter how the investigation turned out, charges, court or no court, Carnes would stand by the man, she loved for unknown reasons.

The jail was located not more than a mile slightly northeast of the headquarters building. At one time, years ago, it was known as "The Castle." It resembled a castle with high, dark, gray stone walls held together with lighter colored mortar, with rounded towers for observation and an arched entrance way on Forrest Street. These structural features were probably behind the nickname.

On the short trip to the jail, I recalled the times when I would hear of prisoners breaking out. During my time in car 105, I rode up the Jones Falls Expressway on two occasions and saw bed sheets hanging from the cell windows, blowing freely in the evening breeze hours after either successful or flouted escape attempts. The windows at the time were large enough for a man to wiggle out That oversight had since been corrected and hence the jail escapes had ceased.

We pulled up to the Forrest Street entrance and were allowed to drive into the courtyard after identifying ourselves. Parking the car, we walked to one of the several yard entrances to the jail itself. Just prior to entering the jail, we passed a screened walkway that led from the jail compound to the jail's cafeteria. Several prisoners were walking from the jail to the cafeteria at the time. They started with the usual shouts and calls, with various ones calling, "Hey, you guys lawyers? I need a lawyer, or would you represent me?" These remarks came almost every time a cop in a suit entered the jail.

At the time, most detectives wore three-piece suits and the sight of anyone dressed that way meant '"lawyer." It was funny, you were not in your natural environment, wearing a suit in a jail made you someone of importance, presumably an attorney. For all intent and purpose, you could have been the arresting officer for the person now yelling that you were a lawyer. Once, on arrival at a crime scene, dressed the same with an additional overcoat, I exited the standard departmental vehicle and heard someone in the crowd of spectators say, "There's the FBI." Clothes impressed the public, especially in poor neighborhoods.

When we reached the locked metal door, a hard knock brought

out the uniformed guard, who seemed to be not very interested He was handed the writ, studied it, read the name of the prisoner and called through a locked door for the prisoner to be delivered. About fifteen minutes later, Lemons arrived and answered to his name when called by the guard. The guard shrugged, and turned Lemons over to us, as the release of the lock on the metal doors sounded and opened. Out stepped a man who looked even smaller than he actually was. The orange jail jumpsuit he was dressed in must have been two sizes too large for him. At first impression, I thought, this could be a man that had desecrated the grave, but not the man who had told his common-law wife that he had killed several women?

He was a very frail man, about 5'6," maybe one hundred and fifty pounds, looking smaller in his oversized jail orange jumpsuit. Lemons answered the guard's name request in a very mild, meek tone, which added to his non-descript appearance. The only thoughts in mind at that time were: Lemons definitely looked harmless, which would allow him to be trusted by women, but unless he talked a good line, they would not freely go with him on his looks. If he was responsible for the acts he claimed, how is it that one or more of his victims did not successfully fight him off? His general appearance was not that of a man who could possibly pick up women during their first meeting. Perhaps if he indeed had victims, maybe they were all prostitutes he had paid and lured to the apartment and overpowered before they realized they were his victims. Maybe he just had an easy approach with them, to allow females to trust him, who knows? I thought he was nothing special, as so many others must have; maybe that was his secret with women. He looked so insignificant that they trusted him, thinking they had nothing to fear from this man.

Returning to headquarters without conversation about the matters at hand, we exited the elevator at the sixth-floor landing with Lemons in tow and walked to the west wing of the building into the our offices. The office was partitioned into three large rooms, containing desks for the detectives. Our sixth-floor wing overlooked the Central Police District; with its roof level several stories below. The west wing outer offices all had windows looking toward City Hall, which was two blocks west. They were reserved for supervisors and were smaller offices generally containing two desks facing each other. In a hall parallel to the larger offices were two small interview rooms about ten square feet each. We learned that one of the two interview rooms was occupied. Day-work detectives had caught a domestic murder before our arrival and were busy taking the wanted confession from the surviving member of the once happy family.

Confessions were always sought after; they made the criminal court case easier. Knowing a confession existed, the lawyers would be anxious to obtain a plea, not wanting to challenge his or hers client's confession in open court. Once a jury heard a confession, it impacted them in two ways: it naturally was difficult for the jurors to forget it existed, and it was rationally believable. Why confess unless you had done the deed? The only time confessions were not deemed to be crucial were in cases where so much physical evidence and or eyewitness testimony existed against the accused that there was not any doubt as to their guilt. Then, the thoughtful decisions about a suspect's court testimony had to be weighed against what possible pitfalls their attorney might create about the statement during the trail. Indeed, a clever attorney could create enough controversy about the confession that the jury could overlook other incriminating evidence.

We settled into the second available room, asked Lemons his full name and advised him of his rights. We stated that we knew why he was presently arrested and that we had talked to the complainants, mother and child. That was a slight lie; we had not interviewed the mother or child, and would not, we were more interested in Lemons growing situation. In his calm manner and with a deliberate low tone, he replied: "I was drunk at the time. I just wanted into the house; I wasn't going to hurt the child. She knows me. She just panicked when I came in the door. I guess I was loud because of my drinking." Lemons had apparently thought about this answer and we had just heard his defense statement, rehearsed for whenever he would see the judge. Who knows, Lemons' minor misdemeanor arrest to date, some liberal judge might believe him? Stranger things had happened.

Asked about the time he took another child to the bus station and was stopped by the police before he could board, he stated, "That was a misunderstanding. We were just out for the day. I was not taking her anywhere. I just wanted to show her the bus station when we were up there. Anyway, the parents understood and dropped the charges." Like every interview before and after, Lemons could in his mind rationally explain the majority of questions put to him. Most of the time he spoke in a calm, collected voice with normal facial expressions, and a controlled response that matched.

We told Lemons that neither of those things were what we wanted to talk to him about. We stated that we talked to his live-in girlfriend and as a result we had responded to the cemetery where he worked, not telling him that we had actually exhumed a corpse. Initially, Lemons denied all of that information we had obtained about that, calling it erroneous and ridiculous, even though he had not been confronted with any of the facts behind the general information.

Both of us gave one another a look, a look that meant we felt Lemons would eventually talk and tell us the truth; he was too easy with his conversation not to keep talking. Trying to defend himself at every step, he would eventually slip up. Talking too much and responding in depth to every question asked, Lemons blurted out, "You don't know anything!" To this day I don't know why, but one thought popped into my head. With all the information we had received from the witnesses, and with the proof that the grave had been desecrated, I said, "I know about the little ghost!" I remembered Lemons had nightmares over that "little ghost." For whatever reason, the dreams, whatever, the "little ghost" had definitely affected him emotionally. Lemons, the small unassuming man, straightened up in his chair and quietly replied, "You do know everything, don't you?" Then without any further words spoken between us, Lemons stated, "I should not go to jail, I need help, I should be seen by a doctor who can help me." In this sentence he had admitted some involvement or knowledge of the crimes being investigated and had given us the psychological answer we needed to approach him in our interview to obtain the truth. I said, "I think you are right. You need a psychiatrist instead of being imprisoned." Lemons nodded his head as if saying yes. From that time on, we had won over Lemons and he had decided to talk freely about whatever was asked, because in his mind he was confident we understood and would help him.

Now that this bond existed between us and Lemons, we started slowly with our interview regarding the suspected deaths. Initially asking questions about his youth, Lemons readily stated he was from Illinois, a small town probably no one knew of. He was an only child; his father left home without warning when he was at an early age. Leaving his mother and him, his mother drank often and ended up with several boyfriends over the years. Then he withdrew and refused any additional information about his childhood, visibly shaken and near tears. We felt that there was more information regarding Lemons' childhood, but he was not going there. Why risk shutting him down at this point? His childhood was a point of discussion for another interview; we would come back to that topic.

When asked about the little hand of the ghost, he responded, "You know all about that. Helen must have told you; she is the only person who knows about it." I replied, "Are you mad or upset with her if she did?" Lemons took no time responding, "No, I love her. I guess she thinks she is helping. She told me I needed help, maybe a psychiatrist." Still trying to sell us on treatment rather than jail, we both continued to agree. Bob asked him to tell us anyway. Melvin explained that he worked at a named cemetery for several years as a night watchman. Probably he would lose his job now because of this arrest. But anyway, he worked there alone and had the run of the entire place. He often wondered what he could find in the old vaults, some of which dated to the Civil War era. They were small walled tombs with locked iron entrance gates. He stated that he liked looking around for valuable articles, anything. He liked looking through vacant or deserted property for anything he could find as well.

One night, he removed a crowbar from the tool shed and went to one of the tombs. He forced open the gate and found the small, mummified hand while rummaging inside. To explain the damage all he had to say was he found some vandalism during his shift. He explained that vandals frequently did the same thing and were never caught. Sometimes during his shifts he would chase youths off the cemetery property. He could explore as much as he wanted without the fear of being caught and fired. He took the child's hand home and showed it to Helen, telling her where it had come from. After that, he continually had nightmares when trying to sleep, with a small baby ghost appearing almost nightly. He returned the small hand to the cemetery and the dreams went away. When asked, he stated that he did not rob any other tombs and would not be able to show us the exact one the small hand had come from, adding maybe the location is in the vandalism report. He did not volunteer the grave desecration when we talked about the small hand and denied any other acts of theft from the cemetery.

We advised him that we had investigated the grave desecration, had identified the victim, located and exhumed the remains. He replied, "Helen must have told you a lot." He stated that on that night he was alone and had the keys to the main office. He had gone in and looked at the burial log and determined where the new graves were located. From the office, he went to the tool shed's location where they also kept the equipment and there mounted a backhoe, which he had taught himself to operate in his spare time. The grave area was already fresh soft dirt from the initial digging and subsequent burial, so the marks from the backhoe would not be noticed. He drove the roads dividing the different sections of the cemetery to the site and dug up the body covered over by fresh dirt. It was a woman buried the same day.

He opened the coffin and climbed inside, lying with the corpse. He did not have sex with her, but he masturbated standing above the open grave. It was cold out. He didn't know why he had such desires and that was one of the reasons he felt he needed a psychiatrist. He added, "She was a nice lady, I like women." He seemed consumed in thought. He stated that afterward he found a piece of plywood, again from the tool shed, and covered the grave and backfilled it with dirt. Lemons denied taking anything from the grave and that was not his intent; he just wanted to lie with a corpse to find out how it felt.

Lemons had confessed to a grave desecration and had substantiated our findings at the time the grave was exhumed. The crime had run the statutes of limitations and could not be charged. He had denied any theft at the time, which could not be established during the daughter's or Helen's interviews. In short, his confession to this act would not result in any type of charge.

He was asked next about his murders and stated "That's the reason why I need help." There was no instant emphatic denial. His facial expression actually softened and he was extremely cooperative in what sounded to be a thoughtful response. A slight grin came over him and he stated: "You guys knew it all, and I'm relieved that you do. Deep down, I knew I would get caught. Maybe this is Helen's way of helping me. We love each other, and I told you I needed help." Lemons almost casually went on to say, "I am responsible for three murders." All of his victims were women in Baltimore City. These murders took place over years and involved three women who were described by him as a black prostitute, an unattached white female, and a young white female co-worker.

With that statement, we decided to discuss the possible victims one at a time to develop enough information on each to be able to identify them if they, in truth, existed. We were still not totally convinced at this point. We knew that Lemons had indeed committed the grave desecration, but was he telling the truth about these deaths? Or was he really a candidate, like he insisted, for the loony bin and the requested psychiatrist based on the reasoning he had for the grave desecration?

The first murder was that of a black prostitute on the west side about ten years ago. He stated her name was something like Sherry or Cheryl. She was in her late twenties, slim build. She had a medium complexion. He picked her up in a west side bar on West Saratoga Street, agreed on the price and went to his home where he lived alone at the time. They went to bed, had sex, and afterward he reached for his club, which was a sawed off baseball bat he kept beneath the bed. It was handy enough that he did not even have to get out of bed. She was small enough that she was handled physically easily. He placed his left hand over her mouth and swung the club with his right hand as hard as he could. The savage blow to her temple knocked her unconscious with just the first blow. He continued to beat her about her head until she was still and he was sure that his victim was dead.

His confidence grew for several reasons; he had killed the woman easy and he felt assured that no one would miss a prostitute. He was positive she had not told anyone in the bar his assumed name, and at the time they left she did not know where they were going. She was just another missing prostitute. What was one less? He displayed a small grin and stated, "I could not believe how powerful it made me feel; it was God like. I controlled her, took her life and felt that no one would ever know. It could not have been easier."

After admitting to the killing, he said, "I cut her open from the base of her neck down her middle, past her belly, below her waist. I sawed her chest plate open and then I lay inside of her until she felt cold. It felt so good. I always wanted to do that. I wonder why I have such feelings. Then I went to work; she was a mess."

He told us he had devised a method of getting rid of the body so that he would not be caught. This method would become his M.O. or, as police and legal authorities called it, Modus of Operandi the method of operation or of the crime. He dragged the body from the bed and placed it in the tub, where he proceeded to dismember the extremities, including the head. Once he flushed the small pieces down the toilet, he wrapped the larger bone portions in newspaper first and then plastic bags from the supermarket. The torso was larger and required more work. He sized the larger portions of the body by cutting off the meat from the torso and then used a hammer to break the bones down into reasonable size and weight. All the parts were wrapped again in newspaper and then plastic bags and put into his freezers, one in the refrigerator in the apartment and one he had in the basement. Lemons cleaned the floor and bed linen. And on trash days, he would throw the separate pieces of the bodies in the garbage truck himself so that no one discovered the body parts.

The second victim was some unsuspecting woman who needed a place to stay and was waiting for a bus. They met on a west side bus and as the bus traveled its route she explained she had just left her boyfriend, leaving him asleep in his apartment. She needed a place to stay while she searched for an apartment and Lemons readily suggested that she stay with him, that he had plenty of room and lived alone. She accepted and they exited the bus near his home and walked side by side to his address and the second-floor apartment. Lemons thought at the time, "How normal we look, and how easy this is." That's when he said he decided, "Why not, no one knows she is even with me." They carried on a long conversation that apparently convinced the woman that Lemons was a reasonably decent person. During the conversation, the women confided in him that she was originally from Virginia. She had married and her husband went off to sea in the Navy shortly after their marriage. The woman grew lonely and hated keeping the house alone without children, or in her mind even without friends. She left her home seeking excitement and initially went to another Virginia town. The soon to be victim admitted that in order to survive financially she became a prostitute and gave up on any aspects of her former life. Eventually, she came to Baltimore and had continued her occupation as a prostitute. The boyfriend that she had left was at first one of her customers. He was nice enough and cared for her, but she did not want to settle down with him and give up the money she was making so she left, bragging that she had taken two hundred dollars from his wallet while he was asleep. The money, as she said, was to get her started in her new life, a new apartment and some clothes. Some day, she would pay him back.

With the announcement that she was a prostitute by trade, it was easy for Lemons to strike a deal for sex with her. Once they had an agreement, he took her to bed. He again resorted to the club when the opportunity arose. This time, it was different; this girl was physically larger than his first victim and wrestled him for control of the club after the first glancing blow. She put up a fierce fight and at times Lemons thought she would win out. He might be the victim. Even this thought excited him. He actually envisioned her taking the club from him and killing him. After all, she was fighting for her life. He finally won the struggle and the girl lie there motionless, apparently dead. Then, he started to begin his ritual of dismemberment and concealment of the body parts. Only this time, something went wrong. He dragged her into the bathroom, placed her nude body into the tub and then was hit hard in the face again.

The girl he considered dead had only been unconscious. She was conscious once again and fighting for her life, delivering a hard blow to his jaw. He shook off the unexpected blow and struck her hard several times in the face until he was satisfied that she was definitely dead. Then the ritual began again, with one addition. He had thought it over and felt that he should remove the victim's teeth; should the skull be found, she could not be readily identified. While removing the teeth, he accidentally lost one under the tub. The landlord would later confirm that he had to replace the tub and its plumbing fittings because Lemons had taken it apart for a reported leak and was unable to reassemble it himself properly. After wrapping the toothless pieces of her skull, he disposed of it by throwing it in the Westside Shopping Center dumpster behind where he worked at the time.

Asked who this victim was he advised she called herself Ann and her last name was Story. He had placed her name in his mother's funeral directory. She was described as being white, 5'8" and about one hundred and forty pounds. After he had killed her, he found the two hundred dollars in her purse, the money she said she had stolen from her boyfriend. The money was really unexpected; he thought she had lied to him about it, what a lucky windfall.

The third victim in our jurisdiction was a girl working at an east Baltimore City restaurant chain, one that Lemons had also worked for as a cleanup man as well as a handyman. He diverted from the subject and stated, "One of their stores' dumpsters is where I put Anne's head, to get rid of it. I told you the Westside Shopping Center." Lemons went on to describe his third victim: "Jessica Younger, she was a young, blond-haired girl, 5'1," just out of high school, 19 or 20 years old, maybe 110 pounds, talkative with a good personality. I talked to her at work for about a month whenever I was at her store, and she was there longer before I got her to go out with me. The manager tried to stop me from seeing her, saying it was company policy that co-workers could not date. She had an apartment about three blocks from the job and I went there two or three times before I talked her into coming to my apartment. We went to bed at my place and I killed her, the same way as the others. I wasn't going to hurt her when we first got there, everything was fine. I looked forward to our sex. Something just came over me and I thought here is the opportunity; she is just like the others, why not?"

The serial killer suspect continued: "That's why I tell you I need a psychiatrist. I love women, but I am unable to stem the desire to hurt them when I have the opportunity. Some doctor could help me, I know. I don't want to go to jail; they can't help. They won't make me well. I love women; they make life worth living, so caring and so understanding. I don't know why I'm the way I am."

I asked if he ever thought about killing his live-in, Ms. Helen Carnes. Lemons thought for a minute and replied, "Of course not. I love her." In response, I said, "No, that's not the reason. All of her family lives within blocks. She would be missed right away." Lemons, quiet for a minute as if thinking about what was said, smiled and had no reply. I was sure I was right.

His drawings were the next topic of discussion, and simply explained by the killer after we admitted we had seen them at his apartment. Lemons had depicted the deaths of his victims in his artwork. He had drawn nude decapitated women as he had remembered them in death, and in one such artwork had written the words, "Welcome to the club." One of the drawings depicted hordes of people being led to a dark triangle at the lower left corner of the drawing. Both of us were unable to determine what the drawing depicted. We asked Lemons what was the drawing's meaning? He gave us a sarcastic look and stated, "You guys are smarter than that. Its two men at the edge of a grave, one is wearing a white robe, one in a black robe. Good and evil, leading people to their grave." Then he stopped talking, seemed to be pondering his next remark and said, "I just don't know which one I am?" Asked if his drawings represented what he had done to the women, Melvin Lemons answered, "I guess they do, that's what I did to them."

After the long interview, we both drove Lemons back to the city jail and saw that he was placed in the lockup. During the short ride back, Lemons discussed his confession to the point of wondering why he did the things he did, remaining calm and good natured, even soft-spoken. Again, he brought up the subject of a psychiatrist for his problem rather than being jailed. I don't know if he feared imprisonment or not, but his answer was a doctor could help instead. Leaving the jail with Lemons back in lockup, we discussed different aspects of the strangest confessions either of us had ever witnessed; impressed by Lemons' confession and the cool manner in which he had discussed the murders, followed by him seemingly devoid of feelings regarding the dismemberment of the bodies. Lemons was after this unemotional confession considered capable of the crimes he confessed, but to date these acts had not been proven and the grave desecration had not led to additional charges.

The murders would have to be proven and, if so, would brand Lemons as a serial killer, Baltimore's first. If not proven, he would be in need of a psychiatrist as he had insisted. We would find out, investigating the information supplied by Lemons in his statement and at the same time granting him his wish. He would most definitely see a psychiatrist; we would refer him to the state board of psychiatry and see if after their examination he was mentally capable to stand trial if any of his statements proved to be true. If Lemons were found to be competent to stand trial, his acts would lead to criminal charges if they could be proven. Found incapable, he would be held in a mental hospital for treatment.

Lemons, in his lengthy and unemotional approach to his gory confessions, had impressed both of us in regards to his deliberate and nonchalant attitude, and left both of us with more questions than answers. The first and most important question, "Did he really commit the crimes he was confessing? Could he have successfully murdered several women over a period of time and gotten away with it? Obviously, he had issues with his mother over his up bringing; could that had caused the crimes he confessed, or were they just a figment of his tortured mind and he was insane? If he was traumatized by his childhood, was he even emotionally stable? Did he actually cut flesh from their bodies and break their bones with a hammer to get rid of the remains? Or was he a mentally deranged soul and his confessions simply delusional? These and many more questions would undoubtedly have to be answered before the whole truth was known. The fact that the grave desecration had been the first proven aspect of this macabre investigation definitely added credence to our case, but were these murders reality?

While we looked into his information, Lemons was taken from

the jail and committed to Clifton T. Perkins State Hospital, a mental institution, for evaluation to determine his sanity for possible trial. The reported findings were no stranger than the case itself. After two weeks, there was a formal dated report. Examination found Lemons to be border line intelligent, competent and responsible for his actions. It was signed by several attending psychiatrists finding Lemons competent for trial should he be charged. Not the answer either of us expected after dealing with him physically and taking his unemotional statement. But this finding was more than a gift to the prosecuting state attorney should Lemons' case reach that stage. It meant not only could he be charged and held criminally responsible for the crime or crimes he would be charged with if proven but it would facilitate the introduction of Lemons' incriminating statements to the police if substantiated.

The first attempted confirmation of Lemons' confession was taken zealously, but was doomed from the start. The area was canvassed regarding the pickup location and hundreds of area people were questioned as to their knowledge of the victim Cheryl or Sherry by name occupation or description. There were now signs of transitions in the area and with that the possibility that if anyone knew our victim they had left the area. After all, we were talking years, ten reported by Lemons, and trying to establish the identity of a prostitute who may have changed her name frequently. The bars in the area had changed owners, sometimes several times, since the reported murder and as usual we could not get the owners and personnel to admit that prostitution had or ever even existed on the premises of the various establishments. Area and downtown vice squads were notified, with negative results; in the hope our victim could be identified.

Previous area arrests of prostitutes were checked by names and physical descriptions. Some of those fitting the physical descriptions were located and interviewed. They named others they thought were possibilities for the girl we sought, but those leads didn't pan out. Uniformed postal deliverymen were asked, resulting with a few leads that proved to be negative. There was even an area firehouse that was checked; the personnel on all shifts were interviewed for anyone with information. Initially, we thought that some of the firemen frequented the bars in the area when relieved from duty. After several weeks in the field and countless interviews, we had not established the existence of Lemons' prostitute much less found anyone who could identify her or put the two in each other's company. There were several possibilities: she moved her working area for whatever the reason; Cheryl or Sherry was not her normal working name on the street with the majority of her clients; or perhaps the right people were asked and for personal reasons failed to diverge helpful information.

Not too many people wanted to get involved as witnesses for the police. Long gone were the days of cooperation from the general public. Along the way we could have spoken to countless friends, associates or even relatives. Not wanting to be involved with police or their investigations had become the street code. In short, the attempts to find the identity of Lemons' first confessed victim fell short. All we knew about her or the reported murder had stemmed from Lemons' confession of the killing. Nothing was developed to confirm his statements, not enough to charge him, much less convict.

Cheryl or Sherry, if even the correct name for her, like most prostitutes had spent her young existence on the streets seeking money for her survival, drugs, pimps or whatever, and had drifted away, or had been murdered by Lemons like he confessed, and was not missed. She was just another lost soul in an occupation that could often result in such a fate. At the conclusion of our attempts to locate this person, all we could do is hope that she had not met the fate described by Lemons. We never received any investigative information that would substantiate this girl's existence or relate to the Lemons confession. The only thing we did establish was that the area was frequented at the time indicated by prostitutes and that the information we had about Cheryl or Sherry was a possibility.

Anne Story, the second victim, was a different situation. She had a previous arrest record for prostitution under the same name, and in the paperwork her hometown was listed as Williamsburg, Va., naming a female relative with an address in that city. Her arrest record physical description matched the one supplied by Lemons. Apparently, we had the right person. The address given would have placed her in the area

Lemons stated they caught the bus together. Her given address was checked and a tenant remembered her. This address was shared with her indicated boyfriend, who was not on the lease, but frequently was there with her. This information also fit with Lemons telling us he had been told by Story that she had just left her boyfriend. The problem was we had no information to lead us to the man that was her boyfriend; the man she had taken the money from and left on the date she was also killed. We obtained the first name of Bob or Bill and his description. We were unable to place him in a vehicle or its description. With the limited information, he could not be located. Finding him would have substantiated Lemons' information about Anne Story and also given us a witness to establish the theft Lemons had related to us. His testimony, if located, would have placed Lemons with his victim prior to her death.

The trip to Williamsburg took about three and a half hours. We arrived at the address of Mrs. Carolyn Henry on a small, well kept neighborhood street just inside what we were later told were the city limits. The neighborhood was shaded by curbside trees and the area in its appearance was middle class and well-kept. It was an older home and, like most in the area, set on a large lot, large enough not to deal with neighbors if desired and ideal for children to safely play. We were greeted at the door by a well-mannered three or four year-old girl. We told her that we were there to see Mrs. Henry, at which time she turned and yelled, "Mommy, someone is here to see you."

A tall, slender woman, dressed in a light colored housedress appeared carrying an infant boy and greeted us at the door. She showed us to the living room couch, seated herself across from us and identified herself as Carolyn Henry, sister of who we knew as Anne Story. We identified ourselves with our ID cards and badges. She dismissed her daughter, telling her to go and play. The child obeyed and promptly left the room. Henry did not want her child to hear about her aunt.

We started the interview by asking Henry where and when she last saw her sister Anne. She stated, "Years ago in Baltimore. I don't recall the address at the time. I was not familiar with the town, first time there. My husband Ben and I went to visit Anne. He's at work now. At least that's the name she wanted us to call her; she made us promise not to mention her real name, especially to her boyfriend. At the time, she was living with a rather nice man, I don't recall his name."

We asked if the boyfriend could have been Bob or Bill. She thought for a while and said she really did not recall for sure, and his last name was not mentioned. Mrs. Henry continued, "I don't know where we were in Baltimore; it was my first and only time there. I do remember that it was near a train museum; his apartment was within blocks of that museum. It was really a nice place, we just rode by, but you could see this great big round house and lots of train engines and old cars visible from the street."

I immediately thought of the Baltimore and Ohio Train Museum and mentioned the large round house at that location. Henry stated, "Yes, I recall seeing that when we drove around." The train museum was within blocks of Lemons' apartment. We realized that Anne Story had just left her apartment and was waiting for a bus when she met Lemons for the first and last time. Henry said she could not recall the boyfriend's name after trying to recall it since we had asked, but he appeared to really care for Anne. She mentioned that Anne had told both her and her husband that he wanted to marry her, but told them she had "mixed emotions about her own feelings about the matter."

Mrs. Henry looked saddened as she added, "I know she is dead. There are two brothers and another sister, as well as my mother, who are still living and we haven't received a card or letter from her in years. She always sent cards and letters on all occasions and, if alive, she would never miss any of our holidays."

"I received a call from the boyfriend shortly after we returned home from visiting Anne and him. He was furious at the time with her, said he was finished with her, she had ran off and stolen two hundred dollars from him. He stated that when we heard from her he wanted his money back." Her statement corresponded with the information we had concerning Lemons taking two hundred from Story's purse after the murder. In as much as we had not found the boyfriend and had no direction in regards to identifying or finding him, Carolyn Henry could confirm the information about the money if needed in court as a state's witness.

The questions then shifted to Anne Story's background and how she came to live in Baltimore. Henry explained they were for the most part all born in Williamsburg. Anne Story was the middle girl and the boys were both older. Carolyn Henry had three other siblings. Their family name was Stoddard; her name was really Anne Stoddard, not Anne Story. I thought at the time Anne had stuck with the same initials, not necessarily what a real pro in her business would have done. Most prostitutes assumed names far from their own and changed them frequently, something else Anne did not do.

Henry continued to detail her sister's life: "As a child, Anne was a daredevil and seemingly craved excitement. She would do anything. Challenge her and she would try it; heights, swims, foot races with the boys, anything. She met and married Donald Jones within a year of their meeting; she was twenty years old at the time. Donald was also twenty and extremely caring at first, they seemed very happy with one another. They immediately moved to Roanoke, Va., as Don was stationed in Roanoke in the Navy at the time. About a half-year later, he was placed on active duty from his shore job and shipped out. Anne was left alone in an apartment without any friends; she had no children to occupy her time, or any money, dependant on Don's service check only. She was unable to find any work she liked. She was terribly depressed, even with me consoling her through phone calls and letters. The next thing I knew was she was in Bristol, Tennessee. She had gone there on her own before even telling me. She called maybe two weeks after our last phone conversation and advised she had left Don, it was no life for her, and she was now living in Bristol. She was thinking of going from there to Baltimore. I asked her what she was doing for money and she told me she was fine, doing quite well, but would not tell me what she was doing. Knowing what I had learned in Baltimore, I think she was prostituting then. I know from their conversations, the boyfriend and her, that's what she did at one time in Baltimore. The next thing I hear she has moved on from Bristol and was in Baltimore. That's when we visited her."

We asked her when she visited Anne in Baltimore. Henry thought for a moment and answered, "Eight to ten years ago." She gave us the last known address for Donald Jones, Anne's ex, who was still living in Roanoke to the best of her knowledge, had obtained a divorce and remarried and worked at some factory in the area. We advised her that we considered her sister to have been killed in Baltimore around the last time she had heard from the boyfriend about her taking the money; without identifying the suspect other than to say we had one, and not describing her death in detail other than she was reportedly beaten. Carolyn Henry was a small-town girl, not used to the daily routine news concerning killings. She reacted by stating, "I thought she was dead because we never got cards, and that's what usually happens to girls in that profession. That's what you read in the papers and hear on the news."

With that, we bid our farewells, leaving our business cards should she or her family have need for additional contact, or should they have any further information about Anne's boyfriend or the street and address when visiting her sister in Baltimore. We had hope that her husband would remember Anne's boyfriend by name, but the best he was able to do was recall the first name of "Bill" and a description of him when they were introduced that matched the one we had. How many countless Bills or Williams were there in our town? He didn't know what the man did or where he worked. It had been eight to ten years since they were in Baltimore. Nothing that would help us find him was remembered. At least Anne's true identity had been discovered and we had someone to substantiate part of Lemons' confession. We could establish the conversation between Bill and Carolyn Henry about the stolen money, the relationship at the time of their visit between Anne and Bill, and that both Lemons and Henry knew of the money theft by Anne. Both Lemons and Anne lived in the same western part of town and could have met on the local bus line as Lemons had told us. Things were starting to come together, except for Bill, who at the time we had not quite given up on finding. There was still a chance of locating him if we found others that knew both him and Anne, but that possibility was doubtful.

We drove to a motel and stayed over before driving back to Baltimore the next day. While at the motel, we had decided that contact with Donald Jones, Anne's former husband was not necessary. Carolyn Henry had confirmed Lemons' confession about Anne leaving her boyfriend on the same date and him finding the money in her purse afterward. Jones had no investigative knowledge of value; all he could tell us was that Anne had abandoned their marriage Anne's first step, leaving Jones for a different kind of life, was her first mistake, one that would ultimately lead to her death. It probably is a good thing that people can't foretell what their decisions can lead too, small or large, important or not, thought out or quickly decided. Anne Stoddard could have simply adjusted to her new husband and stayed home, where in all probability she would have led a long and fulfilling existence.

On the way home, I relaxed while Jansen drove. I closed my eyes and dismissed the case and the necessary moves we still had to make regarding it, thinking about the B&O Railroad Museum, mentioned as a landmark by Henry during her visit to our town. The B&O Museum, with its large, round house, featured engine turn-table tracks used when the property was known as Mt. Clare Shop, where countless engine repairs were performed. Its forty acre yard and buildings, home of numerous aging engines used by the company in past and present centuries, were always on display for the public.

The Baltimore & Ohio Railroad was once known as America's Railroad, the first regular passenger service in the country. In 1844, the first successfully sent telegraph messages were from Mt. Clare in Baltimore to Washington, D.C. Having been born and raised in Baltimore, I had lost track of the number of times I had visited the museum at 901 W. Pratt Street, but I remember always being impressed with the size, weight and strength of the engines created by man so many years ago. What workmanship and labor must have went into building these wheeled monsters? Yes, like most kids and later on life I liked trains, a common interest held by most males I think, but I am still impressed with the ability and workmanship of railroad workers who created these mammoth engines

A bump in the road jarred me back to reality. My eyes opened and the round house faded as my thoughts turned back to Lemons and the case. We were convinced at this point that Lemons was responsible for the grave desecration and for the murder of Anne Stoddard, aka Anne Story. We had confirmed Lemons' account through the money verification, the two hundred dollars, and would use the sister's knowledge to place Anne and him together. Henry also placed the victim in Baltimore at the time of her death. Therefore, we hoped enough collaborated evidence existed to charge Lemons criminally with Anne's murder. The grave desecration was out of statute and Anne Story's case now had witness testimony linking Lemons to her death. But to date, we had no witness placing them together. Lemons' mother's funeral registration for her viewing had to be checked when we returned to see if it bore the name of Anne Story That would require a warrant to obtain as well as Lemons drawings, but hopefully we had substantiated enough of Lemons' confession to allow a judge to grant one.

At the time, only one case in Baltimore without a Corpus Delicti had ever resulted in a criminal conviction. The term Corpus Delicti referred to the evidence of a crime, such as physical evidence or circumstances of the crime. We had no physical bodies, no victims of the crimes, but were beginning to establish portions of the Lemons' confession. But could enough about his confession be substantiated to bring Lemons to an indictment? The first victim, the female prostitute, was lost completely. Our investigation had failed to establish any information about her at all, not even her existence. Our second victim, Anne Story, actually Anne Stoddard, had been established as living in Baltimore at the time of her death. Her sister, Carolyn Henry, and Lemons knew of the stolen money from her boyfriend, and that link placed her in physical contact with Lemons. Investigative work concerning the named third victim, Jessica Younger, was yet to start and at least had a starting point with Lemons telling us she worked in a local city restaurant chain.

We were faced with the burden of proving in any one of the three murders that Lemons had confessed that there had been a physical victim along with enough evidence tied to that or those murders to convict. What it meant legally was we had to prove Corpus Delicti, a crime must be proven to convict the individual responsible. Related circumstantial evidence beyond reasonable doubt was needed to prove guilt. In these murder cases, even with the confession, we had to first prove that the victim was missing. We believed they had been murdered, and then in regards to the evidentiary aspect of each case, develop physical, demonstrative and testimonial evidence. In this case, our first victim's death if it had occurred could not be proven; no physical body, no witnesses, no evidence that a crime had been committed. No possible way Lemons could be charged and criminally indicted.

Detective Howard Corbin had the only similar case to date. His case developed to the point that he had an active participant in the act of disposing the victim's remains, but ended up without recovering the victim's body. Howard was an old time, outstanding detective. He had talked to everyone around any and all of his cases and over the years had compounded a "nickname" book comparable to none. Just about every unit in the department had sought his help in identifying subjects through the use of those countless nicknames linked to their true identities found in that book. He attended all of the funerals and wakes and won over everyone at them. He made friends with the families and everyone who attended, even if the victims were street drug dealers, those truthfully expected to be victims due to their occupations. Howard would win over the survivors in a respectful tone of voice and a sincere look.

He became involved in his case because of a questionable missing person report. The victim was reported missing by two co-workers and fellow roomies living on Preston Street. Because they reported him missing and also lived and worked with him, both were interviewed. During their interviews, they stated that the missing person had not been seen for about two weeks, saying he left their apartment one night to go to a local bar. All of the three reportedly worked for a contractor, installing sewage drains in Columbia, Maryland, a recently developing area that would become its own community and would later be an established town. One of the subjects appeared nervous and uneasy during his interview and seemed to follow the lead of the other when answering questions, showing Howard the stronger and weaker personalities of the two he was dealing with.

Detective Corbin set up another interview of the person who had appeared to be nervous, this time to be held privately at the homicide office, without the knowledge of the other. At this meeting, the man broke down and confessed to his participation in the crime. The victim and the other man interviewed were drinking at the time, became involved in an argument which lead to fisticuffs, and the victim was stabbed. The interviewee indicated that his only part in the occurrence was to help in the disposal of the body. He stated that it was decided to dispose of the body by placing it inside one of the storm drains in Columbia that they were working on. They waited until late at night, removed the body from the apartment, carrying the victim between them while they walked as if the victim was drunk, placed the body in their car backseat, still pretending he was just another drunk, and drove to the Columbia site where they dumped the body of the victim inside one of the unfinished sewer drains, deep enough inside so that any other workers would not discover him. He advised that was the only thing he did, he had nothing to do with the death.

Another statement was taken; the other worker who was now a suspect in the crime denied the altercation and subsequent killing, and the body was not recovered. Det. Corbin responded to the site as directed by the witness and found nothing. By then, where the body had been dumped was a newly working section of the storm drain system. The heavy rains that had occurred after the reported missing person and prior to Det. Corbin's response could have accounted for the lack of remains. Even in this case with the body missing, Corbin had a witness to the killing who would testify to the murder and the disposal of the body. Although the witness was a co-defendant, he had attested to eyewitness accounts of the victim's death. The victim had not been heard from or located since the date of the occurrence.

To date, we had no witnesses or bodies related to the information we were investigating. We had established that the second victim, Anne Story, lived in Baltimore at the time of her demise and that the theft from the boyfriend had happened, and that Lemons had knowledge of the theft and amount involved; that point would be debated easily by his defense counsel. Based on the argument that, at best, they had met and discussed how she had gotten the money, that didn't mean Lemons had killed her for it or for any other reason. If we had been able to locate the boyfriend, it would have given us a witness who had direct knowledge of the money event. The sister's testimony about the money theft would also be an issue for debate when first mentioned by the witness, but would be accepted when also found in Lemons' confession. Carolyn Henry's best testimony would be that no member of the Stoddard family had any contact with Anne or had heard from her since her confessed killing by Lemons. This information would help to establish that, indeed, Anne had been murdered.

The next day we drove back from Williamsburg, Va. We obtained a warrant for Lemons' mother's funeral registration book and the drawings. These items were soon obtained and submitted into evidence after a lengthy explanation to Ms. Carnes that the seizures of the materials were being done legally. We returned to the office and examined the registry and drawings. Bob checked Lemons' mother's funeral registry and found on the page naming the mother the name "Anne Cocks" instead of Anne Story, also on the lower part of the page was printed the words, "Death of deaths." Lemons had told us he knew her as Anne Story, never mentioning the name Anne Cocks. Had he placed the name Anne Cocks in the book just to protect himself? Another stumbling block when it came to court, if the case would ever get there. All of our information regarding Anne was that Lemons knew her as Anne Story; we had her identified properly as Anne Stoddard, aka Anne Story.

We still wondered if we had enough evidence to actually charge and try Lemons for the Anne Stoddard death that he had confessed. On the other hand, Anne Stoddard's investigation had legs now. If the present investigative information was all we were able to establish, the decision to prosecute would be that of the state's attorney.

After finding a quiet room, we went over the Lemons confession and the notes from Ms. Carnes interview, along with the statement from Mrs. Henry. After we had reconsidered aspects of the case, we decided that two more possibilities existed beyond those we had realized. First, we could see if any city employees working for the sanitation bureau were still employed back at the time of the confessed deaths and had worked the trash removal in the rear of Lemons' apartment. Could we possibly find an employee that would recall Lemons personally depositing trash by hand as he had stated? If so, this person would help to establish that portion of Lemons' statement, when he admitted he placed remains in the trash truck personally to avoid being caught, having wrapped the portions in newspaper and plastic bags. The second person to be located and interviewed was the landlord of Lemons' apartment house. Lemons had told us that during the dismemberment of the victim he had lost one of her teeth under the bathroom tub. He disassembled the tub and recovered the tooth, but could not get the plumbing for the tub back together so it would not leak. He called the landlord for the repair. Surely, if this had occurred, the landlord would have questioned the repair problem in the first place and recalled the incident.

Both of us set about these two possibilities that were directed in firming up Lemons' confession. We worked both aspects together so that either or both could testify to the results. First, we attempted to find the worker for the sanitation bureau that may have knowledge regarding Lemons' actions in regards to trash pickups. Stopping at the area office for the bureau that controlled the trash pickups for Lemons' area, we discovered from an elderly office worker the name of a retired employee still living in the Baltimore community that would have been involved in Lemons' trash collections.

Ed Hartley had retired from the city three years ago and was living off of Reisterstown Road in northwest Baltimore. He was a man in his early sixties, and after our introduction, said he had retired because he had his time in and the work was just too physically demanding at his age. He was asked if he could recall anyone on his route making an issue of depositing the trash themselves in the rear loader of the truck on the route that took in Lemons' apartment, without naming Lemons or his address. His reply after he thought the question over was, "Yes, one seemingly odd little white guy. One time for about two weeks on pickup days he would make sure he placed the trash in the truck himself." Asked where this took place, the time it occurred and what the trash looked like, Hartley gave us the block and the man's description. Both the block and description fit Lemons and his apartment address. Hartley added, "I don't mess with these people, God knows what they threw away, dead dogs, cats, all kinds of pets from monkeys to birds, each other, who knows. I just know to mind my own business. This guy wasn't throwing anything big like a body or something like that; he looked worried enough without me asking what he was doing, and like I said, none of my business." Bob asked, "How was it wrapped, the trash I mean?" Hartley replied, "Just paper and plastic bags, normal trash."

We had found another small caliber witness who could confirm that aspect of Lemons' confession. We showed him an array of photographs and Hartley was unable to identify Lemons, but picked him as a lookalike for the man in question. Probably this identification was better than a positive one defense attorney's would have a field day on a positive identification after all these years even if Lemons was the only one Hartley recalled personally dumping his trash.

Next onto the landlord, who we hoped would recall Lemons having him fix his leaky bathroom tub years ago. After we found out that the landlord lived about a block from the Lemons address, we responded to his home. Ed Christenson owned eleven properties in the area, all of which he had rented for years. He was a veteran of the conflicts that come with renters and the damages they somehow manage to cause. After he had related some of the stories about various damages, he ended his controlled anger with a story about a tenant who had called in the middle of the night complaining her apartment was on fire. After Christenson had asked if she had called the fire department, he did himself, slipped on clothes hurriedly and drove to her address. When he arrived, he ran up the stairs to the third floor and, while exhausted, asked a fireman who was standing there waiting for him about the damages. The fireman smiled and said, "No fire, no damage,steam was coming from the radiator in her bedroom. She thought it was on fire." After we both laughed, Bob added, "I see what you mean." Christenson settled down for what he first thought would be no more than an average problem or complaint, because he was talking with two detectives who had sought him out probably trying to locate some wanted tenant.

He was told about the problem with the Lemons tub leaking years ago and asked if he recalled the matter. Without any thought, he responded, "Oh, yes. Lemon's is one of my better tenants. He's been with me for years. A quiet man, no disturbances, no property destruction problems, pays on time always, wish more were like him. "How about the leaky tub, I asked." "Years ago, responded Christenson, maybe eight years ago, he claimed he had dropped his watch between the tub and the wall and could not get it back, so he unhooked the pipes to the tub to get his watch back. Afterward, he told me he was not able to reconnect them without having it leak. I went up to his apartment and fixed the tub." The pipes for the water run parallel to the wall and took a right angle in front to attach to the tub faucets. He claimed his watch fell from the tub rim onto the pipes attached to the back wall. It could have happened that way. I fixed it; there was no damage from the leaking water to the walls or floor." Bob asked, "Were there any stains or other marks or damage around the tub?" The landlord stated, "None that I noticed." With the information gathered from Mr. Christenson, Lemons' landlord, we had established another portion of his confession as being truthful and had someone to attest to it.

On our way to his front door, Christenson related another tenant situation you boys will understand this one. Because the neighborhood is getting worse, I've told my tenants not to announce me as their landlord when we are on the street and to never pay me on the street where some hoodlum would know I had money. Well, that did not work. I stopped to collect at one of my houses. The tenant was seated on the front steps, jumped up, smiled and openly handed me a roll of money. The roll of money looked like it could choke a horse, the actual rent was not much at all, but the payment was all in one dollar bills rolled up and secured with a rubber band. I automatically looked around to see if anyone had seen the transaction or was about to hit me in the head for it."

Both of us laughed as we walked down Christenson's front steps and headed for our car. As we walked to our car, a streetwalker passed us and muttered, "More cops. Even in dress clothes, you guys always look the part." I smiled as we passed her, and Bob commented, "She is pretty observant, but then in her line of work she has to be."

Now we had reached the point that it was time for us to develop as much information as possible on our third reported victim, Jessica Younger. To date, we had been unsuccessful in our two previous attempts at confirming the murders claimed by Lemons and establishing evidence, although the investigation of Anne Story convinced us we were dealing with a killer. His drawings and his explanations of them, along with the grave desecration confirmation revealed his strange morbid behavior.

Acting on the information that our third victim, Jessica Younger, worked at a restaurant chain near Eastern Avenue and Broadway Street, we responded to that location. While driving there, I recalled a strange case that had happened about a year earlier in the same area.

It was summer and, conforming to Baltimore summers, the temperature was in the high nineties and the humidity was unbearable. Detective Timmons and I had received a call for a suspicious death in a second-floor apartment on Broadway Street, the foot of Broadway within blocks of where the city had been founded, Thames and Broadway. Upon our arrival we found a skeleton covered with a wool army blanket, lying on its back, arms at its side, on the kitchen floor of an abandoned second-floor rear apartment. When the blanket was removed and the skeletal remains were examined, it was noted that there was not an inch of skin left on the body. The maggots had eaten away every fragment of flesh from the remains and deserted the body for the corners of the room. This hot, humid room was full of flies and the floor molding was edged with white fat maggots. The apartment was empty of all furniture and belongings. We assumed it was a skeleton of a male based on the size of the remains. Examination of the skeletal remains revealed no indication of foul play. No evidence of bullet wounds, fractures or chipped or cut bone were found. The cause of death would have to be determined by the medical examiner's autopsy.

We learned during tenant interviews that a man and wife lived there with their mentally handicapped son who was about nineteen years of age. The son had a joyful personality and would run errands for the neighbor, but although he got along fine with the neighbors, he was not as fortunate with his father who often beat him and was known as a drinker with a temper. He was known to beat his son with anything he could get his hands on sometimes even with a stick on the public street and often in the apartment, where they heard the young adult screaming apparently from other beatings during their arguments. We found an eyewitness who had seen the apartment abandoned about three days earlier, he had seen a male and female exit by means of the rear fire escape carrying personal belongings, both loaded down with suitcases and household items. He had witnessed them make several trips up and down the fire escape and in and out of the window, depositing their property in the rear alley until they finished; with one or the other standing guard over their possessions so no one else would steal them, while the other went back for more. The witness thought nothing of it at the time, just someone skipping out on the rent. Another occupant identified them as the former residents of the apartment. An alert was broadcast naming them from information furnished by the owner of the apartments. The alert indicated that both of them were wanted in connection with a questionable death investigation in Baltimore City and was broadcast interstate the next day.

The skeletal remains were transported to the medical examiners to determine cause of death. No indication of a violent death was found when the remains were examined. There were no marks on the skeleton. Unmarked bones were the only source for examination, and a violent cause of death could not be determined. Because of the skeletal condition no organs were intact or even available to determine if poisons or drugs were the cause of death. Therefore, examination at the Medical Examiner's Office failed to determine the cause of death and their findings ruled the death "questionable." They did determine the remains as being that of a young male, about twenty years of age. That meant that the only way criminal charges could be placed in this matter would be if either one of the victim's parents confessed to having caused his death violently when they were interviewed.

The parents fled down the fire escape leaving their dead son wrapped in a blanket on the kitchen floor during a heat wave, were eventually located in North Carolina. They told the local police that their son had died a natural death, denying any current beatings from either of them. They had left their son as found because they did not have the money to bury him. Because both parents kept to their story with the local authorities, and because our State's Attorney's Office deemed that the case could not be successfully prosecuted, we did not respond to the town in North Carolina and interview them. Probably they had agreed on what to tell police before they climbed down the fire escape. They were released from custody in that jurisdiction after we declined further investigation or their prosecution. These people were never charged with a crime related to their son's death. The cause of the son's death was undetermined; eyewitnesses to the contrary were never established. Knowledge of his beating at the hands of his father was insufficient in it self and could not be established as the cause of death. The victim's parents were never brought back on charges related to the death of their son, and the abandonment of his body.

Back to the suspected killer at hand, Lemons indicated that he had dated the woman while she worked at the restaurant and that the manager had admonished them about dating because it was against company policy. We arrived at the restaurant and located the manager in the crowded eatery. He was busy serving customer's, but agreeable to making time for us. He identified himself as Randy Berry and when asked, advised that he had worked there as manager for nine years. When given the name of the former employee we were interested in, he remembered that a girl named Jessica had worked there about eight years ago. He was her manager on the day shift from 7:00 A.M. to 4:00 P.M. Although they had shift managers for all three shifts, she generally worked those hours on the day shift. He said that Jessica had left without warning which came as a surprise at the time to him, because she seemed happy with the job and thoughtful enough to give him notice if she was thinking of leaving. In questioning him, he shared that when she was hired she gave the name of Jessica Younger and an address in an apartment somewhere near Broadway up on Fayette Street, 1001 E. Fayette Street. She was always on time for work and a diligent employee. He added that now that we were inquiring about her, he had never seen her since her unannounced departure. Asked if Jessica had a relationship with Lemons, he explained: "I had forgotten about that. Lemon's was a handyman for the company at the time. He was there to fix things occasionally. He worked all the restaurants. He did small maintenance jobs as required, cleaned areas when needed and took excess trash out to the dumpster. He's long gone now. He often talked to Jessica, who did not seem to be interested in speaking with him. I warned them one time that employees were not supposed to date. Jessica apologized for both of them; it did not become a habit."

The restaurant manager went on: "One afternoon, I do remember he appeared without reason late. He was not working at the time; there was no reason for him to be here except for whatever was going on between him and Jessica. He got her attention through the window. It looked like he was waiting for her. It was near time for her to get off. I didn't say anything to either one." Asked was that near the time he believed she quit, Randy answered, "It was about three weeks or so before the time she left without notice. I figured she got another job. The girls are like that; they seldom give notice. But I thought better of her, she seemed respectable, and as I said she was reliable. Never thought she would leave without notice, didn't take her for that type."

After taking Randy's full name and address, we let him know that a statement would be necessary. We obtained a physical description of Jessica from the manager, as well an older female employee who was still there and had remembered Jessica. We interviewed the co-workers present, hoping to learn more about Jessica and Lemons, with negative results. My partner and I also took the names of present and past employees to be interviewed, and requested the employment application for Younger be made available to us. The manager said he would do his best; the records were old. It later proved that he was right; the records had long been destroyed because of age and storage space. Tim showed him an array of photographs and he successfully identified Melvin Lemons as the former employee who had dated Jessica. Randy dated and signed the photograph. We left him our business cards and told him to contact us with any additional information he or employees who know Younger had. Arrangements were made to obtain a formal statement from him relative to our interview and that statement was obtained later on the same afternoon after his shift ended.

Upon leaving, Bob and I drove three blocks north and located the apartment building, marked 1001 Fayette Street, across Broadway Street from Church Home Hospital. The building was large and we learned later that it contained eight relatively large apartments, with an on-site maintenance man. We rang the doorbell marked "Maintenance" and a heavy-set young male responded, dressed in work clothes. We identified ourselves and asked if he had knowledge of a Jessica Younger renting one of his apartments about eight years ago. The man identified himself as John and stated, "My father owns the building and would have been the here at the time. He would know, he had always kept good records on all our tenants. He is retired and lives in another one of our houses not far from here. I'll call him and see if he recalls her." He called his father, who said he would respond in five minutes. When Carl Creekside arrived, he introduced himself and stated that he had leased a second-floor front apartment to a young girl who identified herself as Jessica Younger. She was about twenty years old at the time, maybe nineteen. Younger lived in the apartment, which was fully furnished at the time, for about three months. It was a good deal for her at the time, young and just starting out. Creekside explained: "I remember her telling me she was from another state and had lost her parents, one, her father in a work accident when she was small, her mother later died of cancer. She was a pretty thing, wise beyond her years. She said an aunt had raised her until she graduated from school. I was leery because of her age that she might be a runaway, but she seemed so honest and straightforward that I took her at her word."

Bob asked, "Did she have any friends, male friends while she lived here?" Creekside responded, "Yes, I thought it strange because her male friend appeared to be about fifteen to twenty years older than she was." "Did you ever catch his name?" asked Tim. The former maintenance man stated he had not, nor did she ever mention the name. Creekside replied, "The few times that I saw him, the guy was quiet, almost antisocial toward me." In harmony, both Bob and I asked, "Can you describe him?" Our interview subject answered, "Like I told you, he was an older man, quiet, about 5'6" or 5'7," slender build, white."

Bob and I had just come from the restaurant manager's positive identification of Lemons. We had developed the array during their initial search for the first victim, the black prostitute. We handed the photo array to Creekside and asked, "Can you identify any of these men as the man you saw with Jessica Younger when she lived here?" Creekside said, "It's been a while," reaching for the pictures. He took his time and studied each of the six photographs. He stopped on number four and said, "This may be him; I'm not sure. This is the man I think. It's been so long. He had a gaunt look about him like this guy."

It was the photograph of Melvin Lemons. We had Creekside sign and date the back of the picture for identification purposes and thanked him. This identification at least placed the two Lemons and Younger together, as had the information from Randy Berry, the restaurant manager. "Is there anything else you can think of regarding Jessica?" asked Bob. Creekside thought for a minute and said, "She left without notice, only a few days into her monthly rent. She was such a nice kid I never thought she would do that, especially being paid up to the end of the month. It was in July or August I think. I know it was hot. She even left jewelry and clothes behind. Just starting out on her own, she didn't have much. I'll check my records and be able to tell you for sure."

I asked did he know anything about Jessica besides her involvement with an older man. The former maintenance man replied, "She had mentioned to me that she graduated school in Baltimore County and that she worked at the restaurant at Broadway and Eastern. That's all I know about her; she kept to herself. She was an attractive person. I only saw her maybe ten times once she moved in. After she left, I stopped in where she was working and asked one of the waitresses about her. I was told that she had left there suddenly also, without any forwarding information." Carl Creekside would make a good witness if Lemons was tried, arrangements for his statement was made.

Between the two interviews and subsequent statements, we had developed the following information that corresponded with Lemons' confession: Jessica Younger, perhaps an alias, was a real person. She worked at the east side restaurant and lived blocks away in an apartment when she was employed there. Both Berry and Creekside confirmed that information. Berry established Jessica and Lemons as having a relationship. Creekside placed them together at her apartment house.

Younger disappeared suddenly, leaving her apartment before the rent is due, leaving clothing and jewelry behind, and just as suddenly leaving her job without notice.

Randy Berry and Carl Creekside had confirmed that Jessica Younger had existed, but a search to establish her identity using the name had failed. At least she was not known by that name in any of the Baltimore County school systems for those graduates from 10 to six years ago. The search was extensive. Baltimore County surrounds Baltimore City except on the south side and includes a massive area. There wasn't a Jessica with the last name Younger or a Younger surname found on the rolls whose school photographs could be identified by either Berry or Creekside as that of the person they both knew as Jessica Younger.

Again, another curveball had been thrown at us. What was the reason for this young, outgoing girl to use an alias with her first employee and landlord? Was it trouble with the parents? Was she a runaway, an undesirable boyfriend she was hiding from, her social habits, alcohol or narcotics? No, she always appeared stable and reliable. A desire to be out on her own, a pregnancy, or some other reason, who knew? We knew certain things: we may not ever know the reason she used an alias, never know her real name, but we had two witnesses that not only put her in company with Lemons but also established that a girl known to them as Jessica Younger did exist at the time, and we had Lemons confessing he had killed her.

Additional investigation failed to link Lemons to Younger further. That's what we had. Having information that she may have gone to school in Baltimore County and the approximate date of her graduation, even teachers in the classrooms around the time of her proposed graduation were interviewed. It did amaze me how many dropouts we found from what were considered good schools in good neighborhoods. It made you realize what a problem that situation really was, even in the 1970's.

The missing persons report was checked for people fitting her description and similar names. An article was even placed in "The Sun" newspaper describing her, with the address of her last known workplace and known residential address, as well as asking any parent of a missing girl fitting the description to step forward. None of these methods worked. We were left with the two witnesses we had found, who put our suspect and the victim together, and no further direction regarding the development of any additional information on their relationship or Jessica's true identity was found.

State's Attorney Chuck Lamasa had taken an interest in the Lemons case from the beginning because it was so bizarre, and when Lemons was not held by the state hospital and considered mentally insane, his interest grew. He realized that not only the case was oddly different but also that a trail would be a sensation in regards to the media. A gruesome serial murderer tried and convicted, although the full aspect of the case would not be known because he would not be allowed to link the information about the other deaths, Story and the prostitute Sherry or Cherry, to his case, He was convinced that Lemons was in truth a serial murderer and some leak would announce the fact to the media.

Chuck was the best prosecutor in the State's Attorney's Office at the time. He was tall, dark, handsome and most of all bright and fearless, and a aggressive prosecutor. Lamasa and I got along well having a lot of previous cases reach successful conclusions. Because of this success and being able to work well together, I would seek Lamasa out to handle most of my cases.

A trip to the State's Attorney's Office was required and an appointment time was made with Lamasa. The State's Attorney's Office was located in the criminal court building located at 200 N. Calvert Street. It was a four-story, gray stone building, which encompassed one square city block, located three blocks west of the police headquarters. Actually, before the old police headquarters building was built and opened around 1920, the courthouse served also as the headquarters. The building directly across from this building, the old Central U.S. Post Office building was also now part of the courthouse complex. It held additional courtrooms, added when that central post office and The Postal Inspector's moved to their new building further east on Fayette Street.

I recalled when I was a rookie officer in the Central District that I was detailed to the former main Post Office Building for a civil rights demonstration back in the early 1960's protesters had handcuffed themselves on the iron entrance step railings located on the Calvert Street side of the building. Uniformed police were called and swore an oath to the government of the United States in order to have arrest powers on government property. It came to that, and several demonstrators were arrested. I sometimes thought of that incident and wondered, since I was sworn that day and not notified other wise. Was I still technically a sworn government police officer to this day?

With the appointment scheduled, Bob and I walked up Fayette Street to the State's Attorney's Office to see Chuck and discuss the Lemons case. Arriving at his office, both Bob and I were greeted warmly by Charles "Chuck" Lamasa. It was Bob's first meeting with Chuck in as much as he was new to our unit. We told him in detail of our investigative findings in regards to all the information we had gathered on Melvin Lemons: first, his confessions in the presence of both of us implicating him in the murders of three people at various times; the grave desecration, which was discovered after the statute had ran out prior to the confession about the three murders; and the children's assaults, one leading to his arrest initially which started the entire investigation.

Our complete investigations on all three believed victims, the prostitute known as Sherry or Cheryl and those identified as Anne Stoddard and Jessica Younger were discussed in detail and scrutinized with questions and answers about the three, in order to establish if a successful criminal indictment was possible in their individual cases or on any. By the time of this conference we were sure all the investigative possibilities had been addressed.

After we had thoroughly discussed Younger, Lamasa stated, "Better, it would play better. Her alias would be argued over, but the two named witnesses, the restaurant manager and the apartment manager, will attest to her being an actual person and in company with Lemons at times." Lamasa leaned back in his chair and said, "A hard sell to a jury but one interesting enough to try and peddle, along with his confession." Chuck asked for time to read the reports and advised he would get back to us with his answer. Did they have enough to charge and, as far as he was concerned, again falling into that political web, successfully prosecute Mr. Lemons? Wins were everything, and one loss could destroy a disproportionate amount of a prosecutor's reputation. Chuck, who was now pressed for his next court appearance, left us seated in his office by saying, "I'd love to get this guy. I'm sure he did these things, and if freed would do more."

Lamasa called almost a week later and advised that we should charge Lemons with the murder of Jessica Younger. He advised that he would establish her as a Jane Doe and prove her existence through the two witnesses, as well as her involvement with Lemons, before her sudden disappearance. Lamasa stated that perhaps information could be turned around on some of the defense witnesses to allow additional information to be accepted into testimony. Lemons' family would definitely attest to his strange acts in assaulting the children, if he could get it all into testimony. He stated that since we had established the victim's name to be an alias, we should charge on a Jane Doe warrant. Another matter to argue to the court for him, but he would. We would have to discuss our efforts to find out her real name, and he would present the names of the witnesses who knew her as Jessica Younger to the court in the explanation.

The prosecutor explained, "You have a lot on the Story aspect of the case, but no eyewitnesses to put her with Lemons together, that case would be difficult to prove. The stolen money is good, but the defense could have many explanations for Lemons knowing the amount. She could have even bragged about it on the bus to him. You know whatever excuse for him knowing about it would be presented by the defense. In between time, interview Lemons again to see if he gives us anything more." After the phone conversation with Chuck, Bob turned to me and said, "Lamasa was just on the line. He said it's a go for Jessica Younger, he would take the case."

On a moderately warm day, Bob and I drove to the city jail, took charge of Melvin Lemons again and started our drive back to headquarters. Lemon's was less talkative than usual during the ride and appeared rather quiet and moody. Bob asked jokingly what was wrong, was he tired of prison life?" Lemons responded, "I thought you were on my side of this; I thought you would see I got a doctor? I told you that's what I needed, not jail." I was glad he had responded in the manner in which he did. Now I knew what was bothering him, and if we didn't answer the question, it could hinder our efforts of obtaining additional information from him.

Unless we told Lemons the reason he was in jail and not with a doctor, there would be no reason to interview him. He would not be cooperative. He was upset because in his mind we had not kept our promise. If we did not explain the situation to him satisfactorily, we could turn around now and put him back in lockup. In his mind, we had failed him and were not to be trusted, much less talked to. Unless we reassured him we felt he needed a doctor and we had not failed him, Lemons would shut down and not cooperate further. Why should he tell them anything when they had reneged on their promise?

Both Bob and I started to explain that all we could have done was referred him to a doctor, which we had done as soon as possible, that was why he was at the state hospital. In as much as they had released him back to jail custody, the doctors had decided that he did not require their treatment. Neither of us had any control over that decision. Lemons said he understood and apologized for blaming us, saying he was confused, and even though they had not kept him for further treatment, he wasn't lying; he needed the treatment. He actually yelled out, "I told everyone I needed help from the doctors. I don't know why I do these things. I like women, I do, why won't they believe me? jail would just keep me away from them, the women I mean." Gradually, he calmed down and seemed to ease up rather quickly. Shortly afterward, in a calm, normal voice, he leaned back in the rear seat next to Bob and started talking casually about the weather and looking about, taking in the sights during the rest of the trip as if his angry tirade had not just happened. I continued driving to our office.

Upon our arrival at headquarters, we reassured him that we had nothing to do with the decision made not to keep him in treatment. The doctors had made that finding. Lemons nodded as if he understood and turned to Bob and said, "You guys treat me good, you're alright. I know you try and help me." Bob advised him once again of his rights.

Once again, in one of the two interview rooms, we started our questioning. It was our hope to develop more information on all of his victims and to get him to discuss his motives behind his actions. Lemons appeared much more relaxed and asked, "What more do you want to know?" We told him that we were not charging him in the grave desecration although proven, thinking that would loosen him up for the coming questioning. His reply was, "I don't know why I did that. I just had the feeling I wanted to lie with dead women, you know, just to know how it feels."

Bob and I had moments when his responses truly amazed us; the things he did and talked about so casually. He did seem relieved, and replied, "I like to lie with women; I guess I answered my own question, that's why I did it. I think women have so much power over men. We do whatever they want they always control and plot against us men. My mother was like that, that was the first time I saw how they could be."

My partner pursued this topic further, "You have not told us much about your family life. Tell us about you growing up." Lemons hesitated and said: "I was an only child in a rather poor situation. My father was gone time I was ten years old and my mother and I lived alone in a rather rundown home on the outskirts of a small town in Illinois. It was so far out of town, it was like a farming community. It was isolated from the town, the town was miles away and I didn't have others my own age to play with, few friends my age, nobody really. My mother worked in a factory about twenty minutes away on shift work and drank when she was off. I think now her drinking was to forget about us being poor. After my father left us, I don't know why he did, mother started to date different men from work and from town. She started going to a bar in town when she was not working, leaving me alone to fend for myself with no friends and nothing much to do."

Lemons suddenly stopped talking as if he didn't want to speak further about his youth, appearing agitated and slightly tearful. We both noted his changed attitude and both continued with other questions changing the subject. It was evident that something about his youth was more than uncomfortable just by the way he had shut down and by his facial and body reactions once he had stopped. Bob stated, "We all came from small or large poor families, and our parents all loved us.

They did the best they could. Times were hard; money and work were both hard to come by. Back in those days, women were lucky to find jobs at anything, and she did provide, she probably did the very best that she could." These statements took Lemons back to the childhood discretions. Lemons looked disgustedly at Bob and replied, "Not her, she did things that I can never forget or forgive." We were getting to him about his hard childhood and he was closer to telling us the truth.

After his statement, he appeared to be in thought, still disturbed by whatever he was thinking. He continued: "All right, I've told you everything else. You know what I have done to those women, I might as well tell you why. I told the doctors, and if you asked them, they would tell you. Since you don't know, I thought telling the doctors, they would help me, know that I needed help. My mother did things with me that mothers are not supposed to do." "What kind of things?" we blurted out, knowing Lemons was going to talk about it. He proceeded "She made me sleep with her. She took me to bed with her when I was only twelve years old, and mother told me she was lonely and that it was all right because she was my mother. She showed me what she liked sexually and for years we slept together once or twice a week. She was usually high on drugs or alcohol when she insisted that I did whatever she wanted because she was my mother, and I did. Once in a while, she would bring different men home from wherever and tell them it was all right for me to sleep with them both because I knew them now. Some of these men were as drunken and abusive as my mother was; anything they wanted to do physically was all right with her. Others did not believe her when she told them, then she would just laugh and drop the issue; others would include me. That's why I told you women get what they want. She got anything she wanted from those men and from me. I knew at an early age that what she did was wrong. She not only did what she wanted but she embarrassed and demeaned me in front of the men. She used me sexually and gave me to strangers for whatever they wanted to do. It took me a long time to have a woman in the natural way.

"Sex was not taught to me in the right way. I had mixed emotions when she died. I loved her because she was my mother and hated her for what she did to me. Part of me was glad that she died. When I was little, I thought about killing her for the things she made me do, but then who would have taken me in? That's why I say women get anything they want; they use men just because they can. Why would anybody do the things she did to me, her own son? They are so beautiful and yet they do not respect other humans. Women, all of them, use and humiliate men that's all they are good for. Mother taught me about all women; they are pretty, but they are all devils. Most of them get what they deserve, and I see that they do."

We had just heard what had amounted to a rant on the part of Melvin, and what explained his reasoning for his deep hatred of females and the killing of three. His own mother sexually abused him; she allowed and watched others sexually abuse her son. I wondered if Lemons had discussed these acts with the doctors. Why hadn't they accepted the acts as having impacted on Lemons' psyche and the cause for his state of mind? Had those acts with his mother so disturbed Lemons that he had become a predator of womankind and taken it upon himself to rid the world of those females he thought wronged him? This new information left me thinking, was he right, what he needed was mental and emotional help? Or was he so criminally insane that the doctors at Clifton T. Perkins thought the solution was through incarceration?

With these questions still lingering, three of the four doctors who had evaluated Lemons were contacted later by phone all three doctors insisted that he be criminally charged should the investigation warrant it. They felt him quite capable of the reported murders and would testify that his mother's previously reported influence and sexual conduct with him were contributing causes, but that he was sane and fully aware of his actions, and their ramifications.

After two interviews of Lemons, Bob and I felt that he was disturbed emotionally and was more than eligible for treatment at the state hospital, but the call had been made. It was out of our hands. He had been evaluated and sent back for criminal prosecution as far as the state was concerned; leaving the police with no other alternative, now it was up to the criminal process. They had hit on the psychological causes for

Lemons' killing spree, why he disliked women, why he probably hated them, and why he killed randomly with no apparent remorse. But for whatever reasoning, it was not enough for the professionals who had evaluated him to find him insane or incompetent to stand trial.

After Lemons' denouncement of his mother, we told him that we were going to discuss the three victims he had previously told us about and he agreed. Ninety percent of the information regarding the deaths of the subjects was the same, although information was obtained on Jessica Younger.

Bob asked, "How about the girlfriend you worked with?," and that started Lemons. "Jessica, Jessica Younger?" She will be the hardest to link to me out of all of them," replied Melvin. Then, he told us: "No one ever knew her real name. She was a runaway and never told anyone her correct name. I knew her as Jessica, Jessica Younger. Neither one was really her name. She had run away because she was abused and disliked being forced to go to school. . I started with her by talking to her when I had repair work or jobs at her restaurant. I was a general handyman for the company. Well, mainly cleaning up at the restaurants, like taking out the trash and doing the floors, some repair work that I could handle. Anyway, I was attracted to her. She was very pretty and smiled when I spoke with her and I thought she was different. When she mentioned that she had been mistreated by her parents, I felt we had that in common. Anyway, we hit it off. We saw each other three or four times before she turned out to be just like the others.

"After about a month, I asked her to move in with me. I was alone at the time. She stated that we were just friends, I was too old to go steady with, and she was too young to consider settling down. She told me our relation was just something for her to do, something to do just to occupy her time. I cared for her and she thought I was a joke. I had thought about marrying this one; here she was, just another bitch out for herself. She even said that she wanted more than an older handyman out of her life. Like the others, Jessica did not know who she was playing with. I gave her a chance. I told her I was sincere in my offer and that I really cared for her, that I thought I loved her. She grinned and asked if she had ever given me any reason. She laughed when I said I cared.

Maybe seven or eight days later we went out drinking together at a downtown bar where I had met her when she got off. Afterward, I took Jessica back to my place for the first time and killed her. I was so mad at her for treating me the way she had that I just got the club out when she wasn't looking and began hitting her until she fell dead."

We asked for a physical description of Jessica. Lemons replied and the description fit that previously obtained from the management and employees of the restaurant and the landlord from her apartment; it agreed in detail down to the cute figure and the dirty blond hair.

I asked if he had ever been to her apartment. He hesitated and then replied, "One, two times I think, but I don't know the address." Didn't he realize we had already attempted to obtain her address from the restaurant manager, whose name was not mentioned? But he never commented about it. Perhaps he hadn't thought about that, or maybe didn't even remember it. He never mentioned that he had met the landlord. When he was asked if he had, he could not remember. We didn't necessarily want him to know he had been identified there with Jessica, so that fact was not mentioned.

From the information given by Lemons about Jessica's past, and the limited knowledge obtained from Randy Berry, the restaurant manager, and the apartment landlord, we realized that in truth our third victim, Jessica Younger, may well be formally identified as Jane Doe, when presented in court if the judge presiding accepted the information they had developed. Her true identity might not ever be known.

Next, Lemons was asked about his drawings and his mother's death registry. He explained the drawings by saying, "They explain themselves, that's what I did to them. I drew them because I wanted to show them as they really are: dismembered, nude, embarrassed, tortured and humiliated. All the things they do to me and other men." "And the nude male in these drawings represents you?" asked Bob. "Yes," Melvin quickly replied, "I told you I did those things. That's me with the knife, and in one I have the club. The club that was the thing I used to get even for all the disrespect those women gave me. Damn them all! They are all alike. I showed those three. I tricked them into being with me and I showed them I was one to be reckoned with."

After the interview, Lemons was returned to the city jail. He remained social and in a good mood, stating he was satisfied that he had told us everything, which brought him some amount of relief. After this second interview, we were now convinced that the quiet, small, soft-spoken, unassuming person that Lemons presented physically was indeed capable of the acts he had admitted; and although the doctors had not ruled that it affected him, the sexual abuse he had suffered at the hands of his depraved mother had created the person he was.

The second interview did result in more information that could be used .Lemons had added his reasoning behind the death of Jessica and established that the name she used was not her true identity, explaining why we had not able to establish her true identity. Who knows how many lies she had told to conceal her identity along the way? More than likely, everything she mentioned about her self were falsehoods and helpful in her deceit.

We found ourselves for the second time seated in the office of Charles Lamasa, after our two-block walk from headquarters. Parking was always a problem anywhere in the downtown area, so walking was the answer. Bob and I were slightly early for another scheduled meeting with the prosecutor regarding Lemons.

The office was on the fourth floor, about fifteen by fifteen feet in size, with two chairs in front of a cluttered desk stacked with paperwork. A half-oval glass window, the only one, was located behind the desk and ran from floor to ceiling, taking up most of the wall. Apparently, the office had been sized down at some point and the window preceded the remodeling and was left original. Because the window was not normal height, looking out of it from a seated position gave you the sensation that you would fall onto Fayette Street. Concrete pillars stood on both sides of the window and the exterior of the building design prevented a view. The organized, functionally arranged offices with well-placed law books, viewed on such television shows as "Law and Order," did not exist in the real world of prosecution. As in most large cities with old courthouses, inadequate space, old furnishings and budget restrictions hampered the professional appearance of a law office. The case volume was another problem that leads to unbelievable situations.

Frequently, prosecutors would catch murder cases on a Friday, go to trial on the following Monday, and ask for a quick summary of the different witnesses' information from the detectives sequestered outside the courtroom on the case seconds before the witness would testify. Typical questions were "Who is this? What are they testifying about?"

Chuck bust into the room, walking quickly, and said his hellos at the same pace, with his back turned as he walked around his desk to be seated. We had an hour appointment, which in its self was rare. Seldom did a prosecutor have the luxury of sixty minutes to interview those with information on a case. Chuck would probably be before a judge on some other case in an hour, still weighing this conversation. The two of us took turns interjecting the new information gained from Lemons' second interview about Jessica including the information that Lemons had given about his childhood and mother. Lamasa thought that the information was important in establishing Lemons' mind set, and that he would have to be cautious in the way it was presented to the jury, so as not have them thinking it was a defense for Melvin. Although he felt that Lemons' lack of acceptance to the state mental facility would offset that concept through the examination of the psychiatrist's.

Just prior to running out, Chuck asked, "Is Melvin Lemons capable of the Jane Doe murder, and standing trial for it?" We both agreed the witnesses could establish them together as a couple, and we had Lemons' confessions to her murder. The statements from witnesses and his drawings supporting the means of disposing of the body all made the case makeable. Chuck said, "Let's go with it. See that he is charged in her death and I'll see you two in court with Jane Doe, aka Jessica Younger. If anything else comes to light, let me know."

Roughly two months later, Lemons' murder case went to trial in Part 8 of the city's criminal court on June 25, 1980. The large courtroom was typical of the period in which it had been built. It had twenty-foot ceilings, thick tapestry at the windows running floor to ceiling, with ornate columns and inlayed mahogany wood walls and benches. Chairs and tables were heavy, dark, oak wood, and the judge's bench and surroundings a light gray marble.

Antique paintings of Baltimore's founders and former governors hung on the wall on each side of the judge's bench. The flags of the United States and the Maryland State flag were displayed prominently behind the judge's bench on both sides of his centered, leather, high-back chair; the Maryland multicolored, black, yellow flag stood to the judge's left-hand side against the wall, and the stars and stripes to his right.

The tables for the prosecutor and that of the defense counsel were in front and parallel to the bench. A center aisle that separated the two legal tables with their chairs split the large room. Long benches on each side ran from behind the counsels' tables in parallel rows toward the rear of the room for the use of the general public and witnesses if they had not been sequestered. The wooden benches for the public always reminded me of pews found in churches, and may have been at one time, or copied from their construction.

Shortly after the proceedings started, we were advised all witnesses in the case would be sequestered, meaning that anyone who would be called to testify as a witness in the case could not be physically in the courtroom during any other testimony dealing with the trial. Both Jansen and I testified in pretrial motions. After my pretrial testimony, I found myself seated outside of the courtroom's double closed doors with Ms. Helen Carnes. Although it would be more than a day of testimony before she would take the stand, her steadfast loyalty toward Lemons with what information she probably had withheld from us convinced me that she truly loved him, a living example of the saying love is blind. I thought back about asking Lemons if he would have killed her, and he had to think about the answer for a while before responding. She had no idea that her nearby family was her buffer from her man and what he really felt about women. Family love and closeness has always been important and a mainstay over generations, but in this circumstance to Lemons it meant only that if anything suspicious ever happened to Helen Carnes, like a sudden disappearance, her family would know immediately and name him a suspect. He would not even have enough time to dispose of her body.

There was a strange aspect to this situation. Normally, the wife, or in this case the girlfriend of the accused, and the supporting witnesses of the accused found themselves seated away from the state's witnesses and the police involved in the case. We definitely represented the bad guys to them. Each day of the trial, Ms. Carnes seemingly sought either Bob or myself out; sat near or at least on the same bench and even made attempts at small talk, never commenting about the ongoing trial. She was in a hard place. Carnes wanted to support her man, but because of the two separate assaults on two of her grandchildren at the hands of Melvin, and now him being on trial for this, family ties were strained, even visually. Not one member of her large family testified on behalf of Lemons during the lengthy trial, or from what I understand none of them were named as witnesses on the defense attorney's list.

The fact that the victim was known at the time of this case by an alias was explained to the jury and they appeared receptive. The jurist makeup was seven white and five black, with men nine out of the twelve with one alternate, a female. Bob and I probably averaged two or three hours each for two days testifying to separate aspects of the investigation, as well as on Lemons' confessions and the recovery of the death registry and the drawings. That death registry was going to be used to introduce into the trial Lemons' mother's actions and influence over him, if Lemons himself took the stand and could be opened up to that line of questioning. The witnesses sat outside of the courtroom doors in the marble-walled hallway on what resembled the same type of church pews, waiting their various turns to testify.

The trial lasted five days. Aside from our testimony, others who took the stand included Jessica Younger's apartment and restaurant managers, the owner of Lemons' apartment house, a seventeen year employee of the Bureau of Sanitation, and Ms. Carnes, Lemons' live-in girlfriend. She unwillingly testified under oath to all that she had told us during her interview that was admissible. After her damning testimony for the state, she stepped off the witness stand, walked to Lemons' side at the defense table and kissed him on the cheek, turned to the jury and said, "Who would believe such a nice man could do those things?"

This courtroom experience was as every bit as bazaar as the investigation had been. At one point, Assistant States' Attorney Mark Cohen, who assisted Lamasa, came out of the courtroom and announced that Lemons was seated quietly, his facial appearance typically indifferent throughout the proceedings, but was busy drawing a sketch of him. Ms. Carnes, who was seated there at the time, looked up with a mournful look on her face and commented, "That's not a good sign; he must not like you." Cohen gave a quizzical yet concerned look, forced a smile and said, "Look out for me, guys. Her boyfriend is strange."

At the conclusion of the trial, Melvin Lemons was found guilty of the murder of Jessica Younger alias "Jane Doe" and sentenced to life imprisonment before Judge Hammerman. The defense attorney, D. Eton, thought he had grounds for an appeal and stated one would be filed. We had not witnessed any of the remaining trial after our testimony, but Lamasa had put Lemons and the victim together with the witness testimony and convinced the jury. Evidently, Ms. Carnes in her anxious attempt to help her man had divulged too much information about him during her testimony. Lemons walked from the courtroom, looked at me and asked, "What if it's all my imagination? What if I didn't do these things?" I replied, "You know you did this and the others." Lemons grinned and said, "Yes, I know."

Baltimore's first serial killer had been convicted and had convinced everyone involved of his heinous intentions and brutal acts upon unsuspecting females. The story of the investigation and subsequent conviction went national in "True Detective" and "Master Detective," magazines.

Months after the trial, my family and I went to the movies to see "The Shining," starring Jack Nicolson. Nicholson played a caretaker at a large resort closed for the winter, located in an isolated area. Along with his wife and children, he was charged with the maintenance of the property. Gradually, the solitude of the work and the isolated location played on their relationships and his mind. Jack's character withdrew and gradually went mad. He attacked the other family members with an axe after seeing what he thought was his likeness in one of the ballroom photographs, which dated back to the 1920's. The character froze to death lost in a large maze that fronted the property.

Leaving the theater with my family afterward, I thought about the movie I had just seen and realized it was not nearly as scary as the real-life investigation of Melvin Lemons, the bludgeoned killings, followed by bodies being dismembered and their parts discarded in garbage trucks and dumpsters. Lemons him self was an insignificant person yet capable of premeditated, heinous murders involving multiple victims Those acts were captured in his drawings of nudity and sex so that he would be able to control his desires, all the while seeking out new victims.

The Shoe Salesman

Seated in the homicide office, Det. Howard Corbin and I waited for any calls that would put us on the street responding to a serious assault or worse. Det. Timmons was on leave. After being hours into our shift and working independently on various reports from other cases, the phone rang. Howard answered, speaking briefly and replying in an understanding manner. He hung up and turned to me, "We've got one, it's a dead body not far from the office; let's go."

We drove to the 100 block of Montgomery Street, located just one block parallel to the Inner Harbor on the south side. It was less than a mile from the headquarters building, an area known as Federal Hill. Montgomery Street was located in an upper middle-class neighborhood. Expensive renovated townhouses occupied by educated, sophisticated people with expensive cars parked in front. Those with houses on the north side had added decks on the upper floors and roofs of their homes to provide rooftop views of the inner harbor and downtown. Normally, this was a quiet neighborhood as far as crime activity; the only relatively frequent crimes being burglary and larceny from homes and cars because of the expensive trappings that attracted intruders from the less affluent areas that surrounded them.

Montgomery Street was an east-and-west street that ended at the foot of Federal Hill, intersecting with Battery Avenue. Long forgotten is the memory of a force of one thousand Union Troops who had erected a small fort and pointed cannons toward the heart of the downtown business district in the hopes it would guarantee the allegiance of Baltimore and Maryland citizenry after the Baltimore Riot in 1861 at the beginning of the Civil War. Now known as Federal Hill this hilltop flies a large American flag. Workers send their peaceful lunch hours under the flag's shadow looking down at the angelic view of the inner harbor during the summer months. A place where people can enjoy the weather and overlook the marina, pavilion restaurants and the surrounding promenade, as well as enjoy the city skyline to the north of the Patapsco River Basin.

Just over a mile southeast is Fort McHenry. In the War of 1812, the British sailed into the harbor of Baltimore and attacked the fort. A young lawyer by the name of Francis Scott Key stood on the deck of the British flagship and penned a poem in 1814 that later became our national anthem in March of 1931, "The Star Spangled Banner." Seeing the flag still waving at dawn's light after the bombardment inspired Key. Baltimore was, indeed, rich in history, both local and national, but as I thought back on those events it also crossed my mind that we lived in an increasingly violent community. In the history books, we had rallied against enemies, but now it seemed more so against ourselves.

It was about 9:30 p.m. when we arrived at the scene and the only foot traffic noted was that of the policemen milling about, with emergency lights flashing from several of their marked cars. I thought to myself that in this neighborhood only those in the process of coming home to one of these townhouses would be on the street at any hour after dark. This would reduce the possibility of witnesses. Not like some of the neighborhoods they were called to where the police had to keep the crowds of interested bystanders away from the crime scenes or they would destroy the evidence no matter what time of the day or night. We entered one of the well-kept row dwellings directed by a uniformed officer and met a waiting uniformed lieutenant just inside. The lieutenant without asking provided the following information. The victim was found as a result of one of the neighbors seeing the front door ajar when they came to visit. After calling aloud for the resident, the neighbor entered the home and found the victim lying in the kitchen. Since this woman was a witness now, her name and address was gathered.

The victim from what the witness had told the police was a quiet man in his forties who had lived there for three or more years. His name was Robert Easy. The light in the kitchen was the only light on the first floor that she found on, and upon going into the kitchen area she found Easy on the floor dead. The lieutenant was also informed that the victim lived with a man by the name of Lee Crispy since moving in. Crispy was not to be found nor his whereabouts known at the time.

Robert Easy was laying face down, clothed in multicolored pajamas, matching top and bottoms, and a dark blue bathrobe. A kitchen knife protruded from one of his back wounds. This knife matched a set of knives found in an open cabinet drawer. Utensils from the same open drawer were strewn about the floor. A weapon of opportunity, meaning the killer did not bring the weapon into the house with him and probably grabbed it during the assault on Easy. The weapon of opportunity meant that it was possible that physical harm to the victim was not previously intended. Mr. Easy had suffered multiple stab wounds to his chest and back. Examination revealed defense wounds to both hands as well as to his right wrist and lower forearm. The victim had also suffered facial injuries most likely caused in a fistfight. His right-hand knuckles were bruised and cut. The wounds on his face, hands and body looked to have occurred during his struggle.

Easy was still wearing one bedroom slipper on his right foot. The other was located in the second floor bedroom, inches from the bed. Upon examination of the entire home, it was determined from the disarray that the assault had started in the second-floor bedroom and ended in the kitchen, where the victim had been fatally stabbed. What appeared to be blood smears from a right-handed person and blood droplets were found on a back wall and on the steps in the second-floor area down towards the kitchen. Those stairs were accessible from either the second-floor hall just outside the bedroom or from the kitchen. Items were found scattered around the floor of both rooms, indicating that there had been an altercation prior to the victim's demise.

In the bedroom, the closet was found open and several shoeboxes were open and strung about the floor of the closet and into the room. The dressing and night tables did not contain watches or rings.

Without prior knowledge of what jewelry Easy had, it was impossible to determine if any personal belongings had been taken. Examination of his hands substantiated the prolonged struggle and act of self-defense, when cuts were noted on both of his hands and forearms, as well as the conditions of both the kitchen and bedroom. The scene was processed at our request and direction, with attempts made to develop fingerprints from disturbed items in both rooms, including the overall area as well as the doorknobs in the various rooms. A search of the neighborhood and questioning of residents was conducted with negative results; no one had heard the noise caused by the apparent altercation and subsequent stabbing death nor could we locate anyone who had witnessed any suspicious person or persons leaving the Easy residence. His car was found parked and locked in the same block as his home without evidence of any disturbance. It also was processed.

The identified witness was interviewed. She was a sophisticated, elderly woman living several doors from the victim on the same side of the street with her husband, who had not been in her company when she discovered Easy. She related the same information she had previously shared with the lieutenant. The witness added that the victim was friendly but was not too involved in the neighborhood activities. She did not recall having seen him in weeks. He had lived there quietly for years with his friend named Lee Crispy. Both Easy and Crispy were very nice but kept to themselves. She stammered briefly and then added, "I think you would say they were lovers." She was obviously uncomfortable with trying to explain their relationship. Easy was in shoe sales and Lee was a clerk at one of the stores on Howard Street. She didn't knew where he would be at this hour, but one seldom went anywhere without the other. The information about the victim having been a shoe salesman answered the amount of shoes and shoe boxes found tossed about from the closet. And then the obvious question, "Do you detectives think that Lee may have done this, killed Mr. Easy?" Although we were considering him a suspect once we had learned Crispy was presumed alive, not at the residence and missing, this question remained unanswered.

It's true in a domestic case: Your first suspect is the survivor. They are the one you have to eliminate as a suspect or develop as one if other investigative leads are not answered. The obvious question was where was the victim's housemate? The overkill in this case also pointed toward lovers. Frequently, when one lover kills another the passion is so intense that it results in an overkill situation, more stab wounds, or more gunshots, or excessive beating, whatever the means.

A canvassing of the neighborhood was conducted by the uniformed personnel, including the houses on the block behind Montgomery Street with a view of the Easy home should the residents had seen anyone exiting the rear of the home or heard a disturbance in the past twenty four hours. His car was examined and showed no signs of an assault, or rummaging. The ignition was intact and the car keys were found in the Easy home. There was a possibility that the person or persons responsible for his death had been in his vehicle prior to the murder; therefore, the entire interior was dusted for prints after being towed to the headquarters garage as evidence. If discovered, the prints may lead to the assailant. Names and addresses of those located and interviewed were obtained.

Satisfied that everything possible had been done at the scene, we returned to our office and wrote the initial report governed by what our investigation had revealed to date. Next on our investigatory to-do list: wait for the autopsy findings, obtain the blood-typing analysis returns and do our utmost in locating and interviewing the victim's housemate, Lee Crispy, because of his absence at the scene was presently the most likely suspect. It was standard procedure for the Medical Examiner's Office to perform the autopsies the following morning after the body was delivered in the P.M. The investigative detectives frequently would attend the autopsies for firsthand information about the victim's wounds and cause of death. Both of us attended the autopsy of Mr. Robert Easy.

Finding Lee Crispy was not a difficult task. The next day, when we returned for our shift, a message reading, "What happened to Robert? I want to know what you have found out. Call me whenever you get this. Sincerely, Lee Crispy," with an attached phone number was there waiting for us. Crispy was called immediately and answered with emotion in his voice. Asked where he was at the time of Easy's murder, he stated, "Out of town visiting my parents in Georgia; they live there in a small town." I interjected that we wanted him to cooperate by giving his statement now. Crispy did not hesitate and said anything he could do to help he would. The phone number he had given was located at the Montgomery Street address and he was told that we would pick him up within minutes.

About fifteen minutes later, we rang the doorbell of the Easy/Crispy home. Seconds later, a well-groomed man, proportioned 5' 8," 165 pounds, appeared and opened the door. It was obvious by the look on his face that he was bereaved and had been crying. Crispy identified himself by name when asked. He even looked like a salesman. He was nicely dressed in a suit, shined shoes, and every hair was in place. Crispy showed us into his home and in the light we observed two things: this man was truly handsome and he was destroyed emotionally over the loss of his friend. Except for being so upset, he looked like a candidate for a movie part, probably a starring roll at that, or a politician running for the presidency or head of a elected office.

We explained to him that rather than answer his questions, which came one after the other, it would be better to take his statement first, which would be done at our office at headquarters. Crispy readily agreed to cooperate with our request for a statement by saying, "Whatever you feel necessary. I want to help. I was away until today, visiting my parents in Georgia, to come home and find this." He was ready to accompany us without further questioning, throwing on an overcoat from a rack near the front door. Seated in the back of the cruiser for the short trip to our office, he was visibly shaken and actually sobbed during the ride. Neither of us had the opportunity to talk to one another about Lee Crispi's demeanor, but both later commented that he was not their murderer although he had not been totally eliminated as a suspect at this early date. This man cared deeply for Robert Easy, so much so that if he had been responsible for his death, he would have called the police and confessed immediately afterward.

Upon arrival at the homicide office, rather than the use of an interrogation room, one of the sergeant's small offices was used; the thought being the atmosphere was more conducive to placing Crispy at ease. After the routine questions concerning vitals, which included questions about his employment and residential address, questions concerning his out-of-town whereabouts and his reported travel arrangements for visiting his parents were asked. He was then asked about his relationship with the victim.

Crispy said anything he could do to help in the investigation into the death of Robert Easy he would. He went on to detail their relationship: "We were lovers, have been for years. I work as a salesperson at Hecht's Store on Howard Street; Robert worked there selling shoes. He was so handsome. I knew he was gay, we just knew those things. I approached him and we were compatible from the start. He was the love of my life. We bought the house on Montgomery together. One reason was on nice days we could walk to work both of us enjoyed that so much. Plus, the house, neighbors and area were so nice. We were so happy.

Robert was a wonderful person and my soul mate, if only he could be trusted. Once, after we became close, I caught him with another man. It was just a fling. It almost destroyed us, though. He promised he would never be with anyone but me. He said it made him realize how much we meant to each other, and he wanted only me. Since that incident, I always would remind him about us whenever I had cause to go away. I knew deep down that he cared for our relationship, but I knew it was in him to occasionally wander. I saw the way he looked at other men when we were out. Before I left town to visit my parents in Georgia, I asked Robert to behave, not to get involved with anyone while I was away. I think he got to drinking, found someone somewhere, picked them up and brought that person home. Maybe whoever it was just wanted to get him alone to rob him. Robert was so trusting, he liked people."

All this information was given with sobs coming in between each statement from Crispy. He was questioned as to mutual friends, locations they frequented, associates, known enemies, the property of the victim such as clothes and jewelry etc. We told Crispy that the closet in their bedroom appeared ransacked, and requested he make a list of any missing items. Crispy responded, "Robert was a clotheshorse and had tons of shoes because of his occupation as a shoe salesman. He was attracted to the business for two reasons: it was not only a job, but he collected shoes like a young child would collect dolls." He would make a list as soon as possible. It would be hard under the circumstances, but he understood without us telling him why we wanted it. After gathering all the information we could, we concluded Crispy's statement by asking him if he would take a polygraph to prove the information he had given was correct. He responded immediately, "I told you I loved him. I would never have done this to Robert." Afterward, we drove Lee back to his home and watched as he entered the dwelling. Although he could not be completely dismissed at this time, as he closed the door of his home behind him we felt that our first and best suspect in this case was gone.

Crispy remained our only suspect at the time only in theory because of his relationship with the victim; he would have to exonerate himself by passing a polygraph that would be scheduled, or by us establishing in truth that he was out of town at the time of the murder. The killing was what we called overkill, meaning that there were more than enough wounds on Easy's body to have caused death. Frequently, overkills occurred in homosexual relationships. Was Crispy being truthful, or was he just crafty? Even if he had been out of town at the time of the murder, was he involved, making the arrangements to have Robert killed beforehand? If so, was the joint ownership of the house the motive? Was there a will naming him? Was he the one to have another lover? These were all questions that had to be answered.

Within days we had questioned friends who might have seen the victim during the period of the Crispy absence, and talked to area service operators, owners and bartenders at Robert's haunts with negative results. None of the friends had seen or heard from him, and he was not remembered by name or description with anyone in his company at the known bars on the night of his death. The neighborhood canvases proved negative, no new information was developed. The blood work was completed and did not help; the only blood typing found at the scene was that of the victim. We were hoping that during the altercation the suspect had left us a blood sample from a wound, but whoever the killer was he had not. Fingerprints were that of the victim. Lee's prints naturally were found about the house and in the Easy car, but not in areas disturbed during the assault and murder.

Found in the downstairs living room were prints of a personal friend of both the victim's and Crispy. Crispy remembered the friend having been there days before he left for visiting his parents. The owner of the prints, the mutual friend, had a solid alibi for the date of death, including several witnesses to his whereabouts on the night of the Easy death. He would later pass a polygraph in case his friends had conspired to develop an alibi for him.

Crispy submitted to the earliest date we could set to have him take a polygraph and passed with flying colors. Our only suspect in the case had proven him self innocent and eliminated what little amount of skepticism we had left. One of the questions asked was had he had anything whatsoever to do with the death of Robert Easy. We had checked his travel arrangements with the air carrier and sent the local sheriff to his parent's home unannounced to confirm his whereabouts. He had been seen physically being there by neighbors who visited and actually had dinner with him and his family on the night of the death. Crispy had left Baltimore a week before the murder and returned a day afterward, as he had stated. Our only hope regarding a suspect in this case was exonerated; we had little or no faith after his first interview that Easy's lover was our man almost from the start.

Crispy, once cleared by the polygraph, became focused on finding his lover's killer. He called our office daily hoping for new and different information, and submitting information he thought could help. He itemized the requested list of possible missing items owned by Robert Easy within days and delivered it personally to our office. We established with this list that shoes, an unknown amount, one pair being brown leather cowboy boots, assorted jewelry, including a gold-colored identification bracelet with the victim's name, and perhaps a suitcase which he described as all belonging to the victim were missing. Based on this information, pawnshops were checked for the identifiable items with negative results. The police district in which the homicide had occurred in was checked for similar assaults as far as stabbing robberies, or robberies at knifepoint with negative results.

In short, the Robert Easy case was on the verge of being a "cold case." About two months had passed by this time without a lead on the murder and without new information to be followed up. At this point, if the unknown suspect did not surrender himself and confess to doing the crime, or for whatever reason a witness had not stepped forward as yet, we would be at a loss. We needed a break on this one.

Marty, as known to most, or Martin Donovan, was a fifty seven year-old man rather heavyset in stature, known to the majority of the people in south Baltimore. He was a cheerful sort and liked by most, a fair person who found it easy to make friends. Donovan had been a uniformed police officer for his entire twenty four years on the job. He had been stationed in the southern district for most of those years, in an area that encompassed the Cross Street Market, located on 1065 South Charles Street. Cross St. Market sold just about everything; flowers, fruit, meats, candy, sandwiches, everything fresh that day. Independent owners full of personality operated the different stalls at the market. All of the merchants were known to each other and to the area residents that were devoted to shopping there, as if they were related. The market was a shopping delight, appearing on the outside to be a one-block long, one-story warehouse, and on the inside a throwback to stores in the early 1900's.

In addition to Donovan's present ambitions, he was looking forward to his pending retirement. He had served the department well and was ready to retire, and looking forward to that day that could not come soon enough in his mind. He had roughly less than a year left before reaching his twenty fifth year of service. At the time in the department, you had to serve twenty five years and be fifty years of age. Donovan joined the B.C.P.D. at the age of twenty eight and soon would be fifty three, and like most retirees had already considered another job to supplement his meager pension. He had a relatively uneventful career to date. Involved in a handful of cases he was proud of, like most police, had never been injured severely and had generally enjoyed his job.

At the time, south Baltimore for the most part was made up of decent law-abiding people who caused few problems. Drugs, like everywhere in the city, were becoming more of a problem. Donovan and the men he worked with were not faced with the drug wars that usually followed the usage yet. He had walked his beat long enough to know most of the troublemakers, watching them grow up in the neighborhood. Now that retirement was around the corner, he had but one thing related to his job left to do. He had set about to train Joseph Small as best he could, to be a good street cop. Small was his son-in-law. He had met his daughter, Joy, when they were both eighteen years old. Both of them were extremely happy with one another and married when they were twenty one. Donovan, like any father, was anxious to help his daughter and her new husband. He had talked Officer Small onto the job to offer security for them. They were just starting out and needed steady employment to build their future. Small followed his father-in-law's advice being of age and accidently ended up in the same district on the same shift. Donovan felt it his duty and responsibility to take Joseph under his wing and teach him everything about the job he could before he left. He liked the kid, knew he took the job seriously and wanted him to be safe and accepted by his fellow officers before he retired. So, like a good teacher, whenever the thought struck him on or off duty related to the job, he would discuss with Joseph the techniques and experiences he had learned over the years, things that would also serve his son-in-law. Actually, he felt deep down that helping teach Joseph Small the ropes was the last police work he would do because of his pending retirement.

Susan Woodberry was a seventeen year old girl attending Southern High and working part time at a local flower shop. She was involved with whom she considered her first boyfriend, the first one she had true affection for. His name was Tommy Hines and he lived over on Charles Street, a block behind the market, with some other guys he considered friends. She had met Tommy at an area Friday night dance sponsored by one of the local churches and they were attracted to one another immediately. They had seen each other for about a month before she mentioned him to her mother. He was slightly older at twenty years of age and that created concern about the age-difference with the mother.

Her mother, Jane Woodberry, was concerned they had a month-long relationship and worried that this boy was three years older than her daughter. She insisted, because of these concerns, on meeting with Tommy. And after a talk with her daughter, the mother continually advised her not to become romantically involved with him or any other older boy. Once she saw Tommy Hines in person, she was even further upset with their relationship. He appeared unkempt. Although he said that he worked at a home for the elderly in the area, he showed a lack of manners toward her at times, leaving her with the feeling that Tommy thought Susan and he would go about whatever business they felt like. After the meeting with him, she told her daughter how she felt and told her not to get involved with him. Of course, remembering her youth, telling a young person not to do something was like a guarantee they would do it just to prove the adult wrong. After the meeting, she was more concerned than ever. Her daughter had always been good, but would she be led by her emotions in this relationship by an older boy. There was something more than the attitude of this boy; she just could not accept him. Of course, mothers always want the best for their daughters. This boys cavalier attitude upset her, he was to cocky for his age.

Hines had borrowed one of his roommate's cars and had taken Susan to Annapolis to window shop, have an inexpensive meal and take a walking sightseeing tour around ego alley. That Annapolis, Md. location was a dead-end channel of water that ended at the foot of West Street, the commercial area of Annapolis. Everyone with a boat would make their u-turn so they could be noticed by those walking the docks and nearby. It was located at the base of the shopping area, which stretched for several blocks on both sides of Main Street up a slight hill toward Church Circle. Just to the right of Church Circle was the Maryland Capitol Building which served as the Capitol of the United States from 1783-1784. This building is still in use by the state government.

Susan was more than happy with the sights during their ride and the visit to Annapolis, but just as thrilled to be with Tommy. They walked around the docks overlooking the harbor with its countless sailboats moored in slips and those secured to floating buoys in the harbor, as well as those under sail sliding past. Annapolis, Maryland, is known as the Sailboat Capital of the United States and is more than beautiful to the eye. The happy couple admired the Chesapeake Bay Bridge and U.S.

Naval Academy, and window shopped along Main Street. While they were talking randomly about no particular topic, Tommy mentioned that his roommates had come by a deal on some clothes and shoes. Susan said that was nice and asked, "Where did they get such a deal?" Tommy hesitated for an instant and replied, "I don't know," promptly changing the subject as if he shouldn't have mentioned it. They went on with their day without further conversation about the matter.

Susan had, on one occasion, met both of Tommy's roommates; they seemed nice enough at the time. Their names were Daniel Grant and John Grimes, they were all about the same ages, and mentioned to her that they had originally known one another from a former job. They had become friends with one another and decided to room together to save expenses. Susan enjoyed the evening and kissed Tommy in the car in front of her home before leaving him for the night.

Two days later, she was at Tommy's house with the other two roommates there. The three of them started a conversation about all the stuff they had just bought. One of them actually pulled some clothes from the middle-room closet and showed her. They said that the guy had shoes and clothing for sale and must have been hard up for money to sell the things. Daniel Grant was actually wearing a pair of the shoes he claimed he had bought. They were expensive looking black loafers. Being more than pleased with their appearance, he walked around as if modeling them for her. When she asked where the shoes and clothes came from, and the name of the person who had sold them the stuff, they looked at one another and finally John replied, "Just some guy." Susan was also stumped; both of these guys had been laid off of construction jobs together about a month ago and complained about not having money to make the bills.

A day after Susan had been in Tommy's apartment with his two roommates, Officer Joseph Small on routine patrol wandered into the floral shop where she worked on Light Street just to say hello to the employees and basically let them know he was in the area. One of the things he had considered important learned in the academy, and from his mentor his father-in-law was to learn your people. Susan was behind the counter at the time and smiled at the young officer as he entered.

He had a habit of stopping in most of the stores in the block and she enjoyed talking with him when he came in.

Small and Susan became engaged in a casual conversation because there were no customers at the time. She unconsciously brought up the matter about the guys having clothes and jewelry, not thinking it would get them in trouble but because she could not figure how and why guys that had been just laid off from their jobs could or would buy such things. After about six or seven minutes, Officer Small said goodbye to Susan with a smile and walked out of the shop. As he walked south on the street, he began to wonder about the conversation he had just had with her, and about the logic of three poor young men buying clothes and jewelry when they didn't have rent money. As time passed, the seemingly innocent information gained from the casual conversation with a young girl played on his mind and became questionable to him. Had these guys who could not pay their rent because of being laid off some how stolen the articles they had in their possession and, if so, had they committed a crime? And then his thoughts turned to the W's he had been taught: who, what, where, when, why, which and how? Answer those questions, and if there had been a criminal act, you could solve it. The only recent crime in the area was the homicide of a man up on Montgomery Street weeks ago. What, if anything, was taken?

Small had met his father-in-law for lunch at the market and both were busy with their sandwiches and drinks. Small was still a stone rookie and pondered if he should tell Donovan what he had learned in a conversation a day before. After all, the information probably would not help or didn't mean anything in the first place. Haunting him about the discussing the information was something one of the instructors at the academy had said to the class, "Don't ever rule out any information you obtain. You never know what is important and what is not. If the information is suspicious, it may be important. Let the appropriate people be made aware of it. You never know what could prove to be important." Even on police matters, you have not been given all the information on an investigation. What you have learned if passed on might just break a case.

Well, he may as well take a shot at it. Small spoke up, "Martin, I want to discuss with you some information I heard yesterday." Martin seemed disinterested at the time. He was more concerned with his food but replied, "Go ahead." "Well," Small said, "I talked to a girl from the flower shop up on Light Street when I stopped in there yesterday and during our conversation I kiddingly asked about her love life; she told me about her boyfriend and his roommates over on Charles Street. This twenty or twenty one year-old works at the old-age home on Light Street, and his name is Hines, Tommy Hines. He and his two roommates came by a deal where they got good prices on some clothes and jewelry. She laughed about it because she couldn't see boys getting so excited over such things; she thought just girls would talk that way about clothes and jewelry. They don't have money enough for the things in the first place." "Well, what about it kid?" replied Donovan.

Small looked at him and asked, "What was taken in that killing up on Montgomery Street, anything? You remember, about a month ago." Donovan smiled, rubbed his chin and chewed down a mouthful of his sandwich before he replied: "Kid, I don't recall what was taken, if anything. Let me tell you something, you call homicide with that little piece and they will blow you off. If you're lucky, you won't hear your name mentioned as the caller on the street afterward. Suits are in a world all their own. Those guys are pretty boys playing at being television cops. They work and socialize differently than we do. Because they look good dressed up, they look down on patrol." "I don't believe that," blurted out Joseph. "We are all on the same team. There's so much stuff out there everyone has to help each other," the youngster said. Donovan smiled and answered, "Well, kid, when you catch a gun or knife, call see if a detective ever helps you, and if you ever help one out with information, see if you even get honorable mention."

The discussion was over. Small had been told exactly how Martin felt about detectives, but he had been left with the same problem: Should he or should he not call homicide with what he felt may be important to the Montgomery Street case, or some other active case? If the information he had gotten from the seventeen year-old was important, it should be passed on to the proper unit.

Seated in the homicide office at the time, and still working the Robert Easy case, Det. Corbin and I were listening to a group of other detectives discuss leads they had to run out on a cab holdup and shooting homicide of a cab driver murder that they thought were linked. Cab drivers being killed always aroused public outcry; they were highly publicized by the media and watched over by the command staff. They would break the case through hard work, and luck in the way of a break, if it happened, or through what we called dogged tenacity, never giving up. They had an outstanding supervisor in a sergeant named Rod Brander and, although the solutions seemed far away at present, this one would be in the black at some point. Homicides at the time were charted on a board with the names of the victims printed in black when the case was solved and in red print until they were. Meanwhile, having our case at a standstill, my thoughts turned to positive thinking regarding the eventual solution to the cab case. I was really hoping that the Robert Easy case would be solved somehow and I would see his name in black but at the time had no inkling how.

The phone rang and was answered by one of the detectives in the room who handed the phone to me saying, "It's for you, one of yours." I took the phone and heard a young male voice on the other end that announced himself as "Officer Joseph Small, Southern District." Small continued on by saying, "I don't know if this means anything, but I had a conversation with a girl who gave me some information on guys with clothes and jewelry they got, and when she asked where they got it, they refused to tell her. They live not far from Montgomery Street, on Charles Street, about three-quarters of a mile from Montgomery. I wanted to find out if such items had been taken in that murder?"

I confirmed what kind of property was taken in the Easy homicide and asked for the name and address of the girl he had gotten the information from and thanked Officer Small for the heads-up call. Indeed, clothes and jewelry were taken from the murder scene. Susan Woodberry's address and work location were obtained. She would be interviewed. The officer interjected, "She is only seventeen years old, seems like a good kid." Small was told should her information provide us with a lead, we would advise him. He went on to add that his father-in-law was a cop also and advised him not to call; stating he himself was not sure the information would help. I said, "You never know, it may prove to be the break we need on this one. I'll let you know. And we will have to interview Susan. Like I said, we will let you know. Our names are Steve Danko and Howard Corbin; Howard is my partner on this case." Officer Small hung up after saying, "I hope this is good." The clothes and jewelry aspect was good. Perhaps our first break, the items were in the ballpark; not knowing at the time where it would lead us, but something that had to be followed up.

After the call from Officer Small, I thought about the rivalry that existed between patrol and the detectives. Small had basically brought it up when he mentioned his father-in-law. Patrol officers often had an attitude that we were in soft clothes because we didn't want to work. Little did they realize the long hours we put in? Most of our shifts extended past the normal eight hours. They complained about us dressing in suits as if we did it to belittle them. If that was truly their reasoning, those that complained, why didn't they want to be detectives themselves? They complained, but deep down they liked the stability of eight-hour shifts and possibly the lack of responsibility it brought. They went home after their eight hours. After their reports were in, they were finished their shift and knew they would not be called back in to work until their next day tour started.

Once, on another call, an old timer made several remarks such as, "he won't get that nice clean suit dirty," or "they look like lawyers, dressed just so nice." And for the final insult, he said, "they won't do anything any way, they never do." That was enough; I thought at that point this guy might go on all night with his insults if he was not stopped. I turned to the officer and said: "I wear what I want not only because detectives are supposed to dress in soft clothes, but I pay for the clothes myself. The clothing allotment from the department yearly might buy you a tie. And if I like the lawyer look, it's my business; thanks for the compliment. And as far as solving the cases, most become a problem from the start when the uniformed guys after being told time and time again not to screw up the scene do so before we even arrive. You guys always bitch about detectives, we work ridiculous hours to the point of never being home, one case runs into the next, and there is pressure to solve every one. And if you are so jealous of our dress and what we do, take the test and do it yourselves instead of thinking up cute lines. You're not even too original; we hear the same trash on every call." The patrolman looked at me and turned and walked away without another word, and was not seen again. I know that I lowered myself to his level, but I had grown tired of hearing it over and over. I had given him several opportunities to stop before I said anything, and my tirade had worked. Enough was enough.

The clothes and jewelry information led us to Montgomery Street, the home of Susan Woodberry, across the street and just doors away from the Robert Easy address. Greeted at the front door by her mother, Jane Woodberry, we identified ourselves as detectives. We explained to her at the door why we were there, stating that her daughter had given a uniformed police officer certain information that might have importance in one of our investigations and therefore we would like to talk to her directly about the matter, but in your presents, and that she was not in any trouble. She advised that her daughter Susan was still at work and was expected home afterward at about 8:00 P.M. We left our phone number and business cards, reassured her that her daughter was not in any trouble and that she was welcome to be in her company when the interview of Susan took place.

We left the Woodberry address, returned to the office and waited the call from the mother or daughter. Although the mother, Jane Woodberry, seemed more than cooperative, not having them together when we went to their home would give the two of them time to decide about their cooperation with us. That was the only negative thought at the time. But we were dealing with a youth who knew she had talked to Officer Small, and she knew we expected to hear the same information again from her. We did not want to pick up the girl separately without her mother knowing, for fear the mother would be overprotective. A rule: Do your best not to alienate witnesses if you can help it; they are already weighing the hardships of their commitment when they decide to help the police without undue pressures or situations.

At 8:30 P.M. that day, we received a call from headquarters security that two women were there to speak to us. Evidently, mother and daughter had decided to come to us on their own rather than call for us at their home. This was best for us, because if Susan's information was valuable enough to obtain a statement, we were already at our office. We cleared them with security and within minutes both females were in the elevator that opened on our office floor, with us waiting in the hallway in front of the elevators. We realized by them responding so quickly that Susan Woodberry was coming to cooperate. Susan was polite and seemed rather relaxed considering her position. She had accidentally said something that had sparked police interest and she was not anxious to implicate her boyfriend in anything illegal, but was forthright enough to tell the truth. We ushered them into one of the vacant supervisor's offices, reassured Susan that she was doing the right thing by telling us, and asked her in front of her mother to repeat to us what she had told the police officer while at the flower shop about her boyfriend Tommy Hines and his roommates. She told us their address and said that Tommy worked on Light Street at a nursing home; and shared the story they had told her about how they got the clothes and jewelry failing to identify the seller, and the fact from the way they talked that they did not have the money to buy the stuff in the first place. Her knowledge of the homicide in the block was why she became suspicious and had told the police.

After hearing her information, it was absolutely material to the Easy homicide investigation. Det. Corbin obtained a formal statement in the presence of Susan's mother, as well as my self. The statement concluded with what Susan hoped was a sincere defense of her boyfriend Tommy: "Tom could have never done anything like what happened to Mr. Easy; Tom was a nice, caring person. Perhaps love is blind it's reasonable to believe young or first love is. After all, there is a lack of experience; you want to believe, so you do. Afterward, the Woodberry's were taken downstairs and outside to their parked vehicle; and after advising Susan in front of her mother to stay away from Tommy Hines for a few days, making any excuse she could, we reassured them both that no one would hear on the street about the information Susan had provided. As the two drove away, we turned to each other and smiled, shook hands and without words turned back toward our offices. I'm sure we both felt that we had the break on this case we had needed.

The jewelry, the clothes, the black loafers all fit. The unemployment causing the need for money and material things, the close proximity of the victim's home and that of these subjects all made for the probable cause in justifying a search-and-seizure warrant for the address of Grant, Grimes and Hines.

A day later, armed with a warrant for the premises of 1205 S. Charles Street, we knocked on the door. One uniformed man in the front and one posted at the back to prevent any possible escape, Detective Corbin and my self stood on the front steps with a uniformed officer and knocked. The first man through the answered door was Officer Joseph Small, on the first raid of his career. Based on the keen alertness to his responsibilities as an officer, his reward for a fine job, rookie or not, he smiled with joy and anticipation as he entered. He had given us the information for the search, the information that would ultimately break the case and lead to the answering of more than the questions posed by the Easy investigation. That aspect had not been realized at the time. He had not only done the right thing in this case but in another we were unaware of.

A young man later identified as Daniel Grant opened the door, appeared frightened at seeing us and took seconds to ask, "What do you guys want?" Corbin grabbed him and patted him down for weapons. We continued into the middle room where we found John Grimes seated on a couch. He was so surprised at the sight of us that he didn't move before we were on him. He was checked for weapons with negative results. The rest of the apartment was quickly checked, first for additional subjects, then for the reported clothing and shoes described in the warrant. A check of the apartment revealed they were the only two in the apartment at the time. Tommy was not home. After we were satisfied that no one else was in the apartment, I grabbed the left wrist of Grimes and looked at the ID bracelet he was wearing. Engraved on the faceplate of the bracelet was the name Robert Easy. In that instant, the three-month case with no leads was solved. I announced the name and Officer Small's eyes widened as a broad smile broke on his face. Both Grant and Grimes were young, twenty and twenty one years of age respectfully. Being found with an item of the victim was bad enough, but Grimes wearing the bracelet at the time, it was ridiculous. What was he thinking? No, it was obvious, he was not thinking. I thought at the time he was to stupid too. Could these guys be bright enough to successfully rob and then kill someone, and get away with it for almost three months?

After cuffing the two arrested subjects and securing the apartment, a full search was conducted. During the search, neither of the two suspects uttered a word, but sat with their heads down and appeared seemingly rejected. Their body language said it all, a sight that had become second nature to us on numerous arrests. A closet located on the east side of the room was checked and on the floor a suitcase was discovered. Opening the suitcase, a .9 millimeter loaded handgun was found sitting on top of assorted men's clothing. Both Grimes and Grant denied ownership. The closet also contained a large amount of men's shoes, size 11, and the same reported size of the victim. The mobile crime lab was called, but asked to park a reasonable distance from the first-floor apartment rather than in front because we had learned that the third suspect, the boyfriend of Susan Woodberry; Tommy Hines would be coming home any minute from his job. About ten minutes later, Tommy Hines unlocked the front door and entered. Dressed in scrubs, he was coming from the senior citizen home where he was a nursing aide. Hines was the third person surprised that day, and we didn't have to ask him a thing. When he entered the apartment, both Howard and I looked down: Tommy Hines walked in wearing the victim's brown cowboy boots. Not a match with the light blue scrubs, but like the charm bracelet it was the proper wearing apparel for us. When he noticed that the boots were a topic with us, he piped up and said, "The boots aren't mine, I borrowed them from Daniel." Tommy was the second out of three arrested subjects to have the victim's items on his person. You have heard the term "fruits of the crime." Well, this was the greatest example I have ever seen of that. Hell, I thought this was the fruit tree of the crime.

A cruising patrol was called and the subjects transported to the homicide office. The scene was processed with the recovery of possible evidence, the suitcase, clothes inside, weapon and shoes. With the arrival of Tommy Hines prior to that of the crime lab, they were advised they could respond directly to the front door. Both Hines and Grimes were photographed wearing the articles identified as belonging to the victim Robert Easy and stolen at the time of his death.

Now a fixture at our office because of his continued efforts to help, his personal interest in the case and his likable disposition, Lee as known by most of the detectives by then was elated. He had heard of the arrest and seen the subjects brought in before our arrival. When we entered the office, he ran to us, shedding tears of happiness, shook our hands and hugged both of us. Seldom do we receive thanks on any of our cases, but this was one of the most sincere thanks ever. By now, Lee Crispy was almost a house cat, known by the majority of detectives in the other squads as well. When he settled down, he entered the sergeant's office we were in, walked to the wide window sill base used by many as a seat and plopped down casually, still enjoying the relief he felt by the arrests, content that Robert's killers had finally been arrested. We told him about serving the warrant and that we had recovered items belonging to Robert Easy that Lee had listed as missing after his check of the premises.

Each one of the three suspects was interviewed after advisement of their rights and all three, Grant, Grimes and Hines, all readily confessed to the killing of Robert Easy. They would not implicate each other in the crime as to who or if more than one took part in Easy's death, but having arrested them in possession of the evidence, they had decided individually there was no way out, they were caught. None of them requested an attorney after being advised of their rights, and all of them denied ownership of the recovered handgun. Ballistics would determine if the recovered handgun had been used in any other crimes. The three agreed to statements, which were obtained separately.

Basically, all the statements agreed that they were out looking for someone to rob. They had agreed that the easiest way would be to rob some unsuspecting yuppie on the street when no one was looking. Get someone who looked like he would have some money walking down the street in an isolated area or just getting out of his car. Threaten him; what, with the three against one, what could he do? Unfortunately,

Robert Easy became their prey. Robert was out drinking at a local bar trying to pick a guy up, perhaps any guy. He was at one of the bars we had checked to see if he was a customer the night he was killed, but no one had noticed him there. Tommy engaged Robert in conversation while the other two held back drinking at another table, as though they were by themselves. After a brief conversation, Tommy agreed to leave the bar and go to Robert's home. Tom found time to alert the other two without arousing Easy's interest. Grant and Grimes got the idea then to introduce them themselves to Robert and following several drinks suggested they all have a private party. Robert should have known just by the numbers involved not to agree, but must have been just drunk enough not to concern himself with the odds. After all, his newfound friend Tom would come to his aid if the other two strangers attempted anything.

After their arrival at the Easy home, Tommy acted interested in Robert and went up into the bedroom with him while Grimes and Grant searched through the downstairs looking for valuables. They were overheard by Robert, who must have become suspect of their activities. Tommy had to restrain Robert from going downstairs. The other two came to Tom's aid hearing the screaming on the part of Robert, who realized at that point he was being robbed. It quickly turned into a full-blown fight involving all of them. Three against one, Robert was battered about the head and body; bleeding, he broke away and stumbled down the backstairs to the kitchen, trying to get away from the three. The youthful men ran after him and started the fistfight again, beating Robert about his head and body, wherever the three could land a blow during the melee. During the beating, Robert was stabbed with a kitchen knife grabbed from a kitchen cabinet drawer. None admitted to the actual assault of Easy; all admitted afterward they took the items recovered. Some time before their arrest, they had agreed not to tell who committed the stabbing that led to Robert's death, a strange pact made after theft and killing. All were being charged with the same crime, but two of the three would not try and lessen their own involvement. Why? After their statements, all three were charged in the homicide.

Sgt. Rod Brander came into the office where the detectives and Lee were seated. He congratulated everyone, including Lee Crispy, and asked if he could interview our arrested suspects. Rod, as mentioned before, was an outstanding supervisor and individual. Know for years, I had worked the same radio car, 105, on a different shift from Brander in the central district. He and his regular partner, Steinweddle, relieved our shift. Of course, there was no problem with his request. About four hours later, while we were still into reports and rereading statements, Rod popped into the office and thanked us again, this time for what had just happened. One of the three, Tommy Hines, had implicated Grant, Grimes and himself in two of the cab driver shooting murders during robbery attempts. A quick ballistic check on the .9 mm pistol recovered by us at their Charles Street apartment had matched bullets recovered from both of the bodies of the slain cab drivers. All three were charged with three counts of homicide. Their mutual involvement in the cab murders on the east side of town explained why they had not given up the person responsible for stabbing Robert Easy. They knew all three of them were going to be charged with multiple counts of homicide once the ballistic analyses came back on their recovered weapon.

Officer Joseph Small had not only solved the Easy murder but was credited with the arrest of those who had committed two cab driver murders as well. He received a commendation for his diligent police work. Off. Small, a rookie had made his bones. His peers more than accepted him. He could have made Policeman of the Year, and was up for that honor. God only knows what conversations occurred between Smalls and his father-in-law, Officer Donovan. Small probably had to become a politician to keep the peace in the two families and probably agreed not to ever talk about the advice he received from his father-in-law. Donovan, on the other hand, must have had to explain his original comments toward detectives privately to his son-in-law. I'm sure they came to an agreement not to openly discuss their conversation about calling us in front of the family.

Cold Gate Creek

———◦◦◦◦◦———

The engineer pulled onto the trestle on time, and headed northeast at a slower speed permitted by the restrictions on the overpass. Cold Gate Creek was below them at the time; a trestle relatively short in length over a creek no wider than fifty yards at this location, flowing into the Patapsco River about a quarter mile further on. The first and last trestle to be passed over, the creek constituted the only water on their trip. They were in the process of pulling twenty five railway cars from a loading area of General Motors

Although the brakeman and the engineer were busy talking about the day's workload, the engineer looked down and stopped the already slow moving engine. The reactionary stoppage jarred the other crewman. The brakeman asked, "What are you doing?" The engineer responded, "Did you see that? There's a body floating in the creek just outside of the track line, below the trestle. I saw it when we went over." After stopping the train, both men jumped off and ran to the area where the engineer had seen the body floating.

Just off the rocky shoreline on the northeast side of the tracks was the body of a white female, face down floating in the water. The victim appeared to be nude, her hair floating eerily on the water as if weightless; a sight he later said would always remain in his memory. They did not observe any blood on the body. The body was about fifteen feet from the shore and the two men thought better of going in after it. With the body floating face down in the water and showing no signs of life, there was no doubt in their minds that the victim was dead. They thought if they reached her, they would disturb evidence while attempting to drag her out of the water to the shoreline. The brakeman and engineer returned to the train, called what they had found into their dispatcher and requested that the police respond to the location they described. They were within the shadows of the Port of Baltimore piers just northwest of their location and within feet of Key Highway, which ran parallel to the railroad trestle.

The train's personnel and its cargo could not stand still on the tracks for long. After identifying themselves to the first responding officer and showing him their gruesome discovery floating near the shore, they moved forward and pulled slowly away from the scene. Time restrictions for the tracks had to be obeyed in order that two trains were not on the same track at the same time.

A uniformed officer working the area responded to the call, took the names of the train crew, and called the crime lab and emergency police services through communications to recover the body. The homicide detectives would also be required on the scene. Working day work, my partner Timmons and I had been in the office by 7:20 A.M., waiting for the roll call that morning that we would miss. We had relieved the 12-to-8 shift early. All but two of them were relieved; the two were dealing with a domestic murder and still had to finish the reports. At 7:22 A.M. one of the sergeants had either taken a call from communications or had been told by the detective who had received it that we had a new call for service. We were there and we were out the door before the daily routine roll. At least it was a rare early one, not a mid-shift call.

We responded to the scene in a little over twenty minutes. At that hour, like any metropolitan area, the traffic was bumper to bumper with impatient motorists leaving home just in time to make it to work on time. When we arrived at the scene, a small crowd from the shipyard portion of the area had gathered, attracted by the police action. The section where the body was found was east across the street from the Baltimore Port Authority, and all but that particular area of middle-class mixed separate framed houses and row homes across from the Port of Baltimore was an area known as Dundalk. A portion of what many thought was Baltimore County east of the city is actually our jurisdiction. The area accepted overall as Dundalk was actually a small community called St Helena and was our jurisdiction. It is the furthest section of the city to the southeast. Active and former employees of factories in the immediate area occupied the homes in the area generally. The G.M. plant and Procter & Gamble were the largest employers.

Once Timmons and I made it through rush hour to the location, we examined the body, which was retrieved from Cold Gate Creek by members of the Tactical Unit. We made sure processing of the scene was done, including a larger than normal amount of photographs because of the size of the overall scene area. The body was that of a woman who appeared to be in her late thirties or early forties. She was beaten about the face and had what appeared to be drag marks on her thighs, the back of her legs and spine. There was a black thick substance in a wound at the base of her spine and also at the base of her skull. It had the consistency of soft clay. Neither of us could identify what the substance was and were at that time not considering what it could be.

She was not nude, as she had appeared to be to the railroad engineer and brakeman when pulled from the creek. Her light pink panties were rolled down like you would roll a cigar and were tight around her lower thighs. Her bra appeared to be rolled in the same method completely off her breast and rolled about her neck, but not as if the bra had been used in a strangulation attempt. There were no marks on her neck to indicate that. Both articles were rolled so tightly that they represented questions in themselves as to how they got that way. How could these articles have been tightly rolled? And what was the black substance ground into her back and neck? There were no defense wounds on either hands or forearms, and no scrape marks on her knees.

Further examination of the body revealed that the only jewelry the victim was wearing was a high school ring from Dundalk High, with the year engraved on the side with no initials or engraving inside, which we were sure to check. Fortunately, one of the two crime lab technicians had an instant camera with his equipment. A close-up of the victim's face and school ring was taken. We now had a photograph of the victim to show during our area canvass, and the school ring year for that part of the investigation.

While we worked the scene of the crime, we requested uniform personnel to canvass the surrounding neighborhood and the gathering bystanders to determine if anyone could identify the victim or heard any disturbance the night before that may have been related. Most of the area from the trestle south was buffered from the residents' homes on the east side and from the highway and commercial port businesses on the west by a wooded area along the tracks. Although those methods failed in part, one of the officers spoke with an area resident who had heard noises followed by a short scream around 2:15 A.M. the night before coming from across from her house at the schoolyard. An elementary school was located across from this woman's home, but the first thought the officer had was that it was not relative to the case. The distance from that schoolyard and where the victim was found was almost a half-mile apart. The officer walked over to the school and looked around the playground, smiled and cursed to him self, realizing his initial thoughts were wrong once he made the discovery and called for the detectives to respond,.

We got to the schoolyard and Officer Prentice pointed out a spot on the playground. There was a woman's purse with items from the purse strewn about the immediate area; a small amount of what appeared to be fresh blood on the ground, which was a macadam surface, and fresh scuffmarks as if made by shoes when someone was trying to regain their footing while being dragged. Thinking we would quickly identify the victim, we went through the purse carefully not to damage any possible fingerprints and its former contents on the ground. Nothing revealed the owner's identity; the assailant or assailants had taken anything that would have identified her. No money was recovered and nothing hinted to the identity of our victim.

Now we had a second crime scene and it was at least a half-mile from where the body was found. We decided then on calling the Helicopter Unit to request aerial photographs from the schoolyard to the body location to properly show the distance that separated the scenes. The body found floating in Cold Gate Creek under the railroad trestle north of the schoolyard and their relationship to one another. A direct route between the two locations was the railroad tracks located just west of the schoolyard. The entire area had to be photographed because of the overall area involved. Aerial photographs would help a future jury understand the scene.

The evidence of the crime now ran from the schoolyard to the creek. The schoolyard contained the purse and some personal property of the victim, along with blood and scuffed shoe marks, making that location the point at which the assault on the victim had started. We located a small worn footpath leading from the schoolyard to the railroad tracks. A piece of a woman's dress was found snagged on a bush as we entered the path. The fabric looked clean and was relatively dry from the night's mist. It appeared to be the victim's because of its location and condition. Blood had been found on the tracks, as well as her dress between the school and the creek about seventy yards north of the school yard. The dress fabric matched the piece found on the path leading to the tracks. The dress had the same rolled effect as the bra and panties.

Assaulted on the school grounds, the victim was carried or dragged up the tracks, causing her to loose her dress during the dragging and have her underclothing rolled off by the friction of her body being dragged. This made for one hell of a crime scene; nearly one half mile in its length, there was only one way to display the entire area and that was by air. I thought I had figured the next step out when I turned to Timmons and said we'll have Fox Trout land at the school, and he would replace the observer and show the pilot the entire scene. It was only reasonable that Timmons would agree. Physically, he was the guy for the copter; he was tall and slender, a good flying weight. I was 6'3" and two hundred and twenty five pounds. Tim had been a door gunner in Vietnam and was used to flying in helicopters. Tim turned to me abruptly and stated, "To hell with that. I promised myself after my last flight I would never get in a chopper again, much less 'Foxtrot,'" that was what our choppers were called. "You can forget it, that damn thing is one-third the size of the birds I flew in. It's a Volkswagen with wings," Tim went on. Good reasoning on my part, but how was I to know he felt that way. The thought of him flying had not come up. I would brief the observer either by land if they landed or by radio if they decided to stay aloft. The only thing Tim had ever confided about his Army tour was that he was so frightened every time they flew that on one mission the bushes moved and he opened up on his .50 caliber gun and killed a cow. God knows what those boys saw and did; I understand why they tend toward forgetting instead of remembering. I noticed that almost all that have seen action tell only the lighthearted stories; physiologically, that's all they want to recall. I'm sure the other sights and situations caused dreams and nightmares they would rather forget.

Fifteen minutes later, the chopper arrived, took radio instructions and photographed the scene for us. One thing was sure: Either one strong son of a bitch carried and pulled the woman up the railroad tracks a long way after assaulting her, or there was more than one person involved. The scene was such that once on the railroad tracks, trees on both sides sheltered the suspect or suspect's actions. There was no view of the track area from the houses on the east, and none from the road parallel to the tracks on the west. The only possible witness to the assault would had to have seen the assault as it occurred on the school lot, and then they would have been on the darkened lot across the street south of where it took place, at least seventy five yards away. Without any other knowledge of how the initial assault occurred or what caused it, the surroundings made it look planned at this point. The assailant(s) could have not picked a better location to do the deed; there was just no eye witness view form any point.

During the neighborhood canvass, no one had named anyone fitting the physical description of the victim or when shown our Polaroid. Tim and I drove to Dundalk High, announced ourselves as police detectives from Baltimore and asked the principal if they had a yearbook from the year we found on the ring. Looking through the pages, we found a female's picture that resembled the Polaroid picture we had taken at the scene. Our victim was identified; she had graduated from Dundalk High some eighteen years before her death. Her name was Alice Porches at that time, probably married since, probably had kids, and probably worked. I wondered all the things she had done since high school. It was a good thing that people did not know their fate. At the end for whatever reason, she had been killed either by beating or drowning; we were waiting on the autopsy results to give us the cause of death. She had been discarded in a rather dirty stream, large enough in someone's mind to be called a creek, for whatever mistake someone thought she had committed.

With the first name and description of the victim, we returned to the neighborhood with hope that someone would know the victim well enough to give us her address or had seen her on the night of her death. We canvassed all the area bars with her name and photograph; in those days, it meant a lot of stops. Just like most neighborhoods, there was a bar on almost every corner. A few of the owners and bar workers recognized her, mentioned she had been in, but did not know her by name and stated that she had not been in on the night of her death. That information established her as a local probably living in the area, but we still did not have her home address.

At about midnight remembering when the call came in the thought that at least it was early on the shift and would not cause us to work over had long faded. We walked into another corner bar and the owner walked up to us with a smile on his face. He announced himself as the owner, told us he was an off-duty policeman in the southeast district and that he had expected us earlier than this. The girl that he heard had been killed was probably Alice Jackson, and she lived around the corner on the next street. She had been in the bar the night before, around closing time, 2:00 A.M. We were not only tired from our day thus far, which was now into its sixteenth hour, but flabbergasted. We looked at each other and as if on the same wavelength said, "Why didn't you call us sooner with this information?" Tim beat me to the question by seconds. Our reply basically sounded like an echo, asking the same question one behind the other. The owner and police officer looked blankly at us and responded, "I knew you guys would show up." We didn't tell him how much time we had wasted at the other bar locations finding his, or talking to the neighborhood residents, or going through the high school photographs and records.

We asked if he noticed anything about the victim while she was there, or anyone with her. He stated that she was rather drunk and had left about 1:30 A.M. The bar was really crowded at the time. He looked outside at closing and she was standing near the mailbox out front with a group of guys, maybe three others. The owner continued: "I didn't pay any attention to them. I don't know who they were. Nothing out of the ordinary was happening then. There was a bunch of young guys talking to her; you know, the drinking age had just been lowered to eighteen year olds, good for business, but those kids can't drink a little."

Thanking him for the information, we left after he described the house our victim was supposed to live in. Since we had been to tired to tell Officer so and so off for not calling us right away, we decided we would stop at that point. Another reason was to give the occupants of our victim's home more time to report the victim missing. Whether they did or not would help us determine if they were involved or not. It would either make them suspects for not reporting the victim missing, or concerned friends and or relatives who really did not know her fate. We returned to our office and called it a night.

The following morning at 7:50 A.M. we rang the doorbell of Mr. Jackson. The house was almost directly behind the bar. The bar owner had described the house to us the night before. It was a modest two-story row, with a small covered front porch. A girl of about sixteen or seventeen answered the doorbell. We identified ourselves and asked for Jackson. The girl ushered us in, saying as she did, "That's my stepfather. He is not home. His name is John Jackson. I'm getting ready for school." Tim asked his whereabouts and she replied, "He is working, he works the day shift at the GM plant." "Where's your mother?" Timmons asked to determine if the daughter knew her mother's whereabouts or of her death. Charlene, who identified herself as we spoke, replied, "I don't know where she is; she left after they argued last night and she hasn't come home since." "What were they fighting about?" was the next question. The daughter answered: "They have been married about two years. He's all right, nothing special. I think he cares for her. My mother drinks more and more often. They fight about her drinking up the house money he works so hard for. They fought last night and I think he hit her, I don't know, I was in the other room. It sounded like a slap and she was quiet afterward. She left and he apologized to me about the fight and said he wished she would stop drinking and stay home."

Charlene was asked if her stepfather had gone out last night. "Yes," she responded, after her mother left. She continued, "About an hour later, he just said he was going out. I don't know where." "Did you see him again last night?" I asked. "No, he must have come in after I had gone to bed. It was late, about eleven o'clock, I heard him when he came home. I was sleeping and did not look at the clock for the exact time," she said. "What bar does she frequent?" I asked. Charlene answered, "All of them."

We thought better of telling a seventeen year-old girl about her mother's death at the time, knowing we were going to meet her stepfather in the near future, that job should be his if he was free to tell her after our conversation with him, assuming he would be. He initially may have been a suspect, but with him reportedly home sometime after eleven o'clock and her seen at 2:00 A.M. outside of the bar, he was looking innocent. He was not seen with her or in front of the bar near the hour of 2:00 A.M.

Charlene advised us that her stepfather was probably at work and gave us the location of his employment. Ironically, it was just a few blocks north of where her mother's body had been found. We left the teenager by telling her we wanted to speak to her stepfather about a neighborhood problem, nothing serious, and that he wasn't in any trouble.

Frequently, the initial suspect in a murder case is the spouse. We had questions for Jackson, but with the time difference established, unless he went back out after eleven the night she was killed, he was not our man. He had fought with the victim the night she died. He had left the premises afterward alone. Circumstantial, he could still be our suspect. Perhaps the events of last night just happened and were forgotten as just another failed effort to straighten out his wife's alcoholism, or they were the last straw for a husband who had reached his breaking point. One thing you had to always do was to consider every aspect of the information learned during an investigation. Don't consider it as gospel or accept it on face value; analyze it and consider the different possibilities it presents.

We drove to the G.M. plant, explained the situation to the manager and shift supervisor, and received permission to speak with Jackson;

a proper formality, because he was going to speak with us no matter what. We found Jackson on the assembly line and made arrangements for someone to take his place while we talked with him. He seemed surprised that police had singled him out by name and stated he did not know why we wanted to talk to him. He was of average height and weight, about forty four years of age, and admitted his wife was not home when he left for work. Physically, he did not look like someone who could carry or drag a woman a quarter of a mile after a beating. Not asking to see his hands, I glanced at both of them and did not observe any damage to the knuckles on either hand.

When asked, he stated that he had completed high school and continued the answer by asking us to explain why we wanted to talk to him. I replied by saying we had a few routine questions about his activities two nights ago, not really telling him why. Jackson was asked to explain his whereabouts the night before last and that of his wife. He stated that he was home two nights ago until about 9:30 P.M., after which he went out, looked for his wife, and not finding her came home late and went to bed. He stated he got home around eleven o'clock that night, went to bed, got up this morning and came to work.

Asked why he was looking for his wife, he became reluctant to say. Finally he said: "Because she is an alcoholic. I didn't find her, like I said. You guys here because of her? She hasn't been home since she stormed out that night after we argued about her drinking, unless she's there now. She get locked up or something? What did she do?" We told him that we had just come from his home and had talked to his daughter Charlene. Jackson replied, "So you should have seen Alice then. What you want with me? She wasn't home when I left for work, but she usually wanders in by now." "Did anything else happen that night between you two?" Tim asked.

Jackson looked at us quizzically and said, "What's wrong? You guys in plainclothes, what's wrong?" We told him as respectful as possible that his wife had been found dead. Jackson almost collapsed; he was crying and he swayed as if he was going to lose his balance. He asked, "What happened? Was she attacked? Where, who, what happened?" We explained enough about finding her to satisfy his questions and told him that as of this minute his daughter was not aware. Telling her would be his responsibility.

John Jackson was taken from work and gave a full statement of his activities on the night of his wife's murder. In that statement, he related the argument and resulting fight between them, amounting to one slap to Alice's face. Afterward, she had left home and that was the last time he had seen her. They fought over her alcoholism. His efforts to find her that night were negative. He had checked several of the local bars for her. Jackson was not responsible for her death; he loved her. He didn't know her friends and did not know where she had gone that night. He remained a suspect, but neither of us thought he was actually responsible for her death. The interrogation had turned into an interview looking for helpful information. He readily accepted the polygraph request and was as helpful as he could be. While speaking to Jackson, his schedule and performance at work for the last few days were checked by other detectives who were told that he appeared normal throughout his work period. After explaining the procedure for claiming the body of Alice Jackson, and telling him we would keep him appraised of the investigation, we dropped Jackson at his stepdaughter's high school. He would have to withdraw her from her classes for the rest of the day and explain what had happened to her mother. In one day, she was motherless and in the charge of a stepfather, both destined for a different life from here on out.

Based on the details we had learned from our bar owner's interview, we had determined a timeline in which the death had occurred. The clothing description of the victim when last seen also fit the clothing that was recovered. Our investigation had determined the last time and location the victim had been seen and that she was in conversation with three young men at the time. The bar was a block and a half from the schoolyard. All we had to do was establish who was last seen with her in a bar that had an estimated crowd of fifty to sixty people at the time, who assaulted her, and why and how was she was found in Cold Gate Creek if the assault started on the school playground.

The same afternoon as Jackson's interview, we checked into the findings of the medical examiners. The autopsy had established that the victim had been beaten to death. She had received several cuts on

the face, a skull fracture and a broken jaw in two places by one or more
of the blows. It was the opinion that her wounds had been the result
of a physical beating with a fist and that no other weapons had been
used. The black substance found at the base of her spine and skull was
creosote. The theory was that she had been dragged by her ankles on
the railroad tracks and that the creosote had come from the railroad ties
embedded under the railroad tracks.

There were small particles of wood splinters removed from both her
head and her spine as well, also thought to be from railway ties because
they bore creosote also, but not as yet confirmed. That would explain the
condition of her clothing, the dress with torn pieces on and beside the
tracks at different spacing on the way to the trestle, and the condition
of the rolled underclothing found on the body. It was believed at the
time that the underwear was wound tightly because of the dragging
action of the body. She had been pulled a long way on the tracks, and
violently, to produce the creosote embedded in her body and the torn
and twisted clothing. While being pulled up the tracks, her head would
have struck each and every railroad tie along the way; you could only
hope that she was unconscious or already dead during what would have
been an ordeal if she were conscious.

As mentioned before, we had one solid lead. Someone, perhaps more
than one, had been with her at 2:00 A.M. at the bar owned by our
southeast district hero, and the bar was loaded with patrons at the time
of closing and before. Perhaps one of these customers could lead us to
the last person or persons seen with her. All we had to do was find the
right one of these people and have them be honest enough to tell us the
truth, and fearless enough to be involved. Wishful thinking to expect all
three: honesty, truthfulness and fearlessness, not standard traits found
in people today. Lies came automatically from potential witnesses just
so they would not be involved. We looked forward to a potentially long
period of interrogations of the various bar patrons from that night that
would hopefully lead us to our suspect(s).

Either we got lucky and found our witness early if he or she existed,
or we interviewed each and every one at that bar that evening until we
found the person who could help us. We returned to the bar with our

favorite owner and obtained a few names or nicknames of patrons he remembered as being at the bar on the night in question. With that information, we started interviewing subjects as located at their homes, or work, based on whatever information we had on them. When located and interviewed, they were always asked the names of those they knew to be at the bar on the night our victim was murdered, in order to add to our list of those to be interviewed.

One of the subjects named as being at the bar on the night in question was Thomas Cain, a young man who ironically lived a city block below the victim on the same street. Cain had been named by one of the many subjects previously interviewed as being at the bar. When we responded to his home, his mother greeted us at the front door, not giving her name. We announced that we were police and wanted to speak to her son, Thomas. A loud male voice was heard from upstairs somewhere yelling, "You damn police. Why don't you leave us alone and do your job somewhere else?" I admit I was a little short tempered at the time and this verbal assault without any warning caught me in a mood. I instantly replied, "Why don't you come on down and we will do our job." We never saw Cain's father or heard another word from him; he remained upstairs and quieted down.

Mrs. Cain explained that her husband was tired from working the night shift; he had just come in and probably needed to sleep. "He did not mean anything by his attitude," she stated. "My son is not home." She said that he was nineteen years old when asked and was working at a named car dealership located about a mile away up on Dundalk Avenue near Eastern Avenue. We left our business cards and requested that he call us at his convenience, that we were talking to everyone that had been at the named bar on the night of the woman's murder. By the time we reached the Cain home, everyone knew why we were in the area without much explanation, but we told her what we needed was routine, easing any fears she may have about our appearance at their home.

Thomas Cain didn't call as requested, so after two days we decided to pick him up at work if he was there. We didn't think anything of his failure to call us, most people did not volunteer when requested to call the police. We arrived at the used car lot located on Dundalk Avenue and asked one of the employees of the business for Cain. He pointed out Thomas Cain cleaning one of the cars. We identified ourselves to him and asked to see his manager. After explaining to the manager that Cain was wanted for routine questioning and not in any trouble, we left with Cain in the back seat of our car. Cain was a good-looking nineteen year-old youth, 5'8" and about one hundred and sixty pounds. He was extremely cooperative and outgoing. He apologized when we introduced ourselves to him, and was cheerful during the ride to our office after being advised that we were talking to everyone we could find from the bar. He made small talk during the ride, smiling and laughing.

Once we were at the office, we sat him down and took what amounted to a rather brief statement about his whereabouts and activities on the night of Alice Jackson's death. After he readily admitted being at the bar, we asked him to identify others there by name, or nickname, or by their description to us, which he did by furnishing a few names. Thomas Cain stated he had left the bar at about 11:30 P.M. that night. His motorcycle, which he parked in front of the south window of the tavern, had broken down and wouldn't start when he attempted to leave. He walked it around the corner and to his house, before entering to go to bed. After his statement, he was thanked and driven back to his job. As we drove him back, he acted nonchalant and appeared to be in a confident state of mind. At the time, there was no information available to us to disbelieve any portion of his statement.

About two weeks later, still acting on information from the various customers from the bar regarding those who had been there, we picked up what amounted to the seventeenth subject and drove him into our office for his statement. Another cooperative youth evidently the lowered drinking age had inspired the attendance at this local drinking hole. He told us about those he knew, a few he recognized as locals, and their descriptions. Some he knew from attending school, and the youngster appeared sincerely helpful. But those he named had already been identified and interviewed, most of which knowing nothing helpful or saying they didn't know anything. After his statement, we walked to the elevator, taking him back to his home. At that point, we were just making small talk.

As we rode down on the elevator, the young man stated, "You know, I forgot someone. Thomas Cain was at the bar also." My first thought was of Cain's previous interview about him saying he had walked his motorcycle home at 11:30 P.M. and had gone to sleep at home afterward. The youth added, "He was there with his motorcycle. He walked it home because he couldn't get it started, then he came back." Tim asked, "Are you positive about that?" Our bar patron answered, "Yes, he came back." "What time was it when Tom Cain came back to the bar?" I questioned. He responded, "He came back within minutes. I saw him there off and on until around closing time."

Cain had lied to us. Finally, we had a lead; we had interviewed someone on the case who had deliberately lied to us. Was Thomas Cain involved or was he a witness who didn't want to come forward? We drove the young man home and thanked him for his cooperation, after having him include the information about Cain in his statement.

Cain had to be talked to again. We located him for the second time at work. He looked slightly disturbed as we approached him. We told him we wanted to speak with him again and asked him to come with us. He stated he would, but asked if his father could come with him this time; his father was off and at home. For three reasons this request was denied: his father's combativeness during our first contact, the fact that Thomas was old enough by law to be interrogated by himself without his parents present, and he had lied to us previously. Cain's attitude was different during this ride to the office from the first trip. He was much quieter and appeared lost in thought. For the first time, Thomas was acting as if he was involved in our investigation. But was he a witness or a suspect?

Cain was ushered into an interview room and advised of his rights. There was no sense in talking around why he were there, so we confronted him with the information pertaining to his lie. Cain drew a deep breath and stated, "I am so scared. I've never been in any trouble before, much less anything like this." He tiered up, as he spoke, "My parents won't believe this. I told them I was just there, nothing else." Then, without us asking another question, he stated, "I was there, I was part of it." Tim replied, "Tell us what happened and be truthful, it will help you in the long run if you tell the truth, and it's all correct ." He gathered himself and said, "I was there by accident. I would never have done what was done to her."

"Go ahead and tell us what happened," I replied. Cain continued: "Well, we were all drinking rather heavily before it happened. The four of us went out front at closing time. She was really drunk, Ms. Jackson. I know her from the neighborhood. One of the guys with us was trying to talk her into having sex with all of us. When she refused, the same guy took her arm and started walking her down the street, telling us to come on. We all walked down the street. She was so drunk that I don't think she knew where she was going. He took her onto the school lot and we followed. All of a sudden he hit her really hard in the face, after she refused sex again. He beat her again and again, hitting her in the face. At that point, she seemed like she was dead. She was bloody and unconscious. He turned to us and said we had to help get rid of her, because if we didn't we were just as guilty as he was. We were afraid of him; he is the neighborhood bully. If we didn't help him, he would beat us like he had her. He went through her coat pockets, divided up the change she had and gave the other guy her coat." The coat had not been indicated as missing to that point, but was later confirmed.

Thomas Cain's disturbing tale went on further: "He told us to carry her up the train tracks and we would put her in the woods. The other guy with us did most of the carrying; he is big and strong, not too bright. We dragged her along way and threw her into the creek, Cold Gate Creek. She didn't move at anytime." Tim asked, "Did any of you sexually assault her?" "No, I didn't, no one did, we were too scared," replied Cain. "Look, you have told us the hard part already; you have to tell us the names of the others involved," I said. Thomas hung his head and said, "It was a guy nicknamed 'Rudy' and the other was Ralph. Rudy's the bully and Ralph is the not too bright big guy." "Do you know where they live?" Tim asked. He answered, "Both live around there. Rudy about two blocks away in St. Helena, Mike Grinder maybe three or four blocks away." "All of you were drunk at the time?" I asked. "Yes," replied Cain. "Did anyone other than Rudy assault her?" I asked. Cain answered, "I swear only Rudy hit her. We were afraid of him, and what had happened. No one else hit her, that's why we did what he said to do." "What are their full names?" I asked. Cain cooperated, replying, "Rudy is Ronald or Roy Fields. Everyone knows him as Rudy. The other guy is Ralph Grinder. We call him Mike."

Wanting to confirm everything, I questioned him: "Are you telling us the truth about what happened?" He replied, "Yes, that's the truth." "Did you take her clothes off at any time?" I asked. "We took her coat at the schoolyard, I think Mike kept it. We divided up what little money she had. We didn't try to assault her. She looked dead already. Her dress was torn off carrying her and dragging her on the tracks. Her underclothes must have torn or rolled up as we dragged her; she was almost naked by the time we reached the trestle." "Who was the one who threw her off of the trestle?" Tim asked. Cain answered, "It was Mike, he's so strong and mental, and he'd do anything anyone told him." "Was he told to throw her off the trestle?" asked Tim. "Yes, Rudy told him to. He told us we were involved in her death and would go to jail for it unless we did what he said. He said he would kill us if we told," explained Cain.

By this point, Thomas Cain was an emotional wreck. I looked at him and said, "Are you sure you have told us everything? Is there anything you wish to add?" He answered," I'm sure. I'm so sorry for what happened. My life is ruined and that poor woman is dead. I'm glad I told you, I couldn't sleep anyway." On the basis of his confession, Thomas Cain was charged with the murder of Alice Jackson. His parents were notified by phone of their son's arrest. His father's initial attitude with us was now understandable. Any father would have acted the same. He was just trying to protect his son. The father had been told by his son prior to our arrival at their home that at least he had been at the scene with Jackson, and he had perhaps told him he was involved in her death. Like any father, his first thought was to protect his son, and he had tried. We had not considered the father's attitude at the time as defensive when we first looked for Cain. The mother's explanation about him had disguised her husband's attitude, either deliberately or accidentally.

We had been given the home address of Ralph Grinder and when we rang the doorbell, he answered the ring. He stated, "My mother's not home. She's out looking for a job." We told him who we were and after we identified him, he was told that he was under arrest and had to come with us. With a childish look on his face, he answered, "I know, I really did wrong, about the lady." Ralph was nineteen years old at the time, almost 6' tall and weighed about 190 pounds. He did fit the description given to us by Cain and looked easily the part of a strong kid. The house, a rental, matched the appearance of Ralph; it was old, needed exterior paint and was generally rundown. He was dressed in what appeared to be washed-out old clothes; his shirt and pants were faded and were frayed at the cuffs. Going to the car, he said, "My mother will be all alone. She needs me, and I help her." We responded by telling him that she would be notified. We advised him not to talk to us about what had happened to the lady until we reached headquarters, wanting him to be formally advised at the time of his interrogation, and have his mother present.

Arriving at the office, we placed him in an interview room, advised him of his rights and told him we were going to take a statement about what happened to the lady and those that were with him at the time. He was almost childlike in his mannerisms and responses. We knew the decision to have his mother there was the correct one.

Hours had passed before she was contacted by phone and was advised to come into our office. A local area radio car transported Mrs. Grinder into our office. She was advised of the situation and sat in on the statement, signing Ralph's advisement of rights form also after reading over it, and giving permission for the statement. In general, he told us the same information we had gained in Cain's statement. They were at the bar, all drinking. They went outside at closing and were standing in front. Ralph continued: "Rudy tried to get some lady to go with us. It was me, Rudy, and Tom, and her. The lady was drunk, we all were. We walked her down to the school from the bar and Rudy tried to get the woman to do something she didn't want to. Rudy hit her in the face several times and she was still. She just lay there; she was dead. Rudy told us that if we didn't help get rid of the body, we would all go to jail, I was frightened; Rudy said if we didn't help, he would beat us up. It was his idea to carry her up on the train tracks. When we reached the bridge, he told me to throw her off, I did."

During the statement, he denied ever assaulting the victim and excluded Cain from the assault as well. He admitted taking the woman's coat and some change, saying, "Rudy divided her money, saying we were all involved now." Asked what he did with the coat and money, Ralph said he had given the coat and money to his mother because they were poor and she needed both. Ralph was responsive to all our questioning and told basically the same story as Thomas Cain. He was so deliberate and so childish in his responses to our questions that we were convinced that he was indeed slightly retarded, although his mother refused any comments or an explanation about his problem. She allowed our interview and did not interfere with the questioning. We would have him evaluated later in order to substantiate his confession as being legally obtained because of his questionable mental ability.

We found Rudy's home by its physical description and the verification that Rudy, who had a proper name of Ronald Fields, lived there when we rang the bell and spoke with his mother. Rudy was not home at the time nor would he be located there or anywhere else for more than eight years. We attempted turn ups at his home on several occasions afterward but he was never found. After these turn ups, it was evident that his family was involved in helping Rudy evade the police. During our search for this subject, we received information that he was hiding in New York State, on property held by the family. He was seen at various times in the neighborhood, and arrested in the state of Georgia for another offense, but released before the fingerprints identified him as wanted in Maryland.

On one occasion, we turned up his home and thought at the time we had him. We barged in the front door and found an unidentified youth sleeping on the living room couch; his head rested on a pillow and under the pillow was a kitchen knife with a six-inch blade. The boy, awakened by us, identified himself and explained the knife by saying it was put there by Rudy and he was told by him that if the police came to use it. The kid said, "I told him I would, but I know better. Why would I get involved with cops by doing something like that?" On another occasion, we received a call that he was in the home of another in the neighborhood. We responded and were told by the father of the boy that lived there that no one was home but him; three boys had just left, including his son. He didn't know the others with his son at the time. We got back in our car and witnessed the three walking in a clearing near some woods not far from the home we had just left. We parked and followed.

The boys, seeing us, ran into the woods. We ran after them. Tim shouldered one to the ground before he got to the woods. I chased the other two. When I yelled at the two who continued to run, "Stop or I'll shoot," one of them did a two and half gainer behind a dead tree trunk on the ground and the other found second gear and ran faster into the woods where he disappeared. I knew at that time Rudy had just gotten away. The captured youth from the woods admitted that it was, indeed, our wanted suspect who had escaped. That was the closest in all those years we had ever gotten to him.

I did not have to be told by the youth that he had been with Rudy. Whenever you called for them to stop, they did one of two things: either surrender or, as we say, put it in second gear, which meant they were gone. At the time, I was not going to fire at the two, not knowing which one Rudy was. By the time he sped up, there was no shot to take. Rudy proved over the years to not only be elusive, as noted by the many different locations he was spotted but in character with the information furnished by both Cain and Grinder, exemplified by his random criminal activity while wanted, which included assault and burglaries in various states.

After leaving homicide, I was assigned to the Applicant Investigation Section of the department and was there for several years when I was notified that Ronald Fields, known as Rudy, had been arrested in New York State. At the time of his arrest, our warrant was identified and served. He confessed to the murder of Alice Jackson to the arresting officers at that time, saying, "That doesn't count any more, the statutes have run out." Of course, they had not. There are no statutes of limitations on murder charges. As elusive as Rudy had proven, even with his various encounters over the years he was on the wing he had not taken the time to learn about the law. Rudy's confession was more than adequate and he must have pleaded guilty based on it; neither Tim nor I ever received a summons to testify in the case, and that was the last we heard of him.

Both Thomas Cain and Ralph Grinder had been tried and convicted in their respective trials long before Ronald Fields was ever arrested for the same crime. Both received lesser sentences because they were less culpable in the act and had no previous records of arrest. The third party Fields had previous records of arrest and was accused of being responsible for the death by the two others involved. The courts accepted their version of what happened, partially because Fields had still been on the wing eluding arrest and could not dispute their version. Fields was identified as being responsible for crimes in several states over the years, including burglary and assault, and was periodically searched for in a wooded area in which his family had property and a cabin, as well as his local address at the time of the homicide.

Several years after the arrest and imprisonment of Cain and Grinder, an officer called me at work and asked several questions about one of the subjects in this arrest. He was interested in Ralph Grinder, who was out of jail and who had eventually admitted to him he had done jail time for a murder. I thought back to the case that now was six to eight years old.

Grinder was the poor, strong, slightly backward, easily led kid, who had given his poor mother the spoils of what was a nightmarish crime he had been caught up in. At the time of the investigation and interviews, I felt he was the least culpable of the three involved. When arrested, Grinder was the one who stepped up and told the absolute truth about the murder out of the three of them. One of the others initially lied; the other ran and was on the wing for years. At the time I had hoped they would have found him incompetent to stand trial. Now he had served his time for the crime and had been released. I asked the officer why he was interested, and he responded, "Grinder has married my sister, he's my brother-in-law. They have been married for about a year. He just told me in conversation about the case." I asked, "Is he working and providing, without any trouble?" The officer said, "Yes, he is. I always thought him to be a nice guy, he's good for her." I thought for a second, thinking back on Grinder, and replied, "Then let it happen. He was in the wrong place at the wrong time. He'll be alright." I heard the words,"Thank you'" come over the phone and then the line went dead.

288

A Victim and His Car

———∞∞∞———

Working the 4-to-12 shift, we received a call that a homicide had occurred in the northeast district. We responded to the address given and found it to be a three-story apartment building, housing two individual apartments on each floor. At about 10:45 P.M., we entered the second-floor apartment marked 2A and found a room with four police officers. We asked which officer responded to the scene and secured it. After determining who that officer was, we asked the others to leave. Most uniformed police officers were much to inquisitive. When a hot call such as a murder came across the radio, all of them in the area would respond. In their excitement to see a body, or what had occurred at the scene, they inadvertently destroyed evidence or could by their presence.

The scene officer identified himself as Officer Benjamin Hart, a four-year veteran of the department and the area postman. He had received the call at approximately 10:17 P.M. for a disturbance at 2A. Upon his arrival at the location, he found the door to the apartment unlocked and ajar. Entering, he observed the victim, a man, lying on the living room floor. After examining the victim, he realized that the victim was died as result of apparent head trauma. His skull had been beaten in; blood and brain were strewn about the floor in the proximity of the body. The furniture appeared out of position as if pushed during a struggle. One wooden dinette chair wad been turned over. An altercation had obviously taken place based on the condition of the room.

The officer explained that after checking the body for life, he had knocked on the adjacent door, Apartment 2B, and that the tenants said they had heard noise coming from 2A a few hours before and had called the police. It sounded to them as if an altercation was taking place, but the noise was brief. Officer Hart stated he had already called communications and they had advised that car 435 had answered the call for the fight at 9:32 p.m. while Hart was out of service on another call. Officer Powers in that car called back into service after finding the door to 2A locked upon his arrival and receiving no response when he announced that he was a police at the door. No one identified themselves as the caller when he was on scene after he confirmed the address with communications.

Officer Hart gave us the names of Apartment 2B for further interviews and stated he had already called for the crime lab. He tentatively identified the victim as a Mr. Albert Kid by the name listed on the first-floor mailbox for that apartment number and also by supplying a physical description of the victim to the occupants of 2B without telling them that their neighbor had been killed. The victim's wallet and his apartment key had not been located, and his left rear pocket was turned inside out. Whoever killed Kid had also robbed him in the process.

The victim was lying on his right side on the living room floor. There was a bloodstain under his head on the carpet, with blood spattering and brain particles on the floor near the body. Examination of the body revealed defense wounds on both hands; they were bruised and had small cuts and scratches, as well as skin fragments under his nails. His head had about a four-inch indentation above his right eye and the upper-front right portion of his forehead was pushed inward, revealing a deep skull fracture and gray matter. No other apparent wounds were noted.

All the other rooms in the apartment were intact, not having been disturbed. They appeared exceptionally clean and tastefully decorated. The bedroom and closet indicated one inhabitant only. The room was neat and the variety of men's clothing hung in the closet was all the same size. The front door originally found open by the responding officer was intact, no signs of forced entry. We counted three heavy crystal, drinking glasses on the living room carpet and one still on the top of an end table. The glass near the body appeared to be the murder weapon. It was partially broken and cracked with thick blood on most of it, smudged with fingerprints. The disarrayed glasses would indicate that more than the victim and his assailant had been in an altercation or at least in the apartment at the time of the assault which led to his death.

We were making the assumption from the name on the mailbox that the body on the floor was actually Albert Kid; he was the approximate size of the clothes we had seen in the closet. The crime lab technician arrived and processed the scene. Fingerprints and photographs were taken. The broken drinking glass with the blood and smears was bagged to be examined under greater scrutiny by our lab. The officer stood by awaiting the arrival of the medical examiners to remove the body. I was impressed with Officer Hart; he had made initial scene observations, interviewed potential witnesses, notified all the needed departments, and checked on the last call to the apartment for service, remembering the other officer answering it before he could call back in service. The only problem, although he had secured the scene, was allowing the other officers in the apartment.

From the condition of the scene, we surmised that the confrontation leading to the victim's death took place solely in the living room. The killing was either accidental or spontaneous during the altercation, because the rest of the apartment was not disturbed. There was no indication that the assailant(s) had rooted through the apartment in their search for other valuables. They had either made a hasty escape out of fear of being caught at the scene or because the death of Mr. Kid was not planned. Our suspects possibly numbered three because of the number of glasses found about the room. They represented our best hope for suspect prints.

We went next door to Apartment 2B. Talking to both the male and female residents we discovered from our description that the victim was more than likely Mr. Kid. The tenants revealed that although they didn't see him or anyone else enter or leave the apartment that night, just before they called the police they heard loud voices and what sounded like furniture being bumped against the wall. When asked, they said that Mr. Kid had lived alone in the apartment about a year, moving in after they had. They gave us the information pertaining to the rental agency located at a different address in case our investigation required it. Asked if Mr. Kid was in the habit of having parties, they noticed that once in a while he had small parties, four or five people. Bashfully, they acknowledged that Kid liked men, saying that the parties usually consisted of young to middle-aged males.

After we had exhausted our questioning and felt the tenants had nothing else to add, we returned to the victim's apartment where the lab processing had been completed. The medical examiner had still not responded. Officer Hart stated that in our absence he had received a phone call from a woman who advised she was the sister of Albert Kid and wanted to know why a police officer had answered her brother's phone and why he couldn't? Officer Hart said he told the sister that one of the detectives would call her back. He had not told her that her brother had been killed. The sister had given him her phone number, but said if there wasn't a return call soon she would be on her way there. She stated that she lived about ten minutes from her brother and that her name was Amanda Price.

Mrs. Price showed up a few minutes later with her husband Alfonso Price, before we returned the call. Both were anxiously concerned about Albert. Neither of them was allowed into the apartment because the body had not been removed. After she had calmed down, we went about the explanation of what we had found and the never comfortable dialogue leading to telling Amanda that her brother had been killed. After a period of hysterics at the news, her husband managed to calm her down enough that we could talk with her. This was always a difficult time, but a necessary one. We had to ask her questions that could possibly help in our investigation. Amanda said that she understood and started off telling what she knew about her brother before we could ask. She stated that he preferred men rather than women and that he dated an assorted group, both white and black men, all ages.

Kid's sister didn't know any of his friends personally, saying that he had a habit of running around in different bars and picking up anyone he could. She said his last relationship was with a man named Carl about a year ago that had ended. She did not consider him a suspect because they parted as friends. When asked, she said she didn't know any of the bar locations that he frequented were and she had no knowledge of his present associates. None of this information could help us. We mentioned to her that both his wallet and house keys were missing; therefore, we felt that the altercation that led to Albert's death was a robbery that he resisted. She responded, I've often told him not to pick up people he didn't know. If they took his keys, is his car gone?" Tim answered, "We haven't had time to check if he even had a car. What kind is it?" She replied, "They have parking spaces here for the apartments. It's a light blue Chevrolet. It should be parked outside in the apartment numbered space." Tim checked the parking spot and area for any car matching the description given us, with negative results. There was not a light blue Chevrolet anywhere on the lot, and the designated parking spot for the apartment was empty. We called an emergency DMV number and obtained the tag number of the Kid vehicle, and put out a "locate" on the described vehicle, requesting a hold on all occupants if stopped, and a wanted relative to homicide, and our immediate notification in either case. We left the crime scene shortly after the Amanda Price interview and returned to the office.

We knew we were dealing with a robbery and more than one subject was involved. Solvability was high fingerprints other than the victim's should be found at the apartment, perhaps on the broken glass he was beaten with, and could exist in the vehicle when recovered if the thieve(s) did not burn the car. Either it was a spur-of-the-moment attack on the victim or the suspect(s) were sloppy and panicked, leaving the glasses at the scene for us to get their prints. Taking the vehicle could prove to be another mistake by his attackers. We started the necessary initial report, using our scene notes.

At 1:31 A.M., we received a call from communications that the car belonging to Kid had been located in the central on Robert Street near McCulloh Street. The car was being eyed by the district officer, who had spotted it at 12:17 A.M. The streets were quiet, the car unoccupied at the time, and no one had returned to the vehicle. We advised radio that we would respond to the location and indicated that we would relieve the officer by driving by his unit and waving to indicate our presents. We arrived at the location in an unmarked vehicle at 1:58 A.M. and took up a parked position with the Kid vehicle in sight, approximately seventy feet from our location. We were close enough not to be noticed on the dark street, but near enough to grab anyone who returned to the vehicle. Our wishes had been granted; the car was intact and had not been abandoned and burned before its recovery. It was parked properly on a public street, which added to our confidence that the suspect or suspects would return.

The street was dark except for the standard streetlights. Traffic was occasional and foot traffic was all but nonexistent at this hour. Our car sat in a residential neighborhood, row house after row house with who knows how many occupants in each dwelling. Radio dispatched calls were infrequent because of the hour, but increasing with each hour as the public awoke to face a new day. We kept the radio low, just so we could make out the calls ourselves, but low enough not to be heard on the street. There was nothing to do but sit and wait, and make small talk. We both hoped that someone involved in the Kid murder would return to the vehicle. It would certainly make the case easier and save us a ton of legwork. We had lifted prints for matching at the scene and would probably get them from the car when it was processed, but if they didn't identify our suspect(s) as expected they would, we had nothing. Tracing the victim's last hours and hopefully putting him with his assailants could prove difficult if things went that way. The case looked like a slam-dunk, but bad luck with the prints and no one returning to the victim's vehicle could throw the case in the other direction and cause a ton of work.

We sat there for a little over four hours, talking initially about moves on the case and then a general conversation about complaints about the job, something every police officer could do at the drop of a hat. We discussed the long hours involved with casework, the bosses, promotions, etc. It was long enough to cover an array of topics, and a lot of different opinions on the subjects were expressed. Ironically, we were parked less than a mile west of where I had grown up and about a mile and a quarter northwest of my first post, which proved to include my radio patrol area also. The thought crossed my mind, as a kid growing up just blocks away and never considering being a police officer until just before I joined the department, here I was on a dark street waiting for a murder suspect or suspects to return to their victim's stolen car. Fate is truly complex and unforeseen.

The conversation was about to lead us into a discussion about our separate job experiences, one of which we were involved in at present. Daylight was almost upon us; a faintly lit eastern sky was about to reveal the first hint of sunlight as the darkness gradually lifted. After hours of darkness, we began to see the front steps start to reflect light as the first sunlight struck the marble. Residents scrubbed these marble steps, once famous to Baltimore, religiously every weekend; a consistent timely chore every Saturday during my youth that marked the day and the start of the weekend. By now, both of us were getting the feeling that the victim's car had been abandoned in the block and no one was going to come back to it because of the growing daybreak. The case was not going to be easy. As the day dawned, we both hoped the prints recovered would lead to the suspect(s).

Just then, a youth, small in stature, wearing dark clothes walked steadily toward us on the street. It was not light enough to tell if he had come from one of the block row homes or had walked onto the street from one of the adjacent streets, but there he was. At first, his deliberate walk led us to believe that he would stroll right past the Kid vehicle, and just as I was about to say he wasn't our man, he stopped abruptly on the sidewalk in front of the victim's car, looked up and down the street, and leaned toward the driver's door. His actions caused both of us to slide down in our seats to prevent him from seeing us. At the time, we were parked about six car lengths from where he stood on the same side of the street. After looking both ways, the subject went in his right front pants' pocket as if reaching for car keys and then unlocked the Kid car door on the curbside. We exited our car without closing the doors so as not to have him hear the sound and run before we were near him. With guns drawn, we approached him on each side of the Kid vehicle as he seated himself behind the steering wheel. He was placing the key in the ignition when I tapped the window with the barrel of my snub nose revolver, announcing that we were police. He turned and looked at the gun two feet from his head, released his hold on the ignition keys and raised his hands from the steering wheel, turning toward me with a look of sad acceptance.

Suspect one had been arrested without incident, with the victim's car keys in his hand and him in Kid's car. The only statement we needed from him was what involvement in the act he played. He was one we were looking for, that was established with his possession of the keys, unless he gave us a believable explanation that he could prove. We felt his prints would put him at the scene, but the names of the others involved were needed. We called for the crime lab to process the Kid vehicle, before it was seized as evidence. Transported the suspect to the office and interrogated him there.

Since he was arrested leaving the area in Kid's car, we had no reason to believe the others had any intentions of meeting him there. Identified as Thomas Willington, age twenty, after advisement of rights he told us the standard story that was a proven threat to homosexuals. In their search for companionship, they frequently attracted robbers. People would beat them and take their belongings, and in some rare occasions actually murder the victims. What many did not realize these victims would frequently defend themselves and their property. Often, we found the resulting altercations were quite violent. Sexual preference had nothing to do with a person's ability to defend himself and his desire not to give up his property.

Willington had not yet become a hardened criminal and he willingly gave up his two accomplices. They all turned out to be neighborhood friends who had grown up together in the area where Willington had been arrested. None lived on the block in which the Kid vehicle was found. Turned out by their parents, or their single parent, in their early years, they frequently found their home locked to them and had to learn to survive on the street. Breakfast often consisted of a soda and a bag of chips. Victims of a vicious circle, no parental supervision or control, no one to keep them in school or show them any direction, no one to teach these three right from wrong or just fundamental respect for others. In order to survive, they had initially turned to convenient crime, crimes they had success with and therefore felt confident doing; spur of the moment street robberies outnumbering their victims, house burglaries and larcenies from cars, anything they could trade for cash. With no jobs, money, education or support from anyone, the three had matured into part of the increasingly expanding numbers of street youth destined for a life of crime and eventual prison terms.

Although all were just either over or under the drinking age, they were seated in a bar eating sandwiches and burgers on the east side when a man walked in smiling at all who looked in his direction and seated himself at the end of the bar. Within minutes with their street smarts they all realized they had found a mark. The three were convinced that the man at the bar was not only interested in them but that he liked young men; he would be easy to pick up. One of the three walked up to him and started a conversation with their potential victim. One would talk him into going outside of the bar onto the street; the other two would follow and rob him

Willington admitted he was the one talking to Kid at the bar, and that after a few minutes of chatting they got up and walked outside. Seeing this, his two friends followed them out. Once outside, as they approached what was to be their victim on the spot, Willington had changed the game. He acted as though the two were friends and asked Kid if he would like to party. Willington had made the decision that robbery on the street was far more risky than robbery at his home. The suggestion, Kid smiled at all of them, seemed to size them up and agreed. A party at his apartment sounded fine. His car was just parked a few doors away. All four jumped in and rode to his apartment complex not far from the bar. Kid parked the car and seemed excited at the prospect of having the young men there.

Once in the apartment, he readily poured his guests their choice of alcohol from a small bar, serving them all in heavy crystal glasses. For the next few minutes, they drank and laughed over small talk as Kid probably mustered his courage to solicit one or more of the young men. Kid made his intentions felt; so did the guests. All three lunged at Kid and tried to hold him down while they announced that they were going to rob and beat him if he resisted. Kid pulled away and the fight was on. Kid, to their surprise, was a very strong man who was not going to accept being assaulted or his property taken. The ensuing altercation knocked not only those involved around, but pieces of furniture were pushed and shoved about. After minutes in which it was hard to land a blow on Kid, because three of them were trying at once, he was finally knocked to the floor and stunned.

At this point in his confession, Willington stopped talking and gave us the name of the youth responsible for beating Kid to death. He hesitated and then said: "Alfonso jumped on him with a drinking glass still in his hand and began hitting him several times in the face. Blood started flowing from the guy's head and face. I yelled for him to stop, but he didn't. Afterward, the man moaned and appeared to be semiconscious lying there for a few minutes and then he was still. We took the watch and ring he was wearing, wallet and car keys from his pocket, looked around for anything else we could see, panicked and left. We went down to his car on the lot and I drove us home. We split his money and valuables."

With Willington's confession and with him naming the other two involved, the case was basically solved on the night we had gotten the call. The other two were arrested and charged with the murder and robbery of Albert Kid, as was Willington. Their version of the crime differed only slightly from Willington's in respect to the involvement of each. Naturally co conspirators have a tendency to lighten their own involvement. Bad and fearless to their pears on the street they are cowards when confronted. An injured hand and prints on the murder weapon gave us the actual killer out of the three arrested.

Prints belonging to all three were found in the apartment as well as the Kid car. Tried and convicted months later in criminal court, all three received long sentences. The hoodlums had graduated from their street training with the inevitable results. The only question I had about the situation was why did Albert Kid, the victim, allow a group of unknowns to be in his apartment in the first place? Did he not consider that these strangers could overpower him? His was the mistake in not counting the odds, three against one, and the odds proved fatal. Often people consider their lifestyle and beliefs are the same as others. Having enjoyed fond relationships with family and friends, and having achieved a reasonably comfortable lifestyle, they forget to consider others not as fortunate think of them as potential victims and opportunities.

Months after solving the Kid case, Det. Tim Timmons and I were on Lombard Street parked just outside a high rise that has since been torn down to make way for new two-story row homes. Excuse me for my phrasing they are no longer referred to as row homes, but townhouses. We were in the same block as Attmans and Lenny's Deli's, Baltimore's answer to the famous Kosher New York Deli's. We glanced one more time at a photograph of a particular suspect we were looking for and noted his physical height and weight before stepping out of the car and walking toward the first-floor office of the high rise.

Although we knew without a warrant we had no real chance of obtaining information about the tenants from the office personnel, we walked into the office and announced ourselves as police asking if a girl by the name of Alicia Barnsworth rented one of the apartments there. A dark-skinned thirty some-year-old female stared at us and smiled as she said, "You guys know I don't have to give you that information even if she lived here and even if I wanted to." She leaned back against a counter behind her and gave us a defiant smile that we knew was one of satisfaction. Just then, a voice came from an open office door behind the girl we had asked and echoed, "Ask them their names, they sound familiar. If its Timmons and Danko give them everything they want." The voice in the other room must have been the girl's boss, because she jumped from her casual pose on the counter and changed her sarcastic facial expression, answering "Yes, Mrs." At that point, a well-groomed female walked into the room from the rear office, smiled and said, "I thought it was you . I caught a glimpse when you came in. My family and I have always been thankful for what you did for us. We pray nightly for your protection, and have nothing but gratitude for the help you give us."

She shook hands with both of us, smiling sincerely as she did as we greeted Mrs. Amanda Price, sister of the murder victim Albert Kid. "Give these guys what they want. Yes, Barnsworth lives here and she is not our best tenant." You could count the number of times the general public, much less a city employee with employment rules went out of their way to help police, but this was certainly one of them

On another occasion, with a policeman lying shot in the street, a civilian walked up on the scene and said, "I wouldn't have your job for anything." That was more of the normal attitude and response toward us from the citizenry and I guess an offhanded compliment. When danger existed, we were appreciated and surely needed. While I was responding to a call for a disorderly man, a restaurant owner once told me, "Next time, use the back-door entrance." I saw red and it was all I could do not to grab him once his words were spoken. He was told as nicely as possible at the time that he should handle the situations himself because the front door was the only door I or any other uniformed police officer used. We may be called public servants, with some actually thinking of us that way, but we will not going to be humiliated by anyone in the performance of our duties. We were there to take whatever necessary actions the situation presented, doing a job more dangerous for most but still subservient to many in their minds just does not compute.

As we walked up the steps past the graffiti-painted walls and the stained floors that smelled of dried urine, I thought that the experience we had just had was a big reason why we did the job. Every once in a while you found someone truly thankful, even appreciative We reached the apartment number given us for Barnsworth and knocked on the heavy metal door. A young woman in her twenties opened the door. Seated on a couch in plain view from the doorway was our boy. We rushed forward and grabbed him before he could stand up or reach for a possible weapon. He was checked for weapons and told he was wanted on a warrant. Timmons and I called the wagon for him and shipped him off to headquarters. The arrest was made for other detectives on a tip that the suspect was at that location with his girlfriend; our turn up had been a success thanks to Mrs. Price and her appreciative memories.

The Drug Dealer and His Girlfriend

A nother bizarre case I encountered during my career would be even stranger than the Thanksgiving murder, the father and son wishbone killing. Working day work on the 8-to-4 P.M. shift, Tim and I caught the case early in the morning hours. It was on Payson Street in the western. Once we arrived at the scene in the rear of 1600 Payson Street, a uniformed officer and crime lab personnel met us. We observed a well-dressed victim wearing a suit. The man was dressed in a white shirt, tie and dark shoes, lying on his back in the center of the alley, just above the cross street. The officer explained that at the time he discovered the body he was walking south in the alley. He saw the person lying in the alley and as he approached he thought the man had broken his neck, because the closer he got to the body the more he realized he could not see the victims head. When he reached the body, he realized why, the torso was headless.

The victim's arms and legs were intact, his right hand was bloodied and he was missing the ring finger. His head had, indeed, been severed. A search prior to our arrival had not located the missing evidence, in this case, the victim's head and ring finger. Upon examination of the scene, we observed that blood droplets ran north in the alley from the body. Those droplets were followed north in the alley, west out onto Payson Street and then south on Payson and up the steps of a corner address on Payson Street. The address was on an angle from where the victim was found and no more than twenty yards from his body when discovered in the alley. While we remained at the front of the property, we had uniformed police secure the rear. When they were in place, they reported seeing what appeared to be blood droplets on the rear step of the same address.

Knocking on the front door, we immediately arrested the male that answered the door. Entering the sparsely furnished first floor, we passed the living room and found the second-floor stairs to our left. Coming down the steps at the time was an adult female. We grabbed her and advised that she was under arrest. Following down the steps behind her were two children, a boy fourteen years old, and a girl twelve years old, both still disorientated from just waking. We entered the middle first-floor room and there in the room on the wet floor was a bucket of what later proved to be water, stained red with blood. In the kitchen hanging over the wall cabinet's edge in view was a bloody hacksaw and kitchen knife. Both of the adults were arrested and transported to the homicide office, including the women's two children. The female adult was identified as Beatrice Stone and her boyfriend, as Kyle Brown. The children remain unidentified because of the occurrence and the fact that they played no role in the crime other than being witnesses.

While we were still processing the scene, a call came in from communications. Another piece of evidence had been found on the train tracks nearby. Tim asked, "What possibly could that be?" I answered, "Something obvious, the head or the ring finger; that's all that's missing at this point." We had the victim, the killers, and the weapons used, as well as juvenile witnesses. The victim's head had been placed in a paper bag and thrown onto the train tracks from street level. A gust of air from a passing train had blown the bag off the head, and a civilian walking on the street above the tracks had seen the bloody sight and had called the police.

During the interrogation of the mother of the two children, it was learned that the victim was an ongoing boyfriend, a drug dealer from Pennsylvania, who when in town would call the female, rent her house and stay at her home while conducting business. His fatal mistake was letting another junkie know his business. Little did the drug dealer know that Beatrice had taken up with another man in his absence? Kyle

Brown and her had conspired to rob and kill him when he came into the city, taking his money and drugs before any of his transactions could be handled? To the best of her knowledge, the dealer had kept her address a secret and, once missed, his associates could not trace him back to her.

The dealer called announcing his arrival and the female welcomed him with open arms as if nothing was wrong. They partied and drank the entire day and into the evening, putting the dealer more than at ease and in a drunken state, which she thought made him easier to assault. When our visiting dealer reached a combined alcoholic and drug high, she called for her present boyfriend and told him to come to the house. Once he arrived, the plan went into motion, but it had two flaws. First, the dealer was used to the street wars. A big man, he was much more combative than they had thought his condition would allow him to be. Second, although they had planned the robbery, they had not planned what weapons if any were to be used to subdue their victim. Initially, they thought with both beating him he would have been overcome.

Both jumped the victim in the room we found the bucket of blood. He fought back violently. The battle was on, it was very physical and they were not necessarily winning. The woman remembered some tools that were in the kitchen, broke off from the fight and returned with a screwdriver and a hammer. She stabbed the victim with a screwdriver in his chest and handed her boyfriend Kyle the hammer; he struck the victim in the face, knocking out the victim's right eye from its socket. The struggle continued with the victim's bloody eye rolling and dangling on his left cheek, his face covered with blood pouring from his head wounds. Another hard blow from the hammer to the head crushed his skull and he fell to the floor in the middle first-floor room, semiconscious and dying of his injuries. All the while this savage assault was in progress, the two children watched perched on the stairs leading to the second floor from where they had witnessed the entire gruesome, bloody assault. Mother did have enough compassion to order her two children upstairs before the dismemberment started.

The disposal of the body, which had not been planned any better than the assault prior to the attack, was their next problem. The man weighed too much for the two of them to move. First, Beatrice called the local bar and tried to solicit some patrons to help her. They refused to help; probably after some consideration of the amount of money offered them compared with being involved in a crime. Next, she called a relative, a sergeant in our department, and told him to come over because she had a problem. She must have thought he would willingly help dispose of the body and risk his job as well as jail time for his aid. God knows what she was thinking to call him. The sergeant was contacted and confirmed her call to him. He stated that he was estranged from his cousin because of her drug problem, knew nothing of the killing, and refused to comply with her request for him to help. He knew nothing of her recent activities and had not associated with her for years because of her drug usage.

Having failed to get anyone to help them dispose of the body, she decided on the next step. They would dismember the body and dispose of the pieces separately. Both agreed on that method. She stated she held the victim's ears to steady the head while her boyfriend sawed at the victim's neck. The bloody gore was too much for her boyfriend and he could not cut up the rest of the body, as she wanted. She stated, "If I knew he was so squeamish, I would have done it by myself. He's not a man." She added she was forced to cut off the victim's ring finger to get his diamond ring when it would not slip off. Beatrice was as calm as someone taking out the trash during the statement while describing the dismemberment of another human being. It struck me at the time she was the hardest, most indifferent female I had ever come across. She stated the finger was thrown away with the head, but it was never recovered, probably carried off by an animal or bird, before the tracks were searched. Her indifference to the cool-blooded killing made me wonder, she could have kept everything they stole from the dealer if Kyle would have become a second victim. Asked, she denied thinking that, but I wondered.

At that point, with only the head removed and the desire gone to continue the dismemberment of the body, they waited until nightfall, dragged the remains out the back door and into the adjacent alley. When they dumped the body, they removed the plastic trash bag covering the upper body. Their logic being the police would get fingerprints off the plastic bag. They then walked the route we had to their front door, not seeing because of the darkness they had left a blood trail leading to their front door. While telling her tale, Beatrice was claim and collected. She was far more callous than her boyfriend Kyle, for that matter, more callous than most men. During their statements, the boyfriend said he opened the front door willingly to us only because he expected a door-to-door interview by the police to find any witnesses to the body found in the alley. He intended to act casual and lie about anything asked about the body. This turned out to be the most unusual Thanksgiving Day murder investigation to date, outdoing the father-son wishbone family altercation leading to the father's killing witnessed by the entire immediate family.

Kyle Brown was advised of his rights. The woman's newfound boyfriend was now scared and more than anxious to talk about his involvement. He confessed to the planned murder and basically gave the same information as his girlfriend, adding that she amazed him, "She was really a vicious bitch." He had no doubt in his mind she would have cut the victim to pieces and had no qualms about doing it. He said he thought at the time they were cutting the guy's head off he better watch her, "she could do the same to me, and take all the money and drugs." We felt that if she had the opportunity, we could have been faced with two victims instead of one and perhaps given the medical examiner's office the job of matching more body parts. We certainly had to agree with his thoughts: She was the most vicious, callous minded woman we had ever encountered. Needless to say, this was not a difficult case for trial. We had the body, the scene evidence, the confessions of the suspects, and the statements of the poor children who had witnessed the murder and would have to live their lives trying to forget their mother's act.

Drug Cases

Ron Brews leaned against the building and lit a cigarette. He took a puff and held it down to his side and slightly behind his back so that it was not as noticeable. He was not supposed to smoke while on the door. Ron was a doorman on The Block, Baltimore's famous row of sexually explicit sex clubs and bars known the world over due to the service personnel and seamen that shipped in and out of our port city. Well, they call them doormen, but actually Ron was a barker, his job was to lure men into the scantily clad girly strip shows on stage inside the club that employed him. As prospective customers harried, strolled or staggered up and down his portion of the sidewalk, his job was to call out and convince them that out of all the clubs his had the best show in town.

Ron was a twenty two year-old male and had been holding down this job for six months. He had been a helper on a delivery truck and a stockman in a warehouse as far as previous legitimate occupations. This was not a real job as far as he was concerned, but it gave him a steady income and certainly was easier than the others. Plus, it had enabled him to meet his girlfriend Linda, who he had been seeing for three months now. Ron Brews, like a lot of young people, had run into problems with the law in the past, but in his mind he was past that now. Part of those types of problems had been caused because he was forced to be on his own at an early age. His parents were old school as far as he was concerned, both hard workers and set in their ways.

They provided him with a good home and attempted to pass on their standards and moralities.

In his teenage years, Ron experimented with drugs and it caused more than a small problem with his dad. His father was ex-military, hardnosed and steadfast in his feeling about illegal drug useage. When he found out his only son was involved in drugs, the argument quickly turned from a shouting match between them into a physical beating by his father, which ended in Ron being thrown out of the house. His mother cried and pleaded, but his father's mind was made up. No son of his was going to live in his house and use drugs. The logic of this is questionable. What do parents do in this situation? Help their child with every possible aid available or show him tough love, as in this case. Either way could work. Quite often, it depends on the individual that needs the help and their desire to cooperate. Perhaps what his dad did not fully realize was that putting Ron on the street made his continued drug usage increase even more.

The young man found himself stealing articles of value from those who allowed him to live with them to support his drug habit. Ron seized every opportunity to take anything of value when the opportunity presented itself. He satisfied as well as stole from desperate men risking arrest to have sex with younger men they solicited while prowling the Patterson Park area in their cars. These street activities caused a few arrests, one for theft at a store and two for solicitation in the park area, which brought him to his present occupation. Because of his age and the fact that his parents did appear on his behalf, these minor charges did not result in any detention, but helped to scare him. As he stood there thinking over these experiences, he had convinced himself that the old life was over and that with some effort on his part things would turn out the way he wanted. He had a girlfriend he cared deeply for, would find a steady decent job, stay out of trouble and would make his way through life like everyone else. A good attitude, one you would have to agree with except for one problem he was not truly ready to commit, in his pocket was a small glassine bag of heroin.

The future rosy dreams of a happy life were just flickers in his mind and would be washed away and replaced with the supposed pleasures the drug would bring Linda and him that night. Ron had not awakened to the reality of the dangers of continued drug usage. He could hardly wait until his break: He would run over to the club where she worked and tell her the good news that he had scored some good stuff. Ron knew he would have to convince her to try heroin because she never had, but thought she would agree to it for him.

Linda Barrands was a young, energetic, personable girl ready to spring into her adulthood. She came from a good family, was an excellent student and never a problem to her parents. After graduation from high school, she had no desire to go on to college. Anxious to be on her own, Linda and a girlfriend planned throughout their senior years of high school to share an apartment. Their wishes came true and for about a year and a half they lived together until her friend mentioned she was going to marry her boyfriend and move. Linda found her self solely responsible for the monthly rent and could not find anyone she was compatible with to share the rent. She ended up losing the apartment and moving back home briefly, but again craving her independence. One of the girls she knew from high school was working in one of the strip clubs and had mentioned that she would make enough money for any apartment if she would come to work there.

Linda ended up at the club as one of the dancers. Almost immediately she realized that the management in this kind of business expected much more than she was willing to do. Although more than happy with the money, she was a little uncomfortable even dancing for a living, but the idea of making extra money by selling bottles of cheap champagne, having men paw her, and promise sexual favors to have drunks spend their money and stand around looking for her after hours was just too seedy for her. She was thankful that the management was not pressing her because she was new, but she also knew that day would come in the near future. She either did what was expected of her or would have to leave. Being pretty and young with a nice figure only drew them in the door; the real business depended on how much money you could get from them one way or the other. Right now, this job afforded her extra money, but soon she would have to settle for one that paid the rent but left little extra. The new job allowed her to find the apartment that she loved and furnished the income to keep it, but she knew she thought more of herself than to work for any length of time being sexually exploited.

Ron's break came around 9:20 P.M. He crossed Baltimore Street to visit briefly with Linda and make sure they were spending the night together. Walking in and out past the vehicles in the street, it struck him it would be difficult to get run over on this street, the cars on it moved at a snail's pace. The drivers were crawling along taking in the sights on The Block: the billboards on the walls advertising the nude dancers; the colorful neon signs naming the various clubs hanging above each one, giving the street an overall soft bluish glow; the street crowded with prospective male customers and female workers; women running in and out of various clubs, leaping in and out of cars and cabs in various degrees of dress governed by the time of year. All were either being dropped off by their recent boyfriends or husbands late for work, or they were anxious to flee the area from promises made to jilted customers.

Ron reached the sidewalk, nodded to their doorman and walked to the basement bar and stage area. Linda was at the bar halfheartedly trying to convince a middle-aged man into buying a bottle of champagne for a ridiculous price, reminding her that this job was not the answer to her prayers. She saw Ron as he entered and excused herself briefly from her halfhearted task, telling the man Ron was her brother and she would be right back. Reaching Ron, she laid a quick kiss on his cheek, making sure the man waiting at the bar was not looking. Ron returned the kiss with a smile on his face thinking, "I do like this girl." They quickly confirmed their meeting after work and Ron eased Linda into the idea of experimenting with something new as far as a drug. All they had done together was marijuana and Linda was relatively new to even that. Linda, hearing heroin, raised her voice and attracted a co-worker Anne, who walked over and told them to keep their voices down. Ron lowered his tone and explained he had scored and wanted Linda to try it for the first time. During this three way discussion, he even invited Anne to join them that night when they all got off. Anne declined, saying she had other plans and walked away. The brief conversation ended between the two with a request from Ron for Linda to think about it.

After work, the two met at the only eatery open after 2:00 A.M. on The Block, Pollock Johnny's, a novel establishment because of the variety of customers it drew at that hour and afterward. It was a strange mix: club owners, doormen, bouncers, bartenders, strippers, prostitutes, pimps, and believe it or not, uniformed and plainclothes police officers. The Central District and Headquarters was a block away, the district's entrance on Baltimore Street and the Headquarters entrance on Fayette Street just north. Uniform police working the area and from the district, as well as nightshift detectives, found this was the closest for food, although the Polish hotdogs with the works eaten at night were as deadly to your stomach as a shotgun blast. Actually, even though it made for an extremely strange mix of people and occupations, the idea that someone in there at any time could be a police officer helped hold down potential dangerous situations.

Ron and Linda finished eating, walked outside and hired what was probably a returning cab driver having delivered his first passenger from The Block looking for the later fares 2:00 A.M. in the rest of the city meant the streets had been empty for at least four or five hours and the hope of fares would be found at four places: either the two bus stations, the airport or at Baltimore Street. The happy couple jumped in the cab's backseat, told the driver their destination and fell into each other's arms. As the cab driver glanced in his rearview mirror, he smiled to himself as he watched two kids, in his mind, embrace and seem to generally enjoy each other. They did not look like one of the usual first-night meetings with the drunken man hoping to score and the stripper or prostitute wanting to roll him rather than have sex. The two in the back reminded him of his youth when an embrace brought with it a feeling that all was right with the world.

The couple had requested an address about two miles from where they were picked up, in a part of town that was still relatively nice. It took about twelve minutes before the cabby pulled in front of the address on the 2200 block of N. Charles Street. Ron and Linda stopped necking long enough for him to pay the fare. They thanked the driver and walked toward a three-story row house about four houses from the corner of 22nd Street. The apartment Linda had rented was located on the second floor, with a business being the first-floor tenant. She smiled as they entered, she was just so happy with her place. Ron had been there a few times prior to this and casually strolled into the small kitchen and found a seat at the table. Linda joined him with two beers from the fridge. They talked, drank their beers, reached across the table for each other and kissed occasionally.

Ron perhaps for the first time realized that he truly cared for Linda. Except for his parents, even though his father and he had their problems, Linda was the third person in his entire life that he truly had feelings for. Both agreed that the hour was late and that they should go to bed. After sex, as they lay there Ron brought up the idea of Linda at least trying heroin; that it was only bad if you became addicted to it and the first-time usage would not cause that. Linda was skeptical at the request having never used heroin before, but her apprehensions drifted away with the thought that she trusted Ron and that he would never intentionally harm her. They embraced and kissed for a while and then Ron set about preparing the doses. He shot up himself first, after which he quickly prepped and injected Linda. Both lay back on the bed and talked until the drowsiness set in. They fell asleep in each other's arms. Ron's last thought, almost dreamlike and hard to hold onto because of the influence of the drug, was a question to him self asking how he was going to keep this girl?

He awoke feeling he had been run over and had difficulty thinking through the act of how to actually stand and perform what his mind was telling him. Next to him on her back was the nude body of Linda. He told her as he staggered away that he was going to the bathroom, but she did not respond. Afterward, he walked back into the room and started talking to her again. After she did not answer, he walked to the bed, covered her with a sheet, and thought he was shaking her awake. As he touched her, she felt cold to his touch, and at that point Ron's world with the first love of his life had ended. He rushed into the kitchen, grabbed the wall phone and dialed 911. Crying uncontrollably, he walked into the bedroom after unlocking the apartment door, sat on the bed, stared at Linda and begged forgiveness. The ambulance crew responded and upon examination pronounced Linda Barrands dead at the scene. The responding police officer found Ron Brews in an all but hysterical state raving to both him and the ambulance crew how he had killed Linda. We received the call minutes later and responded to the apartment in twenty five minutes. Ron again readily confessed to us that he had killed Linda. He stated that he had injected her and that it was the first time Linda had ever used heroin. The makings were on the night table in plain view and there was no indication upon examining the victim that she had died in any other manner than Ron had told us. The apartment was in order and there were no signs that an argument or struggle had occurred prior to our arrival. Ron rode to our office with us while the scene officer stood by for the morgue wagon and Linda's removal from her beloved apartment.

At our office, Ron related the same story. Linda had taken the drug willingly that he had injected her with and unfortunately, and more than regrettably, had died as a result. He broke down several times during the interview and at one point he seemed like he needed a sedative to calm him, so we stopped. We had gathered all the information needed. Ron continually confessed to everyone at the scene of his dead girlfriend that he had killed her. He confessed to be exact to five people being the scene officer, two medics and two detectives. He had killed her but accidentally as far as the evidence and his information was concerned. Both had taken the same drug freely and although he was feeling far from it, he was lucky he had survived.

Attorneys from the State's Attorney's Office joined a conference call about the case and afterward agreed that from the information Ron had related to us, a decision on charges would be made after an interview with Linda's co-worker, Anne Cross, to confirm that aspect of Ron's sequence of events. That afternoon at the club, Ms. Cross was located and confirmed that she was part of the conversation when Ron announced his drug buy to Linda and asked her to try some with him that night. She further volunteered that she honestly thought they were lovebirds and that Ron would never have harmed her deliberately. The information was relayed to the attorney's office and it was decided that no charges would be placed in Linda's death. Ruled an overdose by the medical examiner, we could not prove intent.

What we had not told Ron Brews was that there had been three other overdoses as a result of heroin usage in the past two weeks and that narcotics detectives linked all the deaths as occurring on the east side of town. The thought was that a bad batch of heroin had been put on the street. Ron was brought back in for another interview and asked where he had purchased his heroin. Now calm, he was even more cooperative. Ron explained about a year or so ago after he was put out of his parents' home, he started hanging around the Patterson Park area and in his travels met a dealer. At the time, Ron was making his money as a male prostitute for the guys that rode around looking for young boys. Everybody called this guy "Little John" because he was a big son of a bitch. Ron gave us a good physical description of "Little John" and told us where to look for him. That information was later passed onto the narcotics in the hopes it would help in preventing the "hotshots" from reaching their potential victims if indeed Little John was the distributor. After the interview, Ron was told after all the facts into the death of Linda Barrands the investigation had been ruled accidental and the autopsy ruled an accidental overdose. He would not be charged in the case. Ron walked out of our office physically free without any idea or concept of how or when he would be mentally free. Perhaps Linda's death would free him from his drug dependency or experimentation, or because of his emotional guilt, plunge him even deeper.

I know that most police would hear the facts of this case and decide that the victim Linda, because she worked at the time on The Block, was already a lost child and destined to end up as she did. Her death would have come from continual drug use, not just one injection. But what would have happened if she had cleaned up and Ron or some other guy she had met had tried hard to make a life and home. From those that knew her, that's all she wanted. But because of her premature death, none of us will ever know if she would have turned out to be an upstanding citizen and parent or just another social problem. She did not live long enough to find out.

Aaron had two brothers, of which he was the middle one in age, and a sister who was next in age to his older brother just short of two years older than he was. His mother worked as a domestic in Roland Park while his father worked a hard labor job at a scrap recycling business. They had lived for years on the west side, occasionally moving as a result of cheaper available rentals. With both parents thankfully employed, the family was not rich by any means but survived as well or better than most. Like many families in the seventies, the children went without the thrills in respect to some things they felt they wanted. But compared to most in their income bracket, they were considered a stable family.

One afternoon Aaron's father did not return home from work. He did not come in after work the next day or any time after. His mother, who had always been the rock of the family, set them down and almost casually told the family their father had abandoned them and she was convinced their marriage was at an end. She gave the children a reassuring smile as she did frequently and told them all would be all right. Of course, things had to change. Aaron's older brother resented the situation as well as his father and found employment within the week to help the family financially. His sister, although still in high school, became what amounted to the adult guardian at that point. She supervised their school studies, cleaned the house, washed their clothes, made the beds and prepared the meals. Aaron and his brothers chipped in as needed, but being young at the time had to be told what had to be done rather than having them help on their own. His mother's job and the financial help from his older brother's employment kept the family together. But because his mother worked in Roland Park eight hours, six days a week and the bus trips too and from were each an hour, she was either not home or resting when she was there.

Perhaps because of his youth, Aaron found a release from his family problems by playing sports. Whatever sport was in season, he would play up until the next seasonal sport came on the scene. He was not only good at baseball, football and basketball but also dedicated to learning the sports. The youth was hardnosed and actually had a natural ability at whatever sport he was involved in at the time. Area team sponsors and coaches quickly recognized that Aaron was indeed a gifted athlete. It did not take Aaron long to find that his heart was in the game of football. He loved the sport and perhaps because of his natural ability playing the game, maybe the game loved him back. From the ages of fourteen to sixteen he excelled playing football. Truly, he was a natural halfback. His size, speed and the ability to change direction, find holes and take on tacklers made him a pleasure to watch. Aaron had found his place in life; his father and the family problems he had caused were lost in his desire to play the game. As the years passed in his athletic career, he found himself on the area's more prestigious teams, always starting at his position and always performing better each season. Long before high school, he was scouted by most of them in the Baltimore area as well as in Washington, D.C. area

Now an area namesake as well as a potential star athlete, Aaron wanted to stay home and play where everyone knew him, so he went to the area high school. His star continued to shine and he was the starting halfback at the school for all four years, setting records in touchdowns scored and for most yards gained in three of the four years. With such a high school performance, there was no question colleges would seek his services for their football team even more so than the high schools had. Aaron did have a problem as far as his grade average at the end of high school, but most colleges offered tutoring to solve that potential problem, so that hurdle appeared minor at the time for any school offering him a scholarship.

There was one other problem that would loom on the horizon and eventually change the direction of his entire life. Aaron, who would not admit to himself that there was even a problem, surely could not tell any college offering him a free ride or any portion of one. Because of his talent, the young man knew almost everyone in his community. They idolized him for his athletic ability. Most wanted to be included as being considered a personal friend and therefore wanted to impress and do things for him, the various aspects were appreciated by Aaron, but some favors were not true gesture of friendship. For years, Aaron had experimented with variety of street drugs and had graduated to using heroin about a year earlier. To befriend him initially, it was free for the asking. Once he was addicted, prices came into play, which he gladly accepted.

As Aaron's habit increased, he told himself that the drug actually helped him perform better on the football field. By the time he was on the practice field of his chosen college, his game and attitude toward the coaches and his tardiness from classes and some practices all reflected a problem seen before by the coaching staff. Aaron was a talented kid from a rough neighborhood, labeled with a drug habit and having poor grades, coming into a college that would protect their interests before his. His first and last year playing college football was average on the field and poor scholastically, even with paid tutelage. A spot check of his dorm room in the offseason discovered drugs and his college experience was over.

Home again, with the hope that another college would take him because of his athletic ability. He worked odd jobs while waiting for a call that never came. Aaron thought about a junior college to prepare him for another, but knew in his mind that education would always stand in the way of his possible football career, really having no desire toward furthering his education. Back in his neighborhood, he was king of the hill again; men admired him, women adored him. Drugs, drink and the good life were at hand without any college restraints. Still with the same mindset, he used more illegal drugs, including heroin, than ever before. Seeing that no colleges were at his door, he played locally for unlimited teams and finally for a well-known flag football team as his physical attributes waned and he aged. By now, his drug usage was daily and although his family admitted it, he would not.

Aaron was on a downward spiral and like most addicts would not admit he had a problem. The last member of the family that stood by him was his sister, who after having him come home because he had no other option gave up on him when he stole from the house to pay for drugs. On the street, he did what most junkies have to do, steal any way from anybody to get their fix. Out of places to stay because of thefts and penniless because he was unable to hold a job, Aaron found himself indebted to the very people who had led him into his drug abuse. At this point, he had begged for drugs he knew he could not pay for. Living on the street and in an occasional shelter, the once idol of his neighborhood was now just another homeless man sleeping in doorways and begging for coins.

On Winchester St., near Fulton Ave., a man dressed in old tattered clothes, wearing a coat sizes to large for him, staggered up the street

316

hardly able to maintain his balance without falling. His eyes watered and nose running from the cold, he looked up at a house and tried to remember if it was the right place. Slowly, he walked up the short steps to the front door still not sure if he had found the right place. Leaning against the doorframe, he pounded on the door. An old man pushed open the curtain over the small window in the door and, after seemingly recognizing the guest, opened the door and allowed Aaron inside. Gathered in the front room were both men and women seated on the floor littered with old newspaper and on what appeared to be pieces of old and filthy furniture not worthy of keeping. Aaron staggered over to an open spot in the room, sat on the floor, back against the wall and managed to slip into a semi-conscious state. The house was one of his former shooting galleries and the old proprietor who let him in knew him as a regular. The others in the room were all in various states of consciousness from their drugs and would not even realize he was there. It was cold out, he needed the rest, and he did not want to be found.

Across the street when Aaron staggered inside was a young, well-dressed man who paid special attention first to the man he was watching and then to the address he had entered. After Aaron had been accepted inside, he casually walked to the corner and spotting a wall telephone and made a brief phone call. Afterward, he strolled back to his spot on the pavement. Fifteen or twenty minutes later, a new car pulled to the curb just east of the address. The man came across the street, greeted the two seated in the car and pointed to the house. As the man on the passenger's side got out of the car, his coat brushed back and the handle of a revolver could be seen sticking out from his waistband. The three walked to the front door and knocked. The old man answered, looked concerned and stepped aside. The men looked around the room, walked over to Aaron who was sleeping against the wall and while two held his arms to his sides one reached inside his coat and pulled out a syringe. He leaned over and stabbed the needle into Aaron's left forearm saying, "Enjoy, it's your last." After menacing glances at the old man, they turned and quietly left. The old timer took time enough to get everyone out, hurriedly cleaned up as best he could and then went several houses down and had them call the police.

After patrol called it in, detectives responded to the scene and obtained the information that the dead man was a friend of his just from the neighborhood and was followed there by some gang members or drug dealers he had crossed. Three came to the door minutes after his arrival. They gave him a "hotshot" because he either owed them money or had threatened to report them to the police. Whatever it was about, they knew the syringe would kill him. He died within minutes without a word. The old timer added, "That's it, all you get. All I'm saying, those bastards are serious. They don't care who sees them kill. I am not going to be a witness. Lock me up if you want."

Aaron probably had slipped far enough to threaten the identities of his dealers, and a lesson for anyone else that would consider that had been clearly made. A man with the God-given talent to perhaps become a successful athlete, financially help his family out of near poverty and give them a stable life had made one bad choice along the road to success. The old man closed the door as the detectives left the scene saying," He was a hell of a football player. Can't remember his whole name, but his number was 21." The detectives walked down the steps behind the crime lab tech as the morgue wagon pulled to the curb. Maybe there was rhyme and reason behind Aaron's story. Shortly after he lost football, the love of his life, there was nothing left to lose except life itself.

Ralph Brophy walked slowly into the rear alley of one of his secure bedding places, pushing his shopping cart loaded with personal prizes that only he knew their value and need, various articles collected for unknown reasons but important in his mind. When he reached his spot, he carefully pushed the cart into one corner of the six-foot in cove located between two building doorways and settled down on a few layers of cardboard he had previously placed on the ground to insulate him from the cold night concrete. As he slowly stretched out, he realized that his body was more painful than ever. He thought about the problem, smiled slightly and thought the thing that had cost him his family, job and finally his self dignity along with countless attempts to kick was now giving him a second kind of pain and after having to suffer through this stage would probably kill him. Well deserved he thought, caused by his stupidity. He closed his eyes and prayed that the nagging pain and discomfort would allow him to sleep at least for a few hours.

He was awakened by the sound of a gunshots and people running in the alley. By the time he was fully conscious, he realized that one man had already ran past down the alley to his left, but the sound of others running down the alley was to his right. He stood up and as two others passed him running after the first guy, he heard several gunshots fired by the two men running past. He crouched in the corner of the in cove and pulled his dark coat over his head to hide himself as best he could. Shots echoed off the walls of the in cove and sounded like cannon shots as they were fired while the two men ran after the other.

Brophy's testimony went as follows: "Someone must have stumbled or was hit by a bullet, because you heard him cry out in pain as if he had fallen. Shortly after that sound, several more shots were fired rapidly and then there was silence. Two men walked back past me and I covered up again as they passed. It took maybe ten minutes before I had the courage to go see what had happened. The two men did not come back, so I thought I was safe. I got up and walked down the alley toward what appeared to be someone on the ground. I reached the man who was lying on his back and looked down at him. He was shot in the face and several times in the chest from what I thought, because that's where all the blood was. No question about it, he was dead. As I stood over him, police lights came down the far end of the alley; some of the neighbors must have called after hearing the shots. Plainclothes men came and afterward brought me here."

Because the detectives who caught the call were still at the scene, I took Brophy's statement at the office. The shock that I faced was not his information but his physical condition. When I entered the small interview room where he had been placed, a strange odor struck me. I must have reacted with a startled look as I stared at him, because he responded without a word, "It's me. I'm sorry, the odor is me, and I can't do anything about it." Still a little taken back, I responded with a question, "What's wrong?" Brophy sat there looking back at me with abscesses over his hands, neck, and face. Large puss-filled blistered mounds looking as if they were ready to break covered him. I had heard of what caused this skin disease, but had never seen its results.

Brophy was an IV drug user and somewhere along the line had used what we referred to as a dirty needle. He went on to appear to be genially apologetic about his condition, telling me that he had sores all over his body, covering his arms, legs, abdomen, back, groin, scrotum and neck. Occasionally the numerous abscesses would break and cause the odor. He admitted he continued to use drugs because he could not shake the habit. The drug money came from his military pension and was enough if he lived on the street. Doctors had told him he needed to be hospitalized because of his condition, but he would rather stay on the street for drugs than be treated. He told me that his veins were so bad at this point that he would have to shoot up between his toes. He smiled and said, "I deserve this. I used to be bright. I knew it would hurt when you needed a fix, but I did not know it would lead to this. This will kill me painfully."

The above witnessed facts of the homicide shooting were obtained in a cooperative formal statement given by Ralph Brophy. Unfortunately, because of the circumstances at the time of the occurrence, his information basically identified three people that were unknown to him and the crime he had seen. He had witnessed the actual killing, the unidentified victim along with his two shooters. Unfortunately all were unidentifiable because of the darkness As Brophy left the office, I wondered if he would live long enough or even be located if still alive to set the scene if arrest and trial occurred. The case was truly a whodunit at this point, but Brophy's medical condition was not in question.

Drug murders and assaults grew over the years I spent in homicide, as did the distributors and dealers. These people became rich knowingly dispensing sickness, death and heartache to the families and friends of those addicted. And not to forget, they also murder their competition to expand their businesses. The death toll is impossible to determine. I know that the death penalty in most states, as in this one, no longer exists, but what better candidates than the manufacturers and distributors in charge of street dealers. Since the ultimate penalty no longer existed as a possibility, we should send them away for life plus, with no parole.

Unsuccessful Cases

———◦◦◦◦———

You could not always reach a successful conclusion when working a case. Sometimes even solving a case would not result in a successful prosecution. We had a cab murder shooting at the high rises off of Argyle Avenue. Timmons was off and I had a female detective who later transferred to federal government law enforcement. It was her first case in the homicide. She was dedicated to the job and a quick learner, enthusiastic, intelligent and a good cop. Through witnesses, we developed and identified a female resident of a building adjacent from the shooting location who had reportedly seen a suspect run from the cab after the shooting. She had reportedly told them that she knew who the shooter was. Both of us knocked on this potential witness' door leaving our cards in the door frame several times without any response. About the four or fifth attempt, a girl in her early thirties opened the door of the six-floor high rise and ushered us inside with the comment, "I may as well let you in. You keep coming; you'll get me killed. Everyone knows who you are." Meaning others would notice the police there, word would get back to the shooter, he would feel forced to silence the witness, and eliminate them.

Armed with an array of photographs including the person's picture we thought was the shooter, we asked her if she could identify anyone of them. She confirmed that she had witnessed the shooting and then identified the one we had information on as being the perpetrator, signed and dated her identification, and then returned back to her housework she was involved in before we arrived. "Understand, I have to live in here, that's all I can do. Now leave me alone." As we walked into the hall, my new homicide partner was elated about her first case having reached a successful conclusion. I turned to her and stated that's the last time we will see that girl; she was telling us she wasn't going to testify and why, she has to survive here. Court came and went on that case with no sign of our witness. She had left the apartment weeks before the trial, probably when she received the witness notice for the up date. Now, who knew where she was or what identity she was using. When I was new on the job, losing a witness and the case as a result would have upset me. Now, years later with the amount of intimidation and worse, who was I to judge? She had lived in a war zone without a gun, her answer to this situation was to disappear and survive.

The rewards were often small. Of course, like any other job, the outcome to murder investigations was not always positive. It's human nature; you remembered the ones you didn't close, they played on your mind. You recalled what you considered good testimony when you outwitted the defense counsels. You were proud of the good in-fights you mustered with the department supervisors and sometimes the state's attorneys over case problems and testimony when necessary. Of course, you were pleased with convictions. Most of all, I was proud of my personal integrity regarding my job performance. No matter where a case ended, I had done my best to solve it. When people volunteer for such things as community service, athletic coaching, and fundraisers for the poor, etc., I think of the sacrifices and commitment of all that served through the various police departments, and I am personally proud I was one of them. We served our community to a greater degree than most, protecting those who lived in our city so they could carry on their daily pursuits.

Of course, there were always the cases you could not solve. They are the ones you don't let go of and remember frequently over the years. You continually run them over in your mind, what else could you have done? And you revisit them whenever time allows, trying to reach a satisfactory conclusion.

The cases described below are two such cases in my mind, with established suspects but not indicted. To date, the victims of these crimes have not been represented in a court of law nor have the persons responsible for their deaths been tried before a judge. The events in these cases are true, but the names of those involved as witnesses, victims and suspects are withheld in the hopes that the perpetrators, may one day come to trial for their actions.

A woman on one of the numbered streets off of Greenmount Avenue was found shot to death by her husband of over thirty years upon his return from work. She was dressed in a flimsy nightgown, one gunshot wound to her chest, seated in a relaxed position on her living room couch. There were no signs of a struggle or disturbance to the interior of the house, no forced entry to the premises. It was established that the victim was a homebody, neighborly, but not outgoing in her relationships in the community. She would sit out on their front steps with her husband when weather permitted, but when he left for work she was in for the night and not seen until the next day, doors and windows locked. The neighborhood was deteriorating and she was fearful of strangers and of possible nighttime home burglaries

Her husband worked the night shift at a heavy machinery repair company. Most of the machines were so large that they required mechanical work in yards equipped with large cranes. The yard workers were supposed to stay on the premises during their work hours. On the night his wife was last seen alive, the victim's husband left her on the front steps of their home seated alone. She waved goodbye and went into the house, based on neighbor information. It was also learned that she seemed normal during her conversations with the neighbors and never had visitors when her husband was not there. The husband came directly home from work and discovered her body minutes before 8:00 A.M. and immediately called the police. An autopsy report placed her time of death at about 2:00 A.M. from a single gunshot to the chest. The weapon was not recovered, and the husband stated no guns were kept in the house. Everything at the scene was processed, the body, wound, and interior of the house. Only the occupants' prints were identified, the husband's and his wife's. The two lived there alone; they had one adult son who had his own apartment, having moved about a year before.

The son responded to the scene having been called by his father. He provided interesting facts about his mother's habits. She was a very modest woman and would have never been seen in just a nightgown by anyone she did not know. Of course, in his mind, he was not considering an intruder that had threatened her dressed as she was. He confirmed that she locked herself in after the father left for work, as if it was clockwork; she was afraid of staying alone. The only keys to the house were in the possession of husband and wife, and her keys were found on a table inside the front door in the hallway. She was so diligent about security for the house that when the son visited her alone, she identified those at the door before she opened it. When asked, the son thought that his parents got along well; like most long-married couples, they had their routine and seemed happy, they seldom fought.

The husband's interview was held at our office on the day his wife was discovered. It was my second case investigation and I was not the lead investigator assigned. Two other experienced detectives were breaking me in. When questioned, he stated that all was well between them and that when he left for work the night before she appeared normal. He did not suspect anyone nor would he consider any affair. She had packed his lunch, which she did nightly appeared normal when they sat out on the steps and he had left thinking all was fine. He stated he had worked for the company eight years, and he had eaten lunch at about 2:00 A.M. with his named foreman. He confirmed that she would always lock up after he left and was leery about opening the door to anyone at night. To his knowledge, he said there were no other keys to his house; his son did not even have one. The only thing that differed between his statement and that of his son was the modesty of his wife. He did not agree with that.

During the interview, the husband seemed appropriately upset, and forthcoming in his responses to our questioning. He stated that he never had a thought about an affair and did not suspect her of having one, nor could he think of anyone responsible for her death other than an unknown suspect who got her to open the door to them and during the attempted robbery shot her. We had gathered a lot of information in a short period of time. With no forced entry to the house and no foreign prints having been found, the husband appeared to be our most likely suspect.

We set about proving or disproving the information at hand. The husband's story that he had gone to work that night on time, worked a complete shift without leaving during it, never left the premises and lunched with his foreman all had to be checked. He had reportedly left work at 7:30 P.M. and gone right home.

Responding to his place of employment that night, we noted that it was located no more than ten minutes from his home. At night with no traffic, it would take about ten minutes for him to drive home and 10 minutes back. His co-workers indicated that he was not very sociable, a loner with a direct disposition. When the foreman was interviewed about their mutual lunch break, he commented that it was the first time in eight years that the man had eaten with him during a break. He had asked the foreman a few nights before if they could eat together. During the lunch that took place at about 2:00 P.M., he appeared normal with very little small talk between them. The foreman thought the lunch date was requested by the husband because he wanted to promote himself for a job coming open at the yard, but that topic was never brought up during their conversation. When asked if employees left the premises during work, the foreman laughed and said, "There are more ways out of here than the gates; of course they do. Most sneak out up until 2:00 A.M. for drinks at the bars across the street. Too many employees and too many places in the yard for them to get lost in, can't watch them all."

The situation looked as though the husband may have used the foreman for a witness to his whereabouts at the time of the murder, providing the husband with his alibi. With this and the other information gathered, the husband clearly became a suspect. We had to get him physically away from his job sometime during the hours of his wife's death. Only two reportedly had the house keys, the victim and the husband. No forced entry, no disturbance inside. Victim shot while in a comfortable position, wearing sleeping clothes, as if she knew her assailant, let them into the house, and was not afraid at the time the shooting occurred. The house showed no signs of an altercation or disturbance because there wasn't any before the shooting; the victim may have been lounging comfortably just before shot. We checked with all the co-workers to see if anyone saw him leave at any time or missed him during the shift. All modes of transportation were checked, taxi, bus line drivers. Even the reported accidents and traffic tickets between his employment and house were checked, should he have been involved. Neighbors were re-interviewed to see if any had seen him return home any time during that night or his car during the hours he claimed to be working, nothing. None of them had any reason to believe either the victim or her husband was involved in an affair at the time. Days invested and we could not put him physically at the scene or away from work when the crime was committed. Was it possible he hired someone to do it and gave them the house key? That was another angle, another possibility, but if so, they had not been physically placed at the location of the crime.

We decided that a confrontation with the husband was our only possibility at this time; confront him with all the information that seemed to compound his guilt and hopefully he would realize his position and confess. We drove to his home and announced ourselves after ringing the bell. The door opened and he gracefully ushered us in, still presenting a remorseful appearance and demeanor. He greeted us softly with a question, "Have you guys found out anything?" One of us replied, "Yes, that's why we are here." We laid out the information, touching on all the points that made him look guilty or at least involved in his wife's death. Ending in the information about him requesting lunch with his foreman for the first time in eight years, and asking why he had? The husband answered the question by saying he was trying to plug in for a new job, build some rap pore with the foremen. One of us accused him directly of the shooting, and he answered, "Well then, prove it." With that defense response we know he was our man.

As a result of that defiant act, the husband became the focus of our investigation. Bank records were checked, insurance policies, gun permits and the possibility of another love interest. Nothing more was developed. After exhausting all leads and possibilities, we gave the State's Attorney's Office our investigation. Their attorneys decided we were probably correct in our feelings, but that a good defense attorney would bring doubt to all the findings. Enough evidence to implicate and criminally charge this subject had not been developed. In all probability, the individual we felt responsible for this crime has died a natural death by now; he would be in his nineties if still alive.

The second case in my homicide career that went unsolved was that of a young female high-school senior. Her story goes as follows.

Karen Hardwick spread her stance and rose up on her toes to receive the serve. The ball jumped rapidly from the service area on her side to her right. She lunged in the direction of the ball, fully extended and returned an equally hard shot toward the net. The ball tipped the top of the net, but the slight contact did not impede its velocity. The straight hard return landed inches inside the out-of-bounds line and could not be returned, ending the match. Karen ran smiling to the net and congratulated her friend and frequent opponent. She walked to the bench area, set her racquet down and toweled off hurriedly, knowing she had to leave the club within minutes after her shower in order to be home in time for her family's standard dinner hour. Karen took a quick moment to relax and stood erect glancing over the manicured grounds of the club visible from the tennis court area. She was a privileged eighteen year-old blond, blue-eyed beauty, with a slender build. A joy to her parents even at this tender age, she realized how fortunate her life was and looked forward to the rest of her pending college years and future adult life.

Arriving with minutes to spare before dinnertime, she sat down to dinner with the rest of her family, parents Laura and Donald, and her only sibling, her sister Janice, who was fifteen years old at the time. At the evening meal, talk centered on the girls' school grades and potential colleges each wanted to attend. Both girls were anxious about furthering their education and Karen anticipated her college years, although the exact schools changed periodically. After dinner, Janice and Karen retired to their individual rooms to devote time to their respective homework assignments.

At around 7:30 P.M. in the evening, the phone rang and Laura, Karen's mother, answered and called that the phone call was for Karen. Karen put down her book and answered her phone. The caller immediately indicated that he was a representative of some of the most prestigious colleges in the country and was impressed with Karen's scholastic grades and athletic abilities; Karen's status could very well land her in the college of her choice. His company was interested in ladies with her potential for one of their placements. Janice overheard Karen's responses to the caller from the next bedroom and, as often little sisters do, picked up her extension. The conversation continued briefly, filled with continued appreciation for Karen's potential and concluded with the caller advising that he would contact her soon about a possible agent placement.

Karen hung up the phone excitedly and ran for her sister Janice, who was not as taken with the call. The older sister recited the contents of the call and the resulting possibility for her to get accepted by an elite college. Janice said she felt the call was a hoax; the caller seemed more excited than Karen and did not give her time during the conversation to express her feelings; and from the sound of it, it could have been a classmate playing a prank on her. Karen dismissed the possibility that the call was a classmate prank. Janice calmed her sister's enthusiasm and asked the question that was on her mind after telling her she had listened in on the call, "Did you not notice that the caller's voice seemed to change during the call? At first the caller's voice sounded like that of a male; as the call went on, it changed and it sounded like a woman trying to speak like a male." Karen scoffed at the thought, saying she had not noticed any such thing, and kiddingly advised Janice that she was jealous of her newfound opportunity for college.

Janice told her parents about what she questioned about the caller's voice and her mother Laura advised she did not speak to the caller long enough to notice a change in the voice. Her father made no comment about that aspect of the call, dismissing the possibility as only Janice's opinion. Karen, on the other hand, was excited over the possibility; she always wanted a good school, much less a prestigious one. Could this caller who identified himself as Barry Christensen, be the person to open the door of opportunity for her? In her excitement, she admitted she had missed the man's business association, but if he were sincere, surely she would get all the information necessary when he called back, as he said he would be doing. The family openly discussed the possibility of her attending even an Ivy League school, with sensibility toward Karen's excitement over the unexpected news. The conversation ended on a note that the caller, if credible, would call again and all the college possibilities would be identified and explained. Karen smiled and nodded her agreement, knowing college represented a standard family plan for both her and her sister and this opportunity would relieve some of the financial burden. But deep in their thoughts, both parents hoped that the caller was sincere because of her enthusiasm.

Two days later, at about 6:45 P.M., both sisters walked from their tennis match toward the parking lot. Janice, who was riding with friends to a local eatery, gave her sister a hug and kissed her on the cheek, telling her she would not be long and would see her at home. Karen nodded a smiling approval and walked toward her parked car alone. Janice, without any knowledge of the future, could not realize that this moment would prove the last time she would see her sister alive.

As the hours lengthened, the worry grew more intense at the family home, with no call or appearance from Karen. Janice had related their previous goodbye and had told them that no one was around or with Karen when her big sister was last seen walking toward her car. Well before midnight, the frantic parents had called the county police department concerning their daughter's disappearance. They in turn referred the family to the Baltimore City Police, because the club that Karen attended and was last seen at was just inside our jurisdiction. BCPD was immediately called and the family was advised that a lookout for Karen's vehicle would be broadcast as a "locate" and that a formal missing persons report could not be taken until the person was missing for twenty four hours. The officer assured the family that in most cases the person was just late in calling or coming home, and had probably lost track of the time. Nine out of ten times there was nothing to be concerned about. They were advised to call back should she come home so that the "locate" could be cancelled.

The following day, the missing persons report on Karen Hardwick was accepted and the investigation began. Det. John Wagner and I were assigned to the case initially to gather preliminary facts. We responded to the Hardwick home and met with the family. Mrs. Hardwick was all but hysterical at this time. Mr. Hardwick managed to conceal his concern from both his wife and daughter Janice, but confided privately that Karen would never do something like this on her own. Something was definitely wrong. When asked about any odd occurrences or recent arguments with anyone, the family couldn't recall anything. However, Janice mentioned that the only strange thing that had occurred recently was a phone call days ago to Karen, which informed her she was being considered for some quality colleges. Janice went on to furnish the information about the call and advised that the caller identified himself as Barry Christensen. Neither she nor Karen had recalled the company this caller worked for, but she swore that while overhearing the call on the extension the voice of the caller changed from male to female.

We returned to our office and, based on the suspicious nature of the call received just days before Karen's disappearance, we requested some investigative lead way, after all the incident was still a missing person We spent the rest of the day identifying and running down any such agencies or college affiliated businesses that would solicit potential students. None were established and it was noted that acceptance to college was based on grades and applications. Looking through police records and business listings through the phone directory as well, no one known as Barry Christensen could be found, and there wasn't any business affiliated with colleges involved in identifying perspective students. At the end of the day, Karen was still missing without a word, her car not located and the name Barry Christensen looking more like an alias with every attempt to identify the subject.

The following night on the 12-to-8 shift, a southern car received a call for an automobile fire on a vacant lot off of Patapsco Avenue in a wooded area. As the responding officer arrived, he found the local fire company attempting to put out a car totally engulfed in flames. Once the car fire had been extinguished and the vehicle cooled from the blaze, it was discovered that the vehicle identification number and tags revealed that it was registered to Karen Hardwick.

John and I were called at home about the discovery and location. We both responded to the scene and were told by the uniformed officer that the car fire was all they had; no witnesses to the incident and no one identified as the person finding and calling in the fire. Some footprints made by a male's shoe were cast; they had been discovered and considered as possible evidence because they appeared to have been made by someone walking away from the vehicle. The fire was so intense that the car was completely gutted and no evidence of a crime or previous occupant's identities was discovered. With this discovery, the focus of the investigation now turned towards the worse. Logically our missing person now had the appearance of a murder or at best abduction. The potential victim's car was burned to hide the evidence of the crime.

We returned to the homicide office, waited for a reasonable hour and drove to the Hardwick home to personally break the news about finding Karen's car. Prior to that time, we considered aspects of the college call, searched for related cases or similar ones, and pinpointed the physical locations involved to date, home, club and the vehicle recovery location.

We arrived at the Hardwick home and after our announcement about finding Karen's car and its condition the family initially seemed to accept the possible outcome of the situation without saying it. They were truly devastated, each coping as best they could in their own way. Donald Hardwick looked solemn and remained relatively quiet, as though digesting the facts to date as best he could. Laura Hardwick broke down completely and needed her doctor to prescribe a sedative later that day. Janice ran from the room in tears.

The following morning, the worst came to pass. Another southern patrol unit received a call for a body discovered in a field behind some apartment buildings fronting Patapsco Avenue. Two young children playing in a field had found the body and served as the officer's escort to the scene. The officer was led to the body of a female clad only in her underwear, bra and panties, lying on her back in the middle of the field some two hundred yards west of any occupied housing. Her body revealed strangulation marks from an apparent cord or rope marks around her neck; no other marks were discovered on the body at the scene or during the autopsy. The area was covered with low lying, thick brush and grass. There were no distinguishable footprints. Because the brush appeared undisturbed and the body had no scratch marks, it was concluded that she had been carried to the location and placed where found. The autopsy later confirmed death by strangulation. She had not been sexually assaulted, but the nature of her death was intentional. The victim was not strangled to a point of unconsciousness but with such force it fractured one of the vertebrae's in her neck. From the ligatures and bruising found on her neck, it was established the object used was a half-inch rope.

With what little evidence we had based on the families information about what was now considered a questionable phone call, we were looking for either a man or a woman whose voice changed during the conversation; who used the bogus name of Barry Christensen; who could not be found under that AKA; who probably abducted Karen and used her car in the abduction because it was burnt afterwards; liked to inflict pain on his victims; and was strong enough to carry his victim's dead body hundreds of yards into a vacant field. The only considered evidence was that of a man's shoe cast walking away from Karen's burnt vehicle. Was it the suspect's shoeprint and would we ever find the person who made the print?

After we obtained the information discovered from the autopsy, we canvassed the immediate area in which the body was found. Area commercial buildings were checked for potential night watchmen who may have seen anything out of the ordinary. An apartment complex hundreds of yards away from where her body was discovered was canvassed door to door. Inhabitants were questioned as to unusual noises, seeing an unfamiliar young blond-haired girl, and if any of their neighbors had any strange habits that they were aware of. At this time, due to the proximity of the burnt car and the body location, we felt our suspect or suspects were from the area. Who or whoever they were, they knew to use isolated areas not distant from one another to dispose of both the vehicle and the body.

The funeral was a mess, the Hardwick's now had accepted the horrible consequences of their loss, but none of them could bear the realization. All were crushed by the fact that such a young adult with such a love for life and a seemingly unending potential had been taken from them. There was no reason behind this act, a random act of violence that took the life of someone who appeared destined to make her mark, someone who could not wait to prove herself to the world. Someone so gentle in nature that she probably believed whatever words that had been used to lure her to her death. Honestly, hundreds of mournful people attended the funeral, classmates for years, relative, friends, teachers, and those who knew and respected the family. Along with this massive group were eight plainclothes detectives from the homicide office, John and I included. We had obtained a list of those expected to attend and had arranged with designated family members and close friends to photograph and identify any persons unknown to the Hardwick's in the hope that our suspect would be brazen enough to attend. Those unknown signing the register were detained long enough to be properly identified and determine valid reasons for their attendance. But this approach also proved negative: After over one hundred interviews conducted both at the funeral and the Patapsco site, we still had no positive leads in the case. The photography effort at the funeral and gravesite was the only time in my ten years in the unit that we attempted to develop information through the use of that investigative technique.

The voice seemingly changing from male to female during the surprise call from a supposed college agent had not been overlooked, along with the fact that he or she used an alias at the time of his conversation with Karen. At this point, it was a possible lead, perhaps the one we needed. As a result, we checked all nine districts' Vice units for known sexual impersonators, females who had on occasion dressed like or pretended to be males and vice versa. We also asked the vice cops to pass the information onto their respective districts should the footmen know someone fitting the description of the one we were looking for. This approach in an effort to identify Karen's caller led to a slew of new names and subjects involved in all sorts of activity, from S&M to street prostitution to impersonators who made their living in live performances or walk-around shows dressed as the opposite sex. Needless to say, we met, interviewed and learned about a number of several lifestyles, including numerous perversions not heard of in my twelve to thirteen years in the department. After I was exposed to these lifestyles, the only thought I had was," To each their own." We explored this underworld possibility for weeks, but our search for Christensen was no closer to his true identity and still there were questions as to his involvement. If he was identified, we still had the burden of proof as to his guilt. Weeks of investigation had eliminated all people around or known to the victim that we could find. This had proved to be the longest case to date I had worked time wise with no positive direction.

Next, the captain of homicide in conference with several ranking officers decided to call in a clairvoyant. I cannot recall the woman's name any longer. Some questioned the move, but the matter was approached with an open mind by most. Obviously at this point we were grasping for anything that could help, and maybe she could. The meeting with the clairvoyant was held in the captain's office with few others in attendance. She was advised of the case and after dedicated thought could only indicate that she felt the Hardwick girl was abducted by some contrived method by a male who impersonated a female by often wearing a female wig. She was unable to provide any additional information as to how the abduction took place or the location at which the subsequent imprisonment and strangulation took place. No physical description or locations of the suspect, the car fire, or of leaving the victim's body in the field could be added.

The one new point in our effort to identify Christensen or whatever was his true identity was that he was a male and impersonated a woman at times by wearing a wig. The clairvoyant's image of the man wearing a wig furthered the belief that the caller overheard by Janice calling her sister was a man instead of a woman. This additional information sent us again into the world of perversion and impersonators and the countless use of female wigs by odd men. We discovered too many strange acts to discuss or even warrant discussion. Many were unbelievable and others to gross for description. Possibly with the countless interviews, we had talked to someone with either knowledge of the suspect or suspects in this case, but if so it would have been evident to them that a reasonable approach to our interviews and questions would satisfy as their cooperation and minimize their involvement in our investigation. No M.O. fit the crime and after months and hundreds of man hours we had nothing.

This, above all the unsolved cases, has always bothered me personally. First, it occurred within my first year in homicide and I was not satisfied that two of my cases that year were not solved by arrest. In the second place, I questioned how many more cases would be like this one. Did the culprit or culprits plan and carry out what appeared to be a perfect abduction and killing? Was the caller named Christensen even a reasonable suspect, or just a timely prank call that occurred at a crucial time? Or were the culprit(s) just fortunate not to have some witness stumble upon them through a suspicious act, or some odd mistake accidently made would afford us the opportunity to catch them? One thought I still carry is that possibly a planned or random act of violence could be contemplated and successfully accomplished with no linkage to the perpetrator. Anyone in our society with no deference to class or race, being completely innocent and having no rational link to the culprit(s) reasoning could be targeted or randomly chosen for an act of violence. It has been said that a perfect crime is one committed against a person that the perpetrator has no individual knowledge of. Therefore, there is no relationship between them and no reason to consider the suspect as being involved in the crime.

Another case that went unsolved occurred in northeast Baltimore at the home of the victim. The victim was found dead in the basement area of her house by one of her two daughters. She had been struck in the throat and head with a hand axe; the cleaned axe had been placed on an adjacent tool board afterward. The victim was found lying face up on one of her home business upholstery tables. She was partially covered from the waist up with a piece of cloth used in her work. No prints were found during the scene processing, and the axe handle indicated that the assailant was wearing gloves at the time. If DNA were being used at the time, perhaps this case would have become a routine matter because of the evidence that may have been discovered.

The daughter had called the police immediately upon discovering her mother's body. We were able to interview her at the scene; from her information, we learned that she was one of four children, another female daughter and two brothers. She told us of her mother's business and indicated that numerous customers picked up re-upholstered furniture from her often, and she would supply a list of their names. It was not unusual to have the customers in the basement work area because of the sizes of the finished upholstered pieces. The only piece of information to run on at the time of the interview was about one of the brothers, although the sister felt he would never do such a thing. The brother had lost several jobs recently because of his drug usage. His mother had thought he was on a downward spiral and thought some hard love would help in straightening him out. A few days ago, she told him he was unwelcome in her home as long as he used any type of narcotics and could not hold a job. His present living address was unknown to any of the family. Before we were able to locate him, he had called one of the sisters and found out about his mother's death and volunteered to meet with us. After his interview, we confirmed his alibi for the night of the murder and eliminated him as a suspect. He happened to be more of a victim of circumstance than a suspect.

The covering of the body was a psychological act by her assailant. Those who injure or kill another that is loved or close to them think the victim won't be discovered in the condition they left them if they are covered or, in their mindset, buried. Finding the victim covered left us with the possibility that the person responsible was a relative or loving friend. All of the immediate family was checked regarding their individual alibis that were found to be solid, leaving little reason to suspect any.

In one of these interviews, we were told of a male who was in the same age range as her children and who had been taken in some time ago by their mother. This male was described as being from a broken home, having a hard life with his mother who was more occupied chasing men than caring how he was raised. Our victim had all but adopted him about five years ago. They had such a good relationship that he even called her "Mom." She helped him through school and got one or two of his jobs lined up for him afterward. He had been around for the funeral and all, and appeared shattered by her death. Based on the existence of this person and his reported closeness to the victim, he was located and interviewed. During the interview, he confirmed all the information pertaining to the relationship between he and the victim. Adding it was true, she was the only one that helped him grow up straight, and he said, "I loved her." Asked when he last saw the victim, he stated it had been about two weeks ago at her home. Working steady now, he had not enough time for visits, unfortunately. He denied any recent conflicts with the victim, but seemed squeamish when he answered. He emphatically denied being in her downstairs work area recently, which was noted.

We asked at the end of the interview if he would submit to a polygraph. Our request was based on his quick denial about being in the work area and the fact that he had a close relationship with the deceased that may have led to the ritual burial if he had been responsible for her death. The polygraph was requested and he was notified it would take place in four days. We picked him up and sat waiting for the results after the test. The examiner called us to the side and indicated that the test results indicated that he had knowledge of the crime and may have committed the murder; he deliberately answered the questions in sentences and moved frequently, trying in the examiner's mind to disrupt the test. The motion and conversation disrupted the four separate tests ran, but the positives for knowledge and involvement registered on three of the four different tests. But to what extent was he involved? Did he actually kill the victim or was he concealing knowledge of the crime? After the examinations, we took him to an interview room in our office and confronted him with the polygraph results. We talked for nearly an hour, but in brief he was inflexible He didn't kill her, he loved and respected her, he had no knowledge of the crime or who was responsible, probably blowing the polygraph because of his evection for the victim. Knowing that the polygraph was inadmissible as court evidence and that we had no physical evidence linking him to the crime, we transported him to his home and left with an identified suspect in mind. Now how to prove it? His record was checked and showed only one juvenile arrest for assault and no criminal adult record. A friend vouched for the suspect's whereabouts on the night in question when located, but that was a personal friend whose name was submitted to us to support his alibi and could have been schooled.

The investigation dragged on with no new direction or evidence for almost a month. Neighbors were interviewed and they failed to place any visitors, customers or vehicles at the victim's home on the night of the homicide occurrence. One of the daughters submitted a list of recent clients and they all checked out.

About six weeks after the killing, we returned to the home after learning that a check from the victim's account had been written by a female and that the bank had called about it, knowing the victim was recently deceased. Looking in the checkbook kept on the first floor, one of the daughters discovered the check number was much higher than the commercial checking page. Turning to the check page that matched the number, she found the entire page missing. This checkbook was on an upstairs room table and had not been examined during the scene investigation. Motive had been established in our minds, but were the checks stolen? And were they given or taken, found missing, argued over, and subsequently the motive for the murder? These were all questions that had to be answered. The girl that cashed the check was identified as the present girlfriend of our suspect. There was the link to the victim. Was the boy she helped raise responsible for her death over the theft of the checks, or just the theft? The victim may have discovered the thief, and be the reason for him having difficulty with the polygraph? Or did the discovery of the missing checks lead to the argument that resulted in her death? His girlfriend refused to implicate the suspect or cooperate in any fashion. She hired a lawyer, as did the suspect. The girlfriend was tried and convicted for passing a stolen check in Baltimore County Criminal Court. Without physical evidence and without her testimony as to what occurred on the night, or what events lead up to our victim's death, we had little on the suspects in order to charge either with this crime. The polygraph results are not accepted in a court of law, and the State's Attorney's Office refused to prosecute the case. Unlike the other case, this crime occurred in the late seventies. Both of these individuals are elderly now and damn lucky they chose to support each other by not telling the truth as to the extent of their involvement.

In both of these cases, the likely suspects were known. But the acts they committed could not be proven at the time to justify an indictment. Knowing is one thing; proving is another. Having enough probable cause for an indictment and winning a conviction in a court of law is another.

Kidnapping, Rape, Prostitution, Extortion and White Slavery

───────◦◦◦◦───────

onna Grimes came from an affluent family and neighborhood. Born the first daughter of upper middle-class parents, both of which were professional people, at seventeen she was the oldest of three children, a sister two years younger than her and a brother who was now ten years old. The neighborhood was known as Roland Park, old money located in the northern portion of Baltimore, with its spacious large-framed housing, massive manicured lawns and ancient trees casting shade over the walkways. This was a quiet wholesome environment for a young girl to live her existence, consisting of better than average schools, friends and mentors. Her life to this point was a dream: a handsome high school boyfriend who was an athlete, her own life as an accepted pretty cheerleader, and her understanding parents. As she jumped from her own car parked in the driveway of her home and walked to the front door, she thought with anticipation about this Sunday and the concert she would attend downtown. It was a group she had always loved and this would be the first time she would get to see them. She was a little disappointed that Dave, her boyfriend, had refused to go with her because he hated the band playing, but that was all right. She would attend by herself if necessary.

Karen Franks had only one thing in common with Donna Grimes. They lived in a different world, different neighborhoods, friends, houses and communities. They were unknown to one another and would probably never meet, but both were going to the same concert and both were filled with anticipation and excitement about attending. Karen lived in a lower middle-class neighborhood in Baltimore County, east of the city. She lived in a two-story brick row home with a small front porch and a matching small yard. Her only transportation was her dad's car, which was four or five years old and not as available as it used to be because her parents had recently separated. Hopefully, her girlfriend Susan would have her father drive them; if not, they would take a cab to the concert. Whatever, nothing was going to ruin this Sunday for her. School like her grades was just OK, her boyfriend was nothing to write home about, she was upset over her parent's separation, and her only brother treated her indifferently, as most brothers often do. But no matter how they had to get there, Karen and her friend Susan would have a great time and for two or three hours all her problems would be lost in the loud musical sounds, bright lights, colorful costumes, and the defining sound of hundreds of teenage girls screaming their approval after every song.

Neither Donna nor Karen realized that two people unknown to either one of them at the time had far different plans for a few that attended the concert. The two had planned acts that would eventually involve their victims, both girls, and introduce them to a world filled with fear beyond anything either could have imagined. Their simple desire to attend a girlish mundane concert would lead to frequent nightmares and thankful prayers of survival, as well as unspoken and unforgettable memories.

Dawn gradually broke and added light to the small, dingy single room. The room was never dark during the night hours because of the streetlights' reflecting into the room from the various nearby commercial neon signs, which reflected through the dirty windows, making it nearly impossible to find actual darkness. But sleep had finally overcome her as a result of drugs and exhaustion. Karen stirred on her filth-ridden sheets and began to focus on her surroundings and her situation. It all came rushing back to her; it was not a dream and all of it was true. Just three weeks ago, she and her girlfriend Susan were outside of a concert in downtown Baltimore, walking quickly and smiling happily with enthusiasm over the performers they were about to see when they were approached in the youthful crowd by a couple near the entrance, Two smiling people who appeared just as anxious as they were about seeing the upcoming performance. At first, the conversation topic was centered on the concert. The male was a good-looking black man in his twenties. The girl with him had a British accent and appeared to be about the same age. Within minutes after engaging Susan and her in conversation, the couple started talking about partying and drugs. They casually suggested that Karen and her girlfriend meet them after the concert and go party with them; they knew of a happening party that she and Susan would enjoy. Karen begged off but gave the couple her home phone number, saying she would be interested in the future. Another time sounded great. Susan immediately pulled Karen away after declining the party offer and telling the two it was nice talking to them.

She yelled," Karen what is wrong with you; two strangers we just met, giving them your phone number, are you crazy?" Susan asked. As they pushed their way through the crowd, Susan remarked, "Don't you realize that these people are hustlers? She looked like a prostitute from the way she was dressed and he looked like her pimp." Karen now recalled Susan's comments and wished she had listened. Susan asked, "Why didn't they give you their phone number in return?" That question ended the conversation about the two they had just met. Susan and Karen enjoyed the concert, took a taxi home afterward without stopping elsewhere, with no mention of their encounter with the two. As far as it seemed, their meeting with the couple in front of the concert was over and done with, if only that had been the end, and not the beginning?

About two weeks later, a girl by the name of Ely called Karen at her home. She identified herself as one of the two who had met Karen and Susan on the night of the concert. She said that the guy with her was her husband, Sam. She was extremely cordial and upbeat during the conversation. She and her husband had been pleased at their meeting with Karen and thought she was a fun and entertaining person. They had since left Baltimore and moved onto New York, they were rich, and traveled wherever they wanted to go. On a lark, they had decided to take in New York and see the sights. Asked about her accent, Ely stated that she was from England, had met Sam after coming to America, and they had traveled everywhere. She had even taken him back to her home country. They were so impressed with meeting Karen that they wanted her to join them in New York and party with them. If she came, Ely would show her all the sights the town had to offer. They would shop, dine and sightsee, and she and her husband would pay for everything. Karen could take the train up at their expense if she decided to come. Ely would make the arrangements. She did not even have to worry about her clothes; they would buy her anything she needed. Karen ended the conversation with an answer of maybe; she would have to think it over. The offer and the possibilities were so sudden, yet she thought exciting. Over the next few days, Karen continued to receive calls from both Sam and Ely at different times. Both repeatedly offered the free trip to New York to visit with them.

Karen was a seventeen year old, who had never left the state for what she considered any real trip, much less a trip like this. A trip to New York was more than she could imagine, and their proposal was too good to turn down. The glamour of the "Big Apple" overwhelmed her so completely that there was never a thought regarding any possible problems during this wonderful trip. Both had been almost gracious on the phone with her. What was there to fear? There was only the youthful desire to experience something on her own, something she decided on her own. She was going to see the Statue of Liberty, Central Park, Grand Central Station and Times Square, everything the town had to offer, and from what she had been told, buy clothes and eat at distinguished restaurants. The only problem was that she realized that her mother would not allow her to do this. Her mother would nix the idea before Karen got two words out. She would have to leave without telling her mother or anyone prior to taking off. She would leave a note for her mother explaining why and how she had gone to New York and that she would phone her on the same day that she arrived. Karen would introduce the couple over the phone to her mother, and everything would be all right. This way, her mother would know where she was and that she was safe.

During the next call from Ely, Karen agreed to come to meet them in New York. Ely seemed elated. She told Karen that she would prepay a bus ticket for her for the next day. The thought crossed her mind, what happened to the train trip? But Karen didn't care, just as long as she was going to get to New York City. After all, it was a free trip, what's the saying, "beggars can't be choosers." Her new friends had promised her a wonderful trip at their expense. Needless to say, with the excitement of seeing New York with all expenses paid, the skepticism expressed by her friend Susan about these two was not even being considered.

The next morning after her mother left the house for work and her brother was out somewhere Karen packed her only suitcase and waited for the time to leave after writing the intended letter to her mother explaining her whereabouts. When it came time to go to the bus station, she used half of her money to call for a cab and take it to the greyhound station. As she had promised, Ely had a bus ticket on the scheduled trip to New York in Karen's name waiting. Karen was so excited about the trip that she looked gazed out he window the entire time thinking, "I'm looking at sights I've never before seen, even if a lot of it is just normal everyday sights." It was not long, not in her excited state, before she arrived at the New York terminal. Ely was waiting as she stepped from the bus. She hugged Karen and kissed her on the cheek, smiled and seemed genuinely happy to see Karen. Ely was dressed in a nice dress and matching blouse. The thought crossed Karen's mind, Susan had thought Ely dressed like a whore, not true, she was dressed well and just fine for a rich woman. After all, she and Sam had enough money to flip about as they pleased. Later thinking back on their meeting at the bus station, they had appeared as two friends or even sisters greeting one another upon her arrival, nothing out of the ordinary for anyone to remember or even know Karen was one of the two people observed.

They hailed a cab from in front of the bus terminal with Ely giving the driver the address of their destination. It was true what they said about New York cab drivers; Karen was actually frightened on two occasions by his driving. Ely seemed unconcerned, acting like she didn't notice. In and out of traffic they darted, always a little too fast or too close for Karen's comfort. Both girls chatted lightly about seeing one another again and the upcoming events Ely and Sam would treat Karen. The cab driver, even with his reckless driving manner, chimed in that it sounded like Karen was going to have an exciting stay. Little did the driver or Karen know about what was going to unfold?

First impressions of the "Big Apple" had the young girl half-heartedly listening to Ely while she took in the sights. Like all first timers to New York, she could not believe the number of people on the streets everywhere; the way the pedestrians scurried about as if in a constant rush, and the congested bumper to bumper traffic. The car horns were blaring constantly but failed to break the traffic. The cars and buses all but ignored by those pedestrians running wherever they were bound. Karen thought to herself: "This is what I expected and more, a city alive, colorful, and exciting. What a wonderful town." Only minutes later, the girl's thoughts and dreams of the big city would change from her wonderment about being there and her excitement about the trip to her first taste of disappointment and, although she did not realize it at the moment, what her youthful misdirected flight to New York would actually turn out to be.

They pulled up in front of a rundown hotel in a blighted neighborhood. The cab driver gave a disappointed look as though the conversation he had just overheard during the ride was not true. Apparently, he was not used to the area and the rough neighborhood, and it showed in his disappointed tone after listening and responding to their conversation on the trip there. Ely paid him and they exited the cab. The sidewalk and the hotel entrance steps were littered with various pieces of papers cigarettes butts and empty wine bottles. Someone with a broom could have found an easy job; evidently no one had volunteered for weeks. At curb side overflowing trash cans lined the street with trash spilled into the gutter. Older looking cars were parked almost bumper to bumper on both sides of the one way street. A neon sign advertising the name of the hotel had so many letters out on the marquee that the name was unreadable. Concrete pillars at the entranceway were cracked and chipped. The front steps actually had grooves in them from foot traffic over the years. A person staggered up the street carrying all his possessions, another drank from a wine bottle while he slumped down the hotel's front steps. The entire block looked like a row of rundown tenements. The hotel, with its extra floors, loomed over the rest of the block with its full length rusty iron fire escape exposed to the front face of the building. It had landings on each floor level running the length of the windows, and ladders going from each level to the next.

Karen followed Ely into the small lobby area of the hotel thinking all the while, 'What are they living here for?' They said they had money.' When asked, Ely said that the hotel was temporary and that tomorrow they would upgrade. All the nice hotels were booked up. They walked to the hotel's desk and there found an equally unkempt hotel attendant, who was a small seedy looking character dressed in slacks and a shirt that needed both cleaning and pressing. He acted as if he knew Ely, said no more than "Hello," as if Ely deserved little comment. Ely nodded and continued to walk Karen to the single antique elevator. Entering the elevator, they rode to the fourth floor, exited and walked to Room 407. The hallway was narrow with water pipes exposed on the ceiling and light bulbs hanging from exposed wires. Again, Karen thought, 'Why are they in this place?' Sam jumped from a chair to his feet and ran across the small room to greet Karen with a hug and a smile as they entered the room. The room matched the rest of what Karen had seen on her way from the elevator a replica of the rundown hotel, poor lighting, old furnishings, dingy wallpaper, no phone. Small in size, it did have a door leading to a tiny bathroom, and like everything else she had seen upon her arrival, the room was unkempt and in need of a good cleaning. She wondered at the time, 'How old is this place? And is there some heath rule or something that would keep them from renting these rooms?'

Both Sam and Ely continued to entertain their newfound friend and discussed their plans to show Karen a good time. During their conversation, Karen relaxed and was offered beer or whiskey. Sam was more than gracious and smiled at both Karen and Ely as if satisfied at some unknown occurrence. Little did Karen realize at the time it was probably because of her arrival and the fact that she was now in their hands. Karen's thoughts about the present situation she now found herself in made her think, 'What have I done, who are these people, and why did I ever put myself in this position?' She was frightened, but tried not to show it; all the while thinking, "I don't even have the money to go home, don't know where I am, and will they let me go?."

During their conversation they mentioned that they did not have any drugs. Sam suggested that Ely go for some. He mentioned that they knew a lot of people and could get anything they wanted as long as the money was there. Ely casually walked over to a chair cluttered with both male and female clothes and withdrew a short shirt and a halter-top. She casually pulled off what she had been wearing and stripped to her underwear, standing there seemingly unconcerned putting on the different clothing. Yes, she said that Sam was her husband, but she was not modest in front of others. Karen thought back on what her girlfriend Susan had said back at the concert; Ely had slipped into clothes that made her look like a prostitute. Sam laughed and remarked, "That's better. Dressed the way you were you could never score, they would think you were the law." Ely agreed, said she would be right back and closed the apartment door behind her.

No sooner than Ely had left, Sam turned to Karen and said: "I've got some things to explain to you. You're not stupid, so listen up. You can't go home until you pay us back for bringing you here. If you behave and do what I have told you, you'll be alright. If you try to run, we will kill you and your family. They're listed in the Baltimore phone book and I will find them and kill every member of your family. While you are with us, you will not call home or walk up to police for help. If you do, you and your family will die. I promise you, if you obey me, all will be all right. We will let you go home when we make our money. Something else, you will be on the street hooking with Ely most of the time. I will be watching. If you don't see me or Ely, I have friends that are my eyes who will be watching you. If you screw up, your family dies. If you don't make a mistake, everyone and everything will be all right." Startled by the sudden announcement and its ramifications, Karen just stood in the middle of the room motionless and in a state of shock as Sam smiled again. He reached out and took her right arm and started out the door. Karen, frightened and starting to cry, asked where they were going. Sam did not answer her. They reached the old elevator, Sam pushed the up button, they stepped in when it reached four and Sam pushed six. The elevator groaned and started upward with various rattling and banging noises, stopping on the sixth floor. They walked to an unidentified room with Sam still holding Karen by her arm. They entered the room, which resembled the other one floors below.

Sam ordered Karen to take off her clothes, that he just wanted to see her build. Confused and frightened, Karen thought about her life and that of her family's and did what Sam ordered. Karen slipped from the jeans she was wearing and removed her blouse. Sam remarked that she had a decent enough figure and that she would do. He removed a knife from his pocket and told Karen not to make a sound and to lie on the bed as he opened the blade. "I promised I would not hurt you if you do as you are told," said Sam. As Karen lay back on the bed, Sam took torn strips of what looked like towel material and tied her to the bed spread eagle, on her back. He tied Karen's arms, legs and gagged her mouth. He told her again he would not hurt her and then carefully cut her bra and panties off. Karen was defenseless, motionless because of her bonds, and hysterical with fright; it was all she could do to remain conscious through her tears during the assault. After she was tied to the bed, Sam held the open knife to Karen's throat and proceeded to rape her, telling her not to resist him. When he was finished, he sat on the edge of the bed, leaned forward and said, "You'll do just fine." Ely, obviously knowing where the two would be, came into the room with their drugs. She walked to the bedside, knelt over and embraced the sobbing girl saying: "Don't worry. If Sam said you will be all right, you will. He's a man of his word. Just do what he told you." Sam had prepared the drugs while Ely spoke to Karen. He approached the bed and stuck a needle into her left arm saying, "This will help you forget everything." Karen, who wished she were dead at the time, realized that Sam was right. Whatever they had dosed her with sent her into a state of drowsiness in what felt like minutes. Soon, she had trouble thinking about any of it: "Where was she, that she had been raped, that they wanted to prostitute her, what would happen next, how she could get away from these people and what would happen to her family if she did escape?" She had created her own nightmare and one for her entire family. Why had she not listened to her girlfriend? What was going to happen to her? With every minute, she had trouble holding onto these thoughts and then there was nothing as she passed out.

Now Karen was fully awake, her bonds gone, both her kidnappers seated with her; Sam in a nearby chair and Ely at the foot of the bed on the sheet covering the mattress acting as though the events of the night before had never happened. Reality set in fully, she could not imagine even a nightmare being as bad as this. They gave her coffee and donuts and waited until they were convinced that she was fully conscious and clear headed. Sam started with the promise again saying he would never sexually assault her again if she complied with his demands and did as told. He made Karen recite what he had told her about escape, phone calls and her family after which he seemed satisfied.

The daylight hours were spent going over the rules of her new occupation. They ate all three meals and Karen was offered alcohol and drugs whenever her captors used either. After they thought she understood the rules of what they expected, both Sam and Ely treated her like a friend with no apparent problems between them. The two told her that afternoon Ely would take her out for clothes and show her the ropes that night. In the way of training, Karen was told how to dress, act and look to entice her clients: Look out for clean cute, well-groomed young males or females who look about twenty to twenty three; they were probably young cops, new faces sent out on detail to solicit prostitutes. Last but most important, she was schooled in the prices for the various sexual favors expected of her. Although they solicited on the street, there was always a designated nearby hotel that offered cut rate rooms from clerks manning the hotels. Girls would pay ten dollars upfront for a room when you had a mark. They supplied a room for one hour. Neither of them was to ever admit to anyone that they were working together or give any information to anyone about Sam. Ely reminded Karen, "If arrested, say nothing; Sam will bail you out."

The pimp Sam proceeded to advise his new worker: "If you say anything about us to the cops, you know what will happen. We may not get you and yours right away, but we will get them all. If the trick appears too weird and you are afraid, don't pick him up. Don't bring any attention to yourself in street disturbances. Don't give your real name or address to anyone, especially the police. Listen to Ely she knows bad tricks and plainclothes vice cops when she sees them."

Late that afternoon, Ely as promised took Karen to a cheap clothing store and talked her into clothing she would never have bought for herself, but presumably would attract customers. They took a cab to the area they were to work and Ely stayed with her until Karen learned the ropes. The lurid, disgusting clothing Ely picked for her had seemingly worked. The clothes were inexpensive and rather trashy in appearance, enough to make Karen look the part. Short shorts and flimsy halter tops with high heels seemed to be the apparel of the moment. The next day, two days after her arrival in New York when she should have been living her dream, Karen found herself in a horrible nightmare: turned out on to the street to support her new ill-conceived friends by whatever sexual acts her johns paid for. Sam and Ely with their threats, and the strange, sometimes demented street customers, frightened her beyond belief. She was threatened with death from Sam and Ely, as well as the threats made against her family, and on the street disease and possible assaults or worse at the hands of her customers.

Karen with her naïve, almost childlike thoughts of being on her own in the big city, with her independence in front of her, filled with dreams of everything she wanted to do and become, had to face the raw reality of the moment. She had to do as she was told by her two captors, who just minutes before was considered friends, or she and her family might be killed. Her stupidity had created this hell and in her mind there was only one way out. Caught in an unbelievable situation, the only way she saw for escape was to follow orders. Prostitute herself and they promised all would be well, she and her family safe. She would follow Sam and Ely's instructions, convinced that it was the only way for her and family survival. It was the only logical method to follow in her mind to ensure safety. Hopefully, they had told her the truth and she would survive this hell; survive with the two of them and never tell her family and friends what had really happened.

One night while all three of them were in the hotel room, a knock came at the apartment door. Sam opened the door to the little, dirty-looking hotel desk clerk and two policemen in uniform. Karen was lying in a darkened corner of the room on the bed semiconscious from her drug and alcohol usage, but awake. The police asked if there were any runaway youths in the apartment. Karen's hopes leaped with the possibility of being found and returned home safely. Sam casually stated, "Not to my knowledge. That girl sleeping over there is my sister-in law, my wife's sister," motioning to Ely. "She's staying with us." Susan thought about the threat on her and her family and was not going to say anything different in front of Sam and Ely. She lay still as if sleeping without a word. Evidently the police were just going through a routine check for runaways; they never mentioned Karen's name or description or said they were looking for anyone in particular. They accepted what Sam said about her being his relation. The cops were satisfied and began backing out of the doorway. The night clerk gave Sam a sheepish looking grin not seen by the police, as if apologetic for bringing them and closed the door. Susan closed her eyes and thought her first possibility at being rescued had passed her by.

At times, Ely was not with her on the street and she saw uniformed police, but was fearful of approaching them, the threats looming in her thoughts. If her parents had notified the police and put out her description, the cops she saw acted as if they didn't care or did not know to pick her up. On the other hand, she worried that if they knew, one would recognize her; pick her up as a runaway and she would be safe. But what about the threat against her parents if that happened? How would they be protected? And if they were, would the protection come in time? Hell, Sam and Ely could get her or them anytime. If they were not arrested at the same time she was found, they could do anything they wanted. Maybe they would just run from the law if she was found, maybe they would carry out their threats. Maybe they already had someone in the Baltimore area to contact to get her parents. They could be killed before the police could prevent it from happening. Such thoughts constantly flooded Karen's mind, always the fear for their safety was present. Sometimes Ely and she turned over as much as four hundred dollars a day. Sam was keeping his promise not to abuse her further. The death threats were mentioned probably to keep her in line, but she could not take the chance. And when the two girls were not on the streets, Sam shared his drugs and alcohol with them and they acted as if they were all friends.

Ely appeared to relax and accept Karen as a friend, talking about their occupation as if it was just another job. They were on the streets every day, with their main haunt being the lower class areas off Broadway. There were so many prostitutes and johns in the area that the cops seemingly accepted the situation, making both the prostitutes and the johns rather comfortable in obtaining their needs by their presence, but not making arrest. Money and sex and the necessary conveniences to obtain both were readily at hand. Area hotel rooms were available for only ten dollars paid to the waiting clerks who assigned hourly rates to the rooms, as Sam and Ely had stated. The johns were all types: kids together in small groups seeking sex, but afraid of arrest or assault; business men protecting their jobs and images; men of all ages who acted like gentlemen; and freaks wanting things unimaginable, those she definitely refused, they were just to strange. They were the only ones that frightened Karen; they seemed unafraid, which made you leery. What were they capable of? They were so anxious to get you alone they were blind to the moment and their surroundings. Whatever their fantasies, it consumed them, and frightened Karen. You could see it in their eyes, something's not right. They were freaks and for your own welfare you stayed away from those.

Surprisingly, threats were infrequent; Karen figured the johns would be afraid of the pimps beating them up, and the police because they could identify them and in some rare cases ruin their respectability. If violence came to any of the working girls, it was at the hand of their pimps and seldom in public, which would draw attention. It was a trashy perverse world: sex, money, drugs, pimps and demented people; nothing like the movies that for some strange reason romanticized the profession. Whores supplying nothing more than listening sessions to guys that wanted to be heard, what a joke. Even Karen realized that nothing good could become of anyone in this lifestyle.

Six days into her new life, Karen mustered up the courage to risk a phone call. She found herself outside of a fast-food joint with no one close to her, with Ely attending to a trick off in one of the hotels. She hurriedly reached for the pay phone and dialed her best girlfriend Susan, praying for an answer. It seemed like ten minutes in her mind, but finally she heard the word "Hello"; it was Susan and not her parents. Immediately Karen blurted, "Tell my mother I'm forced into prostitution in New York! You were right about the couple we met at the concert. Call my mother, please, no joke, you call, tell her!" Karen abruptly hung up, fearing someone was watching, walking quickly from the area, distancing herself from the call. Minutes later, it dawned on her. In her anxiously rushed phone message, she had failed to identify either Ely or Sam by name and description or tell Susan where she was. She dismissed the thought with the realization that Susan would remember them from the concert meeting. Then, other thoughts flooded her mind: "They don't know where I'm at in New York, where we are staying, how to find me. Did I put my parents and brother in danger?" Susan, please tell them. Help them find a way to help me.

Susan had taken the brief excited call from Karen seriously. She heard the terror in Karen's voice and believed every word, knowing her parents were frantic over her disappearance. Within minutes, she had called Karen's mother and related the information she had received during the phone call from Karen. Karen's mother quickly hung up and phoned her estranged husband to tell him while Karen's brother listened on another extension. Both parents, already concerned about Karen being missing, panicked over the news that she was being held against her will in New York and being prostituted by her captors. Immediately after the disturbing news, Karen's father called the Baltimore County Police with the additional information, having filed a missing persons report on Karen as soon as it had been possible.

The police now had the information about the two approaching Karen and Susan at the concert, and that her assailants and Karen were in New York involved in prostitution. This information for the first time alerted the New York authorities that Karen was being held against her will in their city by two apparent kidnappers, a male and female team and their description. As a result, it ensured that every uniform and plainclothes officer in the New York City Police Department was alerted to the situation and would be looking for Karen and her assailants. At the same time, this information alerted the Baltimore City Homicide Unit to the whereabouts of the two subjects wanted for the abduction and forced prostitution of another girl who was initially lured from the same concert at which Karen had attended and met her assailants. Their investigation was being conducted as a result of a case whose victim was named Donna Grimes. That case had similar M.O. and suspect descriptions.

Hearing what had happened to his sister, the twenty one year-old brother of Karen took measures into his own hands. Jason took it upon himself to drive to New York City and find his sister. Arriving in the city, he questioned people he stopped on the street, showing pictures of Karen and soliciting the whereabouts of areas known for prostitution. Initially, he was unsuccessful in obtaining any information about his sister or in finding her physically. Even in the seedier sections of town, he was impressed with the number and type of people. A city of millions and he was attempting to find and rescue one; still not knowing how he was going to do it, if he was lucky enough to even find Susan. He returned home after two days he had spent in New York without any information pertaining to her or her whereabouts. As wild as the notion, Jason was not going to give up. He returned to New York a few days later in company with a youthful friend who had volunteered to help him. This time, as impossible as it sounds, he observed his sister getting into a cab. Jason began running across the street as the cab pulled from the curb, but in the end frustrated in his failed effort to reach her before the cab drove away. He had at least learned the area in which he would find Karen sooner or later. He phoned the news of her sighting home, told them he would search the next day after staying in a nearby hotel; giving his parents new hope that she was well and they had a chance of finding her. After calling the NYPD with the news of the sighting and explaining the situation, he spent a sleepless night in the hotel, anxious to renew the search for his sister the next day.

The following day was fruitless: no Karen and no one who would admit to knowing her by description. On the second day after first seeing her, Jason stood alertly on a corner, looking in all directions, observing as many people as possible and as the thought crossed his mind that Karen may have moved on, out of a fast food place she walked. Jason ran across the street and grabbed his sister by her shoulders. The impossible had happened, a stroke of luck, God's will, who knows. He had his sister safe and sound. Karen looked at him with concern, "What are you doing here? You'll get me in trouble, let me go." Jason almost yelled back, "Are you crazy? You're safe, come with me." Karen excitedly responded, "You don't understand, these people will hurt all of us. Leave me alone, please. Sam said he would let me go after seventy five more dollars, please." Jason had heard enough; this was their opportunity, his sister was coming home. He grabbed her left arm and pulled her down the street. The brother observed that no one paid them any attention, no one was coming after them to take her away and the escape was flawless. Just take her and run, still not an organized plan, but it was working. Five hours after being found on the streets of New York, Karen was home in the arms of her loving parents, brother and friends. The ordeal was over, she was physically unharmed, but the mental and physical anguish what Karen and her parents had suffered through would cause emotional scares for years to come and mar her life forever.

Karen read in the paper later the next day that two people wanted in Baltimore for kidnapping and forced prostitution had been arrested in New York City the day before. Ely, who was out on bail for prostitution at the time, was arrested again. Sam attempted to bail her out and was arrested on the Baltimore charges he was wanted on. Karen did not come forward as another complainant. Both were arrested and charged with the same crimes that involved her captivity, there was no reason to identify her as another victim and witness. She wanted to forget and stepping to the forefront in their trials would make it harder with family, friends and schoolmates. It would be hard enough, if she ever could, without everyone knowing what had happened. She had been lured to New York by a phone call, and wished to forget the rest. If she never returned there it would be too soon, diffidently she did not to relive the horrors by testifying against those two in open court.

Baltimore city homicide involvement was initiated the morning after the downtown concert. A north Baltimore resident called the office and reported his daughter Donna Grimes missing after she failed to return from a concert held in the city. She had left home for the concert alone and the father was unsure if she had gone with anyone. Donna had failed to return after the concert or call home. Her father had reported her missing minutes before he called through to our office from the central district. With these circumstances it was generally thought that the missing person was just at a party with friends afterward and had stayed over. Not enough hours had passed to consider anything wrong. But after he spoke with us, he received a phone call. An hour and a half after his conversation with the homicide office, an unidentified male who sounded as if he was a young black male called. The caller asked him to identify himself, which he did. Then the caller announced, "We have Donna, she's OK and she will remain unharmed if you meet our demands. I want two thousand dollars for her safe return. Tomorrow at 7:45 A.M. put the money in one of the two phone booths, the one furthest from Maryland Avenue on Preston Street. Do as you're told and you get her back, you'll get her back in one piece. No cops, you do want to see her again." The unidentified caller hung up. The frantic father listened to the dead phone tone and imaged the worst. For whatever reason, the father thought it through enough to walk next door to his neighbor's phone and call us while his wife stood by their phone in case the kidnapper called again. Although the father had called the district police initially and was referred to the homicide, the crime and now the missing persons report was in the central district as was the possible ransom site, and the presumed site of the abduction being the concert location. Now with this news of the kidnapper's call from the father, we were more than convinced that an actual crime had taken place and was in progress. The father was asked his address and requested to stay by the phone for additional calls from the kidnapper. We responded to his home. Some twenty five minutes later, we had Donna's description placed on citywide radio. Arrangements were initiated to cover the requested money drop, if the assailant was not apprehended before the allotted time. These arrangements would involve personal from the central, tactical division and homicide. Donna's vehicle was located in a public parking lot where she had evidently parked for the concert. Although there was no evidence of foul play observed, the vehicle was processed for prints.

At 5:30 A.M. the next morning, a meeting involving all personnel was held at our office regarding coverage on the possible drop location: Maryland and Preston Streets at 7:45 A.M. Donna's father had stated almost immediately that he had the money and would pay anything to get his daughter back. At the time of the meeting, no other calls had been made to him by the unidentified ransom caller. The people who had Donna were afraid we would trace the calls coming into their phone. Everyone at the meeting was in plainclothes so as not to be observed out of place. They were all dressed as ordinary people you would see on the streets at that time of day in that area. Tactical and central had both marked cars, with uniformed personnel for outer perimeter coverage, and plainclothes personnel assigned within the area, including a backup quick response team if needed. One of our own from homicide was disguised as a street drunk and found his way to the northwest corner of the drop intersection prior to the time the money was to be left, where he sat on the curb as if he was intoxicated and could not walk further. Everyone involved knew their respective assignments. The drop location of Maryland and Preston streets posed a reasonable problem. Maryland Avenue was one-way south and Preston Street was one-way west. Heavy morning traffic would be on either corner either stopped or flowing each time the light changed in its favor. Donna's father would arrive in a cab as close as possible before the drop time and place a paper bag with the money in the designated phone booth, then leave in the same cab. He insisted that we use real money for his daughter's safety should anything go wrong. All was in place by 7:00 A.M. and being monitored with radios.

The money drop was carried off as planned within minutes of the allotted time by. Mr. Grimes as directed. He got out of a cab about three car lengths from the booth, walked hurriedly to the designated phone and placed the money on a shelf below the phone. Foot traffic passed the phone booth, a few slowed by their interest in the brown bag they saw, wondering about its contents, but no one entered to check the contents of the bag. I imagine most thought it to be just another deserted empty bottle of wine in its bag, maybe abandoned by our drunken undercover cop on the curb across the street. All of us waited and watched. It was 8:25 A.M. and no one from the various vantage points had observed anyone enter or go near the booth, although views of the booth were occasionally disrupted by the traffic volume The anticipated rush to apprehend the pickup man once he grabbed the money was fading. The elapsed time caused tension and unnecessary radio chatter among the units on the detail. Just as we decided to lift the surveillance, a radio call dispatchers came on the air.

A district call came over the radio and stated that a girl identified as Donna was calling from a North Avenue motel for help, giving details where she was being held. She had untied herself and had called the police emergency phone number. In response to that call, I directed all marked units to stay away from the motel that was no more than a half mile from us and have only one plainclothes unit nearby respond, no marked cars. Marked cars would alert the suspects of our arrival or, if they were not at the motel but watching, keep them from returning to Donna's room. Homicide detective Donald Kincaid was the first on the scene. He freed Donna, who was on the bed tied at her ankles, and then instructed uniformed tactical units to leave the room and scene in order not to announce their presence and to preserve the scene as far as evidence was concerned. A lawful request made by the detective in charge of the crime scene not obeyed by uniformed officers and their superiors ended up costing him two weeks of uniform duty. But that's another story, politics is just politics. Yes, you could be right, but right was not always accepted, just like any other job. Ambitions for promotions and status with bosses was sometimes more important than good police work. A good case, made you notable; the powers to be would appreciate you.

Donna, although hysterical from the experience, was not physically harmed. She was transported to Maryland General Hospital, examined and found to be physically sound, but a victim of a recent sexual assault and had been drugged. Her father had ridden with her in the ambulance. With his calming influence and the time spent in the hospital Donna agreed to an immediate interview as soon as she was coherent. Meanwhile, we learned that the extortion money had been successfully picked up by some unknown person. The only rationale was that the person had successfully leaped from a vehicle at the intersection traffic light, grabbed the money and jumped back in the vehicle in a matter of seconds leaving a bogus bag behind. Of course, Internal Affairs was interested in how the money ended up missing; their investigation later exonerated any departmental personnel. A Day after her hospital release Donna more than anxious to help with her father appeared at the homicide office where she gave us a statement as to the events leading to her kidnapping, extortion and rape.

The distressed young girl stated that she met two individuals at the concert prior to entering. One was a young black male and the other was a white woman with a British accent, both well dressed, both friendly, both conversationalist and very social. They initially talked about how excited they were about the concert. The conversation changed to a party they were going to afterward. They said they knew some of the performers from the concert and they would be there. They stated Donna had the length of the concert to think about it and make up her mind about going, but that she was more than welcome. If interested, they would drive to the nearby hotel party. Thinking about it, she was confident that the two were trustworthy and it was her opportunity to see music stars up close in real life. After the concert, she met the two again in front of the building and walked with them to their car, talking about how good the concert had been and how nice the upcoming party would be. Looking back, Donna had been taught better: think it through, go off with strangers to an unknown location, in her eighteen years, how many times had she been warned? But tonight, these people were fun loving; the party with its promises would be great.

The three got into a nondescript vehicle parked on a nearby lot and drove to the North Avenue Motel. Donna not being that familiar with the city had no idea at the time where she was, but she noted the area was not the nicest, a little rundown looking. She remembered asking the two if music stars would even come there. The guy, who she knew as Sam, laughed and said, "Of course, they do all the time. Most people would not expect to find them in this kind of neighborhood. It keeps the reporters and camera freaks away." Both laughed and Sam turned and unlocked the motel room door and ushered Donna and the girl called Ely inside.

Immediately Donna realized her mistake: there was no party, no band members, nothing but the three of them. Sam and Ely both turned to Donna, and as Ely smiled at her Sam said, "It's unbelievable how easy this is. No fuss, no mess. You're here now and you will do as told. You'll be safe as long as you do." Donna panicked and lunged toward the door. Ely grabbed her by her arm and said, "Sit on the bed, bitch. Everything is all right, just do as you are told, do what we say." Donna did as she was told, feeling drained of all emotion. Weak beyond belief, she staggered to the bed and sat quietly. What had she done? She had gone with strangers, too an unknown place and was faced with an unknown outcome. What did they want? What were they going to do to her? Would she live though this situation? Sam took a syringe from one of the night tables and told her it would calm her down, nothing bad. She screamed and resisted, but both Ely and Sam held her down. Ely muffled her screams with her hand. The last she recalled after Sam gave her the needle was a calm drowsiness coming over her.

The next morning, Donna awoke with an unidentified male lying on top of her forcing intercourse. The man left afterward, paying and thanking Sam who had been seated in the corner the entire time. Donna, still drowsy from whatever they had given her, in her semi-consciousness heard Sam say, "That's all we want from you, girl. Do whatever we tell you and behave, and then we will let you go," as he reached for her arm and injected her again. Once again, drowsiness set in, the room grew dark and Donna escaped her captor for the moment as she slept.

When she fully awoke she was still tied to the bed by her arms and legs. Ely announced that she was looking for tricks in the area and abruptly left the room. Sam checked Donna's bondage and told her he was going to pick up some money he had coming, never mentioning that in reality it was the ransom for her. He gagged her mouth and left the room with her tied to the bed, tossing the bed sheet over her nude body. After Sam left, the room was empty and she managed to untie herself, freeing her hands but not her ankles, taking the gag off and calling 911 for help. Donna thought as she called, 'Why would they leave the phone within reach on the nightstand?' Minutes later, police banged on the door and forced it open when she screamed for help. They covered her nude body and called for an ambulance as she told them what had happened to her in a frenzied, probably incoherent voice.

We obtained complete descriptions on both of her abductors. Asking if they had mentioned anything she could recall that might help us locate the suspects, Donna stated that in conversation among them Sam and Ely had mentioned that they had just come from D.C. and Virginia, and they liked New York. We had missed both: Sam at the pickup location and Ely who had probably watched the marked cars and uniforms swarm the motel parking lot. In their attempt to rescue Donna, they disobeyed an order requesting uniformed personnel or marked units stay away sting that much more. Donna was now safe and reunited with her father, who under the circumstances was delirious about the safe return of his daughter and seemed unconcerned about the botched ransom money. After being told that in all probability every aspect of her kidnapping would be made a focal point in the trial if the two were caught and tried for their crimes, Donna readily agreed to testify against them wanting the two caught and taken off the street so they could not do this to any one.

Donna was correct in her feelings. The two that had abducted her, kidnapped, drugged and prostituted her had to realize the felonies they were committing. We all wondered why they did not guard her at all times, and even consider killing her to do away with her being a witness. These people had committed multiple felonies and had decided to do so after premeditated planning. Maybe the fact that she had freed herself and managed to call for help was the only thing that had saved her life. Were these two that stupid to commit multiple felonies to accomplish their aims, and did they really think they could get away with such acts?

We contacted authorities in both D.C. and Virginia trying to identify either or both of the suspects. In our inquiries we found that the Alexandria, Virginia Police Department had reported a similar crime involving the solicitation of a young female by a couple who claimed to be married, a black and white couple in their twenties. After approaching her and chatting for about fifteen minutes they turned the conversation to prostitution, advising that there was a lot of money to be made and it was easy. The man said he would keep her safe, and the girl advised she would work right with her and be with her all of the time they were working the streets. The girl said she wasn't interested, wondering why these strangers even approached her with such a plan, and called the police. This must have been our people, the M.O. slightly different, but a black and white couple soliciting a young girl for prostitution certainly fit. When this direct approach failed to work, they came up with the method they used on Donna. The description supplied fit, but the information supplied could not confirm their full identities or possible whereabouts.

New York City P.D. was notified by teletype with the description and M.O. of the suspects, and initially had no similar case information. About a week went by and then they notified us that a female prostitute had been arrested for solicitation and that her name was Ely. Unfortunately, they had failed to link this person to our wanted teletype before she made bail. It would be two weeks before she appeared for her hearing on the charges. Ely's photograph was sent to us and Donna identified Ely's photo from a group of five others as the girl involved in her abduction and subsequent crimes. This information resulted in a call to NYPD and the arresting officer for Ely, a vice cop in one of the precincts. During the conversation, he stated that he should be able to pick her up on the street again before her hearing date. That information caused a meeting with our captain. Both Det. John Hess and I attempted to sell the idea of going to New York and arresting Ely when located. Initially, the captain was against the request until we convinced him that the odds of Ely showing for the pending hearing were nil. Why should she show up when she had to figure she was wanted in Baltimore? Our second argument at the time was what if they abducted another girl before we got them? What if the abduction ended in the girl's death? What if every attempt was not made to arrest the two having previous knowledge of what they were doing? It took the captain another day weighing the idea and the means of transportation before he finally agreed. Hess and I were to take an unmarked car to New York City, link up with the arresting officer on Ely and attempt to locate and arrest her and Sam with the assistance of the New York City Police Department.

The next morning, Hess and my self set out for New York City in a motor pool car. After the three hour trip, we drove to their Headquarters building and met with a member of their Commissioner's Squad, a unit that handled VIP threat investigations, security protection, and assisted out of jurisdiction police with New York cases. The detective assigned to us was more than helpful. He had twenty two years on at the time and more than convinced us that he was a well rounded investigator having spent four years in robbery before this recent assignment. He knew the job and the arresting vice detective had been his former partner at one time. He advised that the vice cop was a professional and would gladly assist us in every way possible.

The precinct he was assigned to was located in the heart of a rundown area of bars, shabby three-story apartments, dirty streets and maybe dirtier street people. The precinct itself was straight out of "Barney Miller," the old lighthearted television series, seriously, it truly was. It was a rundown two-story located between three-story buildings, with marked and unmarked cars parked two and three deep in front of the entrance and in both directions above and below the station house. As you entered the building, there was a plywood board with numerous tagged car keys hanging on it. The tags on them indicated the location address where your department car had been parked at the end of the shift before the next started. Parking was so bad on shift changes they had to park as close to the station as possible and walk into the station and hang the keys on the board so that the next shift could walk out, locate their car and start their patrol.

We entered the station and observed a familiar scene: cops uniformed and in plainclothes, yelling arrested subjects, male and female, cops yelling back, old desks cluttered with papers, wanted photos on the wall board and, believe it or not, someone was playing a trumpet in the next building which we heard as we climbed the steps to the second floor. It brought back another familiar scene from "Barney Miller," but true. The series on television must have done its homework; the sights and sounds were there. I could not help but smile as the soft tones filtered through the wall. Perhaps this was the actual station house they filmed "Barney Miller" at, or at least the one they took hints from. I was tempted to ask, but thought better of it, not wanting to embarrass our host.

The cop we wanted was pointed out and we walked over to him while he was talking on the phone. He cupped the phone for a moment and asked his old partner who we were. The detective replied that we were from Baltimore and were looking for one of his previously arrested females. After the call was concluded, the vice cop asked for identification from us. He turned to his previous partner and asked, "Who are these guys really? Who are you running at me, are they Internal Affairs or what?" Hess attempted to explain that we had called him about the prostitute he had arrested. He hesitated for a minute; leaving us thinking he must have remembered our call and would settle down. After he was satisfied that we were who we said we were, he relaxed and was much more than cooperative.

We walked to his unmarked car parked at the curb some two blocks away from the station. Nearly four hours cruising and sitting in the red-light area looking for our girl Ely, but no luck. It was the same world all over: whores soliciting, pimps watching out for their women, tricks and vice cops, and anxious John's deciding whether or not to approach the prostitutes. It could have been the streets in Baltimore as well as in New York, probably the same in every major city in the world. Our vice cop pointed out and named several of the girls and pimps as we rode the area searching. He knew his people. Nothing was mentioned about the vice cop's attitude when he met us until he had left. Once we dropped him back at his precinct and made arrangements for future searches for our two, he parked his car, jumped out and went into the station, leaving us to walk back to our detective's ride. Our assigned detective explained that presently there was an internal investigation involving property detectives telling commercial burglary victims to inflate their losses to the insurance companies in a supplemental loss report and the detectives would write and verify the loss report. That's what his old ex-partner was concerned with? What an outfit, afraid to trust his own former partner. They could have their department and the job. If you could not trust your former partner, who could you trust, and why work in such an atmosphere?

Knowing the area that Ely frequented, we used the commissioner's office and the vice man for two days in our futile attempts to find our girl. If she was out there, we failed. The four of us had missed her or she had moved her business activity elsewhere. Ben, the detective from the commissioner's squad advised that he had to handle another matter out of his office, and the vice cop Ritter advised he would keep trying to locate Ely, but she may have left town. Reporting our unsuccessful attempts on the third day to our captain, we were requested to come home and keep Ely's hearing date in mind, although all involved felt that her court date was meaningless to her.

During the ride back to Baltimore, I thought of Ritter's response at our arrival in his office. It's tough enough to do this job, but how could you do it with so much corruptness and mistrust that you questioned the loyalty of your ex-partner? What an outfit. I guess that with the number of police they have, they have all types. Having missed Ely after a good effort on our part, we had to hope she would be located in New York before her pending court date. Surely, she would leave town prior to that court date knowing she was wanted for part one crimes, and we would have to wait until she turned up again. We drove back to Baltimore, turned in the vehicle and our travel report and receipts and the investigative report regarding our New York effort. We were about to leave the office for our respective homes when we received a call from the New York Police Department. The call was from Ritter and he advised that he had apprehended Ely about two hours ago on the street not far from her previous arrest location. Within a half hour of her arrest, Sam was arrested at the same precinct when he casually strolled in to present her bail money thinking it would be nothing but a routine matter. Ely had called Sam about her arrest and bail money, but had not been told until afterward that she and Sam were wanted in Baltimore in regards to our warrants. When both were in custody, they were advised of the pending extradition to Baltimore and the numerous of felony counts against them.

Within a week, both had been delivered to BCPD. Neither one fought extradition. They both had lawyers waiting in the wings. A local attorney well known to us, who had a reputation for handling scumbags, even realized that in this particular case he had two of the worst. We did get an answer about the ransom money. While under arrest in New York, Ely talked freely. When asked she told Ritter that Sam had jumped back and forth from a cab to get the money, leaving a similar paper bag behind in the phone booth. She laughed about the police finding Donna at the motel. She was walking back to meet Sam there at the time, having no luck soliciting at North and Charles streets. Seeing the marked cars pour onto the lot, she just turned and walked away.

Both were charged and both stood trial on the charges of kidnapping, rape, false imprisonment, possession and use of narcotics, extortion and white slavery. Both were found guilty on all of the charges and were sentenced to life terms. Judge Peter Ward presided and ASA Gary Schemer assigned to the Sex Offense Task Force of the State's Attorney's Office prosecuted the case.

Not only were these heinous crimes with potentially lifelong lasting ramifications to the victims, but it also brought to light just how easy perverted minds could commit such acts. How easy to gain the confidence of any unsuspecting teenage girl, control her long through injected drugs and then prostitute her at will in her semiconscious state, or have her do your bidding conscious of her acts under the threat of death to her and her loved ones. Parents always want to protect their children from any harm, it's natural, but Sam and Ely had proven how easy these criminal acts could be accomplished. Either they did not consider or maybe did not even care that their actions would result in a lifetime of nightmares and the victims' countless remembrances of unforgettable forced horrible acts they would never forgive themselves for, as well as possible subsequent drug addictions. Were life sentences really enough for the two? Thank goodness the laws against crimes committed by them lead to sentencing so severe that hopefully others will consider the harsh penalties and not commit such acts.

Blood Brothers

R obeson County in Southeast North Carolina is the largest county in the state and is the home of the Lumbie Indian Tribe, which is the largest tribe east of the Mississippi River. They represent the ninth largest tribe in the nation. Many of the people of this tribe migrated north for economic reasons and settled in Baltimore City during the mid 60's and 70's. Broadway, located on the east side of the city, became home to a vast majority of those coming into town. This area is noted as the location where the original city was founded in 1729. The Lumbie Indian population grew rapidly and reached from Thames Street at the water's edge on the south to Fayette Street on the north, mainly up the heart of Broadway as well as surrounding blocks east and west. As ethnic groups tended to do during this period of time, the Lumbie's lived among themselves, secure in the familiarities of their lifestyle and beliefs. Like most immigrants in a new environment, they were taken advantage of in regards to housing arrangements and wages.

Crime increased in the area as established property owners either passed away from age or moved out of the area to avoid the poorer laborers moving in. The new population rented single room's which housed several people in their one room apartments with a single bathroom for two floors. They worked hard for low pay, living payday to payday, and like most poor tried to drown their situation in weekend drink. Living, working and financial conditions along with individual temperament led to an increase in assaults. Cuttings and stabbings increased as knives were the weapon of choice; a tool of their ancestors, it was readily available and inexpensive. There were worker pickup points along Broadway frequented by those looking for cheap day labor, with hordes of hopefuls more than willing if only picked. The jobs ranged from people seeking help with home improvements to contractors who paid low and did not need the names of the workers. These pickup sites were always overpopulated by daybreak by those seeking any type of employment, but rarely chosen. A truck would pull up, the driver would point to the number he needed, they would jump on his truck and the rest would hope to be chosen next.

One of the funny stories related to me by a former central officer who transferred to the northeastern told a story of what the neighborhood had become. Working the evening shift, he was strolling south in the rear of one of the Broadway blocks near dusk. No one was visible in the alley or yards as he nonchalantly twirled his nightstick, a lost art to modern policemen. As he walked past a wooden fence, he heard what sounded like air rushing by his ear followed by an almost instant thud sound. Attracted to the sound of the thud, he turned to his right and saw an arrow lodged in a wooden fence. It had missed its apparent mark by inches if he was the target. There was no way to determine from where the arrow had been fired from, what distance or who had shot it. Was it an intended miss or had the arrow not found its mark? The recovered arrow did not reveal any fingerprints when processed. When he told me about the incident, I asked if he was serious, had he actually been shot at with a bow and arrow. He laughed because that was his nature, and then with a straight face swore that the incident was true. I laughed and said, "If it had hit you, hopefully not injuring you seriously, you could have been the first in maybe a hundred years or so in department history to have been shot with an arrow."

By the mid '70s, the Lumbie Indians had gradually moved from the area, returning home to North Carolina or moving into various sections of the city, leaving their original neighborhood to new immigrants from south of the border. The area designated by Broadway was gradually being occupied by people from Mexico and other south American's coming from various locations throughout their homelands. The

Broadway community was rapidly changing and as it did so did the language from English to Spanish in its various forms. The change did not alter the community's basic makeup: still poorly educated people, living and working by their wits and personal trade skills, sending most of their earnings home to help support family members left behind.

Two members of this new immigrant group were brothers known as Jorge and Carlos Ramirez, who had come to this country about two years ago and settled in Baltimore where they worked hard at every opportunity as day laborers. They had been raised on a small farm in Mexico some sixty miles outside of Mexico City, where they had worked with their mother, father and three sisters on an average of fifteen hours a day on depleted land that yielded fewer and fewer crops each year. The decision had to be made: either stay and hope the land would become more forgiving, or both go to America and send back whatever money they could to support the family. Recent weather and overworked land had taken its toll and had eventually made the decision for them. Theirs were the hopes of so many coming to America: labor, support their family and have a better life for all. Both brothers were beyond loyal to one another and their family. They saw no other answer than to bid a sorrowful goodbye.

Just years apart in age, both brothers had strong affection for each other and a loving dedication toward their family and its survival. Whenever possible, they tried to land the same temporary jobs and worked side by side. Existing in the city and working everyday with different and varied work crews at whatever work they were called upon to do, both made numerous and different friends, but nevertheless usually socialized together. Jorge, the younger of the two, had grown up under his brother's wing and, as far back as he could remember, Carlos had been caring and respectful of him. They shared a one-room utility apartment in a rundown three-story row that was divided everywhere possible to allow more renters. A shared unisex bathroom was located down the hall. In all probability, this housing was not legal by heath code standards, but it looked exactly like all the others in the area. They worked as many hours as they could find, and true to their plan sent every possible penny back to their family.

With the influx of Spanish-speaking people in the area, small neighborhood bars seemingly sprang up overnight to accommodate their new patrons. One such bar was a narrow converted storefront on Eastern Avenue just east of Broadway with a Spanish name and music to draw the overworked newcomers. Here they could socialize with their own, speak in their native language, make friends and have a sense of home. The music was loud and the people louder, and on occasion when personalities and alcohol did not mix, altercations took place. Some of the resulting arguments turned into fights and minor assaults, but were usually handled in house without calling the police. The police did not consider this particular bar a bad place. It was not listed for numerous police calls or problems and seemed to run itself. At the time, the department did have a list of the top ten worse bars in town as far as number of calls and seriousness assaults, but this was not one of them, not even close. The bar listings had been developed so that these places received special attention. The Ramirez brothers frequented this bar usually together. If you saw one, you would see the other.

One Saturday evening, both were seated at one of the few bar tables with friends they had met since their arrival in town. All were talking about work and their respective homeland communities. They had drunk freely for over an hour. One of the friends got up from his chair and stated that he had to make a trip to the bathroom. As he reached his feet, the alcohol took over and he stumbled against the chair, lost his balance and accidentally brushed the man seated at the table behind him. The man stood up and reached for the guy still trying to regain his balance. Cursing as he rose, he grabbed the man and pushed him back into his seat, threatening him and reaching for a knife that he had in the waistband of his pants. Carlos, who was a peacemaker by nature, immediately stood and forced himself between the two. He pleaded with the stranger to forget the incident, saying it was no more than an accident. The man now turned his attention toward Carlos, angered by his intervention. He directed his anger and foul language toward him. It took everyone in the general area of the two men to separate them. Carlos was trying to calm the situation the whole time, while the man later identified as Antonio was verbally trying to start an argument with this new foe. Cooler heads prevailed and physically prevented Antonio from actually reaching Carlos. Although Antonio did finally sit down, his face reddened and he continued to hurl comments and threaten Carlos. To avoid any further confrontation, Carlos and Jorge left the bar, with Antonio calling out threats as they exited. As they walked to their rooming house, Jorge mentioned that Carlos had to learn not to get involved in other people's problems. He had often seen Carlos come to the aid of others, but this man Antonio, whoever he was, seemed to mean business. He seemed to be the type that relished bar fights and from what they had seen could not control him self when angered. Jorge asked, "What are you doing, he pulls a knife and you step up against him?" Carlos looked at his brother and said, "It's always been my way and it always works." Carlos had dismissed the matter before they reached the front steps of the row house leading their upstairs room.

About ten days later, Carlos learned from some friends and patrons that were there the night of the argument between Antonio and him, that Antonio was a man to be feared. He had a reputation for brawling, a mean disposition when drinking and reportedly had cut a fellow at one of the other bars. When he was drunk, he would fight at the drop of a hat and would use anything at hand to reach and inflict pain on his victim. Along with this nasty description of the man and his acts, Carlos was also advised that Antonio had put the word out that if he saw Carlos he was going to hurt him. Carlos, after hearing all of this, like he had with his brother's concerns smiled and dismissed the warning. Not seeing any actual threat, he did not mention the new information to his brother Jorge. Nothing would come out of this slight misunderstanding. Little did he know that the information about Antonio was correct? Down to the letter, Antonio had every intention to fulfill the threats he made. Carlos, with his forgiving nature, had dismissed the matter while Antonio was spoiling for a fight trying to locate Carlos' whereabouts.

The following Friday, Jorge walked into thier room after work expecting to find his brother waiting for him. It had almost become a ritual between the two that after a hard week's work they both would spend hours at their local bar with whatever friends showed up. But instead of finding Carlos in the apartment, a brief note on the dresser explained that he had gotten home early and would be at the bar around ten P.M. that night and would meet Jorge there. Jorge flopped on the bed for a while for a well-deserved nap. He woke after some hours, carried fresh clothes to the unisex bathroom, bathed and changed. Afterward, he walked down Broadway and turned toward the bar to meet Carlos. As he approached, he saw an array of flashing lights from police cars and an ambulance pulled up close to the front door of the bar. He continued his normal pace and casually strolled to the entrance where a uniformed officer denied him entry, saying the bar was a crime scene. As the officer held him back, telling him there had been a serious cutting inside for some reason it struck him it was his brother Carlos who had been hurt. Jorge was sickened at the thought.

Just at that moment, the ambulance crew rushed out of the bar with Carlos on a stretcher unconscious and strapped to the stretcher. Jorge felt his body sag and for a second thought he was going to faint. As soon as he could pull himself together physically and emotionally, he announced to the officer at the door that the victim was his brother. The officer grabbed his arm and ushered him to the rear open doors of the ambulance, advising the crew that he was related and he could ride with them to the hospital. As Jorge climbed beside his brother, the policeman advised that the detectives would speak with him at the hospital. The doors closed, the siren started and Jorge found himself seated next to the motionless body of his brother as the medic worked feverishly administering aid to Carlos' wound. In an instant, the reality of the situation struck him. He was calmly walking without a care in the world to meet his beloved brother one minute and the next he was riding in an ambulance rushing through traffic to an emergency room with the thought that his brother could die. As he stared down at his brother, he suddenly realized that whenever he had last spoken with Carlos, whatever those words had been, they might will be the last conversation between them.

The ambulance arrived at the nearby Johns Hopkins Hospital and Carlos was rushed into the emergency entrance while Jorge was ushered to a waiting room. We arrived after the scene had been processed. By the time we interviewed Jorge as to his knowledge of the events that led to his brother's cutting, Carlos Ramirez had been pronounced dead. Jorge had been told and requested to await our arrival. Jorge's grief was more than evident; he was given a sedative before talking to us. During the interview, we advised that from witnesses we had developed a suspect and that his name was Antonio. No last name had been obtained. Jorge readily described the situation in which Carlos and Antonio had words weeks ago and that Antonio had a poor reputation. He could not furnish Antonio's last name, address or possible friends though. There was no reason not to believe him. Even after the sedative, he was barely able to hold himself together.

Investigation at the bar scene had revealed that at about 10:15 P.M. Carlos was seated at one of the small tables with some friends when a large man casually walked up behind him, yanked his head back with his left hand and slit Carlos' throat with a straight razor from left to right. As the startled witnesses watched, the assailant repeated the action and cut Carlos' throat a second time. Then he calmly turned, placing the closed razor in his pocket and walked out of the bar, leaving Carlos gasping for air and trying to speak. Blood gashed from the wounds and within minutes, although several tried to help him, Carlos was unconscious on the floor. The witnesses to the assault were very cooperative and a few of them had knowledge of the previous encounter with threats between the two men. They were only able to identify the suspect by his first name Antonio and furnish a description. It was learned that Antonio had a reputation for fighting and frequented the area bars. Antonio's friends and associates were unknown. All in all, we were impressed with the amount of information we had obtained. Most of the group was new to this country and many feared the police in general because of past experiences in their countries, and present legal status. The Ramirez brothers must have been well liked. For the next couple of days, we ran the bar scene in the area of the killing in hopes to develop leads on the suspect to no avail. Antonio, for the drunken combative ruffian that he was, had been closemouthed about his personal life, giving us the thought that he may well have been in the country illegally and if so flee as a result of the murder.

As it turned out and as was expected, Jorge Ramirez had a better network than we had. The brothers were known and well respected in the community, and those who either had information at the time or developed it afterward told Jorge rather than us. What he did was not expected. Jorge would decide his response and not inform us. He had promised to assist in any way he could to help and apprehend Antonio, but after someone made him aware where to find Antonio, he had made up his own mind what to do.

On a Saturday night, fifteen days after the death of Carlos Ramirez, we received a call to another Broadway area bar for a serious stabbing. It was located only blocks from where Carlos had been stabbed. While riding to the scene, the possibility was discussed that this could well be in retaliation for that murder and the victim could be Antonio. Upon our arrival, a man fitting the description of Antonio was found lying on the floor midway the length of the bar in a pool of blood. The victim had been pronounced dead by the ambulance crew before our arrival. A hunting knife was still protruding from the victim's chest. Examination of the body established that he had suffered stab wounds to his stomach as well as chest where the knife was buried. Visually, the victim fit the description of the man we had been looking for. Recovery of his wallet confirmed he was Antonio Jessie. Hanging in the same area as his former victim had not panned out well. In our minds, before speaking to any of the witnesses, we had a suspect.

When we interviewed the witnesses, they stated that the victim was leaning over the bar when a man entered and walked directly to him. Without a word, the man reached for his right shoulder and spun Antonio to face him. In what appeared to be the same motion, he plunged the six-inch hunting knife into the man's stomach just below the belt line, pulled it upward and out then buried it near Antonio's center chest in the area of his heart. Antonio looked quizzically down toward his belt, grabbed his stomach and let out a scream as the knife was slammed into his chest. He fell back against the bar and collapsed to the floor. The man who had stabbed him stepped back as if admiring his work, stood over the victim and said, "For my brother Carlos." He repeated that several times as he calmly walked for the door. At the doorway, he turned and said again, "For my brother." Then he turned and was gone. When he walked out onto that street, not knowing at the time, he would disappear for years.

No question that Jorge Ramirez was our man; he had even declared to the witnesses why he had committed the act. How we were after the man we had sat with recently at the hospital and tried to console at the time of his brother's violent murder. He was not worried with being identified with the crime, so it was rather clear that he would be difficult to find even minutes after the act. Checking his room within the hour it was evident that we had just missed him; he must have packed prior to the stabbing. The room appeared that he had left hurriedly, but had taken his clothes, toiletries and whatever else had seemed important at the time. A warrant charging Jorge Ramirez with the death of Antonio Jessie was obtained. Three weeks after its issuance, we had no information as to his whereabouts or potential destination. All we knew of the suspect was that he worked at various jobs, which made him suitable for various forms of employment, and that he and his brother had come to America from Mexico, which presented another country for him to hide in. Once back in Mexico working under an assumed name, would we ever find him?

Almost a month later, we received a call from a small farm owner out in western Maryland who had information about Jorge Ramirez. Armed with a photograph of Jorge and his brother Carlos left behind in their room when searched, we rode out to the farm. The farm owner advised that Jorge was indeed one of the men in our photograph. He said Jorge had come to his farm seeking work within a few days of what was his brother's death. He worked with other laborers on the farm up until two days ago, gave notice without an explanation or destination, settled on his earnings and left. The farmer advised that he had been a solid worker, quiet and never a problem. He stated that Jorge Ramirez was not the name he had used while employed there. The owner explained, "Yesterday, another employee and a co-worker of his came to me and mentioned that perhaps he had been wanted by the police because at one time he had admitted that he was working under a false name." That man was interviewed and confirmed the alias, as well as identified him from the photograph. We left there knowing that Jorge had just moved some forty miles from town after the killing, but had decided that staying that close in one spot for any length of time was not the safe thing to do. How would we know where to look, what type of occupation would he now work, and would he make his way back to Mexico?

Almost three years to the day after the investigation of the two related deaths, our office received a call from the Los Angeles Police Department notifying our apprehension unit of the arrest of Jorge Ramirez, who was being held on local charges as well as our warrant. LAPD was contacted, verified the arrest, and arrangements were made for Jorge's extradition back to Baltimore. At the time, it was the policy of the department that one detective from escape and apprehension and one involved in the case from homicide would respond to the jurisdiction where the subject was under arrest and return him to Baltimore where the crime had occurred for trial. I was selected from homicide and Jerome Johnson, "Jerry," a personal friend and former homicide investigator, was assigned from his unit.

Jerry and I flew out of Baltimore Washington International Airport, as it was then known, on the following Saturday with the intention of returning with our prisoner on the following Monday. We arrived in Los Angeles late in the afternoon wearing suits. Jerry and I were surprised to find people walking the streets wearing coats. It was around sixty degrees at the time; we were uncomfortable in our suits and the locals were cold because it was colder than usual. We linked up with one of their detectives and learned how they had managed the apprehension of Jorge Ramirez, who had eluded us for so long. True, but it happens sometimes. What he told us was like one of those odd stories you hear about criminals and crimes when things go ridiculously wrong. After every possible condition and situation of the act has been planned out, because of an unforeseen twist that is often funny, like the guy who successfully flees the scene of an accident just to find out later that he lost his front tag at the accident. Well, this was a similar case.

Jorge Ramirez was arrested after he successfully avoided capture in God only knows how many states for just short of three years, traveled across country, last heard of at the Maryland farm, but on the loose still except for a quirk of fate. No more than him failing to pay a jaywalking ticket in L.A. had resulted in his arrest. Jorge, who had lived and worked in Los Angeles for over two years, had received a jaywalking ticket under an assumed name, failed to pay it in the allotted time and was fingerprinted when arrested for a misdemeanor. He was identified and held for murder. Later he would comment that he had just forgotten to pay the fine. Caught on such a humble, he had been free for so long he probably did not think about being arrested at this point, especially on such a trivial charge.

With Jorge's scheduled release to us set for Monday, we decided to take in some of the sights in a town neither of us had been in previously. On Sunday, we went to the beach and discovered that it was exactly as we had seen it in movie theaters: well-built girls clad in rather small bikinis vigorously skating the boardwalks and sunning on the beaches while muscle bound giants lifted pounds of weights near the boardwalk, open shops showing goods to the roller bladders and beach bums. Everyone governed by their own activities in perfect condition and tan. The weights were so large and numerous that it appeared as if they were left in place on the beach overnight. Strange sight's for easterners to witness, but it was nice to see how the other half lived. During our obvious tourist stops, we checked in with the local L.A. police and their apprehension section to confirm the status of Jorge's release to us on Monday. We were advised at that time that the judge hearing the extradition had not signed off on it and that our return would be delayed until Tuesday.

In compensation for the delay and to entertain us for the evening, the detective assigned to us on the extradition offered to take us to one of the clubs. We readily accepted his offer. That night he picked us up and took us to a large square block, four-story converted warehouse. The place was packed on every floor with a crowd waiting to enter. Uniformed L.A. police working overtime were seen wherever you looked, inside and out, two on every landing platform between each floor. I thought to myself there might be more police in this building than on some full shifts back home. Each floor was so crowded with nothing but dancing and corner makeshift bars to satisfy their thirsts. The majority of those there were speaking Spanish. As we forced our way through the masses, we assumed that whatever comments being made were hospitable. While on the third floor, a knife fight broke out on the dance floor between two men. The detective with us casually said not to worry, the uniformed officers were there for that. Meanwhile, the majority of the party crowd kept on dancing as if nothing out of the ordinary was happening. The detective was right; the battle was controlled before anyone was seriously hurt. The place must have had a thousand or so partiers and at least fifty cops. We were as impressed with the club as we had been with the beach activity. You would have to call out the riot squad should this place go wrong.

Monday came and the judge finalized the Ramirez extradition papers. We flew out of Los Angeles on Tuesday morning after taking custody of Jorge and advising him of his rights. The flight was uneventful. Jorge was a gentleman, polite and sociable throughout the fight. We had no reason to question him about thee charges he faced and did not attempt. During our flight, he freely commented about how stupid it had been for him to forget to pay the jaywalking ticket, but did not comment on the measures he had taken to avoid arrest for such a long period. I thought that whatever hard ships he had faced, he would have never thought that his life would have turned out the way it did. All in all, we had sized this man up as one who had decided that his loyalty to his brother was more important than whatever happened to him after he had decided to act. This for a change was one of the countless homicides that actually had rhyme and reason to Jorge, the suspect, and to ones pursuing him. His brother Carlos was truly loved by Jorge and his senseless murder could not go un-avenged.

Once Jorge had recovered from the shock of his brother's death, he calmly considered a revenge killing. His brother would have done the same had the roles been reversed. He had never intended to become a fugitive, but the death of the man who had killed his brother was the only justice he could imagine. In this case, Jorge decided to become his brother's keeper and carried out what in his mind was the proper response. The old biblical quote, "An eye for an eye," was more than justified in his mind. In the same or very similar circumstances, how many of us would have made the same decision?

Decision Time

—————◦⊙◦—————

I n 1981, I found that I had reached a point of near exhaustion. I was still as busy as ever, still working extra hours, which the job always demanded; still eating fast food with no proper diet; still sleeping whenever I could. Not the best of situations when you added them up. I found myself on the couch the first day I was off, feeling good on the second day, and right back into the fray the next. My wife insisted that I see the doctor and the thought crossed my mind, as usual, that I had not gone to a doctor for a checkup in a good while, so the appointment was made.

Our family doctor was a nice elderly gentleman, with an office in our neighborhood that resembled a private home rather than a doctor's business. His demeanor matched, soft-spoken and personally caring for his individual patients. After the examination was concluded, the doctor who knew my profession and the demands it placed on me turned to both my wife and I and said, "With your work and the pressures it puts on you, coupled with a fast-food diet at all hours of the day and night, you are going to end up with a heart attack." That naturally got me thinking, what to do? Where would I work?

For the first time in my career since coming to homicide, would I consider leaving it, and where would I go? Lorraine turned to the doctor and said, "He loves the job, he will never consider leaving." But I was thinking, heart attack, is it worth the risk? I was forty one years old and the thought of a heart attack registered. She was thinking I would never give up the job; I was thinking where in the department would I go if I decided to leave. It definitely surprised her when I said I was considering my options.

Applicant Investigation

W ith my physical behind me and with the doctor's professional opinion still ringing in my ears, I weighed my situation for days and made what I knew was a heartfelt decision, one that I had often thought I would never make.

A month later, I was detailed to Personnel, the Applicant Investigation Division. This was a result of being asked twice prior to my health problems to transfer to that division. The major had previously been a detective and lieutenant in homicide and was one of the original people to break me in. He had requested that I serve as his driver, as well as in Applicant Investigation. Once a month, he had duty and was responsible for any calls for service that had to be overseen. He wanted someone with street knowledge for those occasions. For the first time in twenty years, I was not working shift work. I was in plainclothes Mondays through Fridays, day work and had weekends off except when the major had duty. I think honestly that this transfer helped civilize me. The investigation of applicants was not difficult and the hours stabilized my home life after too many years of shift work.

I do recall a rather interesting story from my Applicant Investigation days. One phase of the processing of new police officers was an interview in which questions focused on several aspects of their backgrounds. This face to face interview usually ran around four hours. Although we complained about it, the drug-usage questions were the last covered topic during these interviews. If asked first, we may have been able to conduct countless interviews daily. When asked about his drug usage, a young male beamed back at me and commenced to name almost every illegal drug known at the time. Fascinated, I let him rattle on about the number of drugs and personal usage. At the end of what was a confident, lengthy and involved answer on his part, I had to ask, "How is it that you have tried all these drugs?" Without hesitation, the young man responded, "I sold drugs in high school. I had two guys and a girl working for me. I had to try the entire array of products before we sold it. I think with my experience and background that I would make a hell of a drug cop." My thought was he was right; he would make a hell of a drug cop, and no doubt probably a rich and dirty one at that. Charged with leaving the interviewee without answering whether they passed, I casually said that he would be hearing from us. Needless to say, he had just talked himself out of any further tests or considerations for the position.

Another situation that left a lasting impression occurred when I did a neighborhood background investigation on Chelsea Terrace one summer night. I had played racquetball earlier that night, showered, re-dressed and drove to the location. The neighborhood investigation was one aspect of the applicants' background that had to be checked. Randomly, you would speak with five different area residents regarding the character and conduct of the proposed officer and ascertain if we received any negative feedback as to his conduct or attitude toward his neighbors. I pulled up on the block in my own private vehicle and started the interview process house to house dressed in a suit. The block I was in was about one-half mile from where I grew up. The area had shaded walkways, small front lawns, stoned front porches, and two-story row homes. In my youth, it was considered one of the nicer sections in the area.

It was about 7:30 P.M. on a late summer night and just starting to get dark. I walked up the walkway leading to the porch and knocked on the door before seeing the bell, which I rang as an afterthought. From the dimly interior a little old lady came to the door and looked at me suspiciously through the door glass asking, "Who are you, what do you want?" I displayed my badge case with my identity card on the other flap and announced I was a police officer doing a candidate background. She looked at me with a questioning look and said, "What are you doing in this neighborhood at dark? My husband and I lock the doors at night, never come out, and hope no one tries to come in. It's not safe on the street." With that statement she said goodnight, told me to leave the area and walked away from the door. I finished the background checks at other addresses and got in my car.

On the way home I thought about two elderly people who had probably worked their entire lives to buy their home and now felt as though they were prisoners in it. As I mentioned, this was close to my childhood home and, as everyone does, I felt comfortable and secure, it was my neighborhood. But a major drug corner was less than a block from the woman's home. Their situation was a crime in itself, an example that made you wonder how many others felt the same after dark in our city, a complex failure that honestly could not be rectified. So many areas of the city were going from bad to worse.

The next morning as I walked into the office, a co-worker, another man with the first name of Steve, looked up and started without saying good morning, "What the hell are you doing in that neighborhood at night?" Apparently the elderly lady had called. I answered, "Steve, it's my neighborhood. I was born there, no problem." Steve responded, "No, it belongs to the streets now."

Steve Wright was a positive man and fun loving. One morning when he answered the phone, he displayed the comradeship between races in the department. Steve picked up the phone, listened for a brief time and repeated the caller's request aloud, "You are calling to speak to Steve?" He hesitated for another second and then smiled, glancing at me with a devilish look as he spoke into the phone, "Which one do you want, the carbon or the original?" There was no color on the job, no black, white, brown, yellow, just blue, the color of our uniforms.

Internal Investigation

The Internal Investigation Division is charged with the investigation of police wrongdoing. They investigate everything from reported verbal abuse toward the public to allegations of brutality, assault and wrongful actions. The men and women that serve in this division are as dedicated as most, although most police are indifferent toward the unit. Most consider them a necessary evil, but realize they may threaten their very jobs in their investigations. In each case they strive to find truth and the actual facts. It is not a cherished position to those in the department, but most realize that it is a necessary one. Most police would rather have an internal group investigating them rather than a civilian review board. The main reason for that is the thought that those who have done the job could better evaluate the situations they investigate. Naturally, many members of the public support the idea of a civilian board. Both have advantages and disadvantages.

I am writing this section without a pro or con opinion for either internal or civilian police performance reviews. In this segment, I only want to discuss my personal involvement with them during my tour of duty, and admittedly it was a mild one. It does show you another facet of the police officer's life. Consider split-second decisions, sometimes life or death to either the officer or citizen, investigated and judged for an unlimited amount of time until the correct analyzed action is determined and the investigation concluded.

My first involvement with IID came in the 60's, the exact date I do not recall. I was working in car 105 with Ronald Lamartina the same who had been with me on the holdup call I described when the call for an attempted rape came over the radio. The victim was ten years old, a white girl and her assailants were two black youths. When we arrived at the scene, the rear of a schoolyard, two adult men where holding the two boys. The mother of the female child was busy consoling her daughter. The girl's screams had brought the males running and they had grabbed the boys to prevent their escape. The female child reported that the two boys had grabbed her, pulled up her dress, pushed her panties down and pushed at her from behind.

With the information, we had what appeared to be a sexual assault attempt involving a ten year-old victim, two young black male assailants in their teens, and two white male witnesses who observed the assault as they ran to help the victim. Everyone involved in the case was identified at the scene except for the two suspect juveniles because they had no identification, only saying that they were brothers, twelve and fourteen years of age, and offering up their home address. At that time, juveniles of that age were released to their parents if the investigation did not involve a serious physical assault, and this case did not; the female had no injuries at all, and the act had not been carried out. The female was unharmed and the mother was positive of that and declined hospital treatment.

When we reached their nearby home, both the mother and father opened the door to us. We explained the charges, identified the full names and dates of births of the boys, and released them to their parents, advising that there would be a pending trial date probably in juvenile court. At the time, there was no confrontation about the situation with the parents and they seemed satisfied after we answered any questions they had.

About three weeks later, I was in an Internal Investigation interview room, with Ron and I being accused of being disrespectful, abusive and prejudicial in our handling of this matter, with the complaint being lodged by both of the boys' parents. The parents had signed the complaint indicating that when we turned the boys over to them we had said, "You black people can't treat our white women like that." Both of us gave separate verbal statements in the IID interviews regarding how the call was handled. Afterward, we were requested to submit reports as to our individual conduct during the overall case. In these reports, we both denied ever making the reported remark or saying anything that could have been interpreted that way. At the conclusion of their investigation, Ron's complaint was not sustained and my complaint was ruled unfounded. A point of many a laugh afterward, Ron swore the results were different because I wrote better. We were not guilty; that wasn't the issue with Ron. If ever being investigated again, I would write the reports. Both of us had remained in each other's company during the investigation, including at the suspects' home. The only rationale for the difference in their findings must have been that the complaining family described Ron as the person making the statement. At any rate, the investigation was not sustained, the allegations no matter whom it was lodged against were proven to be unfounded, and we knew the entire time that we had not made the implied statement.

Another aspect of this case occurred in juvenile court when the case was tried. The magistrate in juvenile court took exception to the testimony given by the child that was assaulted. During her testimony, she indicated that the boys had grabbed her, pulled up her dress, pulled down her underwear and pushed at her from in front and behind. Hearing the testimony, the magistrate abruptly leaned forward and stated, "If this girl cannot state the facts more graphically, I'll dismiss the charges." Out of reaction to his statement, I jumped up without thinking. Of course, he noticed my reaction and turned to me saying, "I guess you have something to say, Officer?" I replied, "Yes sir. She is a ten year-old child; she is being as graphic as possible for her age." The magistrate leaned back and ordered me to shut up or be held in contempt of court. I was so upset by his interpretation of the child's testimony and the threat of being held in contempt that I shot back, "If I am, the Sun papers will hear why." After a few minutes of silence used by everyone involved to calm tempers, the magistrate resumed the girl's testimony and after an objection from the boys' counsel accepted her original testimony. The boys were both found guilty of the assault. Nothing further was ever mentioned about the matter. No apologies were given by either of those involved in the verbal outburst and no attempts to damage my career were ever taken, at least to my knowledge.

In 1986 my second and last complaint with IID occurred. At the time, I was an investigator assigned to the Applicant Investigation Section of the department. As mentioned earlier, this is the section that investigated individuals who had applied to become police officers. Promotional tests for sergeants and lieutenants were conducted with our office's overview, although the oral interviews were conducted by ranking officers from other police departments. Two members of our overall unit, which encompassed the Medical Section, Applicant Section and the Applicant Investigation Section, had both achieved high test marks on the sergeants and lieutenants list. To someone in high places, this became a matter of suspicion, or as some thought a witch hunt aimed in the direction of our major's position, whatever. At the time, I was not only an investigator but I was the assigned driver of the major. The allegation being investigated was that somehow both test answers had been stolen before the test date making it possible for both to past their respective test with high marks. Person after person was called down day after day to be interviewed by IID; the investigation extended into weeks. It had taken so long that I felt it must be near an end and still I had not been called by IID. Just when I assumed the investigation was concluded and awaiting a report with the conclusion, my phone rang and the major for IID was on the line. Knowing each other, I passed some pleasantries before he got to the purpose of his call. It was an invitation. My presence was requested in their office regarding this matter. I responded by saying I could respond immediately, but knew nothing that could assist them in their investigation. I hung up the phone, told my supervisor I would be at IID and took the elevator down to their office.

I was met at the office by their major and one of their investigators and ushered into an interview room. I was advised of my rights and refused a union representative, talking freely with both as they asked questions about the testing procedures and what safeguards were standard to keep the test from being compromised before the examinations. The latter part of that question I knew nothing about. In short, I told them exactly what I had said on the phone: if the test was stolen by anyone, I had no knowledge who nor did I have any possible suspects. I added that the two who scored high on each of the tests could have done so without any advance knowledge of the answers, both were very bright and good police.

Then I think a thought from left field came to the IID major, who asked, "Why did you drive your major to the test site on Tuesday, the week of the exams? We think the tests were stolen on that night." I responded, "Because the request was made by him. With no knowledge of any problem, I obeyed what I considered a routine request." He retorted, "You should have refused." I fired back, "Then your investigation must have revealed something I still know nothing about. The only way I could disobey a request from a senior officer is if I know at the time of the order it was illegal. I have stated several times I know nothing about the tests having been stolen, if they were at all. Knowing nothing illegal at the time, the mundane order to drive him to the test site was just a request to me." The verbal interview was over in less than ten minutes.

I was requested to submit to a polygraph in the near future relative to their investigation. Thinking back on that request, I answered too quickly by saying, "Let's do it now, today, without representation." Although it was a statement of my innocence, I was convinced that this was a witch hunt. Angered at the attempt to involve me, I felt after I had calmed down I should have prolonged the investigation by asking for an attorney. A few days later, I took the polygraph examination and I passed with no problems, my first and last polygraph I might add.

I was concerned that the investigation results were on my record. At the time, I was near retirement and did not want any ongoing or what looked like adverse or incomplete findings on my record to reflect on pending employment applications. I expressed my feelings several times to their office, was promised verbally I was cleared of being a suspect, but I never received a letter to that effect from anyone. Overall, being active in criminal enforcement for nineteen years of my twenty five year career, my IID experiences were insignificant.

Imagine the threat of job loss, suspension, loss of pay, or actual criminal charges when undergoing an IID investigation, often without foundation because those making the complaints were frequently lying and did solely to initiate complaints.

Retirement

On June 28, 1987, I retired with twenty five years of service. It was the first year that you could retire having a straight twenty five years service instead of requiring that you also be fifty years of age. I was forty seven at the time and one of thirteen retirees. The following year, the retirement age was dropped to a straight twenty years of service with no age requirement, costing me a fair percentage in my retirement benefits, but who could have figured that, It changed the face of the department. My wife and two sons were present at my retirement in the offices of the police commissioner. My thought at the time was that I had mentally survived.

I had witnessed years of every conceivable assault possible, investigated those who killed their own relatives. They had killed innocent strangers sometimes just to murder in robberies and assaults for pennies; every possible low life that walked, those without conscience or any morality, those so lost in drugs that nothing mattered. And in that moment still in the commissioner's office I realized I still liked people. All I had seen and worked through had not affected me in that respect. Along the way, I had seen enough decent acts to still believe. Most people are honest and deserve to be protected in their homes and on the streets from the small percentage that we had attempted to contain. I was a true survivor; I still enjoyed people, even after everything the job had exposed me to, my tour of duty had come to a satisfied conclusion.

Blessed with family and good friends from both my private life and from those in the department, we shared a sit down dinner at a rented hall in northeast Baltimore to celebrate our friendships and my retirement.

My first thought in regards to leaving the department was to work in a different field, a different occupation altogether. It did not take me long to realize that the related field would have to be similar to my police occupation because that was the only experience I had that would support a decent résumé. After retirement, I worked briefly as an assistant security manager at a clothing business, afterward as the chief of security for a large downtown hotel. Both of these occupations were short lived, both were interesting but not exciting. I was still only forty seven years old and looking back on one aspect of the job, which I had failed to consider, was that I had stopped investigating before I should have. While at the hotel, I was approached and interviewed for a position with a national insurance investigative group as a fraud investigator. Actually, my old partner Douglas Cash worked for them at the time and suggested me for the position. I accepted the insurance fraud position because it allowed detective work, and remained there for fourteen years, working with the FBI and the U.S. Postal Inspection Service on case investigations concerning doctor, attorney fraudulent relationships. We worked directly with the supervisors and investigators for the different insurance providers. This was my first exposure to how self rewarding and at the same time frustrating fraud investigations could be. After my retirement from the national company, I accepted a position with a local insurance company as a fraud investigator.

The players who attempt to defraud the insurance groups are in some cases the accident participants themselves, who claim to be in the vehicles when they are not or claim injury when they are not injured; their attorneys, who represent so many scammers they frequently know the accidents are false; their doctors, who the bogus patients are referred, and their runners, the people who set up the accidents and take the accident victims to the professionals for a pay off, they are all involved.

Runners stage accidents and put additional people in the cars. The disreputable attorneys and doctors trade patients to one another, again, for profit. Runners receive a flat rate for their involvement. At the time I retired, they would receive three hundred dollars from the involved attorney for bringing them clients, and the same amount for taking the bogus clients to a chiropractor also involved in the scam. Of course, this money isn't reported earnings. The only responsibility of the runner after the staged accident may be transporting the reported injured too and from their therapy appointments. Frequently, attorneys and doctors are referring clients to each other they know are not injured and often know the accidents are bogus. It's odd how they can keep all this illegal activity straight, organize the frauds in some cases and cannot remember the oath they swore when they became attorneys.

Commitment to the legal profession and dedication to the enforcement of the law has been excused and replaced by their ego and greed. During my investigations of these frauds, I actually had one attorney admit that he had to accept questionable accident cases to stay competitive with the other lawyers he knew were taking known fraud clients and cases. That's a good example of how frequently false insurance claims are filed.

Usually these false claims involve reported soft tissue injuries, which are settled miraculously just below the insurance coverage limits so as not to look suspicious. Various scams are developed and deployed against the insurance companies, costing millions each year in false claims, which increases the cost of insurance to everyone. Once exposed to this type of fraud work, I often wondered why anyone would rob a bank when they could actually receive checks from the insurance company and not use their proper identity in committing the scheme if they were the least bit clever, not having their claim flagged for investigation. After my time with a national insurance company, I accepted an investigative position a local insurance company for just a short ten years. I had intended to retire in another year, but unfortunately I suffered a mild stroke in January of 2011, bringing about my retirement date.

In all my time with the police department, and my two insurance careers, I fought crime and those who committed the acts for forty nine years. I might add that I found many retired police in the insurance business working as fraud investigators and they were just as committed to their new occupations as when they worked in law enforcement.

Insurance fraud, although widespread throughout the country, receives little attention from our judicial system and to a degree from the industry itself. Most executives of the various companies consider their investigative staff a necessity in an attempt to combat the fraud problem. In reality, we save or recover more financially than they realize. Dedicated former police officers and insurance company investigative groups fight the internal politics, where they are seen as a necessary evil. The prosecutors and assigned state agencies charged with combating insurance fraud make a small contribution with infrequent criminal charges. The doctors and lawyers who participate in these frauds using their understanding of the insurance company policies and procedures use our regulations against the companies. An example in the serious acceptance of insurance fraud crime as a major problem is that in 1988 I had to explain insurance fraud or attempted fraud to assistant states attorney's as simply being attempted theft or actual theft when I presented cases to them seeking prosecution.

I recovered just as my neurologist had predicted. It was a mild stroke, thank God, with minor lasting results. Now at the age of seventy four, I am enjoying my retirement, golf, although not playing as well as in the past, and easing into the retired life. Sailing as long as my physical condition allows, yard work, and yes, bus trips at the request of my wife although I do not mentally accept that I'm at that age yet, I go to keep peace on the home front. One such trip was to the Kennedy Center in Washington, D.C. for a musical based on the sounds of Sinatra. After the show, we went to dinner at a downtown Washington restaurant. My wife and I were seated with others from the bus trip; we had not met anyone personally at our table. To my left was a women who appeared younger than her age and who was very social. In conversation, I found out that she was related to the baseball player Al Kaline, who was born and raised in Baltimore. When she asked what profession I had retired from, I answered with my two careers, I kid about three retirements: the police department, which included homicide investigations, and the insurance industry with two fraud investigative groups. Her face lit up and she turned to me with a smile and said, "What an exciting full life you have had, how much you have accomplished, and contributed to our society. How fulfilled you must feel? Thank you."

I thought about what she had just said, and I thought back on the years. She was right. Although not to often put into words, I am very proud. Every one of us who served has given more than most know. These men and women rush in at the threat of harm when civilians flee; they risk their lives daily for the good of society, to help hold it together, to allow the general public enough protection to function in our society in their fields of endeavor. Unfortunately, we are usually only recognized when one of us becomes a fallen hero. All of us are heroes and, yes, I'm proud to have been in the ranks. It is an exceptional profession with dedicated brave people whose only reward is usually self-gratification. God protect all who take the oath and serve at all levels of law enforcement everywhere. May every one of them successfully reach the end of their "Tour of Duty," feeling proud of their commitment and their accomplishments, living a long satisfying retirement, it is justly deserved.

For those that follow, bright, brave and dedicated to enforcing the law and protecting the general public," No matter how difficult their cases and dangerous their duty they will always try again tomorrow, and honor their "Tour of Duty" throughout their careers.

Autobiography/Memoir

B orn and raised in Baltimore, Md., I accepted the position of police officer to help protect and support the people in my community. A far more involved, gratifying and responsible occupation than I had initially imagined, or perhaps even the public realizes. At the tender age of twenty one, I was charged with the working understanding of the law and its enforcement, as well as aspects of training given to legal scholars, doctors, attorneys and psychiatrists. All in order that we could make life or death decisions within split seconds, with only a high school education to qualify us at the time. During my twenty five years, I had personal friends killed and injured in uniform and plainclothes, both on and off duty, while trying to enforce the law. I arrested three armed holdup subjects, purse snatchers, countless thieves, and an unknown number of routine arrests during my uniform and car duties. I witnessed the smoke and broken glass shattered in the streets of Baltimore during the 1968 Riots. My town was a blaze and looked like a war zone.

In 1970 I had the privilege to serve in the elite Homicide Division with some great people. Their expertise, dedication and tenacity directed and assisted in numerous successful case conclusions. During this time I investigated homicides committed in every possible manner for every reason, including a serial murderer who dismembered his victims, an arson homicide that was unintended, as well as a residential killing that lead to cab holdups and additional murders.

I witnessed remarkable acts of courage and sacrifice by both uniformed and plainclothes personnel. In this book I have attempted to relate personal stories and events in an effort to enlighten the general public's awareness to the responsibilities, duties, sacrifices and the professionalism of our police.

Thank them all for their "Tour of Duty." May God bless and watch over each and every one who takes the oath to become police officers throughout the world.

Printed in the United States
By Bookmasters